NOTHING

TO

FEAR

NOTHING

TO

FEAR

ALFRED HITCHCOCK AND
THE WRONG MEN

JASON ISRALOWITZ

Nothing to Fear: Alfred Hitchcock and The Wrong Men
© 2023 Jason Isralowitz

Cover design by Caroline Teagle Johnson
Book edited by David Bushman
Book designed by Scott Ryan

Published in the USA by Fayetteville Mafia Press
Columbus, Ohio

Contact Information
Email: fayettevillemafiapress@gmail.com
Website: fayettevillemafiapress.com
Twitter: @FMPBooks
Instagram: @Fayettevillemafiapress

ISBN: 9781949024425
eBook ISBN: 9781949024432

For Jen, Rachel, and Danny

CONTENTS

Introduction...1

PART ONE: THOSE WHO SUFFERED BEFORE

Chapter 1   Prisoner 95111...10

Chapter 2   "Life Is a Dangerous Thing"...........................28

Chapter 3   Phil the Ghost...37

Chapter 4   The Key to Freedom.......................................44

Chapter 5   Guilt by Association.......................................54

Chapter 6   The "Insoluble" Problem.................................65

PART TWO: PEOPLE V. BALESTRERO

Chapter 7   When the Music Stopped.................................76

Chapter 8   Trial...91

Chapter 9   Stricken Again: The Fight for Compensation.............111

PART THREE: THE WRONG MAN

Chapter 10   "My Basic Fears"..120

Chapter 11   Nothing but the Truth..137

Chapter 12   "I Don't Dare Look"..143

Chapter 13   "Just a Routine Matter"...149

Chapter 14   Prosecutorial Oversight..159

Chapter 15   A Spiraling Trauma..164

Chapter 16   Who Will Listen?...170

Chapter 17   "OK, Manny?"...176

Chapter 18   "The DNA of Its Time"..184

Conclusion..193

Epilogue...201

Acknowledgments...208

Notes...210

Selected Bibliography..238

Index...248

"When you are behind that solid steel door–there is only a little square opening in it to look out, you cannot know how it feels. You think the whole world has shut you in."
–Queens musician Manny Balestrero

"Policemen and the law are my basic fears."
–Alfred Hitchcock

—INTRODUCTION—

Manny Balestrero and sons (*Art Edger/Daily News Archive via Getty Images*)

The newspaper photo suggests a Hollywood ending: a man beams as his sons, ages twelve and five, hug him and kiss his forehead. The man, Christopher Emanuel Balestrero, had just been cleared of charges in the armed robberies of a Queens insurance office. His exoneration came in the spring of 1953, after a man of similar appearance confessed to the crimes. New York's *Daily News* portrayed the guilty party as Balestrero's "double" and used the photo to evoke a restoration of family bliss.

Except there would be no bliss for the Balestreros. The photo itself attests to a fracture in the family: Balestrero's wife, Rose, is missing. While father and sons posed for the press in Queens, Rose remained more than thirty miles away at the Greenmont Sanitarium in Ossining. Rose had suffered a nervous breakdown

1

after Balestrero's arrest. She would remain institutionalized for two years.

In the *Daily News* photo, Rose's continuing absence seems imprinted on the face of her older son, Robert. While little brother Greg smiles unabashedly at the camera, Robert looks haunted and sad. His expression is the face of a family riven by trauma.

This rupture in the Balestrero household lies at the heart of *The Wrong Man*, Alfred Hitchcock's 1956 film starring Henry Fonda (as Balestrero, who went by the nickname Manny) and Vera Miles (as Rose). By the time he signed onto the project, Hitchcock had made many films that featured wrongfully accused protagonists. In the director's breakthrough hit, *The 39 Steps* (1935), tourist Richard Hannay (Robert Donat) is framed for the murder of a woman found dead in his flat. For the rest of his career, Hitchcock returned to the theme of mistaken identity so often that it became his trademark. "I use the 'wrong man' theme a lot because it is something everyone can identify with easily," he said in 1978. "Each of us has at one time or another been wrongly blamed for something we were innocent of."

A factory worker goes on the run after police falsely accuse him of sabotage (*Saboteur*, 1942). A psychiatrist struggles to clear an amnesiac wanted for murder (*Spellbound*, 1945). A tennis pro inadvertently strikes a deal with a sociopath and comes under suspicion for the strangling of his estranged wife (*Strangers on a Train*, 1951). A priest faces ruin when circumstantial evidence implicates him in the murder of a lawyer who had been blackmailing the priest's former flame (*I Confess*, 1953). An advertising executive is mistaken for a government agent and then framed for the murder of a United Nations ambassador (*North by Northwest*, 1959). An unemployed bartender whose ex-wife is murdered becomes the chief suspect in the hunt for a serial killer (*Frenzy*, 1972). All these films use misidentification and false accusation to drive their plots.

While fueled by the same narrative engine, *The Wrong Man* marked a detour for Hitchcock. Here he set out to tell a true story, crafted by screenwriters who drew from extensive field research and a trial transcript. The director chose not to embellish the story with the plot twists and set pieces that marked his ascendance in Hollywood. Instead, he aimed for documentary-style accuracy. "For the sake of authenticity everything was minutely reconstructed with the people who were actually involved in that drama," Hitchcock later told filmmaker François Truffaut in an interview for Truffaut's landmark book on the director. To that end, Hitchcock filmed many scenes on location in Manhattan, where Manny worked, and in Queens, where he lived. Shooting locations included the Queens County Courthouse, the 110th Precinct, local delis and liquor stores, and the New York City subway.

In an early scene, Manny descends into the subway station at East Fifty-Third Street and Fifth Avenue. A screeching Queens-bound E train barrels into the station alongside him, foreshadowing the powerful and impersonal forces that will soon bear down on him.

Hitchcock's use of these city landmarks gives the film a time capsule quality; it allows us to walk the streets, and tour the corridors of justice, of 1950s New York. But what distinguished the film from other crime dramas of its era—and brought it closer to social realism than anything else in Hitchcock's canon— was the decision to tell the story exclusively from Manny's perspective. As the director told the *New York Times*, Hollywood had to that point failed to present false arrest "from the point of view of the person who underwent this ordeal." Instead, most films relegated victims of wrongful arrests to supporting roles while centering their narratives on a crusading lawyer, cop, or journalist. Hitchcock cited two examples of this prevailing approach. The first, *Call Northside 777* (1948), starred James Stewart as a reporter chasing leads all over Chicago to reopen a case involving the murder of a police officer. The second, *Boomerang!* (1947), cast Dana Andrews as a noble prosecutor who restages the shooting of a priest to disprove the state's own theory of the crime. In both films, innocent men languish in confinement, mostly off-screen, awaiting salvation.

In *The Wrong Man*, by contrast, we stay with the Balestreros as they are buffeted by fate without the protection of a heroic lawyer or investigator. Criminologist Nicole Rafter has pointed out that the absence of a "justice figure" sets Hitchcock's film apart from most courtroom dramas, which include "a hero who tries to move man-made law ever closer to the ideal until it matches the justice template." As Rafter observed, *The Wrong Man* has no obvious villain either. Insurance company employees misidentify Manny, but their accusations are well-intentioned, even if tainted by fear. The detectives who arrest Manny fail to conduct a proper investigation, but that failure is not rooted in malice or personal profit.

And so *The Wrong Man* has no conventional heroes or villains, no action sequences, and no Perry Mason moments of courtroom drama. The absence of these elements may explain the film's relative obscurity among Hitchcock's works. It certainly contributed to a poor showing at the box office. The film made only $1.2 million domestically—well below the $4.4 million haul for Hitchcock's other 1956 release, *The Man Who Knew Too Much*. These results pointed to disappointed expectations. "Every moment an eternity of suspense," the Warner Bros. trailer promised. But audiences primed for the Hitchcock brand found something else entirely: a spare, dark account of working-class lives upended by false arrest.

Some critics seemed similarly caught off guard. In the headline for its Christmas Eve 1956 review, the *New York Times* declared that "Suspense Is Dropped in 'The Wrong Man.'" Critic A. H. Weiler praised Hitchcock for doing "a fine and lucid job with the facts," but found only a "modicum of drama" in the film. In Weiler's view, Hitchcock had delivered a "somber case history" depicting events that "rarely stir the emotions or make a viewer's spine tingle." The *Los Angeles Times* similarly praised the "integrity" of the film, but warned that "it is a downbeat, depressing experience" that "proves again that life can be more interminable than fiction." *Time* magazine complained that Hitchcock's "completely literal rendering" drained the story of emotion and that "by sticking to the facts, he missed the truth."

Even Hitchcock later second-guessed his approach. He fretted over the decision to interrupt the story of Manny's experience in the justice system with scenes of Rose's mental collapse. "It's possible I was too concerned with veracity to take sufficient dramatic license," Hitchcock said. Yet in other interviews Hitchcock expressed regret over scenes that deviated from the facts of the case, referring to them as a "mistake." Overall, when pressed by Truffaut to defend the film, Hitchcock claimed that "I don't feel that strongly about it."

Whether because of critical misgivings, poor box office, or Hitchcock's own ambivalence, *The Wrong Man* has drawn little attention compared with the director's other films. The *New York Times*, for example, failed to mention the film in its very long obituaries for Hitchcock and Fonda upon their deaths in 1980 and 1982, respectively. And unlike eighteen other Hitchcock classics, it is not among *The Essential 1,000 Films to See* according to the *Times*.

In recent years, however, *The Wrong Man* has grown in reputation. It airs periodically on Turner Classic Movies, where host Ben Mankiewicz has introduced it as "a different kind of Hitchcock thriller, though still one with a tense and gripping story." Film historians David Thomson and Richard Schickel argued that the film was unfairly dismissed upon its release. Culture writer Glenn Kenny admires its fluent cinematic style and "terrifying attention to detail," while critic Scott Tobias sees it as "an overlooked masterpiece from [Hitchcock's] greatest decade." In 2015, the popular *Filmspotting* podcast devoted an episode to the film after identifying it as a "blind spot" in the Hitchcock canon, with hosts Adam Kempenaar and Josh Larsen praising its artistry and performances.

The Wrong Man's biggest champion is director Martin Scorsese, who has cited the film's camerawork and mood as a major influence on his 1976 classic, *Taxi Driver.* Scorsese has watched *The Wrong Man* "over and over again" across the years. He has singled out "the sense of guilt and paranoia" in sequences where Manny is paraded as a suspect before eyewitnesses. In 2020, in a short film documenting his experience during the pandemic for the BBC Two series *Lockdown Culture with Mary Beard,* Scorsese included scenes of Manny's imprisonment to evoke his feelings of isolation and dread in quarantine. "At first there was a day or so of a kind of relief . . . and then—the anxiety set in," Scorsese says, before cutting to a shot of jail cell doors closing behind Manny.

Despite Scorsese's ardor, *The Wrong Man* remains neglected both as a piece of pop culture and as inspiration for legal commentators. It failed to make the American Film Institute's top-ten "courtroom dramas," a genre that includes "any film in which a system of justice plays a critical role in the film's narrative." Atop that list is *To Kill a Mockingbird* (1962), followed by another Fonda film, *12 Angry Men* (1957), and *Kramer vs. Kramer* (1979).

The Wrong Man similarly failed to make the American Bar Association's 2018 list of the top twenty-five legal-themed films of all time. In fact, the film did not even make the ABA's secondary list of twenty-five honorable mentions. And while law professors have written extensively on films like *12 Angry Men* and *To Kill a Mockingbird*, Hitchcock's film has inspired only limited commentary from legal scholars.

Even with its low profile, *The Wrong Man* isn't just artistic inspiration for filmmakers such as Scorsese. It is also one of the most important movies about criminal justice ever made. By capturing the realities of the legal system of its day, Hitchcock and his team opened a window into New York's history of wrongful convictions. At the same time, the film highlights systemic problems that inform the modern movement for innocence reforms. It both reflects and transcends its era.

Hitchcock's immediate subject was a single false arrest. When viewed in its historical context, however, *The Wrong Man* tells a larger story of how New York's legal institutions responded to several earlier mistaken identity cases. In the most famous of these cases, Long Island resident Bertram Campbell served more than three years in prison on forgery charges, only to be pardoned in 1945 after the real culprit confessed. Today, Campbell is a footnote in American legal history. But seventy-seven years ago, his plight captured headlines across the country, with one paper labeling him "the most famous penal martyr in New York State history." The exonerations of several other convicted defendants drew similar attention.

In vacating their convictions, New York's courts disclaimed any finding of corruption or official abuse. "There has been a wrong done to you, but it was an honest mistake," a judge told one exoneree. Another judge likewise assured Campbell that he had been "tried in accordance with the orderly processes of criminal proceedings" by officials who showed no "malice." Campbell's misfortune, the court said, "was the result of mistaken identity." These statements embraced a narrative advanced by police and prosecutors: wrongful convictions were unavoidable tragedies arising from sincere eyewitness error.

But the record belies this narrative. As discussed in Part One of this book, these early wrongful conviction cases were marked by witness coaching, prejudicial identification procedures, and the withholding of exculpatory information. And in some cases, mistaken eyewitness testimony was not the impetus for the arrest, but the tool used to secure the conviction.

Bertram Campbell's exoneration was a wake-up call for New York's legal institutions. The state's admission that it had incarcerated an innocent person was a shock to the system. Newspapers fueled a push for accountability and reform. A US Supreme Court justice called the case "disturbing." The criminal bar association convened hearings to investigate what had gone wrong. State legislators passed a law allowing Campbell and other exonerees to sue the state for compensation.

In the most significant step of all, Governor Thomas E. Dewey—who as district attorney had prosecuted Campbell—acknowledged the need for additional safeguards against erroneous identification. In 1945, Dewey directed the Judicial Council of the State of New York to study the causes of wrongful conviction and propose corrective legislation. The council was chaired by the chief judge of New York's highest court (the Court of Appeals) and included the presiding judges of the state's four appellate divisions.

But after an extended study period, the council declined to recommend a change in the law. "It is not believed that the problem of erroneous identification can be eased by statute or court rule," the council declared. Its report sidestepped any acknowledgment of official misconduct. In fact, the council failed to address the prevailing identification procedures of the day.

Had the council done so, the course of American legal history might have been different. The evidence of systemic flaws was available in trial transcripts and other records documenting what suspects experienced in police precincts. These records, which underlie the first part of this book, paint a picture of a criminal justice system blind to, and ill-equipped to deal with, the unreliability of eyewitness testimony.

Still, the status quo is not easily disturbed. Without a decisive mandate from the council, reformers had little hope of systemic improvements. And so the cries for change stirred by the Campbell case went unheeded. Authorities neither owned up to their failings nor adopted regulations to reduce the risk of eyewitness misidentifications. Instead, echoing the judicial assurance given to exonerees, prosecutors continued to attribute wrongful convictions to the "honest mistake" of well-meaning witnesses.

In short, while recognizing the tragedies that had befallen the innocent, the state failed to reckon with its complicity in bringing them about.

As a result, when Manny Balestrero came under suspicion for armed robbery in January 1953, eyewitness accusations threatened to seal his fate long before trial. Manny's ordeal is examined in Part Two of this book. In his case, Queens police deployed the same suggestive procedures that contributed to earlier miscarriages of justice. And prosecutors ignored substantial evidence of his innocence. Manny ultimately avoided a conviction only after a juror's outburst that led to a mistrial, followed by the fortuitous arrest of the guilty party for another crime.

Manny's exoneration, in turn, produced the same narrative that came out of the earlier cases: an astonishing similarity between the accused and the real culprit had led eyewitnesses into an unlikely misidentification. Police took no responsibility for the false arrest. There were no demands for improved identification procedures and no scrutiny of the prosecution. New York's investigative business continued as usual.

Released less than four years later, *The Wrong Man* is a rebuke to the state's inaction. The film refuses to exonerate law enforcement officials for their role in mistaken identity cases. Instead, it demonstrates that authorities presumed Manny's guilt based on the word of fallible eyewitnesses. In sequences that attest to the failure to learn from earlier tragedies, detectives subject Manny to a series of incriminating identification procedures, while the assistant district attorney, judge, and jury are impatient to close the case. Hitchcock shows us what the state was not willing to admit: the incarceration of the innocent was as much the product of institutional failings as of the frailties of eyewitness memory and observation.

The Wrong Man was ahead of its time. In the 1950s, American courts continued to invoke the assurance of a leading federal appellate judge, Learned Hand, that "the ghost of the innocent man convicted" was an "unreal dream." Hitchcock makes the contrary case. In fact, the film's most famous line is an ironic reformulation of Judge Hand's premise. "An innocent man has nothing to fear," the detectives tell Balestrero as they interrogate him. But Hitchcock explodes that cliché. His film shows how the routines of law enforcement transformed eyewitness mistakes into a miscarriage of justice.

While many films remain tethered to their era, *The Wrong Man* exerts an enduring power. It is neither dated nor didactic. It has no grand speeches about the presumption of innocence, due process, or police abuses. Instead, in fusing understated realism with striking visual motifs, Hitchcock employs a restraint that aligns with his aspirations of documentary authenticity. He invites us alongside the Balestreros to observe decent people struggling to maintain their bearings in a world turned upside down. By staying with their perspective, the film allows us not only to see what they endured, but also to sense what it felt like.

At the same time, *The Wrong Man* is prescient in exploring issues that have occupied legal commentators over the past sixty years. The issues include the need for eyewitness identification reforms, the assembly-line nature of criminal justice procedures, and the tension between prosecutors' role as advocates and their duty to protect the innocent. The film also strikingly depicts the investigative "tunnel vision" that contributes to wrongful conviction. Legal scholars describe tunnel vision as the tendency of law enforcement agents to reach a conclusion about a suspect early on and "then filter all evidence in a case through the lens provided by that conclusion."

These issues have animated the innocence movement that emerged in the 1990s after the advent of DNA testing. At the forefront of the movement is the Innocence Project, a national litigation and public policy nonprofit whose mission is to exonerate wrongfully convicted defendants. Founded in 1992 by attorneys Barry Scheck and Peter Neufeld, the Innocence Project reports, as of this writing, that 375 people have been exonerated as a result of DNA testing. Almost 70 percent of these cases involved erroneous eyewitness identification.

Forensic advances have thus forced a recognition that the jailing of innocents occurs far more often than jurists had previously acknowledged. As one federal appeals judge noted in 2007, "today, with the advance of forensic DNA technology, our desire to join Learned Hand's optimism has given way to the reality of wrongful convictions. . . ."

That reality hangs over our criminal justice system more than six decades after the release of Hitchcock's film, even as significant strides have been made in recent years. In 2020, the Queens district attorney joined the ranks of other prosecutors across the nation by establishing a conviction integrity unit. For the first time, the office that prosecuted Manny Balestrero had a team to investigate innocence claims. Within eleven months, two men who had each spent twenty-five years in prison—forty-five-year-old Samuel Brownridge and sixty-two-year-old Jaythan Kendrick—were freed based on evidence that discredited the eyewitness testimony against them. Their exonerations drew praise from reformers who saw in the Queens DA's office a newfound willingness to admit mistakes. But their suffering reminds us of the persistence of the forces that led to the imprisonment of defendants like Bertram Campbell.

This is the story of New York's fleeting awakening, more than seventy-five years ago, to the reality of wrongful convictions. It is the story of the falsely accused defendants whose suffering led to early cries for systemic improvements to protect the innocent. It is the story of how the state's legal institutions squandered an opportunity for reform. And it is the story of how Hollywood's most popular director made a work of art that reveals truths that those institutions refused to face.

PART ONE:
THOSE WHO
SUFFERED BEFORE

—ONE—
PRISONER 95111

Bertram Campbell in 1938 (*New York State Archives*)

On the night of May 16, 1938—almost fifteen years before Manny Balestrero would be arrested—a man named Bertram Campbell sat in a jail cell. Campbell, a resident of Freeport in Nassau County, Long Island, was on trial on forgery charges, and the jury was poised to deliberate his fate.

At 10:32 that night, the Long Island Lighting Company deliberately blacked out a portion of Nassau County. The occasion was an air raid drill: the Army was staging war games simulating a bomber attack on an aircraft factory in Farmingdale.

The engulfing darkness portended a dire fate for Campbell and his family as they awaited the jury's verdict.

***

Just four months earlier, Campbell, fifty-two, had been leading a quiet life with his wife, Gertrude, and three young children on Long Island. A native of England, he had come to New York at the age of eighteen. He studied bookkeeping in night school and subsequently worked at various brokerage houses on Wall Street. After the stock market crash in 1929, Campbell struggled to make a living in the securities business. In 1934 he landed a job as an auditor for the Nassau County Employment Relief Bureau, with a salary of $27.50 per week.

By 1937, Campbell had returned to work as a stock and securities dealer. He was also selling trucks on a commission basis for the Freeport firm of Kelly Brothers.

In hindsight, Campbell's address at the time seems laden with dramatic irony: 223 *Independence Avenue* in *Freeport*. Even Dickens might have hesitated to assign such a novelistic detail to a character soon to be stripped of his freedom.

On January 26, 1938, Campbell went to the state attorney general's office at 80 Centre Street in Manhattan. He believed that the attorney general wanted to discuss a securities matter. But upon arriving, Campbell was directed to Detective Archibald Woods of the New York City Police forgery squad. Woods was investigating the passing of forged checks at the Trust Company of North America at 115 Broadway in Manhattan. With Woods were two Trust Company representatives—the president, George Rhinehart, and a teller, Wesley Irvine.

Campbell was mystified. He told Woods that he had never even heard of the Trust Company.

Detective Woods then turned to Rhinehart.

"Is this the man?" the detective asked.

"Yes, it absolutely is," Rhinehart said.

Both Rhinehart and Irvine identified Campbell as the man who, posing as a securities dealer named George Workmaster, deposited forged checks and made withdrawals from phony accounts.

Campbell was not arrested at that time. A little less than a month later, however, Detective Woods summoned Campbell to appear before another Trust Company employee. This time the eyewitness was Rhinehart's assistant, Mildred Morley.

"Do you know this man?" Woods asked Morley.

"Yes, this is George Workmaster, who opened an account in the Trust Company of North America," Morley replied.

Detective Woods then arrested Campbell for forgery and larceny.

Within a matter of hours, Campbell was in the Tombs, the detention center connected to the Criminal Courts Building in Lower Manhattan. Unable to make bail, he would remain there while awaiting trial.

In a desperate but futile bid to persuade the police of his innocence, Campbell took an oath: "I wish my three children to drop dead if I am guilty of this crime."

The case went to trial on May 10, 1938, before Judge Charles C. Nott of the Court of General Sessions of New York County. At the outset, Campbell faced two setbacks. First, a last-minute change in the prosecution's theory left him without an alibi. The original indictment charged Campbell with "forging a check on November 15, 1937, in the sum of $4,576." Based on that charge, Campbell and his lawyer, Charles Conway, believed that the state would argue that Campbell appeared at the Trust Company in Manhattan on November 15. They developed evidence showing that on that day Campbell never left Freeport, where he had been seen shopping by many locals. Shortly before trial, however, the state withdrew the November 15 forgery count. The dates on which Campbell allegedly appeared at the Trust Company were November 19 and November 23. His alibi for November 15 was useless.

But Conway failed to realize he was concentrating on the wrong date. In his opening statement, he promised the jury an ironclad alibi: "It is my contention that Bertram Campbell is a victim of mistaken identity, and on the day the bank account was opened, I shall prove that he was in Freeport, Long Island, all day." These words would later echo in the jury's mind when Campbell did not supply an alibi for the actual dates at issue.

The second bad development for Campbell came when Conway fell ill on the second day of trial. After a two-day adjournment, former US Attorney James Wilkinson, an acquaintance of Campbell's, stepped in for the defense. Before proceeding, Wilkinson asked Judge Nott to instruct the jury not to draw any adverse inference from the change in counsel. The judge agreed. "Everybody knows it is not the fault of this defendant that his lawyer is not here. I do not see how anybody could consider it a reflection on him," he told Wilkinson.

With that assurance, the case resumed. Assistant District Attorney Joseph Brill represented the state. Brill's boss was District Attorney Thomas E. Dewey, New York's future governor.

Under questioning from Brill, each of the three Trust Company employees—Morley, Rhinehart and Irvine—identified Campbell as the man who had opened a phony account under the name Workmaster, deposited forged checks into that account, and withdrew a total of $4,150.

On cross-examination, Wilkinson tried to undermine the reliability of the eyewitnesses. Bank president Rhinehart admitted, for example, that he could not recall how "Workmaster" was dressed. He also admitted that he had never picked Campbell out of a lineup.

But the state had more accusers. Even though Campbell was on trial only for crimes against the Trust Company, the prosecution presented evidence of similar forgeries against the North Arlington National Bank in New Jersey. Two employees from that bank—teller Kenneth Feldhusen and cashier William Gugelman—testified that Campbell, posing as one Morton Sone, presented forged checks that they had cashed. While other alleged crimes are ordinarily inadmissible against a defendant, Judge Nott permitted the testimony as evidence of a "common plan" that was "reasonably connected in point of time" to the Trust Company crimes. And so the jury heard a total of five witnesses identify Campbell.

For his defense, Wilkinson called seven witnesses to vouch for Campbell's good character and reputation. "If ever there was an honest man, Bert Campbell is one," testified Joseph Mackay, a fellow securities broker.

Campbell also took the stand. He swore that he had never been in the Trust Company of North America or the North Arlington bank. But Campbell could not provide an alibi for the dates on which the man posing as Workmaster cashed phony checks at the Trust Company.

On cross-examination, Assistant District Attorney Brill highlighted the conflict between the eyewitness testimony and Campbell's denials:

> Q: You heard Mr. Rhinehart testify that . . . he looked at you while you were sitting at a desk opening the account with Mrs. Morley under the name George Workmaster. Do you recall that testimony?
> A: I do.
> Q: And you say that is not the fact?
> A: That is not the fact.

In his closing argument, Brill told the jury that while Campbell had served "the function of presenting himself to a bank and opening these accounts and completing these withdrawals," he was just one player in "an organized racket." Brill claimed that Campbell was chosen for this role because of his "distinguished appearance" and his "brash brazenness."

No evidence had been presented of any "organized racket" that employed Campbell as its front man. Even so, when Wilkinson objected to Brill's statements as unsupported, Nott overruled the objection.

Brill also exploited the change in Campbell's counsel. He reminded the jury that the first lawyer, Conway, had promised an alibi defense. Brill implied that Conway had bailed out on the case because he thought Campbell was guilty: "I do not wonder that Conway got sick in the course of this trial. I would have been sick too if I had to contend with that kind of case." When Wilkinson objected, Nott overruled him, on the ground that Brill was merely drawing an "inference from the testimony." The judge therefore broke his promise that the change in counsel would not be used against Campbell.

After closing arguments, Nott appeared to steer the jury toward acceptance of the state's theory: "Of course, the jury, in considering whether there is false testimony, or whether the witnesses are mistaken on an identification, can consider the number that made the identification—that is to say, on the theory that five witnesses are less likely to be mistaken than one might be."

The jury began its deliberations at 3:07 p.m. on May 17. At 5:15 it returned with a verdict: guilty. Nott then made his feelings explicit: "I may say I haven't the slightest doubt in my mind that your verdict is correct."

In a handwritten letter before sentencing, Campbell appealed for justice:

> *I solemnly swear by all that I hold holy and by the lives of my dear wife and children that I am absolutely innocent of any participation or any guilty knowledge of the crime of which I was convicted.*

But Nott was not moved. Declaring that Campbell had committed "very rank perjury" during his testimony, the judge sentenced the defendant to five to ten years in prison.

***

And so police took Campbell by train to Sing Sing, a maximum-security prison on the Hudson River in Ossining. There, Campbell was branded prisoner number 95111 and underwent the stark and dehumanizing rituals of prison indoctrination: "He was searched, finger-printed, photographed for the rogues gallery, shaved, bathed, given prison clothes . . . and assigned to a cell."

New prisoners like Campbell were confined in a section of the prison known as the old cell block. This part of Sing Sing dated back to the prison's construction in 1826. Each cell was about four feet wide, seven feet long, and six and a half feet tall. The old cell block featured dark, narrow corridors that rarely saw sunlight. The cells were sweltering and damp in the summer and frigid and damp in the winter. State officials had repeatedly called for the demolition of the old cell block. "The cells are unfit for human habitation, and if a farmer kept his cows in similar quarters he would not be permitted to sell their milk and he probably would be arrested for cruelty to animals," according to a December 1934 report coauthored by the state correction commissioner. A similar report issued in August 1937 renewed this criticism and noted that leaks were so bad during storms that rain flowed steadily into the cells.

Despite these recommendations, the state continued to use the old cell block. In the spring of 1938, Sing Sing and New York's seven other state prisons faced an overcrowding problem. By April 1938, the inmate population at Sing Sing had reached a new high of 2,766, up from 2,408 six years earlier. With more prisoners than cells, authorities resorted to using an open corridor as a "temporary dormitory."

Judge Nott's sentence thus consigned Campbell to conditions that were inhumane by the state's own admission. A new prisoner like him would typically remain at the notorious old cell block for six to nine months, until a cell in the newer part of the prison became available.

In these hellish conditions, Campbell spent many sleepless nights, often sobbing in his cell. He considered suicide. But he put the idea aside based on his love for Gertrude and his children. Perhaps Campbell's knowledge of his wife's suffering fortified his resolve. A Christmas card that he sent to her from prison testifies to both the love that sustained them and the surreal events that had separated them:

To be with you would be in heaven. Yours lovingly, 95111.

To cope with prison, Campbell seized on a self-illusion suggested by Gertrude—the fiction that he was in a hospital rather than behind bars. Gertrude used that same fiction to try to conceal the truth from their eldest son, nine-year-old Harry. But when, six months into Campbell's term, Harry insisted on visiting his father, the fiction collapsed. Harry saw that the attendants in the visiting room were not medical staff, but armed guards.

"What did Daddy do?" Harry asked when they left the prison.

Gertrude tried to explain the accusations against Campbell. But Harry was sure that his father was not a criminal.

"I know my daddy could never have done that," Harry said.

In Freeport, the stigma of Campbell's conviction hung over his wife and children. Locals shunned the family. "I will never forgive the men who did this to my husband nor the friends who turned their backs when we were in trouble," Gertrude later said.

Gertrude and the children soon moved to Baldwin, Long Island. They lived on an allowance of $82.20 a month from the Nassau County Welfare Department. Even so, the family took the train to Sing Sing every week to visit Campbell.

As his sentence wore on, Campbell found new roles in prison—first as an English teacher in the prison school and then later, in a role that evokes Andy Dufresne in *The Shawshank Redemption*, as a bookkeeper. He served more than three years in Sing Sing before being paroled in August 1941.

After his parole, Campbell found a job as a bookkeeper in Haverstraw in Rockland County. The Campbells moved into a two-family home there. In April 1943, however, tragedy found Campbell again when a fire swept through his home. Flames slightly burned Gertrude's hair when she rushed upstairs on the mistaken belief that her daughter was still in the house. While the family suffered no other injuries, they lost many of their possessions. A move to Floral Park, Long Island, followed.

Campbell next landed a job as a bookkeeper for the Plaza Fuel Company in New Hyde Park. But his prison time continued to haunt his dreams. And each week brought an inevitable reminder of his incarceration: a mandatory visit to a probation officer in Mineola.

***

Even as a free man, Campbell dreamed of exoneration. He scoured the papers for forgery arrests, hoping to identify the real culprit. "I knew someday whoever committed the crime I was charged with would be arrested," Campbell later

Bertram Campbell in 1945, seven years after his arrest (*AP Photo*)

told *Newsday*.

Campbell's persistence paid off on March 29, 1945, when he read of the arrest of Alexander D. L. Thiel in the New York World-Telegram. The FBI alleged that Thiel was a master forger whose crimes had taken almost $500,000 from many banks (including twelve in the New York City area) over more than twenty-five years. Given the description of Thiel's technique, it appeared he had committed the crimes for which Campbell had been jailed. With help from a lawyer, Campbell persuaded the FBI to investigate the matter. By July 1945, three of the five eyewitnesses (Irvine, Feldhusen, and Gugelman) who had testified against Campbell swore in affidavits they had been mistaken and that Thiel had committed the forgeries. Rhinehart and Morley declined to retract their identifications.

Thiel ultimately confessed to the crimes attributed to Campbell: "I alone appeared at [the] North American Trust Company Bank on or about November 15, 1937, and signed the signature cards and made the arrangements whereby the account under the name of George Workmaster was opened by that bank." The confession not only cleared Campbell, but also disproved the district attorney's theory attributing the crimes to a forgery "gang" or "racket." Thiel had acted alone.

In response to Thiel's confession, Governor Dewey directed the state parole board to undertake an "immediate executive clemency investigation'" of Campbell. One month later, Dewey granted Campbell a full pardon. The pardon paved the way for the court to vacate Campbell's conviction.

Newspapers at first portrayed Thiel as Campbell's "double." But the resemblance was not significant. The *New York Times* reported, for example, that "Mr. Campbell is . . . tall, erect, and rather heavily built" while "Thiel is a

Master forger Alexander Thiel after his arrest by the FBI in 1945
(*New York State Archives*)

man of medium height and build and somewhat stoop-shouldered."

The *New York World-Telegram* presented headshots of each man side by side on its front page. "Do you think you would have mistaken one man for the other?" the paper asked.

While both men had high foreheads and graying hair, Thiel had thick, dark eyebrows and a thick mustache that twirled up at its corners. Campbell had thin, light eyebrows and a mustache shaped like an inverted V.

The two men's physical frames also were very different. When first imprisoned, Campbell stood over five feet nine inches tall and weighed about 196 pounds—about two and a half inches taller and twenty-five pounds heavier than Thiel.

In fact, Assistant US Attorney John Donovan, who oversaw the Thiel

Photos of Thiel and Campbell on the front page of the
New York World-Telegram on June 30, 1945 (*Library of Congress*)

17

investigation, observed that even at the time of the crimes, Campbell and Thiel "couldn't have looked anything alike." Donovan was the brother of James Donovan, whose negotiating exploits were the subject of the 2015 Steven Spielberg film *Bridge of Spies*.

In a testament to his resilient sense of humor, Campbell noted that "Thiel does not look like me. As a matter of fact he is better looking and much shorter."

Campbell's generosity toward Thiel went beyond compliments about his looks. The two came face-to-face at the Manhattan Criminal Courthouse in August 1945. Thiel extended his hand. To the surprise of onlooking reporters, Campbell accepted the gesture. "There are no hard feelings," Campbell told Thiel. "I don't blame you. I blame the witnesses who identified me."

Were the witnesses to blame? How did Campbell come to be convicted? The answers emerged from an investigation initiated by the New York County Criminal Courts Bar Association after Thiel's confession. Former prosecutor Robert Daru headed the probe.

Daru traced the state's case against Campbell to a mistake that Thiel made in setting up a phony account at the Trust Company of North America. Posing as the "reputable businessman" George Workmaster, Thiel gave his phone number to the bank as Whitehall 4-2567. Workmaster was a real person, but Thiel had accidentally inverted two digits of his phone number. The correct number was Whitehall 4-2657. The one mistakenly given by Thiel turned out to be the phone number for Wesley Mager and Company, a business with which Campbell had dealings. Campbell, who was still active as a freelance securities dealer, used Mager's office often.

After the real Workmaster learned that his identity had been used to open a phony account, police began the investigation that would upend Campbell's life. Investigators fixated on Campbell as a suspect after he was seen coming and going from Mager's office. But the premise of their suspicion was dubious. As Daru observed, it made little sense that the felon, posing as Workmaster, would intentionally use a phone number that would lead police to him. The detectives apparently never considered the possibility that the culprit had made an error with the number.

Having identified Campbell as a suspect, investigators deployed prejudicial practices to obtain the eyewitness identifications. A detailed account of these practices emerged from public hearings that Daru conducted in Manhattan in August 1945. The hearings, which took place at West Thirty-Ninth Street in Manhattan, must have seemed surreal to the Campbells. Gertrude Campbell found herself sitting behind Trust Company employee Wesley Irvine, the bespectacled teller who had unhesitatingly identified Campbell at trial.

Irvine and two other Campbell accusers—North Arlington employees Feldhusen and Gugelman—testified about a series of tactics that had influenced their identifications. Private detectives had first shown these eyewitnesses a photograph doctored to give Campbell a thicker mustache more closely resembling Thiel's—an influential change given that, as Irvine put it, the culprit's mustache was his "most outstanding" feature. Investigators also "pointed out" Campbell to the witnesses as a front man for a forgery ring. "I had been practically assured that this was what you might call a gang operation, and Mr. Campbell was put in the position of being one of the gang," said Feldhusen, the New Jersey bank teller.

Irvine was sufficiently worried about testifying against the "front man for a gang" that he warned his wife to be extra mindful of their children. He also learned from investigators that the suspect about to be paraded before him had spent large sums on the day after the crime. "I was told that Campbell was spending one-hundred-dollar bills in Long Island," Irvine testified. What Irvine did not then know was that several days before the crime, Campbell had received $1,000 in large bills from the sale of stock in a liquor concern. Based on the seemingly incriminating and incomplete information he was given, Irvine believed that Campbell was guilty.

Daru attributed the worst witness coaching to the private detectives who worked for the banks. Their use of the doctored photo, for example, appeared to have occurred "behind the backs" of prosecutors and police. This part of Daru's otherwise stinging report gave state authorities an opening to skirt responsibility. By their own norms, prosecutors had a duty to "examine all the facts and question the witnesses" and to follow up on "any lead suggesting the defendant's innocence." Basic witness interviews would have disclosed the meddling that influenced the identifications of Campbell. For this reason, even if they were unaware of the witness coaching, Campbell's prosecutors had failed to live up to their heralded "obligation to protect the innocent."

Even worse, the evidence showed that state authorities played a direct role in staging suggestive procedures and influencing the eyewitnesses.

For example, Detective Woods and officials in the attorney general's office choreographed the initial display of Campbell to eyewitnesses Morley and Irvine. On January 13, 1938, Woods arranged for the two Trust Company employees to come to the office of Assistant Attorney General Ambrose McCall (head of the securities bureau), where Campbell had been summoned to appear on a securities matter unrelated to the forgeries. The detective told Irvine that a man "under suspicion" for the forgeries would be appearing there. Morley similarly understood that a man suspected of being Workmaster "would be brought to [her] attention" and "pass within [her] line of vision."

In what amounted to a secret identification procedure, Morley and Irvine looked on as Campbell and his lawyer spoke with an assistant attorney general. Campbell had no idea he was on display (this was before he learned that he was a suspect in the forgery case). Once Campbell was gone, both Irvine and Morley identified him as the culprit—even though Morley had seen Campbell only "from the back and the side."

Not only did police tell Morley and Irvine in advance that Campbell was a suspect, but they also allowed the eyewitnesses to hear each other's identifications. At the Daru hearings, Irvine acknowledged that before he identified Campbell he had heard two other witnesses do so. And Feldhusen, one of the New Jersey bank employees, testified that before his identification he received information about Campbell's supposed association with a forgery gang from "people connected with the prosecution."

In all cases, the witnesses were shown Campbell alone, rather than with a group of other men of similar size and appearance. Such individual confrontations—which became widely known as showups—inevitably suggest to the eyewitness that the individual is a suspect. By contrast, a lineup—where a suspect is placed in a group and the witness is asked if they can identify the culprit—may avoid such suggestiveness when conducted fairly.

This is not to suggest that lineups were not in use in 1930s New York. In fact, some police departments had been placing suspects in groups for identification since at least the late nineteenth century. In August 1898, after arresting Staten Island dentist Samuel Kennedy for the murder of a woman found dead in a Manhattan hotel, police summoned a hotel bellboy to the stationhouse, where they had "brought in a number of other people and placed them in the room" with Kennedy. The bellboy had seen the victim with a man before her death. "Will you look around this room carefully and see if you can see anybody that resembles that man?" a police captain asked. The bellboy pointed out Kennedy as the man he had served wine to at the hotel. After a jury convicted Kennedy of murder, however, the Court of Appeals overturned the verdict on the ground that the police captain's testimony about the identification was inadmissible hearsay.

Early-twentieth-century use of eyewitness lineups is confirmed by other court cases. In 1912, in an appeal of a robbery conviction, a New York court referred to an eyewitness's testimony that he and another person went to police headquarters and "there was lined up before them a number of men, of which the defendant was one, and that he . . . was asked to identify the criminal." Similarly, a 1914 ruling by New York's Court of Appeals notes that a defendant accused of murder had been "placed in a line" with thirteen or fourteen others for viewing by eyewitnesses.

The concept of the lineup, or identification parade, as it was once known, dates back even further, to mid-nineteenth-century England. There is a reference to the practice in a police order issued in March 1860, in response to comments by an "Assistant Judge." The use of such "parades" in England grew over time. In a 1930 law review article, a leading American legal scholar, John Henry Wigmore, observed that "the practice of the English police, in lining up the suspect with a dozen or more persons, dressed nearly like him, is a conscientious effort to secure dependable conditions." At the same time, Wigmore wrote that "in the United States it may be doubted whether even that practice is generally followed by police." He subsequently attributed the lack of "adequate precautions" in the

US to "the haste and routine of police and trial proceedings." As one example of the lack of safeguards, Wigmore pointed to a showup where Chicago police displayed two robbery suspects, in handcuffs, before the victim of the crime and asked if she could identify them.

New York authorities regularly used both showups and lineups throughout the first half of the twentieth century. As will be documented in the chapters that follow, both types of procedures were deployed in a way that was suggestive and unfairly prejudicial to the suspect. During this period, legal regulation of the construction of lineups and the use of showups was limited. There were no state or federal laws that mandated the use of any particular identification procedure. There were also no state guidelines on how lineups should be conducted. Authorities did not adhere to what are now thought of as best practices, like using persons to fill the lineup ("fillers") who are similar in appearance to the suspect.

New York state courts occasionally threw out criminal convictions based on questionable eyewitness testimony. But they had not, at the time of Bertram Campbell's arrest, laid down clear rules on how police should secure an identification. The same was true of federal courts. In fact, it would be another thirty years before the Supreme Court, in 1967, afforded certain constitutional protections to suspects who undergo state identification procedures.

At the same time, suspects of this era lacked many basic rights we take for granted today. For example, the Supreme Court had not yet recognized the right to counsel as fundamental to a fair trial in state courts. Only one year after Bertram Campbell's parole, the court ruled that the Constitution did not guarantee the assistance of counsel to an indigent farmer indicted for robbery in Maryland. To that point, the court had recognized an absolute right to counsel only in federal criminal proceedings and in state proceedings when the defendant faced capital charges. It was not until 1963 that the court established, in Gideon v. Wainwright, that all criminal defendants have the right to appointment of counsel. Similarly, the law in place at the time of Campbell's arrest did not require police to warn suspects of their right against self-incrimination. It was not until 1966 that the Supreme Court ruled, in Miranda v. Arizona, that the Constitution requires that a person subject to a custodial interrogation "be warned prior to any questioning that he has the right to remain silent, that anything he says can be used against him in a court of law, that he has the right to the presence of an attorney, and that if he cannot afford an attorney one will be appointed for him prior to any questioning if he so desires."

In this legal environment, innocent suspects were at great risk from unreasonable identification procedures. In the chapters that follow, I draw examples of prejudicial showups and lineups from New York cases that span the period 1925 to 1953 (the year of Manny Balestrero's false arrest). Many of these practices remained hidden from public view at the time.

Still, in his report on the Campbell case, Robert Daru exposed how investigators can manipulate eyewitnesses. His probe revealed that before making their identifications, the witnesses (1) saw photographs of Campbell that had been doctored to match their descriptions; (2) heard incriminating information about Campbell; (3) observed another person identify Campbell; and (4) viewed Campbell alone, rather than in a lineup. Daru concluded that "the procedure and tactics followed which brought about these 'identifications' of Campbell as the forger were so inefficient, reckless and dangerous that almost anybody subjected to the same process would have been 'identified' as the perpetrator of the crime."

For their part, prosecutors disclaimed responsibility for the mistaken identifications. The district attorney's office attributed Campbell's conviction to "honest mistakes" by "honest eyewitnesses." Judge Nott clung to a similar narrative. He told the parole board that at trial he gave "considerable weight" to the eyewitnesses in the case, since (as bank tellers) their "daily work calls for keen observation and detection of impostors." The judge agreed that any errant identification was an honest mistake.

But the record in the Campbell case tells a different story. The eyewitness identifications were not the impetus for the state's theory. Prosecutors had identified Campbell as a suspect based on his connection to the phone number given by the actual forger, Thiel. The state then induced the identifications by using suggestive procedures and by emphasizing that other evidence had been amassed against Campbell. The latter tactic gave the eyewitnesses the impression that their testimony would be only additional proof of guilt. Feldhusen, for example, said the prosecution had conveyed to the eyewitnesses the "unimportance" of their identifications.

The district attorney's office also ignored or rationalized evidence pointing to Campbell's innocence. For example, the original indictment accused Campbell of personally forging the checks. Then prosecutors learned that Campbell's handwriting did not match the writing on the checks. Rather than reconsider its case, the state simply removed the forgery charges from the indictment and proceeded on the alternative theory that Campbell was a front man for a larger operation. Daru concluded that the change in theory fit within a larger pattern of investigative myopia: "Every fact which gave rise to a doubt of Campbell's guilt was discarded to make way for some new pattern and theory, a process wholly proper were we to substitute a presumption of guilt instead of innocence." This filtering of evidence through a presupposition of guilt reflects the problem of investigative "tunnel vision," which modern scholars have recognized as a major cause of wrongful convictions.

Other commentators have referred to the related concept of "confirmation bias." As explained by Preet Bharara, US Attorney for the Southern District of New York from 2009 to 2017, confirmation bias leads authorities to give undue deference to the initial conclusion reached by a respected law enforcement professional. Bharara observes that innocent people often suffer not because of the initial mistaken conclusion, but as a result of "a failure to sufficiently reconsider"—what he calls "the continuing and lazy persistence in the first blunder."

The failure to reconsider infected the Campbell prosecution. Besides rewriting their theory of the case to explain away the handwriting mismatch, the district attorney's office missed the significance of an erroneous eyewitness identification. During the investigation of the Trust Company forgeries, a teller at the Marine Midland Trust Company in New York identified Campbell as the man who, in May 1935, cashed $11,700 in phony checks drawn on the account of a coal company. Prosecutors even drew up an indictment accusing Campbell of that crime. But ultimately they did not pursue the charge because records established that Campbell was at work at the Nassau County Division of Home Relief when the crime was committed.

Implicit in the failure to charge Campbell with the Marine Midland crime was a finding that at least one eyewitness had confused him with a forger. But the state barreled ahead with its prosecution of Campbell, discarding any evidence that pointed to a different suspect.

Prosecutors similarly discounted the results of the police's monitoring of Campbell's behavior. In the month leading to the arrest, detectives kept Campbell and his family under surveillance. During this period, the Campbells "showed no signs of unusual prosperity and appeared to be having financial difficulties." In his interview with the parole board, Detective Woods cast this information as exculpatory. But at the time of Campbell's arrest, the information was ignored. Woods similarly pointed out to the parole board that while Campbell walked with a limp (resulting from the amputation of his left toe), none of the eyewitnesses had ever mentioned such a limp—another discrepancy that the prosecution overlooked.

Detective Woods had doubts about Campbell's guilt. He admitted that "at the time of Campbell's conviction, he was not fully satisfied that the matter was resolved because he knew of related crimes of a similar nature that continued after the commitment of Campbell." Shortly after the conviction, Woods learned that a man using the name Hughes had been arrested in Philadelphia for forgery. The detective proposed bringing two of the eyewitnesses against Campbell—Rhinehart and Morley—to Philadelphia "so that they could observe Hughes to discover whether or not he, and not Campbell, was the real forger." But Rhinehart refused, insisting that he would not retract his identification even if police showed him "a thousand other men." Since Morley also "remained positive" in her identification, "the plan to take them to Philadelphia was abandoned."

The FBI was even less convinced of Campbell's guilt than Woods. Assistant US Attorney John Donovan told Daru that just two days after the jury's verdict, another forgery was committed using the same method attributed to Campbell. Federal agents added this forgery to their file on the crimes for which Campbell was convicted. The FBI kept its investigation open even as Campbell served his sentence.

Aware of the foregoing facts, the New York State Parole Board was begrudging and defensive in its report on the case. Despite Thiel's confession, the board cautioned that "it is impossible today to establish with certainty the innocence of Campbell." The board acknowledged the "complete retraction" by three of the identifying witnesses, as well as support for the pardon from the investigating detective, prosecutors, and the trial judge. But the passage of time made it "difficult to reach an entirely satisfactory conclusion." The board was also careful not to concede any prosecutorial error. The identifications of Campbell had been "clear-cut" and "positive" statements by witnesses "of good reputation and superior intelligence." Campbell, on the other hand, had been "a salesman of dubious stocks for high-pressure groups." The board implied

Bertram Campbell and his family after his exoneration in July 1945
(*AP Photo/Tom Fitzsimmons*)

that such facts made Campbell an inevitable suspect for the crimes. As the *New York Times* observed in an editorial, "the board . . . in this passage seems to be defending those who convicted Mr. Campbell rather than exonerating Mr. Campbell."

Governor Dewey's pardon was no model of contrition either. His statement praised Detective Woods—who "originally investigated and developed the case and arrested Bertram Campbell"—for the "persistence, diligence and devotion to duty" that led to Thiel's confession. Campbell's years in prison, meanwhile, went unmentioned. And like the parole board, the governor admitted no error or remorse on the part of state officials. This omission was not lost on *Time* magazine, which noted: "Only one thing was lacking: no one said: 'I'm sorry.'"

Campbell receives the pardon. Next to him from left to right, are Campbell's attorney, James C. Webster, Assistant District Attorney Brill, and Governor Dewey. (*AP Photo*)

Dewey had political reasons to avoid a mea culpa. He had headed the district attorney's office when it prosecuted Campbell. In fact, Daru attributed the rush to judgment against Campbell to Dewey's desire for a spotless conviction rate. Campbell felt the same way. "It was Mr. Dewey's big clean-up campaign. All he wanted was a record of convictions," he said.

Still, whatever political motivations may have colored the pardon statement, the state was not done trying to make amends for Campbell.

***

At the time of Campbell's exoneration, New York's Court of Claims Act authorized lawsuits by wrongfully convicted persons who had been pardoned on grounds of innocence. But that law only applied to convictions occurring on or after April 13, 1942, and Campbell had been convicted in 1938.

In January 1946, Dewey urged the legislature to pass a special law allowing Campbell to recover damages arising from the wrongful conviction. Without such a law, the state was immune from suit. "Only by legislative act can the State recognize in full its equitable obligation," Dewey said.

The legislature acted quickly. Within several weeks it authorized Campbell to recover lost earnings and "compensation for the indignities and the shame and humiliation and loss of liberty."

On the heels of that enactment, Campbell sued in the Court of Claims. His case went to a hearing in May 1946 before Judge James J. Barrett. Campbell looked on as Assistant Attorney General Arthur Mattison insisted in his opening statement that the claimant's misfortune was not born of malice or unfair treatment. "Mr. Campbell's indictment, trial, and conviction were entirely regular," Mattison said. "All of his rights were safeguarded. He was fairly tried under our law and procedure, and fairly convicted."

In three hours of testimony, Campbell struggled to control his anger at the system that convicted him. "It made me pretty sick when the [trial] judge said I was a brazen liar and lucky not to be in the dock for perjury," he said. Campbell also testified that he was experiencing continuing nightmares that transported him back to Sing Sing.

On June 17, 1946, Judge Barrett issued his ruling. He emphasized that "there was no malice toward him upon the part of any official connected with the proceedings." While attributing the conviction to "mistaken identity," Barrett characterized the state's procedures as "orderly" and recited none of the facts (such as the tainted identification procedures) that contributed to the mistake.

And so Judge Barrett bypassed any searching examination of how justice had gone awry. But he did provide a vivid account of Campbell's suffering:

> He was branded as a convict, given a prison number and assigned to a felon's cell. He was deprived of his liberty and civil rights. He was degraded in the eyes of his fellowmen. His mental anguish was great by reason of his separation from society and from his wife and family and in being deprived of the opportunity to afford them a living which they were compelled to seek from public authorities. He suffered the miseries of prison life and his confinement was doubly hard because he was innocent. He was the victim of a miscarriage of justice but fortunately for him the state has undertaken to rectify the mistake as far as possible.
>
> He served seventy-six days in the Tombs, three years two months and thirteen days in Sing Sing Prison and was on parole four years and six days. Seven years, six months and five days elapsed from claimant's arrest until he was pardoned.

The court ordered that Campbell receive $115,000: $40,000 for lost earnings and another $75,000 in additional damages. Adjusted for inflation, the award would translate to about $1.76 million in 2022.

With new funds in hand, Campbell made several purchases quickly: a new home that backed up to a canal connected to the Long Island Sound, where he intended to go fishing with his sons; a new car; and a bicycle and roller skates for his children.

Campbell also made plans with his lawyer to establish a "national philanthropic foundation" to aid the wrongfully convicted. "I want to help as many of these men as possible, because I know what a terrible thing it is to be imprisoned unjustly," he said.

But time was running out on Bertram Campbell. His health had deteriorated at Sing Sing. Even after his release, the strain of living more than eight years under the cloud of false indictment had exacted a great price. In late August 1946, he suffered a stroke. Only a week later, he was dead at the age of sixty.

Campbell receives his check on June 19, 1946. From left to right are Assistant Attorney General Mattson, Deputy Controller William Pfeiffer, and Webster. (*AP Photo*)

Campbell's doctor left no doubt as to the true cause of death. "There is no question that he died as a result of his imprisonment in Sing Sing. The jail term left its telltale marks on his whole body," the doctor told the *Daily News*.

Campbell had lived only eighty-two days after the court's damage award.

−TWO−
"LIFE IS A DANGEROUS THING"

Elizabeth Wean, formerly Elizabeth Lester, in 1951
(*Star-Ledger, May 17, 1951/NJ Advance Media*)

Bertram Campbell was not the only resident of the tristate area mistaken for a serial forger in the 1930s. In fact, innocent residents of Rochester, New York, and Scotch Plains, New Jersey, fell victim to false charges arising from a forgery spree that spanned a thirteen-year period.

Their stories encompass one of the earliest acknowledged wrongful convictions of a woman in United States history.

***

In 1936, thirty-three-year-old Cecelia Leib was making a living selling cleaners and soaps on the road in the Rochester area. She had once passed a civil service exam and worked for the Veterans Administration, but gave up the job when the

VA moved its offices to Buffalo. With Leib's husband unemployed, her income was the sole source of support for her daughter.

In July of that year, Rochester police arrested Leib on charges that she had passed forged checks in Hornell, New York. The checks were for twenty to thirty dollars and bore the name of the Metropolitan Life Insurance Company. Police made the arrest based on complaints from area merchants who identified Leib from a photograph rather than an in-person confrontation. Over her protestations of innocence, authorities hauled Leib off to the Steuben County Jail. There she remained for five months awaiting trial, unable to post bail.

After the arrest, representatives of Metropolitan Life distributed Leib's photo to police in other cities where similar bad checks had been passed. Leib soon faced six other indictments in New York and Pennsylvania.

But while Leib sat in jail, someone else passed several other forged Metropolitan Life checks in those states. As a result, in December 1936, police began to have doubts about their case. Only then did they engage a handwriting expert, who promptly concluded that the alleged forgeries were not in Leib's handwriting. And when police finally brought Leib before eyewitnesses face-to-face, two of them—a Binghamton tea store proprietor and a Niagara Falls grocer— agreed she was not the culprit.

On December 11, Steuben County Judge Edwin S. Brown declared Leib innocent and dismissed the indictment against her. The *New York Times* reported that "chagrined investigators . . . admitted she was arrested by mistake" and that indictments issued in other cities "were quietly vacated."

Cecelia Leib's misfortune arose from a negligent police investigation. Authorities confined her to prison without arranging an in-person identification by her accusers or examining her handwriting against the forged checks. They would later determine that the woman responsible for the forgeries was Theo Sullivan, once a resident of Elmira, New York. Sullivan was married to Edward Eugene Sullivan, who was known as the Phantom Forger and who passed hundreds of bad checks across a dozen states between 1925 and 1938.

By the time the Sullivans were finally brought to justice, two other innocent people had suffered grievously for their crimes.

***

A minor mistake in arithmetic brought on the ruination of Elizabeth Lester.

A forty-six-year-old widow, Lester ran a boarding house in Scotch Plains, New Jersey. Her husband had died in a New York subway accident, and she raised two children on her own.

In April 1935, Lester shopped at a bakery in North Plainfield and paid with a five dollar check. But she had not correctly balanced her checkbook. There was only $4.30 in her account. As a result, the check bounced.

The baker filed a criminal complaint against Lester for passing a bad check. On the night of April 16, police arrested her in her home. She was released on twenty dollars cash bail.

On April 18, Lester appeared in North Plainfield Police Court to answer the charge. She was accompanied by one of her boarders, forty-seven-year-old Clifford Shephard. A former executive of a Philadelphia fundraising organization and now a salesman, Shephard had lived in Lester's house for about four months.

By the time of her arraignment, Lester had made good on the check, and the baker withdrew the complaint. But police saw Lester's appearance in open court as an opportunity to display her before merchants who had received bad checks from a couple shopping in the area. Lieutenant Detective Elmer I. Henry brought several of the merchants to the courtroom, where Shephard sat toward the back.

Liquor store proprietor John Salva reacted immediately when he saw Shephard and Lester.

"That's the man," Salva said. "That's the woman, too."

Joining Salva in this identification were two local clerks: Andrew Evangelides, of Tom's Busy Corner store, and Martha Longcoy, of the Strong Hardware Company. Longcoy told a reporter on the scene that Lester and Shephard had given her a bad check made out for thirty-four dollars to pay for four dollars worth of grass seed and then pocketed the difference. "Yes, that is the couple," Longcoy said.

By arranging for these eyewitnesses to view Lester in police court, where she was already facing forgery charges, the detective had staged a showup. The procedure resembled the tactics used against Bertram Campbell, who was made to appear alone before multiple eyewitnesses at once.

Lester and Shephard insisted they were innocent, but were nonetheless arrested. They were taken to the county prosecutor's office in New Brunswick. By that time, other eyewitnesses who had received forged checks had been summoned to inspect the couple. In yet another showup, all of them assembled in the prosecutor's office. "There were eight or nine men who stared hard at us as we walked in," Shephard later recalled. These merchants identified the couple just as decisively as the other locals.

The certainty of these witnesses seemed contagious. To Lester, it felt like a "merry-go-round of identifications."

Unable to post the $1,500 bail, Shephard remained confined in the county jail for seven months while awaiting a court date. Lester was held in the county workhouse for the same period.

Shephard and Lester couldn't afford a handwriting expert. Their attorney implored the New Brunswick prosecutor's office to commission its own handwriting study. But that request was rejected.

The case involving the liquor store check charges went to trial on November 12, 1935. The state alleged that on the night of April 6, the defendants purchased seventy-five cents worth of liquor from the Neilson Beverage Company in New Brunswick, paid with a bad check made out for thirty-five dollars, and received

$34.25 back in cash.

Lester and Shephard denied they were in New Brunswick on April 6. Two alibi witnesses, Robert and Carrie Dunn, testified that they had entertained the pair at their home in Scotch Plains on the night of the crime.

But the jury rejected the alibi. After deliberating for an hour, it returned a verdict of guilty. On November 22, Judge Adrian Lyon sentenced each defendant to a nine-month prison term.

Shephard remained defiant after sentencing. Insisting that another man committed the crimes, he vowed that "someday I'll be free to track down that man, and then I'm going to make him confess that he passed these worthless checks."

But as soon as their prison terms were over, both Shephard and Lester were arrested again, this time on complaints by merchants in East Orange. Five of these merchants identified them as responsible for similar forged checks. In June 1936, the pair were convicted of the new charges after a bench trial. Judge Daniel J. Brennan sentenced Shephard to eighteen months in the Essex County prison and Lester to a nine-month term in the county women's detention home.

After serving her second sentence, Lester tried to get on with her life. But with so many unsolved forgeries, she feared that at any time she might be "identified" by other merchants. A walk in town became a dangerous activity. As a result, Lester limited her time in public.

Her fears were borne out by Shephard's third arrest. Having served his second prison term, Shephard was passing by a beverage store in Plainfield on December 28, 1938, when the store's proprietor noticed him. The proprietor immediately phoned police to report that he had seen the man who had passed a bad check about a year earlier. Police quickly arrived on the scene and took Shephard into custody. But this time, the grand jury refused to issue an indictment because it turned out that Shephard was in prison when the check was passed.

In 1939, Shephard finally caught a break. He learned from the Burns International Detective Agency (which had investigated the wave of forgeries) that the bad checks attributed to him used the names of certain aliases of Edward Sullivan, who had been arrested for forgery in October 1938. Experts retained by the agency confirmed that the handwriting on these checks was Sullivan's, not Shephard's.

Sullivan's wife, Theo, was the woman for whom Rochester's Cecelia Leib had been mistaken in 1936. Shephard quickly concluded that Elizabeth Lester had also been mistaken for Theo, while he had been mistaken for Edward.

At the time of this breakthrough, Sullivan was serving an eleven-year prison sentence at Waupun State Prison in Milwaukee. As a result, Shephard journeyed to Wisconsin to meet with the real forger at the prison. There, Sullivan gave a full confession to the crimes for which Shephard and Lester had been charged.

How strong was the resemblance between the innocent pair and the Sullivans? "We sure looked alike," Shephard said of himself and Sullivan. "He was fifty-

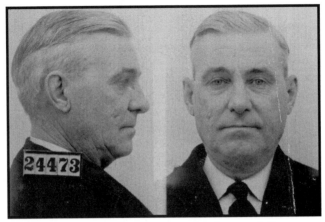

Mug shots of "Phantom Forger" Edward Eugene Sullivan
(*Newark Evening News Archive/courtesy of The Newark Public Library*)

five then and I was fifty-three. We're big and have square jaws and similar facial expressions." Shephard also concluded that Sullivan's wife and accomplice, Theo, "looked a lot like Mrs. Lester"—although photos that appeared in the *Daily News* do not reflect a significant resemblance between the two women.

By securing Sullivan's confession, Shephard, it seemed, had made good on his vow to prove his innocence. And the Burns International Detective Agency had already advised prosecutors in Essex County, New Jersey, that Shephard was not the forger. After Sullivan's arrest in October 1938, the head of the agency's criminal division urged the redress of the "erroneous prosecution."

Yet none of this was good enough for the state of New Jersey. In a maddening display of intransigence, the Court of Pardons in 1940 rejected applications by Shephard and Lester. The court rejected a similar application in 1945. In both cases, the court did not explain its ruling.

It was not until *New York Times* reporter Joseph O. Haff took up Shephard's cause that his bid for exoneration gained momentum. The reporter helped Shephard assemble a third pardon application in 1949. Lester did not join in the filing because she had been ill and decided to await the outcome of Shephard's application.

Finally, in June 1950, the recently established New Jersey Board of Parole recommended the granting of the application. The board cited Sullivan's confession and expert handwriting evidence that vindicated Shephard. On June 14—more than eleven years after the confession—Governor Alfred E. Driscoll signed the pardon.

Shephard, then sixty-four, was working as a porter at a tavern in East Orange. For twenty-one dollars a week, he "scrubbed floors and cleaned spittoons." When he learned of the pardon, he bemoaned the state's failure to act sooner.

"It's too late," Shephard told a *Newark Star-Ledger* reporter as he swept the tavern floor. "If you'd been through what I've been through, you'd be dead."

Shephard hoped the pardon would allow him to get a job more suited to his thirty years of fundraising and sales promotion experience. But no offers were forthcoming. "Nothing has changed," he said in September 1950. "As far as people are concerned, I guess I'm still guilty."

Lester, meanwhile, had remarried after her second prison term and went by Mrs. C. Elizabeth Wean. In May 1951—more than sixteen years after her first arrest—Governor Driscoll pardoned Wean as well.

Wean, then sixty-two, had lost her home as a result of her false conviction. She also had suffered psychological trauma. "I don't care for anything since then," she said. "I think life is a dangerous thing."

Over the years, Wean's claims of innocence had been met with skepticism.

Clifford Shephard after his exoneration in 1950 (© *The Courier News—USA Today Network*)

"It's too bad the pardon didn't come sooner," she told the *Star-Ledger*. "I was terribly hurt—some friends believe me, some just said they believed me."

Less than a month after Wean's pardon, the state of New Jersey awarded Shephard $15,000 in damages— a fraction of the $50,000 payment that a state assemblyman had proposed.

In June 1951, the Governor's office announced that any legislation to compensate Wean would likely not be taken up until the following year. But Elizabeth Wean had little time left. On April 3, 1952, she died in her home in Whitehouse Station, New Jersey. Wean was sixty-three. She was survived by her husband, Harry, and her two children.

Shortly after Wean's death, New Jersey appropriated $1,000 to her estate "for losses, indignities and humiliations suffered by claimant through conviction of crimes and imprisonment therefor." The award was tragically late and astonishingly meager.

Four years later, Clifford Shephard died in Irvington at seventy-one. He was survived by his wife, Nellie, three stepdaughters, and a stepson.

***

According to the National Registry of Exonerations, a database maintained by a consortium of law schools and college research centers, Elizabeth Wean was one of two women wrongfully convicted before 1989 as a result of mistaken eyewitness identifications. The other was Nancy Louise Botts, an Indiana resident who was exonerated in December 1935, only a month after Wean's conviction.

Botts's misfortune can be traced back to late 1933, when Indiana authorities learned that someone was passing forged checks throughout the state. In early 1934, they arrested Marjorie Roberts, a resident of Brazil, Indiana, for the crimes. But several victims could not identify Roberts, and ultimately she was acquitted.

Botts, twenty-seven, lived in the same two-family house in Brazil as Roberts. She was on hand in October 1934 when a private detective came to question Roberts about other forgeries that had recently been committed by an unidentified woman in Kokomo. With the detective were two clerks who worked at stores that had been victimized by the forgeries. The clerks did not recognize Roberts. But they reacted quickly when Botts walked in: in their eyes, Botts was the woman.

Botts had never even been to Kokomo. But the clerks "positively identified" her as the woman who passed bad checks to pay for small purchases. Soon other witnesses arrived and identified Botts in a showup procedure. As a result, Botts was arrested on October 12, 1934. With bail set at $2,500, she remained imprisoned pending trial in the local circuit court.

Botts was pregnant at the time of the arrest. She had a miscarriage while in the Howard County jail.

At trial, seven eyewitnesses identified Botts as the culprit. For the defense, several neighbors testified that Botts was home in Brazil all day on the date of the crimes. And Brazil's chief of police testified that only two hours before the checks were passed in Kokomo, he had observed Botts doing laundry in her home. Brazil is more than eighty miles from Kokomo.

Despite the alibi testimony, Botts was convicted. Perhaps the jury had doubts, since it deliberated for twenty-one hours and recommended leniency. Even so, Judge Joseph Cripe rejected the recommendation and sentenced Botts to two to fourteen years in prison.

In late 1935, the Kokomo chief of police learned that bad checks matching those attributed to Botts were continuing to surface in town. He reported this exculpatory fact to the Indiana State Clemency Commission. The chief also showed Botts's photograph to the forger's latest victims—and they identified her as the forger even though she was in prison at the time.

Based on the continuing forgeries, the clemency commission recommended Botts's release, and Governor Paul V. McNutt pardoned her. The governor explained that the arrest was "through the influence of a private detective, rather than through the regular channels of law." On December 14, 1935, after thirteen months in prison, Botts went free.

Despite her suffering, Botts never lost faith. "I enjoyed being with the girls and helping them," she told the *Indianapolis Star*. "I think a year here should do a girl good. When one has faith it makes no difference where you are."

In July 1937, authorities finally caught the woman for whom Botts had been mistaken. Twenty-nine-year-old Vivian Dorsett and her husband, Fred, were arrested at their farmhouse outside of Indianapolis. The pair, parents of seven children, promptly confessed to passing bad checks over a four-year period.

In 1939, the state of Indiana passed a law allocating $4,000 to compensate Botts for "the injury she has sustained" as a result of her wrongful conviction. The law acknowledged both her miscarriage and her ongoing medical problems resulting from her imprisonment. Unable to finance proper medical care, Botts had "become practically an invalid."

***

Like Bertram Campbell, the wrongfully convicted defendants discussed in this chapter found themselves caught in what looked at first like a nightmarish web merely of coincidence and bad luck. One bounced check put Elizabeth Wean and Clifford Shephard in the crosshairs of a statewide hunt for a pair of forgers. Fate brought Nancy Louise Botts under the same roof as another woman under investigation for passing worthless checks.

The rate of eyewitness errors in these cases was staggering. Dozens of people lined up to swear that Campbell, Botts, Wean, Shephard, and Leib were guilty of passing bad checks.

All of them were wrong.

Yet these tragedies cannot be ascribed simply to chance, or to the fallibility of eyewitnesses. The cases reflected a pattern of institutional failure. Authorities used unreasonably suggestive procedures to secure the identifications. Each of the defendants was arrested after some form of showup—whether the display of a single photograph (in Leib's case) or the in-person display of a single suspect. And even in the face of compelling alibi evidence, police made no attempt to corroborate the identifications. None of the defendants' writing matched the handwriting on the bad checks. But prosecutors did not have the handwriting analyzed until after the defendants had spent time in prison, if at all.

The use of handwriting evidence had vaulted to national attention during the trial of Bruno Richard Hauptmann for the kidnapping and murder of Charles Lindbergh's baby in 1932. The state accused Hauptmann of taking the twenty-month-old child from Lindbergh's home in East Amwell, New Jersey, and then demanding $50,000 as ransom. At trial the state relied heavily on the testimony of eight experts who concluded that Hauptmann's handwriting matched the ransom notes. On February 13, 1935, a jury convicted him.

The Hauptmann case led to increasing judicial acceptance of "examiners of questioned documents," as the experts described themselves. Handwriting evidence emerged as a way to impeach or disprove eyewitness testimony. In 1937, famed New York defense attorney Samuel Leibowitz used such evidence to exonerate a finance company executive of charges that he had swindled Bronx apartment superintendents. At least eight witnesses swore that the executive, thirty-seven-year-old John B. Coughlin, was the con man who had taken their money on the false promise that he would find them better jobs. Coughlin was convicted in the Bronx Special Sessions Court. But after the trial, Leibowitz stepped into the case and retained handwriting experts Albert S. Osborn and his son, Albert D. Osborn, both of whom had testified in the Hauptmann case. The Osborns demonstrated that Coughlin's writing did not match the signatures on the receipts given to the superintendents. Based on this analysis and other evidence assembled by Leibowitz, Coughlin received a new trial and was acquitted in May 1937. Albert D. Osborn also performed the handwriting analysis that helped exonerate Shephard and Wean in 1950.

In these cases, handwriting operated as a forerunner to DNA evidence, which has exonerated hundreds of defendants who had been misidentified by eyewitnesses. But prosecutors of this area did not regularly engage handwriting experts—even in forgery investigations. And the defendants often lacked the financial resources to mount a proper defense. Botts, Leib, Wean, and Shephard were all unable to make bail. None of them had the resources to hire an expert.

In the fall of 1950, after Shephard's pardon, two reporters for the *American Weekly* tracked down the chief of detectives for the Middlesex County prosecutor's office, Charles Collins, to ask about the state's handling of the case.

"Why didn't we ask for handwriting experts? Why, the preponderance of the evidence was so great our janitor could have convicted them," Collins said.

—THREE—
PHIL THE GHOST

Philip Caruso in July 1939 (*New York State Archives*)

On the morning of July 29, 1938—as Bertram Campbell languished in Sing Sing—an armed robbery in Brooklyn set in motion another infamous case of mistaken identity.

The crime evokes a 1930s gangster film. The victim, Eugene Scaramellino, was a clerk for a bookmaker in Jersey City. While out collecting cash for bets, Scaramellino sat in his 1938 Dodge near a cigar store at Fifty-Fifth Street near Fourth Avenue in Brooklyn. Suddenly, three bandits appeared. One of them, holding a gun, opened the car's right front door. The bandit stuck the gun into Scaramellino's ribs.

"Not a word, or I'll let you have it," the gunman warned him.

A second man entered the driver's-side door, squeezing Scaramellino between the two robbers while a third entered the back seat. The bandits then took the $1,400 that Scaramellino had collected, drove for about a mile and a half, and let him out of the car.

The man who had pointed his gun at Scaramellino had a distinguishing feature: a mole on his right upper lip. That mole, like the errant telephone number in the Campbell case, would create a coincidental link between the crime and an innocent man.

***

In this case, the innocent suspect was Philip Caruso, a twenty-four-year-old unemployed man who most recently had worked as a clerk at Blue Eagle Market in Brooklyn. Caruso, whose frail frame and pale complexion earned him the nickname "Phil the Ghost," lived with his parents, six brothers, and a sister at 1957 Seventy-Ninth Street in Brooklyn.

Caruso had no criminal record. But newspaper archives record one previous encounter between Caruso and police. In February 1930, Caruso and two other Brooklyn youths were found in Raritan Township, New Jersey. They had run away from home.

In a fateful bout of bad timing, in late November 1938 Caruso came down with a severe case of the flu. By the time he emerged from a two-week stay in bed, he had a fever blister on his lip.

As Caruso recuperated, he had no idea that police had received a tip from an informant implicating him as a holdup man. A Brooklyn police lieutenant dispatched two detectives to seize Caruso. While the detectives did not have Caruso's address, they knew from the informant's tip that he often hung out at a cafeteria at Twentieth Avenue and Eighty-Sixth Street.

On the night of December 8, Caruso left his house to meet up with friends at the cafeteria. There, he was confronted by the detectives, who arrested him for first-degree robbery.

At a police lineup a short time later, Scaramellino identified Caruso as the robber who sat to his right in the car. But as later reported by *New Yorker* writer St. Clair McKelway, Scaramellino's identification was clouded by doubts. His subsequent description of the gunman to a prosecutor was halting and "confused." Scaramellino could not, for example, coherently describe the man's clothing. Yet when Caruso was brought before him in a showup, Scaramellino told the prosecutor that he was "positive" that Caruso had committed the crime.

Scaramellino's uncertainty became more apparent at a magistrate's hearing to determine whether to refer the case to a grand jury. Under cross-examination, Scaramellino admitted that he had only a "three-fourths view" of the gunman's face. He also could not remember whether the man had been wearing a hat. Even so, the magistrate ordered that Caruso be held for the grand jury, which then indicted him.

At trial in Kings County Court in March 1939, Scaramellino's story continued to morph. Now he testified that he had a "full view" of Caruso's face during the robbery. Under cross-examination, Scaramellino also denied that he had identified Caruso based on any mole or other mark on his face:

Q: Did you notice anything about his face which caused you to form the conclusion that he was the man that held you up or one of the men that held you up?
A: Just I recognized him.
Q: You made no statement whatever?
A: I did not.
Q: Do you remember making this statement to the police officer in the station house: "I recognize him because of the mole on his lip."
A: I didn't say that. I said at the time I was stuck up he had a mark on the lip which could have happened by a scratch which dries up or a mole or something of the kind.
Q: Did he have that mark in the station house on his lip?
A: He did not.
Q: You are positive of that?
A: I am positive.

At the same time, Scaramellino testified that he meant to tell the district attorney that he was "pretty positive" that Caruso was the culprit. But in an apparent fit of impatience, Judge Peter J. Brancato interrupted the cross-examination and characterized the witness's testimony as indicating that "he was positive this was the man."

The prosecution offered no evidence of Caruso's guilt other than Scaramellino's identification.

The defense called three witnesses. First, one of Caruso's former employers testified that Caruso was left-handed. This fact was relevant because Scaramellino said the armed robber held the gun in his right hand. Next, Caruso's father, a shoeshine man, swore that his son was home in bed at the time of the crime.

Then Caruso testified. He denied any involvement in the robbery. He also recounted that during the police lineup he heard Scaramellino refer to the "mole on his lip" as a reason he picked Caruso. "I turned to the detective and I said, 'That isn't a mole; it is a fever blister. I just got out of bed,'" Caruso recalled.

The case went to the jury, which had to choose between Scaramellino's identification and Caruso's alibi.

During its deliberations, the jury asked whether it could recommend clemency. Judge Brancato confirmed that it could. Then the foreperson asked for testimony to be read back concerning "identification at the time the robbery was committed." But the court stenographer was home sick. With Caruso's fate hanging in the balance, Judge Brancato presented two options to the jury:

If you gentlemen can find your way clear to gain information you wish from members of the jury, all right. If there is any serious doubt as to the point involved and you must have the testimony of this witness read to you, you will have to wait a little while until the stenographer comes here. If, however, the testimony you want to have read, the point you have in mind can be solved among yourselves from your own recollection, then you may continue on with your deliberations and may arrive at some agreement . . . .

Given the jury's request for the testimony, it seems apparent that there was "serious doubt." Brancato's remarks thus both appealed to the jury's impatience and reflected his own. The jury took Brancato's cue and found its "way clear" to resolve any doubts without waiting for the stenographer.

On March 9, 1939, the jury convicted Caruso, with a recommendation for clemency. The verdict caught the attention of the *Daily News*, which featured Caruso's nickname in its coverage. "Jury Convicts 'Ghost,' With a Bid for Mercy," the headline screamed.

But Caruso would receive no mercy. A month later, Brancato sentenced him to "not less than ten years and no more than twenty years" in prison.

***

And so Caruso joined Campbell in Sing Sing. After serving four months there, Caruso was transferred to Great Meadow Prison in Comstock.

Then, in July 1939, police reopened the case based on a tip from another inmate in the prison. The tip led to the arrest of the real culprits, Morris Gottlieb and Jack Jacobson, who confessed to the crime.

Still, Caruso was not immediately freed. First there would be a hearing before Brancato on whether to vacate the conviction. Complaining of news reports that he likened to a "motion picture story," Brancato declared that Caruso would need to meet the "burden of proving his innocence." The skeptical judge added that "I know of more than one case where persons with records who have little or nothing to lose have taken the blame for a crime to save another already convicted."

Before the hearing, the judge ordered the production of "all records of police activities concerning the arrest of Caruso." The records revealed that thirty minutes after the crime, Scaramellino told detectives that the gunman had a birthmark on his upper-right lip. This fact was exculpatory since Caruso had no such birthmark. On top of that, a transcript of the lineup proceedings showed that Scaramellino had hesitated in identifying Caruso because the mark that then appeared on Caruso's face (a fever blister) differed from the gunman's birthmark. "That don't seem to be the right mark I seen on his upper lip," Scaramellino said at the lineup.

The withheld records would have eviscerated the state's case, which rested entirely on Scaramellino's identification.

At an August 28 hearing, Scaramellino testified that he now recognized Gottlieb as the culprit based on his birthmark. One week later, the court vacated Caruso's conviction. In doing so, Judge Brancato urged Caruso not to lose faith in the system: "Do not feel bitter against the administration of justice. There has been a wrong done to you, but it was an honest mistake," he told Caruso at a hearing. Brancato assured Caruso that "neither the complaining witness nor the police have any grudge against you. It just happened that way. There was a mistake and there it is."

In fact, like the parole board report in the Campbell matter, much of Brancato's ruling defends the jury's erroneous verdict (and, implicitly, his prison sentence).

The victim's identifications of Caruso had been "assuring and unequivocal." Given Scaramellino's testimony, "any other verdict but that of guilty would have been unquestionably a verdict against the weight of evidence."

At the same time, Brancato criticized the police for withholding the records of Scaramellino's inconsistent statements: "Had the Court then been informed of the contents of those two police reports, I entertain no doubt as to what the result of the trial would have been." Yet by insisting that Caruso had no cause to be bitter, Brancato implied that the court was more a victim of the arresting officers' "damaging errors" than the accused.

The judge also omitted several points that contradict the narrative that Caruso had fallen victim to an "honest mistake" by a sincere witness.

First, Brancato did not address how Caruso came to be arrested. There is no mention of the tip from the "stool pigeon" that led police to Caruso. A lieutenant admitted the informant's role at the hearing on Caruso's motion for a new trial. Police made the arrest before Scaramellino made any identification. This was not a case in which an honest eyewitness mistake had led to a false arrest.

Second, Brancato overstated the strength of Scaramellino's "oft-repeated identifications" of Caruso. Even leaving aside the withheld records, Scaramellino's answers to questions probing for details were riddled with uncertainty. *What clothing was the gunman wearing? Did he wear a hat? Did you ever get a full view of his face?* The witness's inability to recall such details was an obvious warning sign. But Brancato suggested that Scaramellino's identification was consistent and airtight. "At no time did he falter," the judge wrote.

But perhaps the most telling indictment of the court's account lies in an observation made by McKelway in the *New Yorker*. When Scaramellino testified that he had meant to tell the prosecutor he was "pretty positive" about the identification, the judge recharacterized the answer to make it sound more definitive. "He said

Caruso with his father, Frank, and his girlfriend, Mary Senatore, after his exoneration in 1939 (*ACME/Bettmann Archive/Getty Images*)

it meaning that he was positive this was the man," Brancato said. In McKelway's words: "The judge thus effectively erased from the jury's mind the most significant adjective used in the trial—the adjective 'pretty,' which in the sense the witness had used it clearly indicated that he was only moderately certain of his identification of Caruso."

The judge's preoccupation with damage control also shows in his varying statements about how much Caruso and the real culprit, Gottlieb, looked alike. When Brancato saw the two together in court, he said that "there is as much difference between Caruso and this man as the man in the moon." But in his written opinion, Brancato noted that "there is some resemblance in the features of these two men"—a shift apparently intended to lend some cover to the system's mistaken conviction of Caruso.

***

Shortly after his exoneration, Caruso made the news again. In November 1939, he alerted firefighters to a blaze in a rooming house next door to the house of his "sweetheart"; while five people were injured, Caruso prevented any fatalities.

In January 1940, State Senator Phelps Phelps introduced a bill to authorize actions for damages for the wrongfully convicted. "I originally intended to submit my proposal in the form of a claim bill in the name of Philip Caruso, but believe this bill, which will correct the situation for all who are victimized by false charges in the future as well as in the Caruso instance, is more just," Phelps explained.

Two years later, the legislature amended the New York Court of Claims Act to incorporate part of Phelps's proposal. But that law authorized claims only by defendants who were convicted on or after April 13, 1942. Caruso still had no legal remedy.

Meanwhile, Caruso struggled with debts arising from his incarceration. His father had borrowed $895 to pay legal fees. The Carusos still owed more than $2,500 to lawyers. The family also had medical expenses for Phil's mother, who had a nervous breakdown when her son was arrested.

Caruso was unemployed. After his release from prison, he had worked for a month as a shipping clerk making seventeen dollars a week. But he lost that job when his employer's business failed.

Perhaps as a result, Caruso, who had a clean record before his false arrest, turned to crime. In 1944, he was arrested on charges of bookmaking. He pleaded guilty but asked for leniency based on the wrongful conviction. Brooklyn Magistrate James A. Blanchfield, who had presided at Caruso's arraignment in 1938, granted the request and suspended his sentence (a five-day jail term).

About a year later, Bertram Campbell's exoneration put the issue of wrongful convictions back on the front pages of New York's newspapers. Campbell drew comparisons to Caruso, since both men had served time in Sing Sing because of mistaken identity.

Three months after authorizing Campbell to sue the state, lawmakers took up similar legislation for Caruso. The law passed in April 1946. In signing the law, Governor Dewey warned that the state would not provide compensation in all cases in which new evidence led to the vacating of a conviction. "To do so would be to broaden the State's moral responsibility to a point that would be out of reason," Dewey said. But in Caruso's case, Dewey allowed for the possibility that—had the conviction not been vacated—"a governor might very well have exercised the power of executive clemency and have granted him a pardon." Such a pardon would have enabled Caruso to sue under the Court of Claims Act.

Dewey said that Caruso had been imprisoned for five months. In fact, accounting for the period between arrest and conviction, the total time served was almost twice that.

In June 1946, Caruso filed a claim seeking recovery for his loss of liberty, damage to his health, mental anguish, lost earnings, and reputation. He requested $108,750 in damages.

The case was not heard for close to a year. Then came another long delay as Caruso awaited a ruling. Finally, on January 12, 1948, Judge Bernard Ryan issued his decision.

For the damage arising from his wrongful conviction, Caruso was entitled to $5,000.

$-$FOUR$-$
THE KEY TO FREEDOM

Louis Hoffner in January 1941 (*New York State Archives*)

Of all the wrongful convictions discussed in Part One of this book, the one with the most immediate connection to Manny Balestrero's ordeal is the case of Louis Hoffner. Both men were prosecuted by the district attorney's office in Queens. Both were subjected to that office's identification procedures. Both fell victim to a legal culture that exalted eyewitness testimony. And in both cases, prosecutors either ignored or suppressed evidence that pointed away from the defendant's guilt.

The Hoffner case offers a potent lesson in the ruin wrought when authorities lose sight of their duty to protect the innocent. But it is even more striking as an example of how unyielding the legal system can be even when presented with evidence that it made a mistake.

On the afternoon of August 8, 1940—almost thirteen years before Manny's arrest—twenty-seven-year-old Brooklyn resident Louis Hoffner went to Kings

County Hospital to visit his ailing mother, Dora. This was no ordinary hospital visit. Dora was suffering from leukemia, and Hoffner went there to donate bone marrow to her—their second transplant of the week.

As Hoffner gave of himself to help save his mother's life, he did not know that just hours earlier, two eyewitnesses had identified him as a murderer.

***

At 2:35 that morning, a man wielding a pistol entered Christy's Restaurant in Jamaica, Queens. There were three men inside the bar and grill: the owner, William Stotzing; a bartender, Trifon Proestos; and a waiter, James Halkias.

Stotzing and Proestos were counting money behind the bar when the assailant pointed the pistol at them and yelled "stick 'em up."

"Are you fooling, kidding?" Stotzing asked.

"No, I mean business," the gunman replied.

The gunman demanded that Stotzing and Proestos go to the back of the building. Instead, Stotzing made a run for a dark adjoining dining room. Halkias, who had been sitting in a booth nearby, ran out into the street.

Suddenly Stotzing heard two gunshots. He returned to the bar area and found Proestos on the floor, wounded, with blood pouring from his throat and his leg. A scuffle ensued between Stotzing and the gunman, who fired a third shot that pierced Stotzing's clothing but not his flesh. The gunman then fled into the night.

An ambulance brought Proestos to Mary Immaculate Hospital in Jamaica. In a desperate attempt to save him, both customers and employees of Christy's rushed to the hospital to donate blood. But even after several transfusions, Proestos died at 4:15 that afternoon. He was thirty-eight.

That same day, as Hoffner prepared to give his mother more bone marrow, police interviewed Stotzing and Halkias at police headquarters in Manhattan. Both picked out Hoffner's photo from the rogues' gallery—a collection of photos of previous arrestees. Police had started maintaining such a collection as early as 1857. By the end of the nineteenth century, under the leadership of famed detective Thomas F. Byrnes, Manhattan police photographed everyone who had been arrested. The police displayed photos of most-wanted suspects at headquarters and circulated the mug shots among the city's precincts.

Hoffner's photo was in the rogues' gallery because of prior arrests. In January 1934, he was convicted of conspiracy to file a forged registration with the Bureau of Motor Vehicles. Then, in 1935, he was convicted of grand larceny and served more than two years in prison. Now, based on the eyewitness identifications, Hoffner would be arrested again—this time for the murder of Trifon Proestos.

Hoffner lived at 2356 Sixty-Fourth Street with his mother; his father, Abraham, a baker; and three brothers, two of whom worked at the post office. Hoffner worked part-time at a five-and-ten-cent store in Harlem owned by Herman Chalowsky. He earned about eight dollars a week.

Hoffner had a distinctive appearance, with dark, receding hair, and thick black eyebrows. He stood five feet four and a half inches and weighed about 145 pounds. He wore horn-rimmed glasses of the sort popularized by silent film star Harold

Lloyd.

Hoffner did not match the description in the teletype alarm issued by police right after the murder. That alarm referred to the gunman as five feet eight inches tall and 170 pounds. But since Stotzing and Halkias had selected his photo, police staked out Hoffner's home.

Around four thirty on the morning of August 11, Hoffner took his dog out for a walk. He was trailed by three detectives. Moments later, the detectives drew their guns and arrested him. After escorting Hoffner to the Jamaica police precinct, the detectives questioned him extensively about his activities the week before.

About two hours later, police arranged a lineup with Hoffner and three older men. The three lineup fillers were detectives who looked nothing like Hoffner. Detective Harry Woods was thirty-four, five feet nine, and had a streak of white hair. Detective Robert Estabrook stood about five feet eight and had reddish hair. Detective Gerard Grady, thirty-eight, was about five feet eight. All three men were heavier than Hoffner, and all three wore jackets.

Hoffner was twenty-seven and at least three inches shorter than each detective. He wore a polo shirt and green slacks and had two visible bandages on his upper chest from the bone marrow procedure. Hoffner also wore glasses. While one of the detectives (Woods) donned glasses for the lineup, they didn't fit well and, as a result, slid down the bridge of his nose. The other two detectives did not wear glasses.

With Assistant District Attorney John Krogman looking on, Halkias entered the room. He looked at the lineup for about two minutes. But he could not identify Hoffner as the gunman.

Two minutes later, Stotzing, the restaurant owner who had fought with the gunman, entered the room. He approached Hoffner and took a long look. But even though Stotzing had earlier selected Hoffner's photo from the rogues' gallery, he too could not make a positive identification at the lineup.

Ten minutes later, Halkias returned to the room. The lineup had disbanded, and Hoffner now stood by himself. Halkias walked straight up to Hoffner. This time he did not hesitate.

"That is the man; he was in the place the other night," Halkias said.

Based on Halkias's identification, the Queens district attorney charged Hoffner with murder.

Since Hoffner remained in custody, he could not donate more bone marrow to his mother. The arrest had deprived Dora Hoffner of her only remaining chance at recovery. In September 1940, she died of leukemia.

Hoffner had no money for a lawyer. In October, more than two months after the arrest, the Supreme Court for Queens County appointed three attorneys to represent him—John F. X. Sheridan, Joseph Lonergan and Mortimer DeGroot. The three would split a state-paid fee of $1,000.

The trial began on January 13, 1941, before Judge Kennard Underwood. The case hinged on Halkias's testimony. As a result, Assistant District Attorney Albert E. Short added an element of theatrics to his direct examination of Halkias. Short asked Halkias to step out of the witness box and identify Hoffner face-to-face. Halkias walked over to Hoffner and placed his right hand on the defendant's left shoulder.

"This is the man," Halkias said. "No doubt in my mind."

On cross-examination, Sheridan questioned Halkias at length about the lineup. Halkias admitted that he had failed to identify Hoffner at the lineup and made the identification only after returning to the room ten minutes later, when Hoffner stood alone. Halkias explained this delayed identification by testifying that he had seen the killer's face only from the left profile. He insisted that he had no view of Hoffner's left profile at the lineup. After returning to the lineup room, Halkias "looked at his profile, the left side" and identified Hoffner.

The cross-examination also revealed that Halkias had had limited time to observe the killer. Halkias at first estimated that he had watched the holdup unfold over a two-minute period. "I sat there, I sat watching his face," Halkias said of this interval. Sheridan then asked Halkias to pause and tell the court when he thought two minutes had elapsed. "It is about two minutes now, I guess," Halkias said after the pause.

"Let the record show that it is exactly thirty-five seconds," Sheridan pointed out.

After Halkias testified, the defense introduced additional evidence calling his description of Hoffner into question. At the time of the murder, Hoffner had a visible rash on his right cheek, the result of too much time in the sun at Coney Island. This fact was confirmed by Dr. Victor Ginsberg, who performed the bone marrow transplant on Hoffner. "He had [a] reddened mark about the size of a quarter on his cheekbone," Ginsberg testified. Neither Halkias nor Stotzing mentioned this "blemish" in his description of the killer.

The rest of the trial focused on Hoffner's credibility and his alibi. After Hoffner took the stand to maintain his innocence, the prosecution used the prior convictions to impeach him. As for the alibi, Hoffner needed to account for his whereabouts at the time of the murder, which occurred at around 2:35 a.m. Hoffner testified that between midnight and 3:30 a.m., he was with friends at the New Light Cafeteria on Broadway and Flushing Avenue in Brooklyn. He recalled discussing his mother's condition as well as that night's game between the Brooklyn Dodgers and the New York Giants at the Polo Grounds. At around 3:30 a.m., Hoffner went home.

Several witnesses supported Hoffner's alibi. Hoffner's employer, Herman Chalowsky, testified that he attended the Dodgers game and met up with Hoffner and others afterward, around 12:30 a.m. "We were talking about the ball game that I had just seen and Louis was talking about his mother," Chalowsky recalled. He claimed to remember the specific night well because the game featured a ceremony honoring the great Giants outfielder Mel Ott, who was retiring at the end of the season.

Chalowsky said he was with Hoffner until around 3:00 a.m. If this testimony was truthful, Hoffner could not have committed the murder. The prosecution therefore grilled Chalowsky for details about the Dodgers game. The goal was to suggest that Chalowsky had invented his memory of the game to construct an alibi for his friend.

Who spoke at Mel Ott night? Was New York's mayor in attendance? Did anyone hit a home run? What gifts did Ott receive from his teammates? Did they drive a car onto the field and give it to Ott?

Chalowsky struggled to answer the questions. He could not recall whether the mayor had spoken at the game or whether the Giants had presented Ott with a car. The prosecutor did not reveal the answers to the jury. He was content to show that Chalowsky could not recall seemingly major details.

There was at least one inaccuracy in Chalowsky's account. He testified that Dodgers shortstop Pee Wee Reese hit a grand slam, when in fact Reese hit only a single; it was Brooklyn outfielder Dixie Walker who homered and had three other hits. As for the pregame ceremony, Chalowsky correctly recalled the speaking role of Giants pitcher Carl Hubbell but could not remember any of the gifts, which included a sterling silver set and golf clubs (there is no indication in the press accounts that Ott received a car).

Chalowsky's lack of recall featured prominently in the prosecution's closing. It was implausible, Assistant District Attorney Short argued, that Chalowsky could not remember whether a car was driven onto the field and presented to Ott. So Chalowsky must have been lying about both his attendance at the game and his claim that he was with Hoffner talking about baseball at the time of the crime. Short also attacked Hoffner's alibi witnesses for not coming forward earlier.

After three days of the trial, the jury began its deliberations. It returned to the courtroom several hours later with a request to have Stotzing's testimony read back. The foreperson also asked for "another definition of reasonable doubt . . . because we are a little vague on that."

Judge Underwood granted both requests. Then, at 5:45 p.m., the jury retired for further deliberations. Almost six hours later, with midnight approaching, it returned with its verdict.

"The jury find [the defendant] guilty of murder in the first degree under the second count with recommendation for leniency," the foreperson announced.

This verdict betrayed the same uncertainty that nagged at the jury that had convicted Philip Caruso, which also recommended leniency. In a murder case, with no claim of self-defense or other extenuating circumstances, a recommendation of leniency is hard to attribute to anything but doubt.

Hoffner pointed out the jury's mixed message to the judge before sentencing: "There was no reason why they should recommend mercy if I am guilty as charged. If I am guilty I should be sent to Sing Sing and die in the electric chair." Hoffner requested that the judge impose a death sentence, which would also qualify him for a "mandatory free appeal." Hoffner said he would rather face the electric chair than imprisonment for a crime he did not commit.

But Judge Underwood refused Hoffner's request. "I will not play with your life that way," he said. Instead, the judge sentenced Hoffner to life in prison.

Hoffner's conviction was affirmed without opinion, twice—first by the New York Appellate Division in 1941 and then by the Court of Appeals in 1942.

***

Hoffner began his term at Sing Sing but was transferred to Clinton Prison in Dannemora in April 1941. He was assigned to work in the laundry and built a "commendable" prison record. Other than being reprimanded for shouting out of his cell block window to another inmate, Hoffner was a "model prisoner."

As Hoffner served his sentence, two men began a relentless quest to exonerate him.

Bernard Arluck, a young beat cop in Brooklyn, was a friend of Hoffner's late brother Max. Arluck and Max Hoffner had become close friends while working in the Brooklyn post office. After Max died of a kidney ailment in 1940, Arluck remained close with the Hoffner family. Convinced of Louis Hoffner's innocence, Arluck promised to "do everything in my power to vindicate" him. He brought to the effort not only the street savvy of a patrolman, but also the emerging talents of an aspiring lawyer. He attended law school at night and passed the bar in 1944. Arluck teamed with Brooklyn Law School instructor Harry Anderson, a criminal appeals expert who had once served as a Kings County prosecutor.

As part of their investigation, Arluck and Anderson pored over the trial transcript and interviewed Hoffner in prison. They identified new alibi witnesses, who signed affidavits backing Hoffner's story. One of them, a World War II veteran named Nathan Roberts, swore that he had been with Hoffner continuously on the night of the murder. Arluck also located Halkias in San Antonio, Texas, and secured an affidavit in which the state's chief witness conceded that he "could" have been mistaken.

By May 1947, this effort to reopen the case gained the attention of the New York press. *New York World-Telegram* reporter Edward J. Mowery launched an investigative series. Mowery, who had also covered Bertram Campbell's exoneration, would later win a Pulitzer Prize for his reporting on the Hoffner case.

Mowery tracked down some of the jurors who had convicted Hoffner. One juror, Mary Arendt, told Mowery that on the first ballot the jury voted 7-5 to acquit. The ultimate guilty verdict, Arendt said, was a compromise inspired by Hoffner's criminal record. "I thought it might be well to put the boy away for a while because of his previous trouble. I finally yielded to a verdict of 'guilty' with recommendation of mercy," she said.

About two months later, Mowery reported that five other jurors had lingering questions about Hoffner's guilt. "I had my doubts all the way, and I was one of the last to hold out," said Arthur J. Kolb, a veteran.

But the most significant development in the investigation came in September 1947, when Mowery reported that the Queens DA's office possessed stenographic minutes of the Hoffner lineup proceeding. Authorities had not disclosed the minutes before. While the defense never made a formal request for the minutes, one of Hoffner's lawyers claimed that a detective had told him during a trial recess that there was no such record.

The minutes revealed that—contrary to his trial testimony—Halkias had a full view of Hoffner at the lineup when he failed to identify him. With Hoffner standing in line with the three detectives, Captain James Fogarty instructed Halkias to "walk right over and look at those men" and to "go up and down the line." Halkias did so. Then Fogarty said to the men in the lineup, "The four of you turn around," and the men did so. The minutes contradicted Halkias's claim that he had no view of Hoffner's left profile.

After assembling the new evidence, the Hoffner team moved for a new trial in November 1947. When the motion was filed, Queens Assistant District Attorney J. Irwin Shapiro told the judge that "if I had been sitting on the jury, I would never have voted guilty." Shapiro also told the *New York Post* that he did not oppose the motion.

And still the motion was denied. In a ruling that aged poorly, Judge Thomas Downs found no basis for a new trial. He failed to address the substance of the lineup minutes. Instead, Downs claimed that appellate courts had already "exhaustively reviewed" and sustained the adequacy of Halkias's identification.

In 1948, Hoffner's team applied for an executive pardon. As with the motion for a new trial, Hoffner relied on the minutes and other new evidence. But like Judge Downs, the parole board dismissed Hoffner's argument, finding that the minutes were "in substantial conformance" with Halkias's testimony. It offered no specifics in support of this conclusion. Based on the board's recommendation, Governor Dewey denied Hoffner's application in August 1948.

The state's dismissal of the lineup transcript betrayed a reluctance to admit error. Yet four years later, the very same record became the basis for Hoffner's exoneration.

Momentum for the exoneration began to build by September 1952, when Queens District Attorney T. Vincent Quinn reopened the Hoffner investigation. "Nearly two score discrepancies prejudicial to the defendant have been discovered in the handling of the case," Quinn announced. One of his assistants, Peter J. Donoghue, referred to his "uncovering" of the lineup minutes—a curious statement, since Mowery had reported on the minutes five years earlier. The minutes were not new evidence. It's just that Quinn was a new DA. He had defeated the man whose office prosecuted Hoffner, incumbent Charles Sullivan, in the November 1951 election. Sullivan had refused Hoffner's request for a new trial in 1947.

Quinn's office developed new evidence supporting Hoffner's innocence. One witness admitted that he had committed perjury at the trial. Three others lent new support to Hoffner's alibi. Then Donoghue interviewed Hoffner at Dannemora prison and was impressed by his unfailing protestations of innocence. "Close study of this case and a preliminary analysis of my examination of Hoffner at Dannemora lead to one conclusion. There is a grave question as to the guilt of this man," Donoghue said after the meeting.

While at the prison, Donoghue had a flash of insight as he examined the rogues' gallery photos of Hoffner that Halkias had selected before the arrest. The photos, which had been taken when Hoffner was nineteen, provided a frontal view of his face and a right profile view. Donoghue's spine straightened. "There's no left profile in this photo. It's a RIGHT profile view of Hoffner's face!" he exclaimed. Donoghue now had further reason to doubt Halkias's explanation for his failure to identify Hoffner at the lineup. If Halkias had recognized Hoffner from photos without a left-profile view, then he would not have needed a left-profile view at the lineup (although, as the lineup minutes had revealed, he did in fact have such a view).

The state then arranged for a lie detector test for Hoffner. The test was administered by two psychology professors, Dr. Joseph F. Kubis of Fordham University and Dr. Fabian Rouke of City College. After performing the exam at the district attorney's

The left and center photos are mug shots of Hoffner taken when he was nineteen. The photo at right was taken after his arrest for murder in 1941. These photos appeared in the *New York World-Telegram and The Sun* on September 2, 1952. (*Library of Congress*)

office, Kubis and Rouke concluded that Hoffner was telling the truth about his innocence.

***

With the state's support, Hoffner finally had what he needed. In November 1952, Queens County Judge Peter T. Farrell granted his motion to vacate the conviction. The court relied on the state's failure to disclose the lineup minutes showing that Halkias had seen Hoffner's left profile: if the state had disclosed this record, "the course of justice might, in fair likelihood, have been completely different."

Farrell reined in any criticism of the state's handling of the case. In this sense, his ruling echoed the institution-protecting impulses displayed by the judges in the Campbell and Caruso cases. Any notion that evidence had been suppressed was "convincingly disproved by the trial record." While noting that a detective "may" have told Hoffner's counsel that stenographic minutes had not been made (and that Hoffner's counsel may have relied on the "negative answer"), the court emphasized that "nowhere does it appear that any similar inquiry was made of the Assistant District Attorney himself 'for the record.'" The court also failed to name the trial prosecutor, Albert Short, who had died in 1951. Its ruling was not intended as "criticism of a public official who, in his lifetime, was distinguished both for his integrity and a wholesome regard for the rights of the accused."

Farrell's muted tone belied the gravity of his core finding. Had the lineup minutes been disclosed, the trial judge "might have justly found the evidence so far below the statutory standard as to require a directed verdict." This conclusion implicitly condemned the decision to prosecute Hoffner—which rested entirely on Halkias's testimony—in the first place.

Farrell also noted other evidence pointing to Hoffner's innocence. For example,

The front page of the *New York World-Telegram and The Sun* on November 10, 1952 (*Library of Congress*)

bar owner Stotzing, who grappled with the culprit, "would appear to have had the best view of the man, but would not swear that it was the defendant." And while Hoffner had a prominent blemish on his cheek at the time of the murder, "nowhere in the description of the killer is any reference made to such a visible blemish."

It is a testament to the norms of the era that the court did not even mention the unfairness of the lineup. The state's placement of a suspect alongside three older and significantly taller men, all detectives, was not news. But this was a rare case where both the witnesses and the police acknowledged the suggestiveness of the procedure. In a 1948 interview with a parole officer, Stotzing recounted that at the lineup he knew immediately that the younger, bandaged Hoffner was the suspect and that the three older-looking men were police officers. Halkias agreed that Hoffner stood out in the lineup because of the sharp contrast between his appearance and the other men. And Captain Fogarty "was frank to state his recollection that police officers in the lineup looked vastly different from Hoffner, and were carefully and conservatively dressed." Yet Fogarty insisted that "the lineup was as fair as the Police Department could make it" given the short notice.

After Judge Farrell announced his ruling, Hoffner, clad in a prison-issued gray sweater and dark pants, alternatively wept and smiled. He denied any feelings of bitterness.

"How can a man feel bitter when men like Detective Arluck, Mr. Anderson . . . and Mr. Ed Mowery went to bat for him through the years. I don't think this could happen in any other country—that so many people would try so hard to help a man they didn't know," he said.

Hoffner called for changes in the lineup procedures that had led to Halkias's identification. He felt that other innocent men had been imprisoned as a result of these procedures. "The only difference between them and me is they have nobody to help them," he said.

Farrell's decision, standing alone, did not exonerate Hoffner; it only vacated the conviction. But the district attorney had no intention of initiating a new trial. Relying on his office's investigation and the lie detector results, Quinn asked the court to dismiss the indictment.

"It is my sacred duty to safeguard all the rights that are guaranteed to an accused," Quinn said. "Therefore, in view of the dilution of an already weak case by availability of the lineup minutes . . . I moved this court for dismissal of the indictment."

Hoffner was free. He spent his first hours of freedom walking the streets of Manhattan. That night, he slept in a hotel and awoke at dawn.

"I couldn't go back to sleep," he later recounted. "I lay there in a soft bed with white sheets, and the key to that room was on the inside. I had the key. I had freedom and I knew it. Freedom is things like going where you want to and when a door is locked you hold the key."

Having waited twelve years to be exonerated, Hoffner would have to wait several more to be compensated. It was not until 1955 that Governor Dewey approved legislation permitting Hoffner to sue for damages based on the wrongful conviction. That same year, the Court of Claims awarded Hoffner $112,290. Yet the court recognized that "all the wealth of the State of New York could not compensate the claimant for the mental anguish suffered through nearly twelve years of false imprisonment, under the impression that he would be there for the rest of his life."

Hoffner married Evelyn Hayden in 1955, and the couple had four children. While *Newsweek* reported in 1957 that Hoffner owned a Long Island sporting goods store, the business apparently failed. In 1961, Hoffner applied for a pardon clearing his criminal record, which was limiting his employment prospects. But the state denied the request because the murder conviction had already been vacated and because it saw no basis for granting clemency for Hoffner's earlier convictions.

Hoffner died in Ronkonkoma, New York in 1985.

No one else was ever arrested or prosecuted for the murder of Trifon Proestos.

–FIVE–
GUILT BY ASSOCIATION

Thomas Oliver after his imprisonment (*New York State Archives*)

In October 1945, less than three months after the exoneration of Bertram Campbell, two assailants robbed and assaulted a seventy-two-year-old widow living on the West Side of Manhattan. The ensuing criminal investigation showed that the Campbell case had not ushered in an era of greater scrutiny of eyewitness identifications. It also highlighted the heightened obstacles facing Black people in New York's criminal justice system.

***

The widow, Sophie Wright, lived in an apartment at 430 West Fifty-Third Street, between Ninth and Tenth Avenues. At about 2:00 a.m. on October 22, Wright was asleep in bed when intruders broke into her apartment through the kitchen door. Awakened by the noise, she went to turn on the light in her room. One of the assailants then hit Wright on the side of the face with an iron bar. The force of the blows broke Wright's jaw and dislodged her eye from its socket. She was taken to City Hospital and remained there for thirty days. Wright ultimately had to have her left eye removed.

Based on a description given by Wright, police detained a twenty-year-old Black man, Eddie Lee Wilber. At the hospital, Wright identified Wilber as one of the assailants. Wilber confessed to the crime and implicated an acquaintance, Thomas Oliver, a seventeen-year-old Black man. While Oliver maintained his innocence, Wright identified him as the second assailant. Oliver was arrested and indicted on assault and robbery charges.

The case went to trial on February 4, 1946, before Judge Owen W. Bohan of the Court of General Sessions in New York County. Since Wilber had disavowed his confession, he and Oliver were tried together. Wright positively identified both of them in the courtroom. But Oliver had an alibi supported by multiple witnesses: he was home in bed at the time of the crime.

The jury rejected Oliver's alibi and convicted both defendants. On February 28, 1946, Judge Bohan sentenced each to ten to fifteen years.

During an interview with officials at a prison reception center in Elmira, New York, Wilber changed his story again. This time, he admitted his guilt and declared Oliver innocent. Wilber said he had falsely implicated Oliver to protect his actual accomplice—a man Wilber knew as J. Camp. Wilber told police of several local bars that Camp patronized.

The district attorney reopened the case. Detectives soon identified James Campbell (no relation to Bertram) as the new suspect. But Campbell had apparently fled the city. As police sought out Campbell, Oliver remained in prison.

Then an investigator for the DA's office reinterviewed Sophie Wright, who had unhesitatingly identified Oliver at trial. The investigator, Harold Danforth, learned that Wright had testified in great detail about the assailants' jackets, shirts, and pants. Yet during the new interview, Wright conceded that she had little opportunity to observe her attackers. "I had just turned on the light when they knocked me out," she said. Wright also said she had poor eyesight and typically wore a pair of thick glasses—which she was not wearing at the time of the assault. Danforth then asked Wright how she could have described the attackers' clothing given the suddenness of the attack and her bad eyesight. "Well, I had seen them in the neighborhood— they're neighborhood boys," Wright replied.

Danforth realized that Wright's testimony about the clothing was not based on observations made during the attack. "In fact, Mrs. Wright, if you were struck as you turned on the light and you were not wearing your glasses, it would not have been possible for you to have seen their clothes in such detail as you so testified," Danforth said.

Wright had based her description of Oliver and Wilber on past occasions when she had seen them together in the neighborhood. Her identification of Oliver rested on a "mental association" linking him to Wilber.

Wright retracted the identification. Still, without the new suspect in custody, the district attorney was not prepared to seek Oliver's release. And so Oliver languished in Auburn State Prison in upstate New York, even though the only two grounds for his arrest—Wilber's accusation and Wright's identification—had been withdrawn.

Finally, on December 2, 1946, police located and arrested James Campbell. A day later, Campbell confessed to the crime.

On December 6, the district attorney's office announced that Oliver was innocent. He had served 409 days in prison.

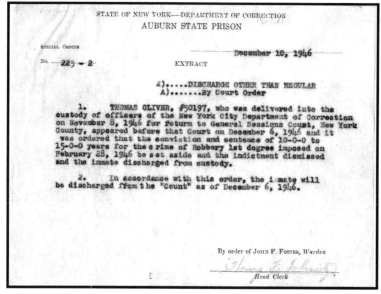

Auburn State Prison discharge order for Oliver after his exoneration in 1946
(*New York State Archives*)

The Oliver case provided more evidence of the need to scrutinize eyewitness testimony. Oliver and Campbell hardly looked alike. Oliver was five feet, five and a half inches tall and weighed 138 pounds. Campbell was at least five feet, nine inches tall (his recorded height as of 1941) and, at twenty-six, was about eight years older than Oliver.

The precise circumstances that led to Oliver's conviction are elusive, because no transcript of his trial is available and because (unlike the cases discussed earlier, all of which involved white defendants) his ordeal received little media coverage. Even so, the case highlights the calamitous effect of crediting an unreliable eyewitness identification. The state's failure enabled Wilber to pin a crime on an innocent person.

The Oliver case had echoes of the wrongful conviction of Manhattan resident William Hansley seven years earlier.

On December 28, 1938, Hansley, a twenty-eight-year-old Black man, appeared as a witness for the state in a trial at the Manhattan Criminal Court Building. After testifying, he went to another courtroom, where two men he knew were being arraigned in the assault of a cab driver.

Upon seeing him, the cab driver told authorities that Hansley had participated in the attack. Even though the other two defendants insisted otherwise, authorities arrested and tried Hansley for the assault. On February 7, 1939, Hansley was convicted and sentenced to fifteen to thirty months in Sing Sing.

Still, a public defender persuaded the New York County District Attorney's Office to reopen the case based on a letter written by Hansley's mother. A subsequent investigation found that the victim's identification was mistaken and that Hansley was home sick at the time of the crime. On April 27, 1939, Judge George L. Donnellan of the Court of General Sessions granted the state's request to vacate the conviction, declaring "there is reasonable doubt as to the guilt of this man, and I am only too glad to grant the motion."

Hansley served seventy-eight days in Sing Sing for a crime he did not commit.

In both the Hansley and Oliver cases, authorities neither tested the victims' identifications nor investigated the defendants' claims of innocence until after they had been imprisoned. And in Oliver's case, even the victim's recantation was not considered adequate to undo the conviction. Oliver remained in prison until police located and arrested Wilber's newly implicated accomplice.

Oliver's exoneration came little over a year after Bertram Campbell's. Given the uproar over the Campbell case, one might have expected the news of a second wrongful conviction to generate similar attention. But that did not happen.

The disparate reaction to the two cases is telling.

In the summer of 1945, the exoneration of Campbell, a white, middle-class professional, drew extensive coverage from all of New York's leading newspapers, stirred cries for reform, prompted an investigation by the criminal bar association, and led Governor Dewey to commission a study on erroneous conviction. The *New York Times* put Campbell's pardon on the front page and ran at least thirty related stories (including two editorials) in the thirteen months after the real forger's arrest.

By contrast, the state's admission that it had wrongfully imprisoned Oliver, a young Black man, barely seemed to register with the media or the legal community. The *Times* relegated the case to a short article on page twenty-three. The *World-Telegram*, which covered the Campbell and Hoffner cases exhaustively, devoted only five paragraphs to Oliver's exoneration.

The coverage of the Caruso and Campbell exonerations featured extensive reporting on the defendants' backgrounds, family, and suffering. In Caruso's case, newspapers like the *Brooklyn Eagle* dwelt on the "untiring efforts" of his "sweetheart," Mary Senatore. Photos in the papers highlighted Caruso's happy reunion with her and his parents.

But the public learned little about exonerated Black defendants. In its brief report of Hansley's release, the *Daily News* described him as "28, colored, of 2524 Seventh Ave." The *New York Times* referred to Hansley as "a Negro who had been convicted four months ago of an attack on a Negro taxicab driver." Neither paper interviewed Hansley or said more about him. This scant coverage is especially revealing because the facts of Hansley's case sound like the stuff of surreal melodrama. Having testified for the state in a pending case, a man is misidentified and falsely arrested in what should be the safest of legal spaces: a courtroom. Then, with the man suffering in Sing Sing, a plea from his mother persuades the district attorney to reopen the case. Had Hansley been white, the tale would have captured the front pages.

Thomas Oliver served significantly more time in prison than Hansley, but received about the same amount of attention in the *Times*: a three-paragraph story describing him as "innocent youth" and otherwise offered no details about him.

As of this writing, the National Registry of Exonerations identifies thirty exonerations that occurred in New York State between 1900 and 1972. None of these thirty records lists the defendant's race as Black (Oliver's race is noted as unknown). Yet in the wrongful convictions acknowledged in New York since 1989, Black people have accounted for more than half of the approximately three hundred exonerees.

It's reasonable to assume there were many other erroneous convictions of Black people in the first half of the twentieth century. Some likely never came to light because the defendants lacked the resources and support required for exoneration. Since 1992, the Innocence Project, a national nonprofit dedicated to exposing wrongful convictions, has provided legal services to the incarcerated on a pro bono basis—meaning that its clients do not pay legal fees. The Innocence Project not only takes on cases without regard to race, but also has identified factors that put people of color at a higher risk for wrongful conviction. The results of the Innocence Project's efforts have been stunning: 225 of the 375 people exonerated by DNA testing since 1989 were Black.

Before the modern innocence movement, a wrongfully convicted defendant's best hope often lay in the possibility that a newspaper would take up their cause. Reporters helped exonerate Bertram Campbell, Louis Hoffner, and Clifford Shephard. But as shown in the coverage of the Hansley and Oliver cases, newspapers in mid-twentieth-century America paid less attention to injustices suffered by Black people.

There was a forerunner of the Innocence Project named The Court of Last Resort, which grew out of a magazine series by author Erle Stanley Gardner (who created the character Perry Mason). Formed in 1946, the Court of Last Resort included a small group of investigators, lawyers, and journalists who looked into suspect convictions and highlighted corruption in the criminal justice system. Unlike the Innocence Project, though, Gardner and his team focused on cases involving white defendants. As Professor Ian Burney has found, the Court of Last Resort steered away from "potentially contentious cases, including those involving race."

Without a contemporaneous investigation, it is hard to prove, based solely on court records, that any given minority defendant was wrongfully convicted. But one can examine old trial transcripts and find reasons to doubt some convictions, especially given what we know today about the unreliability of eyewitness testimony. One such case arose several years before Thomas Oliver's arrest and turned on a fleeting glance during an armed robbery.

***

In the early morning of May 31, 1942, Melvin Simmons neared the end of his shift as a clerk at the Sidney Toggery Shop, a haberdashery store at 437 Lenox Avenue, Manhattan. Sometime between 12:30 and 1:00 a.m., a short man wearing a hat walked in.

"I want to see a shirt," the man said.

Simmons turned to remove the shirt from its case. When he turned around, the man had a gun in his hand.

"This is a stickup," the man said.

The man shoved Simmons and store manager Jack Schoenfeld toward a cellar door behind the cash register. He then frisked Simmons and removed seven dollars from Simmons's pocket.

"Go down in the cellar," the armed man commanded.

Just as Simmons began to descend the stairs, he turned and saw a second man, about six feet from the cash register.

Simmons and Schoenfeld remained in the cellar for about five minutes. When they returned upstairs, the register had been ransacked, and the men were gone.

The victims reported the crime to police. That night, Simmons gave a description of the two men to police. The armed man was a "short dark fellow" who was Black. He wore a dark suit and a hat. The other man was a "tall fellow," also Black, but "lighter than the short fellow."

About a month later, on June 27, Detective Harry Browser picked up Simmons in a squad car and took him to the police station. Browser told Simmons he had a suspect in the robbery. The detective brought Simmons into a room where a single person, Horace Wright, was sitting.

"Do you see anybody in this room that was involved in that robbery?" Detective Browser asked.

Simmons walked over to the suspect.

"That is the man," Simmons said.

On that basis alone—an identification based on a quick look at the man standing at the cash register four weeks earlier—police arrested Wright.

Wright, twenty-four, had no criminal record. He lived with his mother, Mattie Wright, at 2441 Seventh Avenue in Manhattan. He worked as a salesman at Esquire Tailors, a clothing store near his home.

Wright denied any involvement in the robbery. He insisted that on the night of the crime, he remained at work from 7:00 p.m. until 1:10 a.m. before going straight home.

The case went to trial in October 1942 at the Manhattan Criminal Courthouse at 100 Centre Street. For the state's case, Assistant District Attorney Edward S. Joseph called only two witnesses—Simmons and Detective Browser—who testified to the facts described above.

Simmons, who was Black, identified Wright as the "tall fellow" who wore a hat and whose skin was "lighter" than the man with the gun. Simmons testified that Wright was the man he saw as he was about to go down in the cellar:

Q: Do you see that man in court?
A: Yes.
Q: I want you to step off that stand and walk over to where he is and point him out to the jury.
A: (Witness complies and indicates defendant).
Q: Now, Mr. Simmons, are you sure this is the man?

A: I am positive.

On cross-examination, though, Simmons admitted he had given police a spare description of the assailants:

Q: What description did you give the police as to the man who was in the store?
A: The officer that came there, I told him the description: a short fellow and a tall fellow.
Q: What was the description of the short fellow?
A: He was short and dark.
Q: Is that all?
A: That's all I can remember giving that night. I was excited and all I could say was there were two fellows.

Simmons allowed that he wasn't sure if "the tall fellow" had a mustache. Wright wore a mustache at trial and testified he had had one on the date of the crime. Simmons also admitted there were no distinguishing marks or characteristics on the "tall fellow's" face. Simmons didn't "scrutinize" the face: "I just looked at his face and the face I could never forget."

Wright's counsel also cross-examined Simmons on how the detective secured the identification:

Q: Did you have a conversation with Detective Browser?
A: What do you mean, before going there?
Q: Yes.
A: He told me he had some suspects over there, and when he took me over there he took me in a room and showed me this man there and he asked me could I identify the man, and I told him that was the man who was in the store at that particular time.

Simmons said that only Wright and Detective Browser were present when he made the identification.

The defense presented alibi testimony from Wright, his mother, and two employees of the clothing store that employed Wright. Mattie Wright testified that her son had arrived home on May 31 at around 1:25 a.m. The employees, a salesman and a tailor, backed Wright's claim that he was at the store—which was about nine blocks from the crime scene—until shortly after 1:00 a.m. But on cross-examination, both employees struggled to recall the dates on which they had learned of Wright's arrest. Assistant District Attorney Joseph used this uncertainty to suggest that the two witnesses could not be trusted to recall Wright's comings and goings on the date of the crime, which was five months before the arrest.

It appeared the case would turn on the jury's evaluation of Simmons's identification and Wright's alibi. Then, near the end of trial, the state called Detective Browser back to the stand to impugn Wright's credibility. Wright had testified that he was alone in his apartment when arrested. But Browser claimed that he saw a woman in Wright's bed at the time of the arrest.

Joseph featured this discrepancy in his closing. "Now, I don't care to go into the defendant's morals, but when he takes the stand he has got to tell the truth. If he is going to lie about one little thing, you have a right to think that he is going to lie about a lot of little things."

At 4:12 p.m. on October 16, the jury began its deliberations. It returned forty-eight minutes later with a verdict: guilty.

The court sentenced Wright to ten to twenty years in Sing Sing.

On appeal, Wright's conviction was affirmed. But the dissents of two Appellate Division justices highlight substantial questions about the jury's verdict.

In the first dissent, Justice Joseph M. Callahan said the admission of the detective's rebuttal testimony required reversal of the conviction: "The admission of collateral evidence on rebuttal, to contradict defendant's denial of an alleged immoral act in no way connected with the crime charged, was prejudicial error." In fact, District Attorney Frank Hogan admitted in the state's appeal brief that the evidence was inadmissible under New York law. Hogan argued that "it was not so prejudicial" because "no New York County jury would permit evidence to the effect that a man—known to be single—was sleeping with a woman affect its findings on the entirely unrelated question of whether that man had previously committed a robbery." Yet Joseph's closing argument had linked those very issues to attack Wright's credibility.

In the second dissent, Justice Irwin Untermyer voted to reverse and dismiss the indictment—reflecting his view that no reasonable jury would have convicted Wright.

The historical record does not establish whether Horace Wright was "the wrong man." But his conviction was clouded by doubt. The identifying witness claimed to have seen Wright for a fleeting moment as another man pointed a gun at him and forced him into a cellar. The state offered no other evidence of Wright's guilt. In such a case, it is essential that the eyewitness identification be obtained through a nonsuggestive procedure. The showup that led to Wright's arrest does not meet such a standard. Police told the eyewitness they had a suspect in custody. They then brought the witness into a precinct room where only Wright was present. The resulting identification was not a reasonable basis to convict Wright.

***

As the Wright case shows, New York authorities routinely staked their cases on eyewitness identifications of the defendant. But in one prosecution of a Black defendant soon after Thomas Oliver's exoneration, the state disregarded eyewitness testimony that pointed to the defendant's innocence.

In September 1947, an intruder entered the Brooklyn home of fifteen-year-old Selma Graff and beat her to death with an iron bar. The attack awakened Graff's ten-year-old brother, Donald. He witnessed the murder and then took a blow on the head from the fleeing assailant. Five months later, police arrested Samuel Tito Williams, an eighteen-year-old Black man with no criminal record. Williams was initially picked up in a burglary investigation around three thirty in the morning of September 8. Then authorities interrogated Williams over a nearly continuous twenty-four-hour period. Williams ultimately confessed to the murder of Selma Graff. At an arraignment the next day, though, he pleaded not guilty. Williams alleged that police tortured him into giving the confession.

Under cross-examination at trial, the one living witness to the crime, Donald Graff, said the perpetrator was a white man. He had given this information to the detectives during the investigation. Donald also testified that detectives brought Williams before him at school in a showup. Graff failed to identify Williams at the showup and could not do so at trial. A detective also admitted that the police teletype alarm issued after the crime described the assailant as a white man.

Williams was still convicted of murder, and the conviction was affirmed by New York's highest court. But fifteen years later, the United States Court of Appeals for the Second Circuit vacated the conviction on the ground that the confession had been illegally obtained. The court found that Williams had admitted the crime only after "a long and exhausting interrogation by relays of questioners" and only after the police promised he could see his mother if he confessed. The tactics were coercive, especially given Williams's "weakened physical condition and relative youth" (Williams had been discharged from the Navy for medical reasons). The court ruled that "a confession obtained by these methods cannot be introduced against an accused consistently with the constitutional guarantee that his life and liberty may not be taken from him without due process of law."

In 1974, the case again came before the Second Circuit after a jury awarded Williams $120,000 in damages from the City of New York for malicious prosecution. Affirming the judgment, the court found that the methods used against Williams—including "the physical brutality alleged and apparently believed by the jury in the malicious prosecution case"—were "undue means" of the type used to frame innocent men. The court noted that when the police first brought Williams to the station, they had no "evidence to support a reasonable belief" in his guilt—an apparent reference to Donald Graff's description of the murderer as a white man.

As the Williams case demonstrates, eyewitness misidentification was just one of multiple criminal justice issues facing people of color in the 1940s. At that time, the National Association for the Advancement of Colored People (NAACP) and other civil rights groups were engaged in a campaign to highlight and combat police brutality and racial violence in New York City. As scholars have documented, acts of violence against Black people plagued postwar New York, sometimes even resulting in death or serious injury caused by off-duty police officers.

For example, on May 30, 1949, Donald Mullen, an off-duty white police officer, shot and killed a twenty-two-year-old Black man named Herman Newton during what police described as a "quarrel over traffic regulations." Newton had been driving along Quincy Street in Brooklyn with his wife, Lottie, and his sister. Lottie Newton told police that after Mullen's car stopped short in front of her husband's, Herman yelled "What kind of a stop is that?" Both men then left their cars and argued on the sidewalk. During their argument, Mullen pulled a gun and fired four times, killing Newton.

Mullen told a different story. He claimed that Herman Newton had dragged the officer from his car and beat him and that, lying on the road, Mullen pulled his revolver and fired two shots, killing Newton.

A grand jury declined to indict Mullen. But in a subsequent wrongful death action against Mullen and the City of New York, Justice Joseph M. Conroy of the Supreme Court, Kings County, directed a verdict in Newton's favor. "There has been no explanation forthcoming from the City of New York, in extenuation or in mitigation or to explain the way in which this man was shot," Judge Conroy said. The jury then awarded Lottie Newton $50,000 in damages. In October 1951, the Appellate Division upheld the award, finding that "the evidence adduced was sufficient to establish . . . a willful and intentional killing, and a presumption arose therefrom that it was commitment without justification or just cause."

Only four months after Herman Newton's death, a thirty-year-old Black resident of Brooklyn fell victim to another episode of police violence. John Harvey Brown was walking to work on West Broadway near the Canal Street subway stop when two off-duty officers in civilian clothes accosted him. Brown said the officers appeared intoxicated. According to Brown, one of the officers forced him to empty his pockets while the other struck him from behind with a pistol. Brown woke up four days later in the prison ward at Bellevue Hospital with a skull fracture and indications of brain damage.

In a subsequent civil suit, the two officers, Jerry E. Hogan and John Tyson of the Fourth Precinct, claimed that Brown came at them with a knife while they were investigating screams from women nearby. Each also denied they had been out drinking.

A jury found for Brown and awarded $60,000 in damages. The case turned in Brown's favor when Assistant District Attorney Burton B. Roberts testified that about two weeks after the incident, both Hogan and Tyson "told me that they were in a saloon at about 3:30 a.m. . . . and they said that they had drunk about two beers." Roberts thus contradicted the officers' testimony about their whereabouts that night.

During this same era, Black people were subject to horrific acts of violence in racially motivated attacks across the country. Racial prejudices left people of color especially vulnerable to deficiencies in state identification procedures. Even absent malice, innocents were at risk from eyewitness mistakes. Any animus based on race or ethnicity dramatically compounded that risk.

It is also now widely recognized that an eyewitness's identification is less reliable when the suspect is of a different race. This "cross-race effect" has been broadly accepted by experts in cognitive and social psychology. In 2017, New York's Court of Appeals ruled that a trial court had erred in refusing to instruct the jury about the issue in the case of Brooklyn resident Otis Boone, who was charged with robbery after two white men picked him out of lineups. Boone received a new trial and was ultimately acquitted.

According to the Innocence Project, 42 percent of the 375 DNA-based exonerations involved a cross-racial identification.

***

In April 1947, the state formally acknowledged its error in imprisoning Thomas

Oliver. The legislature passed a law permitting Oliver to recover damages, just as it had done for Bertram Campbell and Phil Caruso.

Oliver filed an action seeking $50,000. The New York Attorney General's Office opposed the request and filled its court filing with facts intended to diminish the value of Oliver's suffering, including (1) he had had a poor academic record and, at the age of thirteen, had been transferred to a school for "socially maladjusted children" before ultimately dropping out altogether; (2) he had been found by a psychologist to be "a high grade moron" and a "mental defective"; and (3) he had committed other crimes and was convicted of attempted larceny after his release from prison. The attorney general asked the court to find that as a result of the wrongful conviction, Oliver "has been damaged in the sum of $1,500."

On December 6, 1948, Judge Donald P. Gorman ruled on Oliver's claim. The judge did not adopt most of the state's proposed findings. He found that Oliver "suffered gross indignities, shame, humiliation, mental anguish, and pecuniary loss." For Oliver's thirteen and a half months in prison, Gorman awarded him just $7,200—an average of seventeen dollars a day.

***

The cases discussed in the preceding chapters framed a series of concerns about prosecutions that hinged on eyewitness testimony. In each case, the witnesses swore they were "positive" in their identifications. And in each case, that certainty failed to withstand the belated scrutiny that came with post-conviction efforts at exoneration.

The cases exposed as flawed the methods that authorities were using to secure eyewitness identifications. Bertram Campbell was ensnared by a combination of witness coaching and suggestive showups. Elizabeth Lester and Clifford Shephard endured similarly prejudicial procedures that allowed eyewitnesses to influence one another's identifications. Louis Hoffner was required to stand in a lineup with detectives who looked nothing like him. And, like Philip Caruso, Hoffner fell victim to the state's indifference to the uncertainty of its witnesses.

Despite their obligation to protect the innocent, prosecutors in these cases rushed to judgment. No one bothered to compare Lester's or Shephard's handwriting to the writing on the forged checks attributed to them. Thomas Oliver went to prison because authorities failed to properly interview the victim about her attackers.

Finally, the state withheld or ignored material information that pointed to flaws in its case. The Campbell jury never knew of the role that private detectives played in shaping the testimony of Campbell's accusers. The Caruso jury never knew of the eyewitness description of the bandit that pointed to Caruso's innocence. And the Hoffner jury never knew of the lineup minutes that would have destroyed the credibility of the state's chief witness.

Would these cases spur reform? Would future eyewitness accusations be met with a newfound skepticism? Would the law evolve to provide suspects with greater protection against prejudicial identification procedures? These questions confronted prosecutors, police, and judges as New York approached the second half of the twentieth century.

— SIX —
THE "INSOLUBLE" PROBLEM

The Appellate Division courthouse, where the New York State Judicial Council met,
as seen in 2022 (*Photo by Rich Dubin*)

On the heels of Bertram Campbell's exoneration, reform of New York's criminal justice system seemed on the horizon. State officials acknowledged, as they had never done before, the unreliability of eyewitness testimony and the need for better identification procedures.

But no reforms followed. As a result, innocent suspects remained at risk from the same procedures that had led to the earlier miscarriages of justice. Worse, the state's inaction foreshadowed a lasting trend with respect to initiatives to reduce mistaken identifications.

Before moving ahead to the story of Manny and Rose Balestrero, it's worth looking at how and why the reform initiative failed.

***

In September 1945, Governor Dewey directed the Judicial Council of the State of New York to study the causes of wrongful conviction and recommend ways to protect the innocent. The council was chaired by the chief judge of the Court of Appeals and included four other appellate justices (all active), a total of four legislators from the judiciary committees of the state senate and assembly, four attorneys representing the bar association, and two representatives of the public. The fifteen council members typically met once a month in the Appellate Division courthouse at Madison Avenue and Twenty-Fifth Street. The council regularly advised lawmakers and the courts on how to improve the administration of justice. While an advisory agency only, the council saw 258 of its recommendations enacted into law in its first fourteen years of existence.

Dewey asked the council to "determine the feasibility of erecting safeguards against erroneous identification by legislation or court rule." The push for safeguards found support from State Commissioner of Correction John A. Lyons, who urged a law requiring that a suspect be selected out of a lineup rather than at a showup. Lyons brought strong credentials to the reform effort. He had joined the police department in 1909, rising to second deputy police commissioner in 1938. Now he was serving his fourth term as the head of the state prison system.

Lyons warned that police must scrutinize "positive" identifications rather than yielding to "the desire to break the case."

"I never believed in having a detective show a witness a picture or confront him with the suspect and say: 'Is this the man?'" he said.

Attorney Robert Daru took a similar position in his report on the Campbell case. Like Lyons, Daru had a powerful law enforcement résumé. He had served as an assistant district attorney for New York County and as special counsel to the US Senate Committee on Crime and Racketeering. In February 1946, Daru proposed several reforms: (1) the viewing of a suspect by a witness should immediately follow the suspect's arrest and detention and should be supervised by a magistrate or other judicial officer; (2) the magistrate should arrange to have the suspect placed in a group or lineup; and (3) authorities should make and disclose a stenographic record of the identification proceeding.

With the support of Daru, Lyons, and other officials, New York appeared poised to outlaw the procedures used against Bertram Campbell.

***

It took the council almost two and a half years to conclude its study. And when it finally released a report in February 1948, the council's core conclusion disappointed advocates of change: "It is not believed that the problem of erroneous identification can be eased by statute or court rule."

The study's ultimate failure to produce reforms offers a potent lesson in institutional reluctance to confront and admit error.

At the outset, the council acknowledged that the Campbell case was not "an isolated instance." It cited a 1932 study of wrongful convictions by Yale Law Professor Edwin M. Borchard that documented sixty-five "miscarriages of justice" from across the country—forty-four of which had resulted in whole or in part from a mistaken eyewitness.

Next, the council outlined the factors that make eyewitnesses prone to error. Some have the obvious limitation of poor eyesight. But beyond that, a witness's perception of an event depends on various other physical and emotional factors. Fundamental to the "keenness of the original perception" are "the distance and size of the object and the conditions of illumination." Another factor is the "emotional state" of a witness, who may experience "strong feelings of excitement, fear or terror" from the crime. Witnesses also may have unconscious biases—"business, religious, political, social or family"—that inform their perception. Then there is the degree of attention paid at the time of the incident—did the witness have a chance to prime themselves to observe, or was the incident "without warning" and of short duration? Finally, "the element of suggestion" arising from statements by others—including other witnesses—may influence an identification.

Judges and legal experts often note that a human memory is not a videotape. The council made a similar point, using a metaphor that surely seemed cutting edge at the time: "a human being is not an observation robot."

Turning to state identification procedures, the council explained that "the danger of suggestion is generally greatest at the time the suspect is confronted by the witness." It therefore addressed whether suspects should be shown as part of a "group"—i.e., a lineup. On that issue, the council agreed that "the showing of a single suspect is more highly suggestive than the showing of a group of persons of generally similar appearance in which the suspect is included."

The council's study anticipated modern legal commentary on erroneous identification. Scholars seeking to diagnose such mistakes have identified two sets of factors: "estimator" factors, which involve limitations on human perception and memory and the particular circumstances of the crime, and "system" factors, which involve police interaction with eyewitnesses, lineups, and other elements under the control of the criminal justice system. The council report provides an early template for this approach.

In addressing system factors, the council endorsed procedures used in England to minimize "the element of suggestion": (1) the lineup should be arranged by an officer who was not in charge of the investigation; (2) the witness should not see the suspect before the lineup; (3) the suspect should be placed among persons of the same general height and appearance; (4) the suspect should be permitted to have counsel present; (5) witnesses should not be allowed to communicate with each other; and (6) a detailed record of the lineup should be created. As the council observed, England's practices aligned with Daru's proposal. The council recommended that "those in authority" use these procedures to prepare regulations to reduce suggestiveness in lineups.

But this was a recommendation, not a mandate. The council provided various reasons why arranging a fair lineup, and the other protections, should not be required as a matter of law. Even with the safeguards, there would remain "an element of suggestion" inherent in the lineup because the witness "will have the idea that the culprit is there." There may be "practical reasons" why a lineup cannot be convened.

Mandating a lineup would give it "additional weight" in the eyes of jurors, who find other elements "confusing" and therefore may "fall back on the only factor involved in the identification which is required as a matter of law."

Fearful of "exalting" lineups in the eyes of a jury, the council concluded that it would be safer to continue the status quo with respect to legal requirements. This reasoning reflects a curious preoccupation with the imperfection of the proposed reforms, without recognizing the relative improvements that they would effect. Lineups were, after all, proposed as an alternative to showups, which the council agreed were inferior. And some of the council's concerns about suggestive lineups could have been allayed by other reforms. For example, the administrator can instruct the witness that the perpetrator may or may not be in the lineup and that the witness should not feel compelled to make an identification. Similarly, while the council feared that a statutory requirement would cause a jury to overemphasize the value of an imperfect procedure, any such risk could have been mitigated by jury instructions and by the safeguards that the council otherwise endorsed. The council failed to weigh the possibility of undue jury influence against the proven risk that juries would convict defendants like Campbell who had endured suggestive procedures.

Beyond that, the council overlooked more nuanced legislative solutions. Rather than requiring lineups in all cases, the state could have established a minimum baseline of fairness for any lineup that was conducted. Or rather than simply recommending the adoption of lineup protocols, the council could have proposed a law requiring them (the New York State Legislature ultimately passed such a law, but not for another seventy years).

The council may have sincerely believed that law enforcement officials would adopt the recommendations in the report. But with no change in law, neither police nor prosecutors had any obligation to do so.

The council report lacked urgency for another reason as well: it failed to address the specific identification procedures used by New York authorities, either in their day-to-day affairs or even in the state's most notorious wrongful convictions. In fact, the council did not discuss any New York exoneration other than the Campbell case.

This void at the center of the report was not for want of evidence. In fact, by 1945, several cases that had come before judges on the council supported a direct link between problematic state procedures and erroneous convictions. One such widely publicized case involved the conviction, near execution, and ultimate exoneration of a Buffalo man accused of murder.

In the early evening of August 12, 1925, three men wielding guns burst into the Art Metal Workshop in Buffalo. One of them shot and killed the shop paymaster, Ward J. Pierce, as he prepared to distribute wages to the employees. As the culprits fled the scene with the payroll cash, they passed Dorothy Littlewort, a fourth-grade schoolteacher who was waiting outside for her father. Littlewort observed that one of the men wore large, dark, horn-rimmed glasses; a cap; and a dark suit with light stripes.

More than five months after the crime, detectives brought Littlewort to police headquarters to view a suspect in the case, twenty-seven-year-old Edward Larkman.

The procedure was a showup. As Littlewort later told the grand jury:

> *They brought him out and had him walk up a little step and stand on a little table . . . and there was a light full on his face. They had him put a cap on and take it off and put dark glasses on and take them off.*

Littlewort identified Larkman as the man in the dark glasses who had fled the murder scene.

The trial hinged on whether jurors believed Littlewort or Larkman. Littlewort testified that she was sure about the identification, while Larkman insisted that he was at a wedding on the day of the murder. Seven witnesses supported Larkman's alibi.

During forty-three hours of deliberations, the jury sent Justice Charles H. Brown a series of questions about the identification procedures used by the police. But Larkman's lawyers had failed to elicit detailed testimony about the showup, and so the questions went unanswered.

After fifteen ballots, the jury convicted Larkman, and Justice Brown sentenced him to death. In November 1926, in a 5–2 ruling, New York's highest court rejected his appeal. Still, since two justices registered their doubts, Governor Alfred E. Smith commuted the death sentence.

Six years later, after an investigation by Yale Law School Dean Carlos C. Alden, Governor Herbert H. Lehman pardoned Larkman. The pardon followed a confession by another man, who admitted his role in the robbery and swore that Larkman was not involved. But it was also based on Alden's finding that the showup was too suggestive. "It is far beyond guesswork to conclude that had this method of identification at Police Headquarters been revealed to the Jury, there would have been a disagreement and not a verdict of guilty," he concluded.

The council's failure to mention the Larkman pardon is glaring. The case offers an obvious example of how a misguided procedure can lead to a miscarriage of justice. The police showup—shining a light on a suspect as he stood on an elevated platform while clad in dark glasses and a cap to match the witness's description—is so suggestive as to border on caricature. And given the jury's unanswered questions, the handling of the eyewitness was material to Larkman's conviction.

Why then did the council ignore the Larkman case? It wasn't the age of the case, since the council cited a mistaken identity example from late-nineteenth-century England as well as the beheading of an innocent man in Napoleonic France. The most likely explanation lies in institutional self-protection. The Court of Appeals had upheld Larkman's conviction. If not for Governor Smith's commutation of the sentence, Larkman would have died in the electric chair. Presumably the judges on the council did not wish to highlight such a case.

Larkman's conviction was not the only available example of the use of prejudicial state procedures in capital cases. In fact, about five years before the council launched its study, another death penalty case based on eyewitness testimony gripped the public's imagination.

On October 31, 1938, thirty-three-year-old firefighter Thomas Hitter was returning to his Brooklyn firehouse to distribute the payroll when a gunman fatally shot him twice and robbed him of $3,400. The murder occurred in daylight, with families and children across the street. There were several eyewitnesses, including fellow firefighters James W. Ryall and Richard J. Kavanagh and Kavanagh's wife, Alice. Two of them told police the gunman wore a gray overcoat and a gray hat.

About six weeks after the murder, police summoned the eyewitnesses to the parole board office to view a suspect—a twenty-six-year-old ex-convict from Brooklyn named Frank Davino. Detectives directed Davino to a room where the three witnesses sat. After Davino entered, each of the three witnesses left the room, one at a time, to provide their reactions to two detectives who waited outside. First, Ryall stepped outside and told the detectives that Davino was the man who had killed Hitter. Then, when their turns came, both of the Kavanaghs expressed some uncertainty. James Kavanagh told police, "I think that is the fellow," but he was not positive. Alice said she could not identify the man.

The next day, police had Davino don a gray overcoat like the one worn by the killer and stand amid a group of seven other men, all of whom were either police officers or firefighters. Davino was made to pull his hat "down over his eyes" to match the appearance of the gunman. James Kavanagh said the hat and clothing "had some part" in his "becoming positive."

On the strength of these eyewitness identifications, Davino was arrested, tried, and convicted in April 1940. He was sentenced to death.

Eight months later, the Court of Appeals reversed the conviction. The court outlined the identification procedures described above and ruled that "the identity of the defendant as the person who committed the homicide was not in this case shown with sufficient certainty to preclude a reasonable possibility of mistake."

Given the suggestive use of showups and clothing, the Davino case was another obvious candidate for discussion in the report. But the council mentioned it only in passing and ignored the prejudicial police procedures.

The council also ignored an appellate ruling on showups that illustrated another factor contributing to misidentification: the pressure that all detectives are under to close a case and move on.

The case grew out of an armed robbery in Buffalo. On September 25, 1937, an armed man in a dark gray suit, wearing a hat pulled tight over his eyes, walked into the Lin-Nor Pharmacy on West North Street. The man held up the pharmacist, Robert Ritter, at gunpoint, and fled with $78.83. That night, Ritter told Buffalo police that the culprit was thirty-five to forty years old, with a husky build, a dark complexion, and pockmarks on his face.

Two days later, Detective Raymond Bundschu went to the home of Salvatore Gerace to question him. Gerace had prior convictions for petit larceny (in 1932) and bookmaking (in 1937). Gerace did not fit Ritter's description of the holdup man. Gerace was twenty-two years old, not thirty-five to forty. He was slim, not husky. He had no pockmarks on his face.

Gerace insisted he had nothing to do with the robbery. He agreed to come with the detective to the police station.

Police then summoned Ritter to the station. "We have a suspect who we want you to look at here," a detective told him. "I think we have the man who held you up."

Ritter entered the police reserve room and saw Gerace alone, seated at a table. Ritter hesitated. Detective Bundschu then had Gerace walk back and forth before Ritter to try to secure the identification.

Ritter told the detective he was "pretty sure," but not certain, that Gerace was the man.

Rather than taking Ritter's statement, Bundschu "gave him time to think it over, as to whether or not this man . . . was the man."

"I was trying to clean up the whole thing, which I get paid for," the detective said later, in a veiled admission that he had yielded to a desire for closure.

Two days later, Ritter signed a sworn statement identifying Gerace as the bandit. On that basis, police arrested Gerace.

After a two-day trial in the fall of 1937, the jury returned a verdict of guilty based solely on Ritter's eyewitness identification. Justice James E. Norton sentenced Gerace to fifteen to forty years in Attica.

About five months later, though, the Appellate Division for the Second Department overturned Gerace's conviction and ordered a new trial. Writing for a unanimous court, Justice Harley Crosby highlighted the discrepancies between Ritter's original description of the suspect and Gerace's appearance, as well as the procedures used by the detective. Crosby observed that "if ever there was a case where the identifying witness should have been given an opportunity to select his man from a group of men, this was such a case." The state elected not to pursue the charges further.

New York courts later cited the Gerace ruling for the point that showups are not reliable. But the council report doesn't mention the case.

*****

The council did not make a single finding—or even offer an example—of *how* New York authorities secured eyewitness identifications. This omission showed a reluctance to confront the state's mistakes. While the council agreed that suggestive procedures may influence eyewitnesses, its report is not anchored by real-world examples. The council seemed reluctant to probe the inner workings of police precincts and prosecutors' offices.

Even in discussing the Campbell case, the council ignored the state's conduct. It observed that private detectives had doctored a photograph of Campbell and used it to influence eyewitnesses. The council emphasized that this episode occurred "before the District Attorney received the case." Yet the police had staged showups that were arguably as suggestive as the tactics used by the private detectives. Beyond that, the district attorney's office either knew or should have known how its own witnesses came to identify Campbell. Prosecutors had a duty to account for the resulting danger of false indictment as part of their obligation to protect the innocent. It was unreasonable for the state to mount a case that rested on witness tampering by private interests.

The council also emphasized that Campbell's lawyer had failed to elicit evidence of the private detectives' actions. Implicit in this point was the suggestion that Campbell's woes arose more from inadequate assistance of counsel than from any failing on the state's part.

In the end, the report called on prosecutors and police to adopt "regulations" to create safeguards against erroneous identification. It urged officials to use "caution and prudence" in their investigations. But since the council never reckoned with the state's role in past wrongful convictions, this admonition likely landed more as a generic reminder than a call to action.

***

The council's failure is apparent from the reaction of the New York County District Attorney's Office, which had prosecuted Bertram Campbell. In a public response to the study, DA Frank S. Hogan ignored the council's recommendations for lineup regulations.

Hogan's response came in a report covering his office's affairs from 1946 to 1948. The report acknowledged "public discussions and speculation about the number of innocent persons convicted in criminal cases." It then suggested that such concerns were overblown: out of all 27,288 felony convictions in the Court of General Sessions between 1938 and 1948, only three ("one-one hundredth of one percent") were "proved" to be erroneous. This comparison ignores the practical barriers to exoneration, which presumably create a wide gap between the actual number of wrongful convictions and the number of cases proven to be so.

Hogan acknowledged that "it occasionally happens that an innocent man is convicted of a crime." In his account, though, the criminal justice system was not to blame. Instead, "these infrequent tragedies are almost invariably the result of *honest* mistakes on the part of *honest* witnesses who, never having seen the defendant prior to the criminal incident, subsequently identify him erroneously but in *good faith*" (emphasis added). The sentence labored to limit the state's role and to show that the system had not been corrupted by malicious outside forces.

Hogan noted that the jury had convicted Campbell based on "the eyewitness testimony of five responsible citizens, all bank employees." Left unmentioned were the showups and other tainted tactics exposed by the Daru hearings. In fact, Hogan did not admit any misstep in the prosecution. His report continued the public relations effort reflected in the parole board report and Governor Dewey's pardon statement. Hogan may have feared fueling criticism of Dewey's tenure as DA, given the power the governor still wielded in the state. Daru had attributed Campbell's conviction to a misguided quest by Dewey for a spotless conviction rate. "District Attorney Dewey's goal of 100 per cent convictions and his having attained 98 per cent will be shown as one of the principal causes of what happened," Daru alleged.

Hogan attributed the "unfortunate" wrongful convictions to "the human equation." But by ignoring the procedures used to secure the eyewitness testimony, prosecutors implicitly removed themselves from that equation. That strategy spilled over into a selective reading of the council report. Under the heading "What Is The Solution?" Hogan noted that the council had "made a detailed study of the problem of erroneous identification" and rejected a proposal to require corroboration of eyewitness testimony in all cases. Yet the council had appealed directly to prosecutors to adopt lineup regulations aimed at reducing misidentifications. Hogan ignored that recommendation and cited the council's report as support for the conclusion that "the entire problem is a baffling one—and perhaps insoluble."

***

Had the judicial council produced reform, the lives of Manny and Rose Balestrero, along with so many others, might never have been upended. Instead, the state practices that contributed to earlier wrongful convictions continued—clear evidence of the council's failure. In fact, a Staten Island police investigation conducted within months of the release of the council's study presaged the treatment that Manny would receive.

On September 22, 1948, Florence Brennan was the only employee at the Taft Cleaners and Dyers at 273 Richmond Avenue in Port Richmond, New York. At about 4:00 p.m., a man came into the store. He had blond hair and a dark complexion and wore dark glasses. He was wearing a camel hair sports coat.

The man asked about the price of cleaning a suit. After Brennan responded, the man said he would return in a few minutes with his clothing. He did return in a few minutes, but without clothing.

"This is a stickup," he said.

He pushed Brennan into a room at the rear of the store. When Brennan screamed, the man jumped over the counter and left without taking any money.

The police arrived soon after. Brennan provided a description and told police she did not recognize the man from any previous encounter.

The next day, Brennan was back on duty in the store along with a clerk, Sue Tafuri. Around 5:45 p.m., a man entered the store and handed Tafuri a laundry ticket to claim his cleaned laundry. As Tafuri retrieved the clothes, she noticed Brennan motioning urgently to her.

After the customer left the store, Brennan explained herself. The man was the culprit who had tried to hold up the store.

"That's the man; he must have come back to see if I would recognize him," Brennan told Tafuri.

Agitated by the apparent reappearance of the holdup man, Brennan left the store. Later, Detectives Hawkins and Bowen from the Staten Island police department came to the store and asked Tafuri if Brennan had seen any suspects. Tafuri then gave the detectives the name and address of the man who had come in to claim the laundry. James Francis. 1840 Forest Avenue.

The detectives then called Brennan at her home. She told them Francis looked like the holdup man.

Armed with this information, the detectives set out for Francis's home on Staten Island, where he lived with his wife and baby. Francis, twenty-nine, was a route man for Hathaway Bakeries.

Shortly after 9:00 p.m., as he was heating up milk for the baby's bottle, Francis heard a rap at his door. The two detectives stood before him.

"Are you James Francis?" Hawkins asked.

"Yes," Francis answered.

Hawkins identified himself and his partner as detectives. They then posed a series of questions to Francis. *What time did you get home from work yesterday? Had you been drinking? Do you have dark green glasses?*

A mystified Francis answered the questions. He then asked the detectives to explain themselves. Hawkins obliged.

"A terrible thing happened yesterday," Hawkins said. "There was a holdup, and you're the man we are looking for. You will have to come down to the station house to be identified."

Francis agreed to go to the local precinct. But first, the detectives inspected his wardrobe. They told Francis to bring along a light tan jacket that was lying on his sofa.

At the precinct, the detectives put Francis in a room in the back part of the station house. Around 11:00 p.m., Florence Brennan arrived for the identification. The detectives then told Francis to put on a pair of dark green glasses that sat on a desk at the station house. As Brennan, standing outside the room, observed Francis through a window, the detectives instructed Francis to take off the dark jacket he was wearing and put on the tan jacket.

Francis's mind raced. Since the arrival of the police at his home, he had had visions of "being railroaded" and sent to Sing Sing. His fate now rested on Florence Brennan's next words.

"He's not the man," Brennan said.

James Francis exhaled. He was free to go.

Francis's brush with the police reflects the continuation of procedures used against Bertram Campbell.

Acting solely on the word of a witness, the police had brought Francis into custody for identification. They then required Francis to put on the same type of coat and glasses worn by the culprit. Francis did not wear glasses.

More than a decade earlier, investigators had enhanced the mustache in Campbell's photo so that he more closely resembled eyewitness descriptions. The eyewitnesses later said that the doctored mustache influenced their erroneous identifications. In the Francis case, the dark green glasses and light-colored jacket were intended to serve the same function—to make the suspect look more like the perpetrator.

The tragedy of Bertram Campbell had spurred much talk of reform. It had led a governor to promise greater protections for the innocent. It had led New York's preeminent jurists to issue a report on the causes of erroneous identification.

But it had not led to action.

The procedures used against James Francis placed his fate on a knife's edge. On the night of September 23, 1948, police were poised to arrest him. Had Florence Brennan uttered three simple words—"That's the man"—Francis would have faced a trip to Sing Sing.

Instead, Francis returned to his wife and baby that night. The accusations against him dissipated, like a thundercloud that rolls by but never erupts.

Manny Balestrero would not be so lucky.

PART TWO:
PEOPLE V. BALESTRERO

—SEVEN—
WHEN THE MUSIC STOPPED

The Stork Club, New York, 1947 (*Superstock/Alamy Stock Photo*)

At the end of the daily commute from his blue-collar neighborhood in Queens to Manhattan, Manny Balestrero stepped into another world.

In 1953, Manny resided in Jackson Heights with his wife, Rose, and their two sons, twelve-year-old Robert and five-year-old Greg. Manny was forty-three. He worked evenings as a bass player at the Stork Club, an exclusive nightclub at 3 East Fifty-Third Street. An epicenter of status and glamor, the Stork Club routinely welcomed America's social, cultural, and political elites. Its guests were the kind of people identifiable by their last names: Sinatra. DiMaggio. Monroe. Bogart and Bacall. Hoover. Kennedy. In fact, Hitchcock himself repeatedly visited the Stork Club long before the events that gave rise to *The Wrong Man*.

Actors Humphrey Bogart and Lauren Bacall at the Stork Club, 1949
(*Masheter Movie Archive/Alamy Stock Photo*)

By the beginning of 1953, the club's owner, Sherman Billingsley, had parlayed its status into a television series. In an early masterstroke of brand promotion, the show featured celebrity interviews and musical performances live from the club.

On Saturday night, January 10, Billingsley invited viewers into the club for a party in honor of pop music phenomenon Perry Como. The forty-year-old singer had found smashing success with his cover of the country song "Don't Let the Stars Get in Your Eyes." Como's record had recently surpassed one million sales.

Performing the hit live, Como assumed the perspective of a man separated from his love, who implores her to remain true:

If I'm gone too long, don't forget where you belong.
When the stars come out, remember you are mine.

The lyrics reflect the narrator's anxiety at being apart from his love for a long time.

On the night of Como's Stork Club party, Manny Balestrero had no frame of reference for such a predicament. He and Rose had lived together, in the same Jackson Heights home, for twenty-one years.

Just four days later, Manny stepped into a nightmare that would separate him from Rose for more than two years.

***

Before the nightmare, Manny Balestrero had built his life on two pillars: music and family. He was born on Manhattan's West Side in 1909 to Italian immigrant parents: Peter Balestrero, who had immigrated in 1906, and Maria Rosa Cereghino, who had come over in 1904.

Manny's initial time in America was brief. By 1915, his family had returned to Italy, and remained there until after World War I. Peter served as a translator for the Italian army during the war. When Manny was eleven, the Balestreros journeyed by boat back to New York, arriving in December 1920. The family, which by then included a younger sister, Olga, lived in an apartment on Manhattan's West Side.

Peter worked mostly as a freight elevator operator. But he was also a self-taught musician and moonlighted as a drummer in a local band, playing weddings and other affairs at Italian clubs. This part-time job ultimately set the course for his son's career.

After Manny completed eighth grade, Peter decided it was time for his son to start contributing to the family income. Manny already had a marketable talent: he was a music prodigy. He had started playing the violin at the age of five. He taught himself to read and write music and became a skilled musician. "I was a puny kid—always just scratching on the fiddle," he later recalled.

As a teenager, Manny joined Peter's band as a violinist. He soon taught himself to play the saxophone and clarinet.

In 1930, Manny's music brought him together with Rose Giolito, who had emigrated from Italy eleven years earlier. The two met at an Italian affair in New Jersey where Manny played and Rose was a guest.

After two years of courtship, Manny and Rose made plans to marry. Rose's father, Bartolomeo ("Bartholomew"), tried to dissuade her from the marriage. With Manny working nights and weekends, Bartholomew worried Rose would get lonely. But despite her father's warning, Rose married Manny in New York in 1932. Both were twenty-two years old.

Manny and Rose moved into a two-family house in Jackson Heights that Bartholomew owned. Rose's sister Tilda lived downstairs with her husband, while Manny and Rose lived upstairs.

The house where Manny and Rose Balestrero lived, as seen in 2021. (*Photo by Rich Dubin*)

In 1935, Manny joined the local musicians' union and began playing a broader variety of venues, including clubs in Greenwich Village. Around this time, he took up the double bass (also known as the upright bass or just the bass). Manny played for various Latin music orchestras and bands. Rose, meanwhile, worked as a dressmaker.

In 1940, the Balestreros had their first child, Robert. Greg was born about seven years later.

During World War II, Manny had a medical deferment and worked for a Long Island contractor that made machine-gun sights for bombers. He resumed his music career after the war, playing many of New York's leading nightclubs and hotels. By May 1951, he had steady employment at the Stork Club playing bass for the Peter Rotonda rhumba band (also known as the club's Latin band).

Manny enjoyed his daily routine. He

spent his days with Rose and the boys before reporting to the Stork Club between 9:00 and 10:00 p.m. His commute to Manhattan was easy: a two-block walk from his home to the Victor Moore Arcade complex on Roosevelt Avenue, where he caught the subway to Fifty-Third Street in Manhattan.

Manny was known among his friends and at the Stork Club as a gentle soul. As described by Herbert Brean, a *Life* magazine writer who later became his friend, Manny was "quiet, inoffensive, peace-loving" and "had never been in a fight in his life." Manny was also a devout Catholic who attended church regularly. After his Saturday night performances at the Stork Club, he would go over to West Forty-Ninth Street for the 4:00 a.m. mass at Saint Malachy's Church. By that time, St. Malachy's had become known as the Actors' Chapel, since the early mass accommodated actors and others in show business who worked (or partied) into the wee hours of the morning and could pray there before going to bed.

In early July 1952, with the Stork Club closed for a week, the Balestrero family took a train to Cornwall, New York, for a four-night vacation at the nearby Edelweiss farm. The days were filled with family meals in a large central dining room, walks into Cornwall village, and games of pinochle and bocci.

July 9 brought intermittent rain to Cornwall. With little else to do, Manny and the boys accompanied another guest at the farm, Karl Wuechner, as he drove to the post office to mail a letter. The Balestreros then had lunch with other guests at the farm. Later, after a game of cards, Manny, Robert, and Greg went into town again to get the train schedule for their return trip. They then walked back to the farm, even as the rain resumed.

With such mundane activities, July 9, 1952, seemed like an uneventful day in the lives of the Balestreros.

But as Manny prepared to have lunch that day, a crime was unfolding some sixty miles away, only two blocks from his Jackson Heights home.

***

Each day, thousands of Queens commuters like Manny passed through the Victor Moore Arcade complex to board buses or subways. The second floor of the complex housed various offices and businesses, including the Jackson Heights branch of the Prudential Insurance Company.

At 12:30 p.m. on July 9, a tall, thin man walked into the Prudential office. Clad in a tan sport shirt and with a coat draped over his arm, the man approached the cashier on duty, twenty-six-year-old Constance Ello of Long Island City. Ello was sitting behind a clear glass panel at a public window where customers paid for their insurance.

"May I help you?" Ello said.

"The cash," the man said.

"I beg your pardon?" Ello replied.

"You heard me. Get it. Don't ring any bells or say anything," the man said.

Ello then noticed that the man was waving his right arm, which remained cloaked within the coat, as if he had a gun.

"Come on, come on, get it," he said.

The Victor Moore Arcade building circa 1942. A sign for Prudential is visible in a window to the right. (*Courtesy of the Queens Borough Public Library. Archives, Thomas Langan Collection*)

Ello hurriedly gathered stacks of five-dollar bills and handed them across the counter. As she did so, a fellow Prudential employee, Yolanda Casagrande, entered the office. Casagrande, a twenty-two-year-old resident of Woodside, asked Ello to unlock the gate that divided customers from employees.

"Let her in," the holdup man said. Ello complied.

As Casagrande passed through the gate, she heard the man say "cash." She saw that Ello was clutching the counter, frightened. Sensing a problem, Casagrande hurried over to her supervisor, Wallace Doubleday, who sat in an office off the main floor.

"I don't like the looks of the man out there," Casagrande said.

By this time, the bandit was gone. He had collected $200 and disappeared into the crowds surrounding the Victor Moore Arcade.

Within minutes, police arrived at the scene. After interviewing the witnesses, detectives circulated the following description of the holdup man: "White, 35, 5'10", 160 lbs., slim, black hair, fair complexion, tan sports shirt." But they could not identify any suspects.

About five months later, the bandit returned.

It was 12:20 p.m. on Thursday, December 18. Ello was again stationed at the cashier's public window, this time alongside fellow employee Catherine Di Clemente, a twenty-two-year-old resident of Corona.

The holdup man now wore a blue coat over a blue suit, with a red tie and gray fedora. With his right hand in his pocket, he walked up to Ello's counter and handed her a folded note.

"You, look up this policy," he instructed Ello.

Ello, who recognized him from the first robbery, opened the note and read it. "THIS IS A GUN I HAVE POINTING AT YOU. BE QUIET AND YOU

WILL NOT BE HURT. GIVE ME THE MONEY FROM THE CASH DRAW."

Ello handed the note to Di Clemente, who was counting cash at the time. Di Clemente got as far as the word "GUN" before realizing this was a holdup.

She handed over the money she was counting and the cash in her drawer (a total of fifty-eight dollars). The man then turned to Ello.

"You go in your drawer," he directed her.

Ello took thirteen dollars from her drawer and gave that over as well.

The bandit took the money and left the office.

After the robbery, police circulated a description of the bandit that varied from the one from the first robbery: "White, 37, 5'8", 150 lbs, navy blue coat, blue suit, grey fedora, red tie, dark hair, sallow complexion, dark circles under eyes."

Each of the robberies made front-page news in the *Long Island Star-Journal*. But Manny Balestrero hadn't learned of them. And so he had no idea when he visited the Prudential office on January 13, 1953, that he was walking into a crime scene.

***

Manny's visit to Prudential was born of financial distress. In mid-December 1952, two of his wisdom teeth became infected and had to be removed. On the heels of this expensive procedure, Rose learned in January that she needed $325 worth of dental work. Since Manny's take-home pay was about eighty-nine dollars a week, the family needed a loan. Manny aimed to borrow money against Rose's insurance policy to pay the bills.

The Balestreros had several life insurance policies with Prudential: a $2,000 policy covering Manny, a $1,000 policy for Rose, and $500 policies for each of the children. With the Victor Moore Arcade so close to his home, Manny had been to Prudential's office several times in the past to pay the annual premiums on his and Rose's policies. For the children's policies, a Prudential agent normally came to the house each month to collect the premiums. In the winter of 1951-52, though, Manny made those payments in person too because the agents were on strike.

At about 2:00 p.m. on January 13, Manny arrived at the Prudential office and presented Rose's life insurance policy to an employee with a question: how much could he borrow against the policy? The woman behind the public counter told Manny at first that she could provide that information only to the policy owner (Rose). The woman then asked Manny to wait while she spoke about the inquiry to others in the office. After several minutes, the woman returned and advised Manny that he could likely borrow $300 at an annual 5 percent interest rate.

Manny thanked the woman and left. He shopped for groceries nearby and returned home.

Life seemed to continue as normal.

***

The Prudential employee who waited on Manny on January 13 was Joan Kopp. While she had not been at work on July 9, Kopp was at her desk during the second holdup, in December.

After greeting Manny and listening to his request, Kopp stepped away from the counter and found her supervisor, Ms. Miller. "That looks like the man who held us up," Kopp said.

Kopp and Miller shared Kopp's belief about Manny with Constance Ello, who was sitting about six feet away from the cashier's window.

"Look at the man at the window," each of them told Ello. "Is that the man?" Ello looked and concluded the man at the counter was the holdup man.

Kopp and Miller each told Ello it was the same man.

"I'm not getting up from this desk," Ello said.

Catherine Di Clemente was sitting near Miller as these events unfolded. She heard Kopp say she recognized the man at the window as the holdup man. Di Clemente looked toward the window and came to the same conclusion.

After Manny left, Miller reported the suspicions of Kopp, Ello, and Di Clemente to Doubleday. He in turn alerted Prudential's home office in Newark, New Jersey, setting in motion a chain of events that would lead to Manny's arrest.

***

On January 14, Manny went to Union City to see his aunt and uncle, who were visiting his parents. He arrived home around 5:45 p.m. and went to take out his keys. He then heard a voice from behind him.

"Hey, Chris," the voice said, using a variation on Manny's given name, Christopher.

Manny turned around and saw three men in suits approach. They were detectives from the 110th Precinct. The men showed their badges and told Manny they wanted him to go with them to the precinct.

"It's all right, Chris, just a routine matter," one of them said. "Come down to the station and we'll tell you about it."

Manny never made it inside his house. He took the detective's statement as an order. Without alerting Rose, he got in the men's car and went to the precinct.

Detectives Matthew Herberich and Leigh Wilson handled the interrogation. They told Manny they were investigating a series of neighborhood robberies. At first they did not mention the insurance office robbery. Their working theory was that the Prudential holdup man had robbed various stores in the neighborhood. They wanted Manny to come with them to the stores to appear before the victimized proprietors.

"You have nothing to worry about," one detective said. "This is just for identification."

Manny was shocked.

"I told them that the situation was ridiculous and that I honestly could not have been involved in any such actions," Manny later recounted.

The detectives assured Manny that "if he had done nothing he had nothing to fear." They then drove around the area and paraded him through different liquor stores, drug stores, and delis. At each stop, Manny was required, in his words, to "enter and leave the stores under the gaze of the different proprietors." None of the proprietors identified him.

Back at the 110th Precinct, the detectives then revealed that Prudential witnesses

The entrance to the 110th Precinct, where Manny was arrested and booked, as seen in 2021 (*Photo by Rich Dubin*)

had identified Manny as the man who held up the office in July and December.

Now Manny was even more stunned. It was incomprehensible that someone would accuse him of a crime. That the crime had taken place within the Victor Moore Arcade complex only added to his astonishment. Not only did Manny pass through the complex every day on his commute, but on the way home he routinely stopped at a cafeteria on the first floor, Bickford's, for breakfast at around 4:30 a.m.

Manny told the detectives he was innocent. He said he had gone to Prudential the day before to seek a loan, and he had visited the same office in the past to pay the policy premiums. The idea that he had held up the office was preposterous.

The detectives again assured Manny that if he was innocent, he had nothing to worry about. But they declined to let him call Rose.

Instead, the detectives directed him to put on his maroon scarf, gray tweed coat, and hat—the same clothes he had worn to Prudential's offices the day before. They placed Manny in the open doorway of a lighted room. Across the hallway, in a dark room, sat two of the Prudential employees who had witnessed the July and December holdups: Constance Ello and Yolanda Casagrande. The women watched for several minutes as a detective repeatedly positioned the hat on Manny's head at different angles.

After telling Manny that an assistant district attorney was on his way, the detectives required Balestrero to write the note that the robber had handed to the clerk during the second holdup. They instructed him to use block letters.

At the detectives' direction, Manny wrote the note six times. In the sixth version, he misspelled "drawer" as "draw"—the same error made in the actual holdup note. This mistake cemented the detectives' belief in his guilt.

Assistant District Attorney Thomas P. Cullen then arrived at the station. Cullen told Manny that the eyewitnesses had identified him and asked Manny to admit his crimes. Manny refused. He implored Cullen to bring the women in so that he could convince them they were mistaken.

Instead, Cullen directed Manny to stand in a lineup with about six other men. The men formed a semicircle.

Viewing the lineup from across the hall, Ello and Casagrande again identified Manny as the bandit.

Cullen confronted Manny and again asked him to confess. Not only had the eyewitnesses identified him, but Manny's note was "identical" to the actual holdup note.

Over Manny's continuing protestations of innocence, police booked and fingerprinted him and placed him in a holding cell for the night.

Too terrified to sleep, Manny prayed for deliverance.

***

When Manny did not return home at the expected hour, anxiety began to course through the Balestrero household. Rose had no idea that Manny had been intercepted right in front of their home. Around 8:00 p.m., she called Manny's parents and learned he had left for home several hours earlier. Now frantic, Rose had Manny's brother-in-law, Gene Conforti, call all the bus lines that ran from Union City to Manhattan to find out if any accidents had been reported.

"There was a lot of crying in the home because he didn't show up," recalled Greg Balestrero in an interview for this book.

The mystery of Manny's disappearance was explained when a detective showed up at the Balestrero home.

"Manny sent me to get his blue overcoat," he said. The detective, who was seeking evidence linking Manny to the eyewitnesses' description of the holdup man, told Rose her husband was at the precinct station.

"Manny's never had a blue coat," Rose replied.

She then showed the detective the closet with Manny's clothes, which did not include a blue overcoat.

At that point, the detective revealed he was investigating charges that Manny had held up the Prudential office. Stunned, Rose confirmed that Manny had visited the Prudential office, but only to ask about a loan.

Later that evening, with Gene Conforti's help, Rose learned that Manny had been arrested and would be arraigned in Queens Felony Court the next morning.

***

On the morning of January 15, police moved Manny through the postarrest rituals of New York's criminal justice system. Around 8:00 a.m., they put him in a van with other prisoners and drove him from Queens to Manhattan. There, at police headquarters, Manny was put in the daily lineup of arrestees and photographed. From there, police took him to the felony court in Ridgewood, Queens, where he was arraigned at 1:00 p.m. before Magistrate Thomas Gray. This was the first time Rose had seen her husband since he had left to visit his parents the day before.

As Manny walked into the courtroom, he silently mouthed the word "Rose" and shook his head to signal his innocence. Bail was first set at $7,500 and was later reduced to $5,000.

After that appearance, Manny was handcuffed, shackled with other suspects, and taken by van to the Long Island City prison. Once inside the prison, Manny was ushered by guards to the cashier, who confiscated his belongings, put them in a small sack, and made out a receipt. Manny was forced into a small holding tank and directed to remove all his clothes. Guards searched his entire body to confirm he had nothing concealed on his person. After that, he dressed, was given bedding, and was put into an individual cell.

Around 5:00 p.m., a guard brought Manny a dinner of noodles with sauce, hot chocolate, bread, and stewed pears. Still overcome by anxiety and panic, Manny could barely eat.

A short while later, he heard a guard call out his name.

"Me, that's me!" Manny screamed.

He was being released on bail.

Guards escorted Manny to a courtroom in the same complex as the jail. There waiting for him were Rose; his sister, Olga; Gene Conforti; and Manny's Aunt Candy. When Manny saw them, he was overcome with emotion. Sobbing, he fell into Gene's arms.

Earlier, Gene had learned that a bail bondsman would accept $2,500 to secure a bond in the full amount of Manny's bail. Rose's sister Tilda supplied the funds, which secured Manny's release.

As Manny returned home, his neighbors were stunned to read about the arrest in articles in the *Daily News* and the *Long Island Star-Journal*. Ironically, both papers misspelled his name as Bolestrero, and both erroneously described him as a "jobless musician."

Manny retained Frank O'Connor, a former state senator, as his lawyer. O'Connor was not a criminal lawyer. Most of his experience had come in the surrogate courts, which hear cases involving wills and estates. While the Balestreros did not know O'Connor, their family doctor recommended him.

In a disquieting coincidence, O'Connor's office was in the same Victor Moore Arcade complex as Prudential's. Less than fifty feet separated the two offices. That fact elevated the role of the complex in Manny's predicament to the surreal. On the same floor of the complex was the office of the Household Finance Corporation, where Manny had secured loans in the past. And there was one more extraordinary coincidence, whose significance would soon emerge: Manny had seen a dentist in the Arcade building twice within a week of the December 18 Prudential holdup.

On Sunday, January 18, after attending church, Manny and Rose met with O'Connor in his office for more than ninety minutes. Manny described his experience with the police in exacting detail. And Rose insisted her husband was incapable of the crime. "Manny would walk five blocks out of his way to avoid an argument," she said.

By the end of the meeting, O'Connor was sure Manny was innocent.

"He was too simple to be lying," O'Connor later told *Life* writer Herbert Brean. "Both of them would have had to be putting up a hell of an act to sound and look like they did. She was so utterly sold on his innocence that she sold me."

But as the Balestreros awaited a potential grand jury indictment, Rose was soon overcome with anxiety about the prospect of losing Manny. In fact, by 1953 she had experienced several devastating personal losses.

***

Rose Balestrero with her sons, Robert (left) and Greg, before Manny's arrest
(Life Picture Collection/The Life Picture Collection/Shutterstock)

Like Manny, Rose was a child of Italian immigrants. Unlike Manny, though, Rose was without her parents for much of her childhood.

In 1909, Rose's father, Bartholomew Giolito, came to America to establish residence while his wife, Domencia, remained in Italy. Domencia was then pregnant with Rose, and she gave birth later that year. In 1913, Domencia too left for America, leaving Rose and her brother Luigi to be raised by her aunt. Rose ultimately arrived in New York in January 1919. She came down with influenza on the trip over and had to be quarantined at Ellis Island.

Rose spent her early teenage years in Neptune, New Jersey. Her father had a farm there. Bartholomew Giolito had received only a third-grade education and was not inclined at first to see his children attend high school. Still, Rose was a smart and eager fifteen-year-old and, with the support of her mother, began ninth grade in the fall of 1925.

Then tragedy derailed Rose's high school career only weeks after it began. On September 26, 1925, her mother died of pneumonia at the age of forty-six.

"She dropped out of school, and life really got dark after that," Greg Balestrero said.

Another devastating blow followed in January 1931, when Rose's brother (who then went by Louis) died in a car crash in Flatbush. Louis was crushed against the steering wheel when another, heavier car crashed into his. The driver of the other car was charged with homicide. Louis was only twenty-four.

Rose found joy with the birth of her son Robert in 1940. But in 1945, she lost a baby who died just after birth.

The Balestreros' second son, Greg, was born in 1947. While still a toddler, Greg was hospitalized with pneumonia and nearly died.

And so by January 1953, Rose had suffered multiple traumas. Now she faced yet another loss, in a horribly surreal and distorted realization of her father's warning about marrying a musician. "You'll be lonely," Bartholomew Giolito had warned his daughter.

For Rose, the prospect of Manny's incarceration was too much to bear.

"She was seeing a lot of loss and a lot of crisis in her life. So when my dad was arrested and she looked at the potential of the kids being without a father and she being alone again, she just retreated," Greg Balestrero said.

Before her husband's arrest, Rose presided over the household with a steady hand. Like Manny, she was reserved and gentle. Rose was more decisive, though. She typically had the final say when it came to things like spending, social events, vacations, and planning for the children.

"She was my right hand," Manny said.

Rose's behavior changed soon after Manny's arrest. The Balestreros' lawyer, O'Connor, noticed the change. While at their initial meetings Rose had been assertive and engaged, by January 23 she "seemed to be in a state of depression."

In the days that followed, Rose became increasingly withdrawn and unresponsive. She blamed herself for Manny's arrest because he had gone to Prudential to seek a loan for her dental care. "She began to accuse herself for sending him to the Prudential Insurance office where he was 'identified' as a bandit. It preyed on her mind and we could both see her slipping away from us," O'Connor later told the *Long Island Star-Journal*.

On February 20, Manny appeared at O'Connor's office with bruises on his forehead. He told the lawyer that "Rose had struck him with a large vanity mirror." By this point, Manny was desperate. He feared for Rose's sanity and doubted his own ability to continue with the case.

Several days later, Rose was examined by Dr. Ralph Banay, a forensic psychiatrist and former director of Sing Sing's psychiatric clinic. Banay found that Rose was "deeply despondent." Banay did not believe she was a threat to her family. Since the one time Rose hit Manny, she had become "entirely quiet and withdrawn." She was coherent and understood what was being said to her. But Rose showed no interest in her family or in the resolution of the charges against Manny.

Banay recommended that she be committed immediately to Greenmont Sanitarium, an institution he owned in Ossining, New York.

Heeding this advice, Manny moved Rose into the sanitarium on February 26. She had, in Manny's words, suffered "a complete nervous breakdown and collapse."

***

Out on bail, Manny returned to his job at the Stork Club several weeks after the arrest. The club's owner, Sherman Billingsley, was convinced of Manny's innocence. So the celebrities who dined and danced at the club in the first several months of 1953 were entertained by a man whom the State of New York had branded as a criminal.

Manny was deeply shaken and distraught over both his own predicament and Rose's absence. He was too afraid to take the subway. A trumpet player in the band drove Manny to and from work.

Manny's mother moved into his home in Queens to take care of Robert and

Greg. His extended family was in a state of upheaval. Most of his family members and friends knew that Manny was a gentle and soft-spoken man incapable of violence or criminal activity. Still, not everyone felt certain of his innocence.

"It was like tossing a hand grenade in an Easter dinner, where there is a house filled with people and it explodes," said Greg Balestrero. "There is absolutely no way to say it didn't impact everybody, down through first cousins. Everybody had to choose: guilty or not guilty. There were people who started to take sides, and that affected us in a big way."

Meanwhile, O'Connor tried to get Prudential to withdraw the criminal complaint. He visited the Prudential office manager, Wallace Doubleday, at least three times in January and February. Each time, O'Connor recounted the evidence that he believed proved his case. But each time, Doubleday said the Prudential employees could not be wrong.

O'Connor then made the case to the press that Manny was a victim of mistaken identity. He likened his client to Bertram Campbell, who had been exonerated about seven years earlier.

Despite O'Connor's efforts, on February 18, 1953, the grand jury indicted Manny on multiple counts of robbery, grand larceny, and assault.

With Rose institutionalized and Manny near collapse himself, O'Connor asked the district attorney's office for an early trial date. That date was ultimately set for April 21, 1953, before Judge William B. Groat of the Supreme Court for Queens County.

In advance of the trial, O'Connor arranged a lie detector test for Manny. Lie detector results were not admissible evidence in 1953 (and still are not today). Even so, prosecutors routinely used the tests in evaluating suspects. In fact, only three months before Balestrero's arrest, Queens District Attorney T. Vincent Quinn had arranged a lie detector test for Louis Hoffner, the Brooklyn man imprisoned for more than twelve years before his exoneration in 1952. Quinn relied on the results of that test in moving to dismiss the indictment against Hoffner.

O'Connor retained Dr. Fabian Rouke, the same man who had administered Hoffner's test, to handle Manny's examination. Rouke scheduled the test for February 23 in his office on West Ninety-Eighth Street in Manhattan. Given Rouke's role in the Hoffner case, the district attorney's office would have no cause to question his credentials.

Yet Manny himself doubted the test. He feared that the polygraph machine would join the circle of his accusers. With the exam about to start, Manny suffered a near-panic attack.

"What will happen if this machine says I'm lying?" he asked O'Connor, clutching the lawyer's hand for support. Manny "began to shake like a reed in the wind," in O'Connor's words.

The test proceeded. Rouke posed questions about basic facts (such as "Were you born in New York City?" and "Is your mother living?") and questions relating to the alleged crime (such as "Did you ever stick up the Prudential office?" and "Were you in the Prudential office on December 18?").

Manny's anxiety was soon eased: he passed.

O'Connor provided the results of the exam to both Prudential and the district attorney's office. But the new information did not change their minds. The prosecution would proceed.

***

O'Connor prepared for trial, with a focus on Manny's alibis for the dates of the two armed robberies: July 9, 1952 and December 18, 1952.

On the first date, the Balestreros were vacationing at the Edelweiss farm near Cornwall. Rose had remembered that as early as the arraignment. In February 1953, Manny, his sister, Olga, and his brother-in-law, Gene, went to Cornwall to speak with the farm's owners, Enrique Ferrero and his wife, Mariannina.

"I'm in trouble," Manny told them. "You've got to help me."

Enrique Ferrero reacted immediately when told of the charges. "But that's impossible—you were here on July 9," he said. Ferrero had a reason for such a specific recollection—July 9 was his wife's birthday, and he remembered preparing a special cake for the occasion. Ferrero also gave Manny the names of other guests who were at the farm on that date, more potential alibi witnesses.

But then came news that must have stoked fears of a cosmic conspiracy: within seven months of their vacation at the farm, two of the potential witnesses—men who sat with Manny at a card game on July 9—were dead. One, a thirty-four-year-old man named Boltero, died after falling on ice during a walk in the park. The other man, Molinelli, died of a heart attack. Manny learned of the deaths when he tried to call on the men at their last known addresses in the city.

Still, O'Connor pieced together a powerful alibi defense from statements by living witnesses. He and his associate, Raymond McKaba, first went to Cornwall. There, Enrique Ferrero agreed to sign an affidavit swearing he had served lunch to Manny and his family at 1:00 p.m. on July 9 (just about thirty minutes after the Prudential office had been held up in Jackson Heights).

O'Connor also tracked down two other guests at the farm who confirmed Manny's presence in Cornwall on that date. The first was Karl Wuechner, who co-owned an auto repair business. Wuechner recalled that on July 9, he and his young daughter, Rita, drove to the Cornwall post office to mail a letter to his mother in Germany. Manny and his sons came along for the ride. The party of five had left for town around 11:00 a.m., drove to nearby Newburgh after mailing the letter, and returned to the farm around twelve thirty—right around the time that the Prudential office was being held up. In the afternoon, Wuechner played cards with Manny. Besides confirming these points, Wuechner gave O'Connor the envelope that he used to mail the letter to Germany.

Another alibi witness, Joseph Dallacqua, signed an affidavit swearing that on July 9 he saw Manny at lunch and then later at the card game.

For December 18, Manny's alibi turned on evidence that he had a swollen jaw on that date—a condition not mentioned by the Prudential eyewitnesses who described the bandit to police.

Manny remembered that he had developed the two impacted wisdom teeth in mid-December. His dentist, Dr. August J. Bastien, prescribed penicillin for the infection with an eye to removing the teeth. But Manny had an allergic reaction. His left jaw swelled up significantly. In fact, a Stork Club piano player told O'Connor that he recalled noticing the swelling from his position in the band, some twelve feet from Manny. O'Connor confirmed through Dr. Bastien's records that Manny's jaw was extremely swollen when he saw the dentist at the Victor Moore Arcade complex on December 15—three days before the second Prudential holdup. The records confirmed that the jaw remained swollen as of a December 22 follow-up visit to the dentist. Several weeks later, after the infection had been treated, Dr. Bastien removed Manny's wisdom teeth.

Bastien signed a statement swearing to these facts. But O'Connor didn't stop there. He then enlisted the pharmacist who filled Manny's penicillin prescription. Like Bastien, the pharmacist agreed to testify at trial.

O'Connor also learned that one of Manny's cousins, Marie Faverio, had visited the Balestrero home at 1:00 p.m. on December 18, about forty minutes after the robbery. She recalled that Manny was wearing pajamas at the time.

Finally, O'Connor interviewed Manny's older son, Robert, about his father's whereabouts on the dates of the holdups. Robert remembered the ride into town with Wuechner on July 9. He also recalled coming home from school on December 18 around 12:15 p.m. and having lunch with Manny, Rose, and Greg. After the interview, O'Connor praised Robert as "a bright young boy" who recalled facts well and gave "honest and spontaneous answers." He pondered the idea of calling the boy to testify to support his father's alibi.

"It's my impression that Robert would make an exceptionally fine witness," O'Connor wrote in a memo.

***

With trial nearing, Manny approached a breaking point.

His time was split among playing at the Stork Club, caring for the children, visiting Rose in Ossining, and meeting with O'Connor. He was under enormous stress. It wasn't just a fear of conviction. Manny also worried that Rose might never recover and that his family would never be reunited. From his frequent visits to the sanitarium, Manny could tell that Rose's condition was not improving.

He lost weight. Sleep eluded him, even with the aid of sleeping pills. He fell into a state of physical and emotional exhaustion.

At the Stork Club, Manny had been known as a steady performer who never missed a day of work. But now, as he stood on stage, performing for revelers into the early hours of the morning, he sometimes drifted into a fog and missed his cues.

Worse, Manny felt terrified just being out in public. At times he became overwhelmed by the fear that a police officer would seize him and return him to prison.

And so for Manny the weeks before his April 21 court date became their own trial, a battle against exhaustion, fear, and despair.

−EIGHT−
TRIAL

Long Island City courthouse, where Manny Balestrero was put on trial, as seen in 2021.
(*Photo by Rich Dubin*)

Most of Frank Crisona's opening statement came as no surprise.

Crisona, an assistant district attorney, read the indictment to a jury of ten men and two women. He described each of the robberies. He promised that four "young ladies" who worked for Prudential would positively identify Manny as the holdup man.

But before yielding the floor to O'Connor, Crisona made an accusation that jolted Manny.

"This defendant admitted to the detectives that he was in financial difficulties, that he had to borrow money, not to go to the racetrack to bet, but he had to borrow money to pay off the bookies in New York. He was in trouble with the bookies," Crisona said.

No evidence supported Crisona's claim about the bookies. It's true that Detective

Matthew Herberich claimed that Manny said during the interrogation that he "was betting on horses." And Manny himself acknowledged that he occasionally went to the track with friends. But he did not gamble regularly or have racing debts. Instead, Manny liked predicting the winners for fun.

"He would take a newspaper going home and look at the races the next day and he would select the winner," Greg Balestrero recalled. "I think they took that and tried to make it into something that it wasn't."

In his opening, O'Connor did not address Crisona's claim about the bookies. But he portrayed Manny as a family man, the father of two young children and the holder of a steady job as a professional musician.

O'Connor promised that "five or six reputable people" would testify that Manny was at a farm sixty miles from Jackson Heights at the time of the first robbery. He chose not to preview Manny's alibi for the second robbery. "I don't want to tip my hand," O'Connor told the jury. He planned to wait until one of his cross-examinations to reveal that Manny had a visibly swollen jaw on December 18.

***

Crisona's first witness was Constance Ello, the young Prudential cashier who signed the criminal complaint. Ello described the July 9 robbery in great detail. Crisona then solicited her identification of Manny with an element of theatrics.

"Will you look around this courtroom and tell us if you see the man who was in your office on July 9 in this courtroom?" Crisona said.

"Yes, I do," Ello said.

"Will you step down and point him to us?"

"Right there," Ello said, gesturing toward Manny, who was seated next to O'Connor at the defendant's table.

Ello wanted no part of the confrontation that Crisona was staging. But the prosecutor persisted.

"Step down and put your hand on his shoulder," Crisona said.

Ello trembled with fear. She stepped off the witness stand and walked over to Manny. As Ello placed her hand on his shoulder, Manny was shaking. He clutched O'Connor's hand under the table for support.

The confrontation was a moment of terror for both accuser and accused. Ello had twice been robbed at apparent gunpoint. The trauma left her scared of being "bumped off" if she testified. Crisona's theatrical gambit made her anxiety spike to a point where she nearly fainted.

After returning to the stand, Ello described the December 18 robbery and again identified Manny as the bandit.

On cross-examination, O'Connor focused on the description of the holdup man that Ello gave to police after the first robbery.

"Did you tell the detectives that the man who robbed you on July 9 had blond hair?" he said.

"I said brown—blond or light brown hair. In fact, I said something like mine, something like that. I don't remember," she said.

"Well, now, please, Mrs. Ello, will you try to recall and tell us exactly what you said to the detectives that day?"

"I said blond or light brown. Very light brown, I said."

"Do you recall distinctly using that particular phrase, blond or light brown hair"?

"Yes, I do."

As Ello testified, the jurors turned to look at Manny. His hair was, in one reporter's words, "quite dark, almost black."

Ello also admitted she told police that the culprit was about thirty-five. Manny was forty-three.

O'Connor then questioned Ello about the identification procedures used at the 110th Precinct. Ello was one of the two witnesses there the night of Manny's arrest. The other was Yolanda Casagrande, who had passed by Ello's counter during the July 9 robbery and realized a holdup was in progress.

Ello admitted that before the lineup, the detectives had told her and Casagrande that the suspect would appear before them. She and Casagrande sat in a "darkened room" across a hallway and observed Manny standing in a "lighted doorway."

O'Connor then secured another admission that made the police identification procedures look even more unfair to Manny.

"Was there anyone in that lineup that you knew before that night?" O'Connor said.

"I don't remember, sir."

"Mrs. Ello, I ask you to think that question over carefully. Was there anyone else in the lineup, the six or seven or eight men that were in that lineup that night, was there any one of them that you knew before that night?"

"Oh, yes," Ello said.

"Who?"

"When the detective came to pick me up at the house, I was nervous. I didn't want to go down alone, and my husband came with us, and they put him in the lineup. I remember that," Ello said.

"And your husband was one in the lineup, is that so?"

"Yes, one of the men," Ello said.

This admission highlighted a fundamental problem with lineups of the era. A proper lineup aims to test an eyewitness's ability to identify a suspect from among a group. Minimum fairness requires that the "fillers"—the term used for those members of the lineup other than the suspect—must be unfamiliar to the witness. The placement of Ello's husband in the lineup violated this basic principle. And, as O'Connor intended to show later at trial, the lineup also included police officers whose uniform pants were visible.

The police did not use the lineup to test Ello's identification. At best, they were just checking a procedural box. At worst, they were arranging the lineup to eliminate any chance that Ello would pick someone other than Manny.

O'Connor had shown the jury the suggestiveness of the lineup procedure. But his questioning failed to shake Ello's confidence in her identification of Manny. Despite her obvious nerves, Ello betrayed doubt only once. The moment came when Judge Groat followed up on Ello's testimony that she was "positive" Manny was the holdup man.

"Could you be mistaken in that or are you sure?" the judge said.

"Well, to my knowledge I'm sure, Your Honor," Ello said.

"'To my knowledge, I'm sure,'" the judge said, as if to emphasize the hedging for the jury.

Crisona tried to limit any damage. "Well, is there any question in your mind about it?" he said.

"No, sir," Ello said.

***

Crisona next called Catherine Di Clemente to testify about the December 18 robbery. Di Clemente had been stationed alongside Ello and had handed over the fifty-eight dollars in her cash drawer.

Crisona moved through the examination quickly. When he asked Di Clemente to step off the stand and touch Manny's shoulder, Judge Groat put an end to the theatrics.

"That isn't necessary," he said.

Instead, Di Clemente identified Manny by his location in the courtroom and his clothing. "Navy blue suit, red tie, and white shirt," she said, pointing to him.

Toward the end of the direct examination, Judge Groat asked if Di Clemente was "positive this is the man."

"Yes, sir," she said.

During a short cross-examination, O'Connor cast doubt on Di Clemente's memory. She had testified that she never saw Manny before the December 18 holdup. But Manny had paid the insurance premiums in person in January 1952. O'Connor established that Di Clemente had initialed the payment receipt. In confronting her with that record, O'Connor suggested to the jury that she had seen Manny at least once before the December 18 holdup but had not remembered him from that visit.

O'Connor otherwise made little headway with Di Clemente, who remained firm in her identification.

As the first day of trial ended, Manny faced a terrifying prospect: a return to a jail cell. Under the prevailing custom for serious alleged felonies, a defendant was remanded—meaning that he would be held without bail—once the trial had started. O'Connor requested a hearing in the judge's chambers to plead for an exception in Manny's case. During that hearing, O'Connor advised Judge Groat that Manny was undergoing "psychiatric treatment."

Back in the courtroom, the judge announced his decision on the remand issue.

"I will continue the bail temporarily, and we will see later on what develops," he said. "But this is a rare exception."

Manny exhaled. He could go home, at least for the night.

***

The trial resumed the next morning with the testimony of Detective Hugh L. Sang, a handwriting specialist assigned to the police lab. Sang had been with the police for six years. He was now an "examiner of questioned documents."

During their interrogation, the police condemned Manny when he made the same "spelling" mistake as the holdup man (writing the word "draw" instead of "drawer"). Assistant District Attorney Cullen likewise told Manny that the handwriting on the two notes was "identical." O'Connor therefore expected Sang to give an expert opinion that Manny's writing matched the actual note.

But here came the biggest surprise of the trial so far: Sang did not claim that Manny wrote the note.

Instead, Sang testified that "the specimen handwriting submitted to me with the note in question [the actual holdup note] does not show enough similarity to, say, to give a positive opinion that he did write it, and on the other hand there is not enough dissimilarity with these specimens to show that he did not write it."

In a short examination, Crisona left no doubt about the limitations of Sang's testimony.

"Are there any similarities between the letters in People's Exhibit 1 and People's Exhibit 2?" Crisona said, referring to the actual holdup note and the notes that Manny wrote.

"There are," Sang said.

"But is it your opinion that there aren't enough to form a definite conclusion one way or the other?"

"That is correct."

While Sang's testimony did not advance the prosecution's case, Crisona had a defensive purpose in mind. He knew O'Connor had his own handwriting expert, one who would testify that Manny did not write the note. Crisona wanted an expert to tell the jury that a handwriting analysis could not rule out Manny.

Judge Groat was not impressed by Sang's testimony. He tried to guide O'Connor to the conclusion that there was no reason for a cross-examination.

"You haven't any questions, have you?" he said to O'Connor.

But O'Connor surprised him.

"Indeed I do, judge," O'Connor said.

"Go ahead if you have," Groat said. "I didn't think you had any after that testimony."

O'Connor had prepared for a long battle, and he was determined to have it. Despite Sang's admission, O'Connor posed more than 100 cross-examination questions. He drew out the "points of similarity" between the specimens, with Sang testifying that nine E's in the holdup note were similar to the E's in Manny's specimens. That led to an extended debate between O'Connor and Sang on certain differences in the E's, but without any apparent payoff.

Near the end of the cross-examination, O'Connor directed Sang to an excerpt from a book written by handwriting expert Dr. Albert S. Osborn: "If two writings cannot be identified as the same, then necessarily they must be identified as having been written by different hands." This principle, if accepted, was crucial to O'Connor's argument, since Sang had admitted he could not say Manny's note matched the holdup note.

"Do you agree with that statement?" O'Connor asked Sang after reading the excerpt aloud.

"In part," Sang said. In a garbled answer, Sang explained that "if we are going to take two handwritings and I submit two handwritings to you, they are not meant to look the same and they are written by the same person, and just because they look different, are you going to say two different people wrote them?"

It's unclear whether Sang's partial admission landed with the jury. But it soon became clear that at least two jurors were losing patience with O'Connor's extended questioning.

***

Prudential employee Yolanda Casagrande had given her direct testimony, including her identification of Manny, near the end of the first day of trial. Casagrande had passed by the holdup man during the July 9 robbery and then saw him again on December 18. After Sang was excused, Casagrande returned to the stand for cross-examination.

O'Connor set out to prove that Casagrande had little opportunity to observe the holdup man during the first robbery. On July 9 she had returned from the ladies' room and realized a crime was in progress when she heard the man at Constance Ello's window say the word "cash."

O'Connor got Casagrande to admit that she didn't look at the holdup man until she had returned to her desk, about fifteen feet from the window. She testified that she then looked at the man before reporting her concerns to the office manager, Wallace Doubleday.

But Casagrande's account of precisely *how* long she looked at the bandit kept changing.

"How long did you stand there, Miss Casagrande, looking at the robber from the time you first turned toward him as you arrived at your desk and the time you started to walk into the district manager's office?" O'Connor said.

"Long enough to see what was going on," Casagrande said.

"How long did you look at him?"

"I wouldn't know the time. No."

"Well, do you think it was a minute?"

"Probably a little more. I was quite upset. I just waited there."

"You were quite upset and you stood there looking at the defendant?"

"And Mrs. Ello. They were both together," Casagrande said.

It was implausible that Casagrande would just stand at her desk watching a robbery in progress. And Ello had testified that the entire holdup took only two minutes. But Casagrande seemed determined to inflate how long she stared at the holdup man.

"Do you think it was more than a minute?" O'Connor said.

"Probably a little bit more than a minute. Yes. I stood there for a while."

"Well, would you say it was a minute and a half?"

"Two minutes, let's say about."

"It's two minutes?"

"About a minute and a half, two minutes, yes."

"And you stood there looking at him for two minutes?"

"Yes, I was quite scared, let's say."

The witness's waffling caught Judge Groat's attention, leading him to initiate a courtroom bit out of a movie.

"When I say 'Start,' you tell me 'Stop' when you think two minutes have passed, please," he instructed the witness.

The judge said, "Start." The courtroom went silent.

After a short period, Casagrande said, "I'd say that's how long I looked at the man."

"That is exactly thirty-five seconds," Judge Groat said.

Having punctured Casagrande's credibility, O'Connor turned to her visit to the 110th Precinct. Casagrande said there were "six or seven men" in the lineup and she recognized Constance Ello's husband as one of them.

Casagrande explained how the lineup worked. The witnesses were "told to count" off the men and to identify the man they recognized by his number in the lineup. O'Connor then pressed her on whether the other men in the lineup (including the man in the "number one" position) wore an overcoat, like Manny.

"Did the number-one man have an overcoat on?" O'Connor said.

"As far as I can remember, they were all dressed the same."

"Do you remember whether or not he had an overcoat on—the number-one man?"

Judge Groat interrupted: "She said as far as she knows they were all dressed the same. Next question, please."

"Well, Miss Casagrande, approximately how tall was the number-one man?"

"If you know," the judge said. "If you do not, say so."

"No, I don't know," Casagrande said.

"Approximately how much did he weigh?" O'Connor said.

Again Groat interjected: "If you know, say so; if you do not, say so."

"No, I do not know," she said.

Suddenly, O'Connor heard a whispered remark from the jury box.

"Do we have to listen to this nonsense?" a man said.

That comment eluded Judge Groat. But then another juror rose from his seat and erupted in bored frustration.

"Your Honor, do we have to sit here and listen to this?"

The speaker was juror number four, an engineer from Kew Gardens named Lloyd Espenschied.

Judge Groat admonished the juror.

"The court will rule on what is proper evidence, Mr. Juror. The court is the sole judge of what is proper evidence. When the case is submitted to you, you will be the sole judge of the facts," Groat said.

O'Connor did not react at first and instead proceeded with his cross-examination. But he quickly realized that he had grounds to move for a mistrial. The basis for the motion lay in apparent misconduct by the two jurors. Their complaints had signaled their impatience with Manny's defense and suggested they might have prematurely decided he was guilty. A mistrial would enable O'Connor to start over with a new jury.

On the other hand, O'Connor doubted his client's ability to go on. Manny would have to repeat the trial process from the beginning, including the torturous courtroom identifications. O'Conner feared Manny was on the verge of a complete breakdown.

In the end, O'Connor felt he had no choice. After the lunch recess, O'Connor moved for the mistrial. He told Judge Groat that he had heard juror number five, Alfred Anderson, complain about the cross-examination to Espenschied before the latter's outburst. A newspaper described Anderson's comment as a "clearly audible stage whisper."

"It seems to me that both of these jurors have given a very clear indication of a very extreme and undue patience with the cross-examination of counsel, which indicates a formation in their minds of some kind of an opinion concerning the probable or possible guilt of the defendant," O'Connor argued.

At first, Judge Groat disagreed.

"I do not think it in any way indicates on the part of the jury or either one of the two mentioned any opinion concerning the guilt or innocence of this defendant," he said.

But the judge also acknowledged that "there has been no known incident of a similar nature around here." He declared a recess to give himself time to consider the motion.

Back in court the next morning, the judge asked juror Anderson whether he had said something to Espenschied. Anderson said he did not recall. But Crisona confirmed that he too had heard Anderson's comment. Even more importantly, Crisona told the judge that he did not oppose O'Connor's motion.

Judge Groat then declared a mistrial. He noted that the two jurors "had nothing but the best intentions" and that their remarks "came as a result of what to them might have seemed prolonged cross-examination." But he ruled that O'Connor's motion was well-founded given that both attorneys had heard Anderson's remark and that Espenschied's remark was on the record.

"The court must say that it is sorry that it has to take this step, in view of the time which has already been consumed, but the court is always the guardian of the rights of a defendant," Judge Groat said.

***

The juror who caused Manny's mistrial, Lloyd Espenschied, had somewhere else to be.

Espenschied worked as an engineer at AT&T Bell Laboratories in New Jersey. He was also a prolific inventor. In 1929, Espenschied and fellow engineer Herman Affel invented coaxial cable, which enabled long-distance phone service and laid the foundation for television transmission. He later invented the radio altimeter, which used radio airwaves to gauge the distance between airplanes and other objects.

Three weeks before Manny's trial, Espenschied made plans to attend the International Scientific Radio Union in Washington, DC. The weeklong conference was scheduled to start on April 26, and Espenschied planned to depart for Washington the day before. And so, on April 23, as he watched O'Connor cross-examine Yolanda Casagrande, Espenschied knew his plans were in serious jeopardy. The prosecution had not yet rested, and O'Connor had promised at least five witnesses for the defense. The trial would not be finished in time for Espenschied to make his trip to DC.

There's no record of Espenschied ever explaining the reason for his outburst. But it's hardly a leap to link his impatience to his travel plans.

Espenschied's interruption of the trial also reflected his personality: he was abrasive and not shy about airing his opinions, including those tainted by bias. In 1944, for example, he expressed anti-Semitic views in a meeting with an investigator from the War Department named G. E. Schwartz. The incident is recounted in author Jon Gertner's exhaustive history of Bell Labs. During the meeting, Espenschied acknowledged his opposition to America's involvement in World War II and blamed it in part on "Jewish propaganda." Espenschied told Schwartz he did not like Jews "because of their racial characteristics." Espenschied recorded these comments in a memo that Gertner found in the AT&T archives. In the memo, Espenschied noted that when Schwartz probed further about the reasons for his dislike of Jews, "I responded that he would have to ask the Jews themselves that question, looking him straight in the face as the Jew that he appeared to be." Espenschied described the meeting as "an American-Jewish-Gestapo incident."

Given Espenschied's outspoken opposition to the war, Bell Lab's leaders barred him from any projects relating to the war effort. "I spent the rest of the time in the Laboratories completely isolated from the majority of the work going on," Espenschied later wrote.

The Bell Labs episode followed a visit by Espenschied to Germany in 1938. In a journal exploring his family's German ancestry, Espenschied referred to the Third Reich as "perhaps the most dynamic . . . and efficient state in the world," praised its annexation of Austria, and ascribed anti-Hitler sentiment in the United States to "antagonistic news channels, influenced . . . by the Jews." Espenschied later acknowledged that his German sympathies alienated members of his Kew Gardens community and made him "a marked man, especially on the part of the rapidly rising Jewish contingent in the neighborhood." While his anti-war positions led some to suspect him "of having been a German agent," Espenschied complained in a September 1953 letter that "I'm yet to be recognized as the true American patriot I thought I was when opposing Roosevelt['s] involvement, his building of Russia and his catering to the Jews."

Ironically, the day after causing a

Lloyd Espenschied, left, in 1949, seen here with Herman Affel *(Courtesy of AT&T Archives and History Center)*

mistrial in an armed robbery case, Espenschied wrote to the police to request that they "keep an eye on my home" while he was in Washington. The reason for the request, he said, was that his house had been broken into four times before.

As a victim of these break-ins, Espenschied had a potential bias in the prosecution's favor. Whether he disclosed the information before trial is unknown. The transcript does not include the questioning of prospective jurors (known as voir dire). But Espenschied's eruption cast doubt on a strategic decision that O'Connor had made during the juror selection process. Attorneys were permitted a certain number of "peremptory challenges" to potential jurors who might have a bias in favor of one side or the other. Rather than exercising any of his challenges, O'Connor accepted each of the twelve jurors whom Crisona approved, including Espenschied.

At any rate, the revelations about Espenschied underline the fragility of the criminal trial process. Innocent defendants face not only the threat of misidentification from eyewitnesses, but also the reality that the jurors deciding their fate have personal agendas that inform their reception of evidence. Those agendas may arise from undisclosed biases. Or from travel plans that make extended cross-examinations an intolerable inconvenience.

***

Did the other jurors share Espenschied's contempt for O'Connor's cross-examination? Would Manny have been convicted had the trial gone to a verdict?

O'Connor claimed that most jurors told him afterward that the prosecution's case was "very weak." But the *Daily News* reported that a poll of the jury, after the mistrial was declared, "revealed it would have convicted him on the testimony of the four girls." *Long Island Star-Journal* reporter Robert Bigelow, who covered the case extensively, felt the jury would not have believed Manny's alibi witnesses.

In preparing for *The Wrong Man*, researchers met with two of the jurors. One of them, a salesman at a men's clothing store, claimed he was the only juror who believed Manny was innocent. The other juror, a bank executive, said he hadn't "made up his mind," but praised O'Connor's performance. Both jurors recalled that Manny hardly changed expression during the trial. The salesman noted that Manny "appeared as a man in a daze," while the bank executive described Manny as a "completely whipped and beaten" man who "never . . . changed expression."

These comments pointed to another obstacle to a favorable jury verdict: Manny's mental state. He was on the brink of emotional collapse. O'Connor feared Manny's anxiety would prevent him from testifying effectively—and perhaps from even taking the stand at all.

Seeking an escape after the mistrial, Manny, his sons, and their Uncle Gene traveled to a resort in Goshen, New York, for the weekend. "It was like a *Dirty Dancing* vacation spot," Greg Balestrero recalled, alluding to the fictional Kellerman's resort in the film.

But the second trial loomed. On April 29, 1953, Judge Groat set the date as July 13.

On the afternoon of April 29, Manny and his sons went to see Rose at Greenmont. During the visit, Rose pleaded with her husband for a permanent reuniting of the family.

"Take me home," she said.

"I can't because it's not over yet," Manny replied.

Before he left, Manny asked Rose to pray for him, and Rose promised to do so.

***

Shortly before eleven o'clock that night, a thirty-eight-year-old man named Charles Daniell walked into a deli at 42-20 Thirty-Fourth Avenue in Queens. Daniell was an unemployed plastics molder who had served as a sergeant in the Army. After ordering some cold cuts, he pulled a gun on the woman behind the counter, Frieda Mank, and demanded the money in the cash register.

Rather than comply, Mank grabbed a butcher's knife and assumed a defensive posture. She then stamped her foot on the floor to signal her husband, Joseph, that there was trouble. Joseph, who was in the cellar, called the police. Moments later, two armed detectives and a police lieutenant burst into the deli. One detective tackled and subdued Daniell. His gun, it turned out, was a toy.

Daniell quickly confessed to forty robberies, including the Prudential holdups. He told police he had read of Manny's arrest and did not want another person to suffer for his crimes. "I was going to try and clear him. I didn't know how, but I was going to try," Daniell said.

Charles Daniell, after his arrest, heads to court escorted by Detective William Amendinger, on May 1, 1953. (*Art Edger/Daily News Archive via Getty Images*)

Manny was on the job with his band when the Stork Club received a call alerting them to Daniell's confession. It was about 1:30 a.m. A piano player from another band ascended the bandstand and pointed at Manny.

"They got the guy!" the piano player said. "They got the guy!"

Manny kept playing. He "was in a fog" and lost in thought about the afternoon visit with Rose.

"I couldn't let go of the fiddle. The drummer grabbed my bass and told me,

101

'Damn it, get down off the stand. Don't you understand?'" Manny later recalled.

Shortly after 2:00 a.m., Manny went to the police station in Astoria. There, he came face-to-face with Daniell.

"Do you know what you did to my wife?" Balestrero said, with fists clenched. Daniell did not answer.

The next night, three of the four Prudential employees observed Daniell in a lineup. One positively identified him as the holdup man. While two others told police they were uncertain, they also admitted they no longer were sure of their identification of Manny.

"I never wanted to send an innocent man to jail," Constance Ello told a reporter from *Life* magazine. "I did my duty. I did what I thought was right. I still think it is right."

The Queens district attorney's office did not immediately drop the charges against Manny. "We are going to reexamine the case in the light of rather startling developments yesterday and last night," T. Vincent Quinn said. Quinn allowed that "if there is any possible miscarriage of justice," his office would "gladly" join in a motion to dismiss the charges.

Manny, meanwhile, recalled his discussion with Rose from hours earlier.

"It was an answer to those prayers," Manny said.

***

On June 15, Daniell pleaded guilty to the Prudential holdups and the other robberies. With Judge Groat attending a labor conference in Europe, the indictment against Manny remained on the books. That indictment was dismissed when the judge returned on July 15, 1953. About two weeks later, Daniell was sentenced to five to ten years in Sing Sing. Judge John F. Scileppi imposed the maximum sentence because Daniell "almost caused irreparable harm to another man . . . and never confessed until after he was caught."

The period between Manny's arrest and his formal exoneration was six months, and unlike Bertram Campbell and other falsely convicted defendants, Manny did not serve a prison sentence. Yet the experience was devastating to his family, which remained fractured with Rose still at the sanitarium.

Rose's continuing absence was the subject of a November 1953 article in the *Long Island Star-Journal.* An accompanying photo shows Manny in the kitchen giving six-year-old Greg his dinner. Both are smiling. But Manny was heartbroken. "I have to believe that she'll be home with me and the boys some day," he said. Prospects for such a reunion remained uncertain, though. Manny acknowledged that during his recent visits to the sanitarium, Rose "doesn't say much about coming home."

While running such human interest stories, the New York press gave little scrutiny to the state's handling of the case. Newspapers presented Manny as the victim of misfortune and dutifully reported police statements that he "looked enough like Daniell to be his double." Under the headline "Double's Arrest Clears Musician," the *New York Times* reported that Balestrero had a "striking resemblance" to Daniell. The *Daily News*, the *Long Island Star-Journal* and the *Long Island Daily*

Press all referred to Daniell as Manny's "double" or "twin." Headlines in papers across the country also used the word "double."

Reports of the resemblance proved greatly exaggerated. Daniell was five years younger than Manny. It's true that each man had a high forehead and receding dark hair. But Daniell's recession was more conspicuous, with thin wisps of hair marking a trail reaching farther back on his head. And the similar foreheads and hair color hardly explain the eyewitness mistakes, since Daniell wore a hat (obscuring his forehead and hair) during one of the two robberies and Manny wore one during his January 14 visit to Prudential.

Manny Balestrero, left, and Charles Daniell
(*INP Soundphoto/Bettmann Archive via Getty Images*)

Daniell did not bear a strong likeness to Manny. A more accurate comparison lies in the words of *Life* magazine writer Herbert Brean, who saw a "fleeting resemblance between the two men, particularly in the set and expression of their eyes."

In short, Manny was no double of a criminal, and his arrest cannot be excused on that basis. A closer look at his case reveals a prosecution that failed to meet the judicial council's plea for "caution and prudence" in matters of eyewitness identification.

***

Manny's arrest occurred shortly after the exoneration of Louis Hoffner. The office that prosecuted Manny was headed by the same man who urged Hoffner's release: District Attorney T. Vincent Quinn.

But Queens authorities had not changed their ways. They instead continued to use suggestive and unfair identification procedures.

First, the detectives forced Manny to parade through the neighborhood stores that had been robbed. Then, back at the precinct, they displayed Manny alone, in a lighted doorway, before the Prudential witnesses. The detectives positioned and dressed him to re-create his appearance from the day before.

Since Manny readily admitted he had gone to Prudential on January 13, there was nothing probative about the procedure.

The next phase of the identification process was just as prejudicial. At a detective's direction, Manny again put on his overcoat, hat, and maroon scarf. He was then placed in a lineup that included police officers, with, in O'Connor's words, "their uniform trousers clearly visible below the hastily-donned civilian overcoats." Thirteen years earlier, Hoffner had stood in a similar lineup alongside three detectives who were obviously older and taller. But Manny had it even worse, since one of the men in his lineup was the husband of an accuser, Constance Ello.

The prosecutor who presided over the lineup was Thomas Cullen. Manny's case was not the first time Cullen had used a lineup filler known to the eyewitness. After the arrest of notorious bank robber Willie Sutton in 1952, Cullen supervised the procedure at which a Queens bank manager identified Sutton. One of the lineup fillers Cullen chose was a lawyer who knew the bank manager. At trial, Cullen, who appeared as a witness for the state, admitted that he knew the eyewitness and the filler were acquaintances. Cullen said he paid little attention to the identity of the fillers and instead focused only on their height. While Sutton was convicted, Cullen's admission shows how injudicious prosecutors were in constructing lineups.

In Manny's case, Cullen filled the lineup with an eyewitness's spouse and uniformed police officers—a procedure so suggestive that it bordered on farcical.

At the same time, the detectives failed to scrutinize the facts that had led the Prudential employees to identify Manny. Had they done so, they would have found substantial cause for doubt.

To recap those facts, four Prudential employees identified Manny:

> Constance Ello: She handed over money to the holdup man during both the July 9 and December 18 robberies.
> Yolanda Casagrande: She saw the bandit from a distance at each of the robberies but was not in the Prudential office when Manny appeared there on January 13.
> Catherine Di Clemente: She did not witness the July 9 holdup. She was at the public counter next to Ello during the December 18 robbery and handed cash to the bandit.
> Joan Kopp: She was not in the office on July 9. She was at a desk toward the rear of the office during the second holdup and saw the bandit from there.

A fifth employee, referred to at trial and in other records only as Miss Miller, the supervisor, was never identified by the state as a witness to either robbery but was at the office during Manny's January 13 visit.

Only Ello signed the criminal complaint against Manny. But based on the trial testimony, the first employee to identify Manny on January 13 was Joan Kopp. She set off a chain reaction in the office. After waiting on Manny at the public counter, Kopp hurried over to the supervisor, Miss Miller, to relay her suspicions about him. Miller was standing at a desk near Di Clemente and Ello. Di Clemente saw Kopp make "a motion that she recognized" the man at the counter. When Kopp conveyed to her and Miller that the holdup man was at the counter, Di Clemente looked over at Manny and told Miller that "it was the same man." Di Clemente's endorsement of Kopp's conclusion was almost instantaneous:

> Q: *How long after Miss Kopp pointed Mr. Balestrero out to you did you tell Miss Miller that you thought it was the same man?*
> A: *A few seconds.*

Kopp and Miller also told Ello to "look at the man at the window." As Ello recounted at trial, "they called my attention to the fact that he was there, and they said, 'Is that the man?'" Ello waffled on whether Kopp and Miller *asked* her if Manny was the holdup man or *told* her Manny was the man. Her answers to Judge Groat's questions suggest that the other two women pressured her to join in the identification.

> Q: *Then what did they say to you?*
> A: *"It's him" or "Is it him?" or something like that. They were both sure it was him, or something like that.*
> Q: *And what did you say?*
> A: *I said, "I'm not getting up from this desk. I'm not taking the window," or something like that.*

Ello said she looked and saw "the man I had seen on the previous occasions."

It seems unlikely that Ello looked at Manny for more than a few seconds. She was paralyzed by fear. "I was afraid and I stayed at my desk," she testified.

Manny fell victim to a group mentality. Ello and Di Clemente identified him only after Kopp's suggestive gesturing and comments. In fact, Kopp played a decisive role in Manny's arrest. She pointed to Manny and asked the other women, "Isn't that the man?" much like detectives handled showup procedures.

Kopp did not witness the first robbery. During the second robbery, she was far from the public counter where the holdup man stood. Yet all the accusations against Manny can be traced to her.

These facts counter the state's explanation for Manny's false arrest. Four Prudential employees did not independently identify Manny as the bandit. Rather, a single employee (Kopp), who had never been close to the real culprit, suggested to the other women that Manny was that man.

The police had evidence that cast doubt on the reliability of the Prudential eyewitnesses. Manny was older than the holdup man they described at the time of the crimes. His dark hair did not match Ello's statement to police that the bandit had "blond or very light brown hair." And a search of the Balestreros' home turned up neither the blue overcoat worn by the bandit nor the "notebook" from which the robbery note came.

Despite these warning signs, the arresting detectives, Matthew Herberich and Leigh Wilson, quickly accepted the employees' identifications. Before questioning Manny in detail, they conducted the showups at the neighborhood stores. Their rush to pin the other robberies on Manny presupposed that he had committed the Prudential robberies.

The detectives also ignored evidence that tended to clear Manny. In an example of "tunnel vision," they concluded early that Manny was guilty and then elevated the importance of any information that seemed to "build their case" against him, while disregarding or dismissing contrary evidence.

For example, before Manny's arrest, the detectives believed that the same man who held up the Prudential office had committed many other local robberies. That's why they paraded Manny in front of the proprietors whose stores had been robbed. No proprietor identified him—a fact that pointed to Manny's innocence. But rather than reconsider their belief in Manny's guilt, the detectives merely discarded the theory linking the Prudential holdups to the other crimes. The abandoned theory turned out to be correct: Daniell confessed to thirty-eight other robberies.

Beyond that, Manny's behavior made the accusations against him implausible. He went to the Prudential office and asked about a loan on his wife's policy. He accurately identified himself and his policy information. This is not the behavior of a man who twice held up the same office at gunpoint. But the police presumably concluded that Manny (1) was brazen or stupid enough to seek to conduct legitimate business at Prudential or (2) had intended to rob the office a third time but aborted the plan for some reason.

Similar thinking would lead to a false arrest in Queens some forty-eight years later. On November 19, 2001, a man robbed a Chase Manhattan branch office in Woodhaven. He passed a note to a teller that read: "This is a hold-up. I have a gun." After the teller handed him $7,791, the man fled. Four days later, thirty-year-old Jack Schreiner visited the same Chase office to open an account. Bank employees concluded he was the holdup man. As a result, Schreiner was arrested and jailed, with newspaper accounts mocking his stupidity for returning to the bank so soon after the crime.

Schreiner was exonerated several weeks later when detectives confirmed that he was repairing a freezer compressor at a Manhattan restaurant at the time of the robbery.

In Manny's case, the best example of the detectives' tunnel vision lies in their reaction to his spelling mistake. Manny re-created the holdup note six times. It was not until the last version that he wrote "draw" (like the actual robber) instead of "drawer." The detectives seized on this error and, in O'Connor's words, "'knew' they had the right man."

In fact, Manny's handwriting samples were evidence of his innocence.

Unlike the holdup man, Manny knew how to spell "drawer." He wrote it correctly five times. The appearance of "draw" in the sixth version should have been treated as an inconsequential mistake made under stressful police questioning. Manny had made a similar mistake in one of the first five samples. While Daniell's note said "THIS IS A GUN I HAVE POINTING AT YOU," Manny wrote "POINTED" instead of "POINTING."

On top of that, the dropping of the "er" from "drawer" is not a distinguishing characteristic among New Yorkers. Many people in New York and elsewhere in the

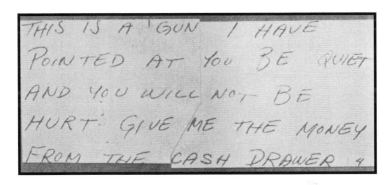

The holdup note written by Charles Daniell (*reprinted by special permission of Northwestern University and the Journal of Criminal Law and Criminology*)

One of the handwriting samples given by Manny Balestrero to detectives in January 1953 (*reprinted by special permission of Northwestern University and the Journal of Criminal Law and Criminology*)

Northeast pronounce the word as "draw." Even courts have confused "draw" and "drawer." In an opinion published in 1997, the Supreme Court of South Carolina recounts in the same paragraph that a murder victim "opened the *cash drawer*" during a robbery and that the defendant then "took the money from the *cash draw*."

The police had other reasons to reconsider their conclusion. Their expert, Detective Hugh Sang, could not say the handwriting was Manny's. At the same time, the expert retained by O'Connor, Ordway Hilton, reached a definitive conclusion: based on repeated differences in lettering, Manny did not write the note. While Hilton never testified because of the mistrial, he prepared a detailed analysis that was later included in an article in the *Journal of Criminal Law and Criminology*. Hilton demonstrated "repeated, small differences" between the holdup note and Balestrero's specimens that "proved conclusively that Balestrero did not write the robbery note."

As just one example, Hilton showed that Manny's writing of the letter G differed in an obvious way from the same letter in the actual note. G appeared three times— in the words "GUN," "POINTING," and "GIVE." Manny's G's reflected two

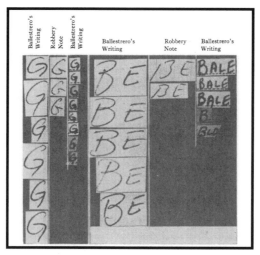

Excerpt from Ordway Hilton's handwriting analysis (*reprinted by special permission of Northwestern University and the Journal of Criminal Law and Criminology*)

separate pen strokes: he wrote the C portion, lifted his pen, and then wrote the horizontal and downstroke to form what looked like the number 7 (or what Hilton described as an inverted L). By contrast, the culprit wrote his G's in a continuous pen motion. Hilton also showed that the G's in Manny's samples matched the G's in tax returns he had prepared a year earlier—proving Manny had not tried to alter his handwriting at the interrogation. The differences in G's alone, Hilton showed, were "sufficient to give rise to a serious doubt" that he wrote the note.

The state cannot ordinarily be expected to defer to the defendant's expert. But Hilton was no ordinary expert. He had served as the Chicago police's first "document examiner" as well as a US Navy handwriting specialist. A leader in the field, Hilton lectured on "The Examination of Questioned Documents" at a 1950 course attended by seventy-eight prosecutors from twenty-six states, including New York. Hilton's mentor and former partner, Elbridge W. Stein, had been regularly consulted as a handwriting expert by the New York County District Attorney's Office.

Despite Hilton's conclusion, the state clung to its theory that Manny wrote the holdup note. The police lab later confirmed the handwriting was Daniell's.

Then there were Manny's alibis. O'Connor told the district attorney's office of the witnesses who placed Manny in Cornwall at the time of the first robbery. These witnesses had no reason to lie. Their accounts were consistent and supported by minute, verifiable details. Yet prosecutors did not seek statements from them until *after* Daniell's confession (the mistrial had occurred before any alibi witness had testified).

Finally, Queens authorities ignored the results of Manny's lie detector test despite their acceptance of the test in other cases. District Attorney Quinn said in August 1952 that he had "great faith" in the lie detector. He also relied on the test in the Hoffner case.

In requesting dismissal of Manny's indictment, Quinn said he had "learned" that Manny passed a lie detector test. This public statement falsely implied that the lie detector result was new information. In fact, O'Connor had the results sent to Quinn's office long before the trial.

In short, like the prosecutors who put Campbell, Caruso, and Hoffner behind bars, Queens authorities had substantial reason to abort Manny's prosecution long before Daniell confessed.

Another thread connecting Manny to falsely convicted defendants lies in the state's response to his exoneration. Newspaper accounts reflect no admission of a mistake and no apology. Quite the contrary: one of the arresting officers, Leigh Wilson, later disclaimed any responsibility in the matter. Wilson said that if he were to meet Manny:

I'd shake hands with him. . . . I have no reason to do otherwise. My job was to make the arrest. I am not a judge or jury.

Wilson acknowledged that "we didn't advise [Manny] of his rights, because it wasn't necessary in that day." Presumably, Wilson was referring to the period before the Supreme Court's landmark 1966 Miranda ruling, which requires that police inform suspects of their right against self-incrimination and their right to an attorney. At the same time, Wilson boasted that Manny "never accused us of . . . mistreatment" because "we treated him well." Wilson also noted that "there wasn't a finger laid on him," as if the absence of police brutality should not be taken for granted.

Detective Wilson's comment was curiously defensive. No one ever alleged police brutality in Manny's case. Perhaps Wilson saw fit to preempt any suggestion of the use of force because his partner, Detective Herberich, had once been indicted for the alleged assault of a burglary suspect. In June 1945, a jury acquitted Herberich and two other officers of the charges.

Herberich had served in the 110th Precinct since 1933 and for many years led Elmhurst detectives in the number of arrests. But the way he and Wilson handled Manny's arrest was not uniquely aggressive. Eyewitness accusations, standing alone, were routinely treated as sufficient to support an arrest without much investigation. And once an arrest was made, there was no looking back. The defendant's fate rested, in Wilson's words, with the judge and jury.

Wilson lost no sleep over his role in Manny's case. "We forgot about it until they made a movie out of it," he said.

The detective's untroubled conscience reflects a common mindset about erroneous convictions. Criminal justice expert James Doyle has observed that in such cases, rather than apologize or examine their own role in the matter, state agents advance a fatalistic view that portrays the outcome as "God's will." Doyle cites the example of Boston Police Commissioner Edward Davis, who, as a detective, had arrested an innocent man who spent nineteen years in prison before his exoneration. While Davis told the *Boston Globe* that he felt "terrible that the system did not work," he saw no reason to apologize because he "didn't do anything wrong" and had instead worked with "victims who were convinced that this was a man who did this."

The narrative that the authorities were just "doing their jobs" found acceptance in the media, which did not challenge the decision to arrest or prosecute Manny. For example, a *Long Island Star-Journal* editorial lamenting Manny's plight acknowledged "there was a strong case against him . . . a case too strong for the prosecution to disregard." The editorial focused on Balestrero's inability to use the results of his lie detector test at trial.

Similarly, in his *Life* magazine account, Herbert Brean wrote that Manny "had been given every right of the American judicial system" and "had been treated with fairness and impersonal consideration." Brean ascribed no blame to prosecutors or the police. This is a telling reflection of the deference shown to state officials in 1950s New York. Brean had probably researched Manny's case more heavily than any other person. He had reported on the prejudicial procedures deployed at the 110th Precinct. By June 1955, when he completed a draft of the treatment that served as the source for *The Wrong Man*'s script, he had become close with Manny. Still, he presented the arrest and prosecution as the inevitable result of the eyewitnesses' accusations, as if authorities had no duty to investigate the matter independently. "The police actually were acting as agents of a complaining witness," he wrote in the treatment.

Even Manny didn't criticize the police. "They couldn't help it," he told Brean. O'Connor went a step further and publicly exonerated the prosecution. While asserting that the "young girls" who identified Manny "made a horrible mistake," he conceded that the police and the district attorney's office "only did their duty once the complaint was made." O'Connor added that "our preliminary investigation of this whole mess rather clearly shows that the Prudential company was behind this action, approved it and was instrumental in getting one of its employees (Ms. Ello) to sign the complaint."

O'Connor's statement may have been a strategic attempt to set up a lawsuit for damages against Prudential. It may have also reflected a calculation by a future prosecutor with political aspirations: O'Connor would soon run for Queens district attorney (an election he won) and later for governor (an election he lost).

Whatever his motives, O'Connor's comment aptly sums up the state's narrative in wrongful conviction cases: The police and prosecutors had only done their duty.

—NINE—
STRICKEN AGAIN: THE FIGHT
FOR COMPENSATION

Manny Balestrero with his sons in June 1953
(*Lisa Larsen/The Life Picture Collection/Shutterstock*)

"ALL'S WELL THAT ENDS WELL," the *Long Island Star-Journal* declared on its front page the day after Charles Daniell's confession.

The phrase not only understated the horror of Manny's ordeal, but also implied a family restoration that had not yet occurred.

Rose remained at the sanitarium in Ossining, where, as one reporter put it, she lived "in her own hazy world of self-incrimination." The trips there were wrenching for Manny and his sons.

"When I visited her, it was really not a lot of engagement," Greg Balestrero recalled. "I remember how difficult it was at the time to reach her. And at the time they were reaching her through electric shock therapy, so it wasn't a really pleasant experience."

Greg said Rose was at times in a state of "complete withdrawal." She experienced a "kind of removal from reality" and stopped speaking before her hospitalization. According to Greg, the condition today would likely be considered acute depression and would be more readily treatable with medication.

With Rose still in Ossining, Manny was raising his sons on his own while working nights. He did the cooking and shopping and got the kids ready for school. When Manny went off to the Stork Club at night, his sister-in-law minded the boys.

It was a time of financial duress for the Balestreros. The Greenmont Sanitarium charged $125 per week—which exceeded Manny's weekly take-home pay of $89 from the Stork Club. As the months after his exoneration passed, the cumulative cost of Rose's care approached $5,000. Manny also had debts from the criminal prosecution. The costs of the lie detector test, handwriting expert, and other trial preparation added up to about $6,300.

In an effort to ease his financial situation, Manny sought legal damages for his false arrest. But in his second odyssey through New York's court system, justice again proved elusive.

***

Intuition would suggest that Manny had a clear legal right to compensation. After all, there was no denying that Manny had been prosecuted for a crime he did not commit and that he and his family had suffered mightily as a result.

Even with innocence established, though, Manny's options were limited. Exoneration alone did not make out a claim for false arrest against the city. Instead, a plaintiff had to show that at the time of the arrest the police lacked probable cause to believe that the person had committed the crime. New York courts had long held that a positive identification by a crime victim supplied adequate cause. In Manny's case, the detectives acted on multiple identifications. In addition, the grand jury indictment created a presumption that the detectives had a lawful basis for the arrest. To defeat that presumption, Manny would need to show that "fraud, perjury, or suppression of evidence" led to the indictment. These requirements made any false arrest claim against the city an uphill battle.

An alternative target was Prudential. The insurer had, through its employees, accused Manny of armed robbery. It stood behind the charges even after Frank O'Connor shared the exculpatory information.

Under New York law, Prudential was liable for wrongful ("tortious") acts committed by an employee within the scope of their employment. If O'Connor could prove that a Prudential employee had engaged in actionable wrongdoing, he might be able to reach into the insurer's deep pockets for damages.

The best available theories for suing Prudential were false arrest and malicious prosecution. But it would not be enough to prove that its employees erroneously identified Manny as the bandit. As one New York court put it, "the victim of a crime does not act at his peril in making an identification." For false arrest, O'Connor had to establish that the defendants had instigated or procured the arrest without reasonable justification. For malicious prosecution, he had to prove "malice"—

which required a showing that a complainant knowingly or recklessly gave false information to the authorities.

These principles reflect a judicial attempt to balance competing values. On the one hand, false arrest is a horrific wrong that cries out for compensation. On the other, every free society needs the cooperation of its citizens to police crime. If eyewitnesses face liability for sincere mistakes, they will be reluctant to come forward. A failure to insulate such mistakes may therefore impede law enforcement.

Despite the daunting legal hurdles, Manny sued Prudential and Constance Ello (the employee who signed the criminal complaint) in the Supreme Court for Queens County in September 1953. He sought $500,000 in damages for false arrest and wrongful prosecution, on these grounds: (1) Prudential and Ello wrongfully accused Manny of crimes; (2) as a result, Manny experienced false imprisonment and prosecution, and suffered public humiliation and embarrassment; (3) the arrest caused Rose "to suffer a nervous breakdown and to become mentally and physically ill"; and (4) Manny, in turn, was deprived of Rose's "society and companionship" and forced to pay large sums for her medical expenses, along with his legal expenses.

Attorney Frank O'Connor, left, with Manny Balestrero after Manny's exoneration in 1953 (*Art Edger/Daily News Archive via Getty Images*)

The complaint alleged that Ello testified falsely at Manny's grand jury proceeding. While Ello had said she picked Manny out of a lineup, O'Connor alleged that she "maliciously and wantonly concealed" that (1) she was at first not sure that Manny was the holdup man; (2) before the lineup, police allowed her to view Manny "as he stood framed in a lighted doorway" and informed her that Manny was the suspect; (3) during this preliminary viewing opportunity, Manny wore a distinctive maroon scarf and gray tweed coat—the same clothes he wore as he stood amid the lineup fillers, none of whom had similar clothing; and (4) the lineup included her husband. Had Ello disclosed these facts, O'Connor argued, the grand jury would not have indicted Manny.

At first it appeared Manny's case would turn on his ability to prove that Prudential and Ello procured his arrest and indictment through malicious or otherwise unjustified actions. But a separate legal issue quickly came to the fore, one with roots in an assault case from forty-eight years earlier.

***

On April 27, 1905, a fight broke out in the town of Orleans, New York, between one Herbert Hutchinson and one Sigmund Stern. In a lawsuit filed soon after in the Supreme Court for Jefferson County, Hutchinson alleged that Stern had, without provocation, beat him on the head with fists and then, while brandishing a knife, chased him and threatened to "cut [Hutchinson's] heart out." Stern, in his defense, countered that Hutchinson had initiated the incident by using "insulting language and epithets" and then punched Stern in the face.

The truth of what happened in the Hutchinson-Stern fight is lost to history. But the litigation is not, thanks to a court ruling on Hutchinson's alleged damages. His wife, Lillian, was "present and nearby." She was pregnant at the time. Upon witnessing the alleged assault on her husband, Lillian experienced "great distress." As a result, she "gave premature birth to a stillborn child." Then Herbert Hutchinson "was put to great expense in the care of and doctoring of his said wife" and "was deprived of the services of his wife . . . to the plaintiff's damage in the sum of One thousand dollars."

Stern and his lawyer presumably recognized the potential impact of these allegations. They moved to strike the part of the complaint describing the harm to Lillian, on the ground that it was "irrelevant and redundant." The motion argued that a defendant accused of assault is not responsible for harm suffered by his accuser's wife.

A Jefferson County trial judge granted Stern's motion. On appeal, the Appellate Division affirmed that ruling. "We are not referred to any case which sustains the contention . . . that the plaintiff, in an action for assault, may not only recover the damages sustained in his own person, but also the damages sustained by reason of injury to the wife, occasioned by fright, and consequent loss of services of the wife." Such damages, the court said, were "too remote" to be recoverable. As support for its conclusion, the court noted an 1882 ruling by the Iowa Supreme Court. In the Iowa case, a man brought a malicious prosecution claim alleging that in reaction to the indictment against him, his wife "became sick, nervous, insane and utterly helpless." The Iowa court ruled that damages for the wife's suffering were not recoverable because that harm was not "natural and proximate consequence" of the alleged wrong.

The court's ruling against Hutchinson—denying him recovery for harm suffered by his wife as a result of a wrong done to him—remained good law in 1953. Only a year earlier, New York's Appellate Division reaffirmed the underlying legal principle. In Roher v. State, three youths brought a false arrest claim after a state trooper had mistakenly accused them of larceny. While the court upheld their claim against the state, it denied related claims brought by their parents for their emotional distress from the false imprisonment. "There is no cause of action for mental anguish in such circumstances," the court said.

This point of law gave Prudential an early chance to try to narrow Manny's suit. In October 1953, Prudential moved to strike from the complaint all allegations relating to Rose. At a hearing on the motion, Prudential's lawyer argued to Justice L. Barron Hill that no medical evidence established that Rose's illness resulted from

Manny's "unfortunate experience."

Justice Hill said at the hearing that false arrest is "one of the worst experiences that could happen to anyone." Even so, on November 19, 1953, he ruled that Manny could not recover damages for harm suffered by Rose as a result of his arrest and prosecution. Justice Hill cited the "general rule" that "the right of recovery for mental suffering resulting from injuries is restricted to the person who has suffered the hurt." He ordered that all references to Rose be stricken from the complaint.

After this defeat, Manny moved Rose to a less expensive facility—the Seton Institute in Baltimore. Even then, the cost was at least seventy five dollars per week.

In the meantime, O'Connor appealed Justice Hill's order. On March 1, 1954, the Appellate Division affirmed the ruling against Manny. Citing Hutchinson and other cases, the court emphasized that the acts described in the complaint "were directed against [Manny] alone." Since Rose had no right to recover for the harm she suffered as a result of those acts, Manny had no derivative cause of action based on Rose's injury.

O'Connor promptly appealed to the state's highest court—the Court of Appeals. On July 14, 1954, that court denied the appeal in a unanimous two-sentence opinion.

Court of Appeals Justice John Van Voorhis would later describe the holding in Manny's case this way: "causation was not established between mental derangement and arrest of the subject's husband on a charge of crime."

This statement is not intuitive. Although Rose had experienced traumas in the past, she had been managing well as a mother and wife before January 1953. Until the arrest, she had never been treated for any mental disorder. As Manny put it, "never—not once—did Rose show any signs of mental difficulty before I was arrested. She was badly frightened for me, and that's it!"

The arrest sent Rose into a spiral. If the law merely required "cause and effect" in their ordinary meaning, then her anguish was attributable to the wrongful arrest.

In the context of tort claims like false arrest, though, "causation" required more. The victim and her injuries had to be within a foreseeable zone of harm created by the defendant's conduct. By focusing on the causation requirement, the courts sought to rein in theories that might otherwise flood the courts with derivative actions based on mental anguish. In fact, Justice Van Voorhis cited the ruling in Manny's case for the idea that "if the door is opened to establishing causation by speculative testimony in mental illness, the quantity of litigation of this nature is likely to be almost unlimited . . . ."

Still, it's hard not to read the court rulings as a symbolic erasure of Rose's plight. The rulings declared her suffering irrelevant, as if to underline the state's seeming indifference to the effect of its wrongful prosecution. Rose would not be included in the story told in court.

After the Court of Appeals ruling, O'Connor and Manny pondered their next steps. Rose's medical expenses continued to mount. Manny had spent close to $10,000 on her care and treatment.

O'Connor then moved to expand Manny's lawsuit. In late July 1954, he filed an amended complaint adding the City of New York as a defendant. The new complaint accused the city, too, of false arrest and malicious prosecution. It alleged that Manny's imprisonment was "unlawful, wrongful, malicious, without lawful warrant or legal process, and without any probable cause."

Given the congestion on the judicial calendar, Manny's day in court remained far off. Cases in the Supreme Court for Queens County took an average of forty-two months to get to trial—a delay untenable for Manny. So O'Connor asked the court to prioritize his case.

As with the battle over Rose's role in the lawsuit, that request led to a legal and symbolic blow against Manny.

***

In September 1954, O'Connor moved for a "preference" that would give Manny a quick trial date. While cases were normally heard in the order of filing, New York's Rules of Civil Practice permitted courts to grant a preference where "the interests of justice will be served by an early trial."

In support of the motion, Manny submitted an affidavit detailing his financial predicament. He had borrowed a lot to stay afloat. The loans included $1,500 from his father; about $1,300 from each of his sisters-in-law; $1,150 from his father-in-law; and $864 from a cousin. Manny's total debt stood at $6,500—about $72,000 in 2022 dollars. Given his modest salary and the continuing sanitarium costs, Manny told the court, he was "completely destitute."

The city and Prudential opposed the request on several grounds. They argued that because Manny could not recover damages for Rose's injuries, the court could not base a preference on her medical expenses. They claimed that financial hardships from Rose's private care could not justify a preference because she had a right to free care in New York's public institutions.

Prudential also pointed to income that Manny received from the sale of rights to his story. *Life* magazine had published Herbert Brean's account of Manny's arrest and exoneration in June 1953. A condensed version of Brean's piece appeared in *Reader's Digest*. Manny's story was also adapted for an installment of the television show *Robert Montgomery Presents* that aired in January 1954.

For these projects Manny received a total of about $3,000. All the funds went toward Rose's care and had not erased his debt. In Manny's words: "As fast as these moneys were received they were immediately turned over by me, either to Dr. Banay or to the Seton Institute, for the care and treatment of my sick wife."

On October 14, 1954, Justice James T. Hallinan ruled that Manny was entitled to a preference on the trial calendar: "While plaintiff may not recover the expenses of his wife's illness as an element of damage, such expense is very relevant here on the question of plaintiff's financial condition and his need for a preference in the interest of justice." Justice Hallinan noted that Manny did not want public care for Rose: "I know of no law which requires a citizen to become an object of public charge if he prefers to pay his own way." He also pointed out that if the Balestreros accepted "public charity," they would automatically qualify for the preference under a recent appellate ruling for a plaintiff who was "on the relief rolls of New York City" after a car accident.

Justice Hallinan set trial for November 8. But the case fell off the calendar when the defendants appealed his ruling, returning the case to the Appellate Division.

On January 31, 1955, the Appellate Division ruled that Manny was not entitled to a preference. It gave only the following rationale:

> *The granting of the motion under the facts disclosed in this record was an improvident exercise of discretion. Concededly plaintiff is gainfully employed at a salary in excess of $100 a week.*

Of course, Manny's salary was only one part of the picture. While Manny was then making $105 per week, most of that was used to pay for Rose's care and treatment. The Seton Institute charged a minimum of seventy-five dollars per week and in Manny's words, "This weekly expenditure increases very substantially when the highly specialized shock therapy treatments are given to her."

In a punishing sequel to its earlier ruling, the Appellate Division again erased Rose from the narrative. It ignored the issue of her medical expenses and did not mention her at all. It also ignored Manny's heavy debt.

With so few details in the opinion, the court's reasoning is elusive. It may have felt that preferences should be reserved for the most extreme cases. It may have silently accepted the defendants' argument that Manny should have moved Rose to a public hospital. Or it may have been influenced by published reports referring to the motion picture rights to Manny's story. "It is a matter of common knowledge that such dramatic rights command a very high price when sold to a major studio for world-wide distribution, particularly as it was reported that Frank Sinatra was being considered to play the part of [Balestrero]," Prudential told the court in its appellate brief. Columnist Dorothy Kilgallen noted in a January 12 column (less than three weeks before the court ruling) that "Warners would like to cast Frank Sinatra as Manny Balestrero."

Even with a potential film deal on the horizon, the Appellate Division's decision is hard to fathom. The law allowed preferences that served "the interests of justice." This standard was intended to allow trial judges to exercise discretion based on the facts of the particular case.

Before the court stood a man who had been falsely arrested, indicted, and tried. His wife was in a sanitarium as a result of the arrest. He was financially underwater because of the cost of her care. He and Rose were victims of a stunning failure by the criminal justice system.

These facts made Manny an exceptional plaintiff. But not in the eyes of the Appellate Division.

Faced with the adverse rulings, and still mired in debt, Manny bowed to financial reality. He had refused before to have Rose in a state institution. In May 1955, though, Manny moved her to Kings County Hospital in Brooklyn—the same hospital where Louis Hoffner had donated bone marrow to his mother.

By that time, Manny had left Jackson Heights and was living with family in Jersey City. He could no longer bear to stay in the home he had shared with Rose for twenty years. "That's where it happened," Manny said. "I had to get away from that house."

Manny ultimately agreed to settle his litigation and received a $7,000 payment from Prudential.

It was not until September 1955—more than two and a half years after Manny's arrest—that Rose was declared "well enough" to go home.

"My life did not start over again when I was cleared," Manny said seven months after Rose returned to him. "It started again last September."

***

One week after Manny's arrest in January 1953, a new play premiered on Broadway. The play turned on false accusations that spread terror throughout a Massachusetts community. Even as innocent men and women faced imprisonment and death, the head judge continued to insist that the "uncorrupted" had "nothing to fear."

The play was Arthur Miller's *The Crucible*. Few works of art have grappled as hauntingly with the corrosive harm of false indictment. And had Manny walked over from the Stork Club to Broadway to see the show, he may have seen in the retelling of the Salem witch trials a refraction of his predicament.

But Manny could not have foreseen that his nightmare would inspire its own retelling, through the lens of Hollywood's most famous director.

PART THREE:
THE WRONG MAN

—TEN—
"MY BASIC FEARS"

Vaughan Glaser, left, and Robert Cummings in *Saboteur* (*Album/Alamy Stock Photo*)

In Alfred Hitchcock's 1942 film *Saboteur*, Barry Kane (Robert Cummings) is an innocent man on the run. Falsely accused of sabotage, Kane escapes police custody and takes refuge in the home of a stranger named Philip Martin (Vaughan Glaser). Kane conceals his handcuffs at first. But he quickly realizes that his welcoming host is blind.

Soon Martin's niece, Patricia (Pat) (Priscilla Lane), arrives. As the three prepare for dinner, Kane drops his knife and inadvertently exposes the handcuffs. Pat is poised to warn her uncle about Kane. We brace for a confrontation. Surely Kane will need to take flight.

Then comes the Hitchcock twist.

"What's the matter, Pat? Have you just seen his handcuffs? I heard them as soon as he came in," Martin says.

Martin has known all along that Kane was a fugitive. And when Pat insists that such a dangerous man must be turned over to the police, Martin refuses.

"It is my duty as an American citizen to believe a man innocent until he's been proved guilty. . . . I have my own ideas about my duties as a citizen. They sometimes involve disregarding the law," Martin says.

***

In *Saboteur*, a blind man senses what agents of the law cannot see: the hero's innocence. While a brief interlude in a chase film, the scene points to themes that recur throughout Hitchcock's canon. The director once observed that his films "usually follow a pattern of the innocent man who gets involved in bizarre situations." He saw this pattern as the key to audience identification with his protagonists.

Hitchcock's police often hastily reach the wrong conclusion about the hero. In his earlier films, that plot point propels the narrative. In *Saboteur*, police target Kane after discovering that a fire extinguisher he handed to a coworker during a factory blaze was filled with gasoline. Within the first fifteen minutes, the chase is on. Even after police catch up with Kane at a ranch outside of Los Angeles, the resulting arrest is only a respite from the action. Kane escapes from the back seat of a police car and leaps off a bridge into a river below. The chase resumes.

Saboteur repeats the structure of Hitchcock's earlier mistaken identity tale, *The 39 Steps*. In that 1935 film, the police first appear shortly after tourist Richard Hannay has narrowly escaped from foreign agents who have murdered a woman. The discovery of the victim in Hannay's apartment leads to front-page reports of his disappearance. "There's enough evidence there to hang any man," observes a police officer as he reads the news. Soon enough, police are chasing Hannay across the Scottish moors. As in *Saboteur*, the end game is escapism. The film uses Hannay's "wrong man" status to drive the action, but never pauses to explore the trauma of false arrest. No sooner is Hannay captured by police than he escapes by crashing through a window. Later, Hannay winds up handcuffed to a woman whom he must convince of his innocence. As the couple banter while eluding both the police and a spy ring, the film nearly morphs into a romantic comedy.

Unable to see the hero's innocence, Hitchcock's police are just as bad at unmasking the guilty. Even his more patient and sympathetic detectives prove ineffective. And in several earlier films that foreshadow elements of *The Wrong Man*, their mistakes are tied to eyewitness misidentification.

In *Shadow of a Doubt* (1943), rather than rushing to an arrest, two detectives, Graham and Saunders, pose as survey interviewers as they investigate Charlie Oakley (Joseph Cotten), a suspect in the nationwide hunt for the "Merry Widow Murderer." Oakley is staying with his family, including his niece (also nicknamed Charlie, and played by Teresa Wright) in Santa Rosa. Even though Oakley sees through their ruse, the detectives take a photograph of him and wire it back east for identification. "The minute the witnesses see that picture we'll know whether or not Oakley's the man," Saunders says. But no eyewitnesses identify Oakley. Instead, the police mistakenly attribute the murders to another man, and the detectives leave town. In their absence, the heroine, Charlie, is left to grapple with her murderous uncle in a climactic showdown on a train.

In the film's final scene, Detective Graham (Macdonald Carey) says of the world that "sometimes it needs a lot of watching. It seems to go crazy every now and then." This observation not only describes the mayhem that Hitchcock depicts, but also underlines the detectives' failure. They watched the chaos unleashed by a serial killer, but could not restore order.

The elements of mistaken eyewitnesses and an ineffective detective also figure in *Rear Window*, Hitchcock's 1954 classic starring James Stewart and Grace Kelly. In that film, L. B. Jefferies (Stewart) implores Detective Doyle (Wendell Corey) to search the apartment of a neighbor whose wife has disappeared. Jefferies (aka Jeff) suspects the neighbor, Lars Thorwald (Raymond Burr), of murder. The detective resists, appealing to the need for sufficient evidence to support a search warrant. But at Jeff's behest, Doyle investigates the matter and returns with a report that appears to exonerate Thorwald: a building superintendent and two tenants saw Thorwald and his wife leave for the train station on the morning after the night of her supposed disappearance.

As Jeff and Doyle spar over Jeff's theories, a thread in their dialogue anticipates the interrogation scenes in *The Wrong Man*. Thorwald should welcome a police search, Jeff argues, since if he's innocent, he has nothing to worry about. "If you find something, you've got a murderer, and they won't care anything about a couple of house rules," Jeff says. "If you don't find anything, the fella's clear." The idea that a suspect would benefit from a search that exonerates him is a variation of the detectives' mantra in *The Wrong Man* that the innocent "have nothing to fear."

But unlike the police in Hitchcock films who rush to judgment, Doyle acts with restraint. Urged to presume Thorwald's guilt, Doyle defers to legal norms. He is an inversion of Dirty Harry. By the end of the film, Jeff's suspicions about

From left: Detective Tom Doyle (Wendell Corey), Lisa Fremont (Grace Kelly), and L. B. Jefferies (James Stewart) in *Rear Window* (*cineclassico/Alamy Stock Photo*)

Thorwald have been borne out, and Doyle and his eyewitnesses have been proven just as ineffectual as their counterparts in *Shadow of a Doubt*. But along the way, *Rear Window* delivers a potent warning about the precedential effect of permitting furtive invasions of our neighbors' homes. The film suggests that Jeff's attitude toward police discretion would create a culture of surveillance and encroach on the affairs of the innocent.

Hitchcock thus often weaved themes of misidentification, guilt, and innocence into his plots. Before *The Wrong Man*, the director explored false accusation most strikingly in *I Confess* (1953). In that film, a priest named Father Logan (Montgomery Clift) stands trial for a murder he did not commit. The plot hinges on a dramatic contrivance. A man who works in Father Logan's parish accidentally kills a lawyer named Villette during a botched robbery. The man then confesses the crime to Logan. Bound by the sanctity of the confessional, Logan cannot disclose his knowledge of the killer. As a result, the priest himself becomes a target of the police investigation headed by Inspector Larrue (Karl Malden).

There is no direct evidence of Logan's guilt. But the circumstantial evidence is compelling. Two young girls tell the inspector they saw a man wearing a priest's cassock exiting Villette's apartment shortly after the murder. A cassock with blood (planted by the real killer) is discovered among Logan's possessions. Father Logan has no alibi for the estimated time of the killing. On top of that, the murder victim had been blackmailing Ruth Grandfort (Anne Baxter), a woman Logan had a relationship with before becoming a priest.

In depicting Logan's arrest and trial, *I Confess* previews themes that would be explored in *The Wrong Man*, including the perils of eyewitness testimony.

For example, the two schoolgirls interviewed by Larrue can supply only one fact about the man they glimpsed leaving the victim's apartment: "He was a priest." But they saw the man only from behind, so had no view of his face. One of the girls notes that it was "very dark." Despite the scant details, Larrue doesn't ask the girls to explain the basis of their conclusion that the man was a priest. While a brief flashback implies the man was wearing a cassock, the inspector never secures that information from the girls. And in the flashback we see that the man was wearing a hat—another detail the inspector fails to elicit (Logan does not wear a hat).

After he interviews the girls, Larrue is convinced the killer is a priest. The inspector never scrutinizes the girls' account because it seems to support his preexisting suspicion of Father Logan, whom Larrue had seen meeting Ruth the morning after the murder.

At the ensuing murder trial, Hitchcock explores both the stigma that accompanies false arrest and the disavowal of responsibility that often follows it. The jury finds Logan not guilty, but announces its misgivings. "While we attach grave suspicion to the accused, we cannot find sufficient evidence to prove that he actually wielded the weapon that killed Monsieur Villette," the foreman says. The judge then gratuitously piles on: "Michael Logan, while I have no doubt that the jury must have reached their conclusion in utmost fairness and solemn regard for justice, I cannot help expressing my personal disagreement with their verdict."

After the verdict, Hitchcock cuts to an alarmed Inspector Larrue, who is seated next to the prosecutor. "They've ruined him," Larrue says. "Why couldn't they have said 'not guilty' simply and let it go at that?"

They've ruined him. Larrue fears the begrudging acquittal will stigmatize Logan. Yet it was *Larrue* who was singularly responsible for the arrest. He then persuaded the prosecutor to put aside his doubts about the evidence. The inspector's blindness to his own role evokes the comment of Detective Leigh Wilson in Manny's case that the judge and jury bear ultimate responsibility for a defendant's fate.

The fallout from the false arrest continues after the verdict. Hissing and shouting angry judgments ("Take off that collar!"), the spectators trail Logan out of the courtroom—a potent visual symbol of how accusations shadow even an acquitted defendant. As the priest descends the stairs and heads toward the exit, he faces the unrelenting, judgmental stares of onlookers. Outside, an angry mob has surrounded the courthouse. When Logan struggles to get to a car, the mob threatens to overwhelm the handful of police engaged in crowd control. One youth breaks through and shoves Logan, causing the priest's elbow to crash through the car window.

While Father Logan is free, he faces ruin from the suspicion that hangs over him. He has been acquitted, but not proven innocent.

I Confess might have delivered an even more powerful message had the film used the ending that Hitchcock wanted. In the original treatment by Hitchcock and his wife, Alma, Father Logan is found guilty and executed. This proposed ending tracks the 1902 French play that inspired the film, *Nos deux consciences*. Hitchcock opposed the death penalty and, according to biographer Patrick McGilligan, conceived of the priest's story as "an anti-capital punishment thriller." But Warner Bros. insisted that Hitchcock change the ending.

Even without the wrongful execution climax, *I Confess* reflects Hitchcock's lifelong preoccupation with the state's power to incarcerate the innocent. "Policemen and the law are my basic fears," Hitchcock once said. The director traced these anxieties back to an episode of his childhood when his father arranged to have a local constable lock him in a jail cell for a short while. According to Hitchcock, the episode was intended to teach him what imprisonment felt like. "I was terrified, even though I knew it was not real," he recalled.

Hitchcock saw in Manny's case not only a vehicle for exploring his own obsessions, but also the opportunity to break from convention by presenting the story from the perspective of the accused. "It may be an expression of my own fear, but I've always felt the drama of a situation in which a normal person is suddenly deprived of freedom and incarcerated with hardened criminals," he said.

By staying with Manny's perspective, Hitchcock would give audiences an unsparing look at what it meant to be wrongfully accused in America. This narrative decision flowed from the truth of what happened. No one came to Manny's rescue. No police officer tirelessly worked to investigate doubts in the state's case. No reporter shined a light on an indefensible rush to judgment. And no lawyer performed electrifying feats of cross-examination. Instead, only a juror's outburst and the subsequent capture and confession of the actual culprit—whether the result of chance, fate, or prayer—returned Manny to his family.

Hitchcock was no stranger to juror impatience. Twenty-three years before Manny's trial, the director depicted the vagaries of juries in his third sound feature, *Murder!* (1930). The foreman in that film starts the deliberations by announcing that "I really don't think it will be necessary for us to examine all the evidence again in detail." It's not long before he collects "guilty" and "not guilty" ballots and flippantly deals them into competing piles, as if he is presiding at a game of chance. Worse, the foreman and other jurors then browbeat the protagonist into putting aside his doubts about the defendant's guilt—a realist's version of *12 Angry Men* (which was released less than four months after *The Wrong Man*).

Of course, there were other true stories of wrongfully convicted defendants that Hitchcock might have chosen. Like the press, though, Hollywood was more likely to tell the story of one type of victim of the justice system. Manny was white, a devoted family man, and gainfully employed, with no previous criminal record.

The unusual elements of Manny's case held inherent interest for Hitchcock, who once said he regretted not being a criminal lawyer. But the director was also drawn to Rose's story. In films like *Rebecca* (1940), *Suspicion* (1941), and *Notorious* (1946), his female protagonists suffered from emotional or psychological torments of varying kinds. With *The Wrong Man*, there was also a hidden connection between the director and the lead female character: Both had lost a parent at an early age. Rose's mother died of pneumonia when Rose was only fifteen, while the director's father had died suddenly of emphysema when Hitchcock was fourteen. Author Edward White has linked the death of Hitchcock's father to the recurring theme in his films of "a seemingly happy home cruelly torn asunder." As White observes, this theme marks not only *The Wrong Man* but also *The Paradine Case* (a 1947 Hitchcock film in which a lawyer's infatuation with his client imperils his marriage) and *The Man Who Knew Too Much* (which the director first made in 1934 and then remade in 1956, with both versions turning on the kidnapping of a child). Rose's breakdown intrigued Hitchcock as much as Manny's incarceration.

Warner Bros. had the rights to a treatment of the Balestreros' story by *Life* magazine writer Herbert Brean. Since Hitchcock owed Warners one film under an expiring contract, the director and the studio agreed in April 1955 that *The Wrong Man* would be their final project together. Under their agreement, Hitchcock would get a share of the film's profits, but no salary.

To do justice to the story, Hitchcock turned to two artists who had extensive experience with themes of innocence and wrongful accusation. The first was a writer who had grappled with one of the most infamous legal trials of the twentieth century. The second was an actor who had appeared in several films with legal themes and who had a personal connection to Manny's experience.

***

Maxwell Anderson was a Pulitzer Prize-winning dramatist who had written two plays involving wrongful convictions. The first, *Winterset* (1935), depicts the toxic legacy of the conviction on not only the victim's son, but also the sentencing judge, who is driven mad by his role in the affair. Anderson's inspiration was the Sacco-Vanzetti case, which saw Nicola Sacco and Bartolomeo Vanzetti, two anarchists of

Italian descent, executed in 1927 for murder in connection with a payroll robbery in Massachusetts. There remains substantial debate, to this day, about their guilt or innocence. But there is little debate about whether they received fair treatment. In 1977, Massachusetts Governor Michael Dukakis declared that "any stigma and disgrace should be forever removed from [their] names" because of the procedures that led to their conviction.

According to scholar Donald Spoto, Hitchcock wanted Anderson on the film because Winterset "dealt with the moral implications of false indictment in the Sacco-Vanzetti case, and because of Anderson's keen sense of grotesque evil in his Broadway adaptation of William March's novel *The Bad Seed* a year earlier." Joining Anderson on the project was writer Angus MacPhail, who had written Hitchcock's *Spellbound* (1945) and had performed uncredited script work for Hitchcock's remake of *The Man Who Knew Too Much* (1956).

Anderson's role highlighted a thematic link between Manny's ordeal and the Sacco-Vanzetti convictions. Both cases involved grossly suggestive identification procedures. In fact,

Author Maxwell Anderson in 1937
(AP Photo/John Lindsay)

future Supreme Court Justice Felix Frankfurter noted that Sacco and Vanzetti "were shown singly" to potential witnesses and forced to "simulate the behaviors of the Braintree bandits." Frankfurter, then a Harvard law professor, condemned the state's showup procedure as a "farce."

Anderson drew on these elements directly in *Gods of the Lightning*, a drama he cowrote with Harold Hickerson in 1928. As in the real Sacco and Vanzetti case, the plot springs from the murder of a paymaster during an armed robbery. *Gods of the Lightning*, however, leaves no doubt about the innocence of the suspects, two labor organizers named Macready and Capraro. Tried by an unscrupulous prosecutor before a biased judge, the defendants are wrongfully convicted and executed.

In the drama, the state's handling of two eyewitnesses foreshadows themes that would resurface in *The Wrong Man*. Both of the witnesses—Mrs. Lubin and a man named Bartlet—have identified the defendants in prejudicial showup procedures. But when the defense lawyer, Gluckstein, seeks to explore this issue at trial, the judge shuts him down:

Gluckstein: When you identified Capraro as the man who leaped into the murder car, Mr. Bartlet, what was the procedure followed? Were there other

> *men in the room, or was Capraro there alone?*
> *Salter: Objection.*
> *Judge Vail: Sustained. The method of identification should not concern us here. We assume that every precaution was taken by the police against the possibility of error.*
> *Gluckstein: I do not assume that, Your Honor.*
> *Judge Vail: Then you have not properly prepared for the question. We are not investigating the methods of identification customary in this state.*
> *Gluckstein: Your Honor, my point is that the methods of identification employed by the State in securing evidence for this trial were arbitrary, unusual, and deliberately prearranged to incriminate the defendants.*

In the world of *Gods of the Lightning*, then, the showup procedures are "customary"— just as they were in New York at that time. Judge Vail's remarks evoke the impatience of Judge Peter Brancato at the 1939 trial that led to Philip Caruso's wrongful conviction. Brancato and other judges of that era failed to question the identification methods used by the authorities.

In *Gods of the Lightning*, the police not only use showups, but actively coerce the eyewitnesses. "They told me I had to," Mrs. Lubin says of her identification. And the prosecutor, Salter, is flat-out corrupt. When Mrs. Lubin seeks to retract her identification, Salter threatens to reveal scandalous personal information about her to her son. He also threatens to accuse her of being an anarchist sympathizer. Likewise, when Bartlet admits his doubts about his identification of Capraro ("I couldn't say it was him"), Salter directs him to give misleading testimony: "You don't have to say it was him. . . . You'll say it was the dead image of him." Bartlet uses this exact phrase at trial. When defense counsel tries to probe the meaning of "dead image," the judge, again, cuts off the cross-examination.

The corruption depicted in *Gods of the Lightning* would not appear in the Anderson-MacPhail script for *The Wrong Man*. There was no evidence, after all, that police knew that Manny was innocent and set out to frame him. But the earlier drama shows that Anderson saw incriminating identification procedures as part of a process that contributes to wrongful conviction.

***

For the role of Manny, Hitchcock turned to Henry Fonda, who had starred in a series of films exploring social issues. Fonda was best known for his Oscar-nominated portrayal of Tom Joad in John Ford's *The Grapes of Wrath* (1940). At the outset of the film, Joad has just been paroled after serving time for killing a man in self-defense. Joad joins his family as they complete an arduous Depression-era journey to California.

Joad is, in the words of film scholar Joseph McBride, a "noble outlaw," a man who stands outside the law yet is fighting for a better society. He and his family must overcome desperate economic conditions faced by migrants during the 1930s. The police in the film are instruments of injustice, using the force of "law" for the exploitation and mistreatment of the dispossessed. The film charts Tom's journey

Henry Fonda, left, as Tom Joad in *The Grapes of Wrath*
(*PictureLux/The Hollywood Archive/Alamy Stock Photo*)

from a loner preoccupied exclusively with his family's interests to a man devoted to the larger cause of social justice. Tom's defiance ultimately makes him a hunted man, but he remains committed to social engagement. "Wherever there's a cop beatin' up a guy, I'll be there," Tom tells his mother, during one of cinema's most memorable monologues.

Having seen *The Grapes of Wrath*, Hitchcock expected that Fonda would bring "a sense of moral outrage" to his performance as Manny. In fact, Fonda had earlier twice played characters who were wrongfully convicted. In *You Only Live Once* (1937), Fonda starred as an ex-con named Eddie Taylor who is framed for a deadly armored car robbery shortly after his parole. Two years later, in *Let Us Live*, Fonda portrayed a taxicab driver wrongfully convicted of murder.

Let Us Live anticipates *The Wrong Man* as a film based on a real miscarriage of justice arising from mistaken eyewitness testimony. In the real case, three men wielding guns burst into the Paramount Theatre in Lynn, Massachusetts, on January 2, 1934. One of the men shot and killed a theater employee. The men stole $200 and escaped the scene in a taxicab. Three days later, police arrested two cab drivers, Clement Molway and Louis Berrett, and charged them with murder. The men were "positively identified" by six witnesses. It appeared that Molway and Berrett were headed for the electric chair when, in late February 1934, one of three men suspected of robbing a bank in Needham confessed that the three were responsible for the Lynn job.

In *Let Us Live*, Fonda plays taxi driver Brick Tennant, who was based on Clement Molway. As in the real case, a theater is robbed, and the culprits flee in a taxicab. As a result, police bring in cab drivers en masse and parade them in front of the eyewitnesses. "That's him, that's the fella!" a woman declares when Brick appears. While one witness says "he don't look to me like . . ." he is drowned out by definitive

128

cries of recognition by others. Then another witness comes around: "I guess you're right. I didn't recognize him before. Yeah, that's the man!" Based on the chorus of identifications, Brick is arrested even though he had been with his fiancée, Mary (Maureen O'Sullivan), at the time of the robbery.

Brick is at first naive and idealistic. Even after his arrest, he seeks to calm Mary by noting that "those witnesses made a mistake—you can't blame the police for that." He assumes that all he must do is tell the judge he's innocent. Brick's idealism is quickly crushed as he and another man are tried, falsely convicted, and sentenced to death.

While *Let Us Live* was in production, Massachusetts officials warned Columbia Pictures that they would sue the studio if the film referenced the actual events in the case or criticized their police or courts. In fact, they insisted that the credits not even mention the title of the *Harper's Magazine* article ("Murder in Massachusetts") upon which the film was based.

Even so, *Let Us Live* has real bite. When confronted with exculpatory evidence, the prosecutor is unyielding and dismissive ("The jury has convicted them, and my job is getting convictions"). And Brick's identification parade is mirrored by a late scene in which the eyewitnesses identify the actual guilty parties. "That's him, that's the fella. Now that I see him, I know him. He's the one," declares one witness. "These are the right ones," another woman chimes in. The scenes highlight not only the unreliability of the eyewitnesses, but also their vulnerability to a mob mentality.

Fonda's filmography made him a natural choice to play Manny. But according to Fonda biographer Devin McKinney, there was a deeper connection between actor and role. In February 1950, Fonda's estranged wife, Frances, had a nervous breakdown and moved into a sanitorium in Beacon, New York. Little more than two months later, Frances committed suicide by slashing her throat with a razor blade. McKinney writes that Fonda's interest in *The Wrong Man* had "everything to do with the man obsessed by the memory of his dead wife." According to McKinney,

Henry Fonda as Manny (*Photo 12/Alamy Stock Photo*)

Fonda's memory of Frances "haunts" the film.

Fonda himself acknowledged his personal connection to the material. "It was a part I could really get into," he told author Charlotte Chandler. "Tragedy had touched my own life with the death of Jane's and Peter's mother."

Whatever his motivations, Fonda fully committed to the role. He even learned to play Manny's instrument, the bass, to meet Hitchcock's demand for authenticity.

***

When cast for *The Wrong Man*, Fonda had acted in over forty films. By contrast, the actress tapped to play Rose Balestrero was a relative newcomer. Vera Miles had made only a handful of screen appearances. She had worked with Hitchcock once before, though, as the star of the very first episode of the television series *Alfred Hitchcock Presents*. The episode, titled "Revenge," aired in October 1955. While only twenty-five minutes long, it features elements that would appear in *The Wrong Man*.

Miles stars as Elsa Spann, a woman living in a trailer park with her husband, Carl. One day, Carl returns from work to find Elsa beaten. She is barely responsive. Elsa tells him that a stranger had entered the trailer unannounced and asked for money. "I refused him," she says, just able to get out the words. "And then he grabbed me . . . and I screamed . . . and he choked me."

The police learn that a neighbor saw a stranger come into the park. "About six feet tall, gray suit, dark hair" is the extent of the description. When Carl implores the police to find the man, a detective observes that "we can't just pick up every man wearing a gray suit."

On a doctor's advice, Carl takes Elsa to a local hotel. While they are driving, Elsa sees a man in a gray suit walking into the hotel. "There he is," she tells Carl. "That's him. That's him."

Seeking revenge, Carl takes a wrench from his car and follows the man to his room. He enters through the unlocked door, approaches the man from behind, and pummels him with the wrench.

With the attack seemingly avenged, Carl and his wife drive off. As they pass through another town, however, Elsa looks out the car window and registers recognition of another man. "There he is," she says. "That's him. That's him." Carl realizes that Elsa is still in a state of shock. Her identification of the first man was no more reliable than this one. Sirens blare in the background, foretelling Carl's inevitable arrest for killing an innocent man in a fit of vengeance.

With its chilling twist ending, "Revenge" warns of the danger of rushing to judgment. The tale brings together several elements of the real mistaken identity cases: the eyewitness description ("gray suit, dark hair") that lacks meaningful details, a victim too traumatized to provide a reliable identification, and the incantation of a phrase—"that's him, that's him"—that dooms an innocent man.

At the same time, Vera Miles's performance previewed her turn as Rose Balestrero. In an interview with director and film historian Peter Bogdanovich, Hitchcock said the shock suffered by Elsa had "the same element" that would mark Miles's character in *The Wrong Man*. After the attack, Elsa is in a nearly catatonic state. Miles would assume a similar demeanor in certain scenes depicting Rose's collapse.

Vera Miles as Rose (*Album/Alamy Stock Photo*)

Hitchcock's relationship with Miles was the most controversial aspect of the film's production. According to Donald Spoto, the director required Miles to rehearse the scenes depicting Rose's breakdown over and over "until she was nearly sick with exhaustion." Spoto also writes that Hitchcock (who had been married for almost thirty years to his wife, Alma) lavished unwanted attention on Miles, wooing her with roses and "strangely ardent greetings." While Miles found this attention "unwelcome," their working relationship ultimately got back on a "cooly professional keel" after the actress married Gordon Scott (star of the Tarzan series of movies at the time) during a break in shooting. Miles would work with Hitchcock again four years later in both *Psycho* (1960) and the television drama "Incident at a Corner" (discussed in Chapter Eighteen).

***

The rest of *The Wrong Man*'s cast had a range of experiences on the film. Frances Reid, who was cast as Frank O'Connor's wife, displeased the director to the point where her part was cut. Reid was to appear in a scene in which Mrs. O'Connor tells her husband that she made an appointment for him to see Manny. But Hitchcock chided her for using obvious gestures that he believed were not worthy of an actress "when she was in public school."

Harold J. Stone, who played Detective Lieutenant Bowers, was on the set when Hitchcock dressed down Reid.

"Let me tell you, the sweat came on," Stone recalled in an interview with *Classic Images* magazine. "I was dying because I had a big 12-page scene with Henry [Fonda], interrogating him. Anyway, I ran out. I went to the next set to calm down . . . ."

Stone overcame his anxiety and performed a long part of the interrogation scene in one take. Hitchcock was pleased.

"Anything Mr. Stone wants, he may have," the director announced. Hitchcock also told Stone that "from now on you may call me Hitch."

Still, one element of Stone's physical appearance raised concerns for Hitchcock: the actor's height. Stone was about four inches shorter than Fonda, who stood six feet, two inches tall. Since Hitchcock wanted Bowers to appear as tall as Manny, the filmmakers ordered Adler shoes, which had an "elevator" line that promised short men that they would be "almost 2 full inches taller instantly" (Adler's ads enticed men by asking, "Want to be *taller* than 'she' is?"). Until the order arrived, Stone had to put wooden blocks in his shoes. "In the cold, it was almost impossible to walk," he said.

Hitchcock came to the set with a precise idea of what he wanted from his performers. As with his other films, the director carefully storyboarded scenes and shared them with his actors. Laurinda Barrett, who played one of the eyewitnesses, recalled that Hitchcock showed her the pictures of the police lineup scene and instructed her to adhere to them strictly.

"I remember offering to move, and being told that I couldn't move a muscle, and do exactly what you're told," Barrett told author Murray Pomerance. "He showed me the shots and he said 'That's what every shot is.' He didn't do anything else but what he drew on those pieces of paper. They were all followed systematically and to the letter."

Fonda similarly said of Hitchcock that "he blueprinted every scene he did carefully with the production man and the assistant director and the script supervisor, so that any one of the four of them could have lined up the shot and shot it."

Fonda, who said he loved working with Hitchcock, was so comfortable on the set that he sometimes dozed off between shots.

According to actress Peggy Webber, who played eyewitness Alice Dennerly, Fonda "believed that one should fall asleep rather than get tensed up by watching them getting everything set up. He told me that was the best thing—learn to fall asleep, try not to get excited about everything."

In Webber's case, though, Hitchcock wanted the actress as amped up as possible for her one scene, in which she waits on Manny at the Associated Life office.

"Hitchcock kept telling me to 'keep the fear up, keep the adrenaline up, keep that going, don't drop it,'" Webber told *Scarlet Street* magazine.

Besides professional actresses like Webber, several actual participants in Manny's case were hired for the film. Harold Berman and Charles Gulotta both played themselves in the roles of the court reporter and head courtroom attendant, respectively. Their casting advanced Hitchcock's pursuit of authenticity in the production. Influenced by the neorealist movement in Italian cinema, the director aspired to re-create Manny's ordeal on film with as much fidelity to the facts as possible.

"The film must breathe reality," Hitchcock said during filming.

Achieving that goal required extensive field research at the Queens and Manhattan locales where the events unfolded. The Balestreros, who had sold Warner Bros. the rights to their story for $22,000, were involved in the research. But by

1956, they had moved to Miami. "I figured if we're going to really get a fresh start, everything's got to be different. We left our friends, our relatives, our home, our furniture, everything, to come down here," Manny told the *New York Post*.

At first, as the filmmakers worked to reconstruct the facts of the case, they interviewed the Balestreros by telephone. In February 1956, for example, associate producer Herbert Coleman quizzed the couple about a detective's visit to the Balestrero home while Manny was being interrogated at precinct headquarters. According to a letter from Hitchcock to Anderson, Manny "got quite nervous again" during this call. As a result, Rose took the phone and provided Coleman with the details of the visit.

Then, on March 20, 1956, the Balestreros and their children met at their home in Miami with Fonda, Miles, and technical assistant Constance Willis. While only eight at the time, Greg Balestrero recalled a limousine pulling up in front of the house that "looked like a cruise liner."

"Vera Miles and Henry Fonda wanted to get to know my parents. And they did for the couple of hours they were together with them," Greg recalled. "Part of it was to find out how my dad carried himself on stage, and how he played . . . and how he held the bass. Henry Fonda went in and watched my dad play for a while."

Over the course of the two-hour meeting, Manny described the routines of his daily life in great detail—including his route home from the Stork Club, how long he would typically wait for the subway, and his preferred early-morning meal at Bickford's, a cafeteria at the Victor Moore Arcade complex. No detail was too granular, as evidenced by a description of which subway car Manny boarded and how "he always sat facing the way of the train and propped his right arm against the window-ledge."

At the same time, Manny's memory of his interrogation, incarceration, and trial was clouded by trauma. He described the events as a "nightmare" that continued to haunt him. He also referred to the false arrest as "the thing," as if the euphemism was needed to keep the nightmare at bay.

"Manny's wife was out of the hospital by then, but she was still shaken by the thing, and we were warned not to talk to her about it," Fonda later recalled. "She just sat there at the table, silently, with her hands folded in her lap."

While Rose met with the actors, her father and her sister Tilda declined

The house in Jackson Heights that was used for the exterior of the Balestrero home in the film, as seen in 2021
(*photo by Rich Dubin*)

to give permission for their names to be used in the film. In March 1956, Tilda told Coleman that she and Bartholomew Giolito "wanted nothing to do with the picture." They took this position even though Hitchcock intended to portray them positively and show their loaning of money to Manny for bail. As a result, the filmmakers did not use Manny's former home at 41-30 Seventy-Third Street in Jackson Heights (which Rose's father owned) and instead shot the exterior of a home about five blocks away.

The preproduction research went much further than meetings with the principals. Among those interviewed were: Manny's attorney, Frank O'Connor; Manny's parents; his sister, Olga, and brother-in-law, Eugene Conforti; Dr. Ralph Banay, the psychiatrist who diagnosed Rose; Dr. Fabian Rouke, the expert who administered the lie detector test; the Ferreros, the couple who owned the farm in upstate New York where Manny and Rose were vacationing at the time of the first Prudential holdup; two men who sat on the jury; and several of the Prudential employees.

The filmmakers were stymied, though, when it came to the cooperation of the police. Associate producer Coleman at first met secretly with the detectives, but soon after that a directive came down precluding further cooperation.

"We had hoped we might be able to get some actual data from the detectives in the case, but apparently the Police Commissioner—a Mr. Kennedy—feels that grave secrets might be given away if we asked a detective whether he blew his nose loudly or softly while interrogating a suspect," Hitchcock told Maxwell Anderson in a February 28, 1956, letter.

"Mr. Kennedy" is a reference to Police Commissioner Stephen P. Kennedy, who became the city's top cop in August 1955 after twenty-seven years in different law enforcement jobs. Kennedy's refusal to cooperate with the filmmakers was no surprise. Hitchcock's request came at a particularly sensitive time for the police, as New York City saw a record number of crimes in 1954. In August of that year, Kennedy's predecessor, Commissioner Francis W. H. Adams, had declared that the city was "on the verge of becoming a community of violence and crime." Adams attributed the crime surge to the lack of adequate funding. He called for the hiring of at least seven thousand more police officers.

As *The Wrong Man*'s research team worked to reconstruct Manny's case in early 1956, Commissioner Kennedy continued his predecessor's campaign for a "larger and better-paid police." The request for budget was partly about image, which the police department had become increasingly conscious of since adopting a formal public relations policy in 1949. "Public relations, insofar as it relates to the Police Department, is the sum total of the attitudes, impressions and opinions of the public in its relationship with the Department," the Department Manual of Procedure stated.

As part of this effort, Kennedy simultaneously sought to assure the public that he would rid the ranks of graft and vice, such as gambling, while affirming the model of the virtuous officer. "Our police are a law enforcement agency which scrupulously observes the civil rights of the peoples it serves and carries out its functions in accordance with due process of law," he announced in a policy speech.

Given Kennedy's effort to burnish his department's image, it is little wonder that he wanted nothing to do with *The Wrong Man*. The film's very title promised a plot set in motion by a police mistake. Even though Manny's arrest did not occur on Kennedy's watch, the commissioner no doubt loathed to give currency to a project that might suggest that New York's finest were not scrupulous in their observation of civil liberties. As Coleman recalled, the police "wanted no part of the Balestrero story" because "they were trying to keep secret the fact that their forces had severely violated Balestrero's civil rights."

Still, the rebuff from Kennedy did not discourage Hitchcock. He and Coleman hired a retired detective, George Groves, to act as technical adviser. They also hired O'Connor, who was then Queens district attorney, for the same purpose. O'Connor had hoped to play himself in the film, but Hitchcock instead cast Shakespearean actor Anthony Quayle for the role.

While the New York City Police Department refused to help, the Transit Authority was more accommodating: it made a four-car subway train available for the scene showing Manny's commute home. With Hitchcock and Fonda on hand, police had to keep the crowds away. Hitchcock told a reporter that despite his avowed fear of the police, he remained at ease "because these policemen I know are temporarily benevolent."

Filming took place in March and April 1956. The production had to overcome several obstacles apart from the police department's lack of cooperation. Hitchcock developed a very bad cold. A camera used for three days of shooting was found to be slow. And the first actor hired to play Judge William B. Groat could not remember

Alfred Hitchcock directs actor Henry Fonda in a scene filmed for *The Wrong Man* in a New York City subway car. *(MARKA/Alamy Stock Photo)*

his lines owing to the lingering effects of a stroke he had suffered a year before. Hitchcock replaced the man with actor Dayton Lummis. "It seemed that everything was going wrong," actor Harold Stone recalled.

Then, tragedy struck in June 1956. Lola D'Annunzio, the actress who played Manny's sister, died in a car crash in Kansas. She was twenty-six. Shortly before the accident, D'Annunzio had completed her role in the film, including appearances in the trial sequence.

That sequence had been shot in the Queens courthouse where Manny had actually been tried. Judge Groat approved the use of his courtroom—but only after Hitchcock had agreed to speak at the local Young Republican Club.

In an interview published in the French magazine *Cahiers du Cinéma* after filming, Hitchcock recalled an exchange with Judge Groat as an example of "how people's memory can be unreliable." The judge insisted that the placement of a large table in the courtroom was incorrect. But his assistants told Hitchcock otherwise: "You know, the judge is mistaken. We remember very well that the table was in this position." As a result, Hitchcock left the table as it was. When Judge Groat returned to find his instructions had been ignored, he expressed irritation. The director shrewdly deflected the complaint by insisting the table's placement was dictated by the lighting needs of his cameraman.

In another interview, Hitchcock recalled that during filming, people kept telling him, "'The judge is wrong. The judge is wrong.'"

Surely the irony was not lost on Hitchcock. Judge Groat had presided at a trial that turned on the memories of several witnesses who swore that Manny held up their insurance office. He was a symbol of a system responsible for reconstructing the facts of an event and arriving at the truth.

"The judge is wrong. The judge is wrong."

Fearful of alienating Judge Groat, the assistants whispered the phrase to Hitchcock. So their rebukes did not echo in the Queens courtroom. But perhaps they echoed in Hitchcock's mind as he finished *The Wrong Man*.

—ELEVEN—
NOTHING BUT THE TRUTH

Hitchcock and Fonda during the filming of the trial sequence
(*World History Archive/Alamy Stock Photo*)

The first image we see is a man's silhouette illuminated by a band of light that streaks toward us from the top rear of the frame. The silhouette casts a distorted shadow whose shape resembles an inverted bowling pin.

"This is Alfred Hitchcock speaking."

There's no visual evidence to corroborate this claim, to prove that the voice we hear belongs to the figure cloaked in darkness. But we accept the claim on faith. And so, in a precredits prologue, *The Wrong Man* induces an act of identification whose reliability is open to question. In truth, as scholars William Rothman and D. A. Miller have observed, we don't know if the shadowed figure is actually Hitchcock.

This point of entry is fitting. For the next 105 minutes, the film will force us to grapple with questions of truth and identity and to consider whether the criminal justice system can discern either. At the same time, the visual of a man standing alone, framed in light, evokes the police tactics used against Manny and other suspects who were placed in incriminating positions for identification.

As we look at this image, Hitchcock's voice tells us that *The Wrong Man* is unlike his past "suspense pictures" because of its basis in fact. The elusive image of the silhouetted figure itself signals this departure. By 1956, Hitchcock's appearance had long been a central part of his persona. As Edward White observed in an astute recent biography, "Hitchcock's physical self was . . . a promotional tool" and "a walking, talking logo" for "'the Hitchcock brand,' a riveting fusion of his personal fame and mythology and the themes, aesthetics, atmosphere of his movies." The director advanced his brand with not only cameos in his films, but also appearances that bookended each episode of *Alfred Hitchcock Presents*. That television series also featured the iconic silhouette of Hitchcock's profile at the end of the opening credits.

But the silhouette that opens *The Wrong Man* is not so recognizable. The director's larger-than-life presence is diminished by the camera's distance, the figure dwarfed by its shadow. Withholding the Hitchcock we've come to expect, the shot announces that what follows will be off-brand.

The director's voice then promises us that "this is a true story. Every word of it."

Given Manny's story, Hitchcock's assurance is loaded with irony. How, after all, can "every word" in a film about false accusation be true?

***

The truth is that most of *The Wrong Man* aligns with the historical record, as reflected in the following plot synopsis:

After the Hitchcock prologue, a title card orients us in time. It is January 14, 1953—"a day in the life of Christopher Emanuel Balestrero that he will never forget." We first see Manny playing the bass at the Stork Club. Upon his return home, Rose breaks the news that she needs her wisdom teeth removed and the cost will be $300. Manny resolves to borrow the money against Rose's insurance policy. The next day, he ventures to the offices of the Associated Life of New York to seek the loan. During the visit, several employees conclude that Manny is the man who previously robbed the office.

After meeting with the employees, three detectives intercept Manny as he is returning home from visiting his parents. The detectives take him to precinct headquarters and advise him that he matches the description of a man wanted for a series of neighborhood holdups. They take Manny in and out of two local stores for potential identification by the proprietors. Then, back at the precinct, the detectives advise him that Associated Life employees have identified him as the holdup man. Based on their identifications, and an error he makes in writing out the holdup note, Manny is arrested. He spends the night in jail. The next day, Manny is released on bail.

The Balestreros hire Frank O'Connor to defend Manny. At O'Connor's suggestion, the Balestreros try to locate witnesses who can verify that Manny was vacationing in Cornwall at the time of the first robbery. But they learn that the two people who could have provided such an alibi are dead. This discovery compounds Rose's escalating anxiety about Manny's predicament, which ultimately induces Rose to have a nervous breakdown. On a psychiatrist's recommendation, Rose moves into a sanitarium.

Manny's case goes to trial, where the first two witnesses positively identify him. O'Connor struggles to discredit them. During a seemingly ineffective cross-examination, a juror rises and exclaims, "Your Honor, do we have to sit here and listen to this?" The judge declares a mistrial.

As Manny prays for strength, a man attempts to rob a local deli. The man is captured and brought to the same precinct where Manny was booked. A detective realizes that the man in custody looks like Manny and places the man in a lineup before two of the Associated Life employees. The employees identify the man, whose arrest results in Manny's exoneration. But Rose remains in the sanitarium. A closing title card tells us that two years later, she was "completely cured" and that the Balestreros were living happily in Florida.

***

Few films even aspire to the standard of absolute truth announced in the prologue. Fewer still come close to achieving it. *The Wrong Man* comes a lot closer than most, even though it sometimes veers from the record.

Hitchcock showcases an exacting attention to detail in an early sequence—one that also displays his penchant for striking images that advance his thematic interests.

Fonda, seen here as Manny in the Stork Club, learned to play the bass for the film. (*Album/Alamy Stock Photo*)

We watch as Manny leaves the Stork Club and heads toward the subway. Two police officers pass by the club at the same time. Manny is then framed between the two officers, his back to them. He will soon have cause to react with distress at any sign of the police. But for now Manny goes about his routine in blissful ignorance and descends into the subway, never looking back at the officers. The image evokes the confidence that every citizen would like to have in the justice system. It's a visual expression of the *ideal* that the innocent have nothing to fear.

In preparing for this sequence, associate producer Coleman and coscreenwriter MacPhail retraced Manny's commute home. They departed the Stork Club at around 3:30 a.m. and went to the E train station. There they noted how many people were waiting at the platform (about seven), how many were in each subway car (thirty to thirty-five), and what kind of advertising adorned the walls of the subway cars (including, apparently, one directed at women by the Brand Names Foundation that asked, "Can you trust your husband with shopping money?"). Upon exiting the subway, the pair completed Manny's routine by eating at Bickford's cafeteria. All this fact-finding informed the portrayal of his commute, condensed to two minutes of screen time.

Many other details are rendered with similar rigor. As reflected in the script files for *The Wrong Man* at the Margaret Herrick Library, the research was exhaustive. Coleman and MacPhail re-created not only Manny's routines, but also his nightmarish experience with the detectives. For example, they visited the deli where Manny was paraded before the proprietor—enabling MacPhail to script a scene that, in Hitchcock's words, "represents what really happened there."

The director's enthusiasm for re-creating reality had its limits. As Professor Marshall Deutelbaum has observed, the film understates O'Connor's role in developing the defense of the case. It omits his witness interviews, his retention of a handwriting expert, and Manny's lie detector test. It also implies that the only two alibi witnesses died.

As Hitchcock was quick to point out, the death of the witnesses was no invention. "If we had been doing a fiction story, we wouldn't have had *two* dying off," the director said. "It would have looked phony." Still, Hitchcock could not resist amplifying the impact of the deaths. The film suggests that no one else at the Cornwall farm was available to verify Manny's presence there near the time of the first Prudential holdup, when in fact O'Connor lined up three such witnesses.

In a larger sense, though, this omission jibes with the reality of Manny's predicament. The police never investigated or credited his alibis. To the state, O'Connor's witnesses were as invisible as they are in the film.

Hitchcock had another narrative purpose for his handling of the alibi issue: to highlight Rose's escalating anxiety. The Balestreros' discovery of the deaths marks a transition from the focus on Manny's case to Rose's condition. As Hitchcock told coscreenwriter Maxwell Anderson, "the scenes of the preparation of the defense should begin to be interrupted by an unexpected element, i.e., the decline of Rose, so that the mechanical details of alibis, etc. become obscured by this growing process of Rose going insane." In a March 20, 1956 letter, the director explained that "the middle section of the picture has been deliberately designed to allow the story of

Rose to take over, and thus swamp the details concerning the buildup of Manny's defense."

Hitchcock also made a calculated decision to compress the trial. As Professor Mark Osteen has noted, Anderson proposed a longer trial sequence that deviated from the record and presented the juror's outburst as a response to extended testimony by the state's handwriting expert. Hitchcock rejected this version because "if we allowed the juror to interrupt at this particular moment, it would seem to be a major contradiction of the actual events, and could be so easily used in hostile criticism of the film." The director also warned Anderson about the need to get "clearances" from the trial participants. "We have had to stick to parts of the actual transcript of the trial, because this fact, and the words they used, cannot be disputed."

At the same time, Hitchcock feared that sticking to the transcript made for a "dull" drama. He had a longstanding skepticism about courtroom sequences. In explaining the extended jury room scene he conceived for *Murder!*, the director noted that "the public is weary of the trial scene and my opinion is that you cannot get it over on the screen really successfully." For *The Wrong Man*, Hitchcock fell back on the animating idea of the project: to show the ordeal of false arrest from the perspective of the accused. He framed the limited trial action through Manny's eyes ("what he sees from his viewpoint") and reactions. Even during O'Connor's cross-examination, Hitchcock wanted to focus on "Manny's state of desperation—on his feeling that everything is against him—that he has no friends in the world." For this sequence, the testimony and attorney sparring became secondary.

And so *The Wrong Man* has no detailed reenactment of Manny's trial. It also deviates from the facts surrounding his exoneration. But even when his fidelity to the record wavers, Hitchcock never ceases to illuminate the perils that confront the innocent in the criminal justice system. His film's enduring value is linked to issues that have infused modern legal discourse:

- Eyewitness identification reform. The role of eyewitness errors in false convictions drew increasing attention in the decades after *The Wrong Man*'s release. By capturing the police identification procedures of his day, Hitchcock pointed to flaws that would spur cries for reform by social scientists and legal scholars. According to the Innocence Project, almost 70 percent of the 375 convictions overturned by DNA evidence included at least one mistaken eyewitness identification.

- "Crime Control" and "Tunnel Vision." Eight years after Hitchcock's film, Professor Herbert Packer coined the term "crime control" for one of two competing models of the criminal justice system (the other being "due process"). Packer described the crime control model as an assembly line requiring police to make quick determinations of probable guilt. This mindset animates the behavior of Hitchcock's detectives. Their handling of Manny dramatizes a model that would inspire extensive legal scholarship. It also illustrates the related problem of "tunnel vision," which imperils the innocent. As explored by law professors like Keith A. Findley and Michael S. Scott, tunnel vision refers to the tendency of law enforcement agents to become fixated on a single suspect early on and then "select and filter the evidence that will 'build a case' for conviction, while ignoring or suppressing evidence that points away from guilt."

- Prosecutorial Duty. Where does the duty of prosecutors lie—in the securing of a conviction or in the search for truth? The Queens district attorney's office put Manny on trial despite signs of error. Yet after the exoneration, its actions went largely unquestioned. Even Frank O'Connor absolved the prosecution. Echoing the state's narrative, O'Connor said the authorities had only done their jobs. The film defies that narrative and shows how prosecutors violated their duty to protect the innocent.

***

In mining these themes, Hitchcock resisted the plot twists and action sequences that mark his other films. This decision may explain the critical refrain that the film is relentlessly grim. Film scholar James Naremore, for example, calls it "one of the bleakest movies ever produced in Hollywood."

Admittedly, as we see the Balestreros' lives unravel, *The Wrong Man* can be painful to watch. Its most visceral moment comes as Manny leans against the wall of a jail cell after his arrest. The camera starts circling him in a manner that, according to the film's art director, Paul Sylbert, was based on the concept of a Ferris wheel. As the rotations gather speed, we experience a disorienting sensation that reflects Manny's psychological state. The camera's evocation of a Ferris wheel gone haywire also recalls the out-of-control carousel at the end of *Strangers on a Train*, which, as Donald Spoto has observed, is one of Hitchcock's "images of order disrupted, of harmony destroyed."

Manny's head spins around to the point that it seems about to be ejected from the frame. If, as film critic Roger Ebert observed, movies are machines that generate empathy, this scene is the cinematic engine on overdrive. The screen fades to black before the movement stops, implying that Manny will not get the relief that Hitchcock's cut provides to us.

We don't get all that much relief, though. *The Wrong Man* withholds the crowd-pleasing elements of conventional exoneration stories. There's no stirring lawyering, no comeuppance for those responsible for Manny's arrest, and no on-screen repair of his family's fracture.

But not every great film delivers a great time. And by creating empathy with the Balestreros, *The Wrong Man* challenges us to interrogate the reasons for their suffering.

—TWELVE—
"I DON'T DARE LOOK"

Fonda, as Manny, and Peggy Webber, as Alice Dennerly, at the Associated Life office
(*cineclassico/Alamy*)

As *The Wrong Man*'s opening credits unfurl, the camera slowly pans across the Stork Club's interior. The club's well-dressed patrons, seated at tables, fill the foreground while behind them couples dance to music provided by a rhumba band. Then the camera stops. At the very rear of the shot stands bass player Manny Balestrero. Manny is so far back in the frame that he is barely identifiable. He is alternatively obscured by the heads of the dancing couples and the letters of the credits. When "*The Wrong Man*" appears on the screen, the right side of the "H" bisects his profile.

A series of dissolves captures the passage of several hours. The dining area thins out and the dance floor empties. By the time the words "Directed by Alfred

Hitchcock" disappear from the screen, our view of Manny is finally unobstructed, but still distant. Only a cut to a close-up shot of the band brings Manny, standing to the left of the frame, into focus.

The scene foreshadows the tale that follows. The camera's inability to see Manny anticipates the inability of eyewitnesses and the police to distinguish Manny from the holdup man.

Hitchcock's use of the camera to explore misidentification is even more striking in his depiction of Manny's visit to the insurance office. The scene sets up a central theme of the film: the willingness of Manny's accusers to condemn him without truly "looking."

Manny walks into the offices of Associated Life of New York to ask about borrowing against his wife's insurance policy. The face of the employee behind the counter, Alice Dennerly, registers recognition and fear. As Manny reaches into his coat pocket to remove the policy, a series of quick cuts between the employee and Manny put us inside the employee's head: *Is this man reaching for a gun?*

Since we know from the title that Manny is innocent, we have been primed to focus on the origins of his predicament. To that end, Hitchcock shows us not only the literal perspective of the accusers (their views of Manny), but also the gap between that perspective and the conclusions that they draw. We see both what the eyewitnesses see and what they cannot see.

For example, Dennerly confides to another employee her suspicion that Manny is the man who previously robbed the office. That employee, Miss Duffield, is wearing glasses and sits about twenty feet from the counter where Manny is standing. Hitchcock frames her supposed identification of Manny in three rapid cuts. First, we see her eyes peering barely above Dennerly's shoulder. Our own view of Duffield is blocked by that shoulder, which blacks out much of the frame. Next, we get Duffield's perspective on Manny, obstructed by the front of Dennerly's body. This is followed by a much closer shot of Manny, which emphasizes his distance from the employees.

The two women walk over to the desk of Ann James, who also witnessed the robberies. As they huddle around her, Duffield relays to James that "Peggy thinks that he's one who held you up." James reacts with a look of terror.

"I don't dare look," James whispers fearfully.

"It is the same man," Duffield insists, even though she's not yet had an unimpeded look at Manny.

Even after Duffield implores her ("Look at him!"), James says, "I don't think I can," and warns that "I think I'm going to faint." She has to be propped up by the other women, who then force her to look at Manny. The image conveys an element of coercion in James's identification. And when Duffield holds the insurance policy in front of James to appear occupied with business, the document functions as a symbolic script, as if James is reciting an accusation prepared for her.

The scene is true to Manny's visit to Prudential on January 13, 1953. Dennerly stands in for Prudential employee Joan Kopp, who first misidentified Manny at the public window and then shared her conclusion with others. Ann James is based on Constance Ello, the employee who was twice held up by Charles Daniell. In her performance as Ello's stand-in, actress Doreen Lang captures the abject fear of a woman who, in real life, was so terrified of the bandit that she worried that she might be "bumped off" if she identified him. (Lang carved out a niche for portraying distraught wrongful accusers. In Hitchcock's *The Birds* (1963), she appears as a woman at a diner who, in a moment of hysteria, accuses Tippi Hedren's character of causing the otherwise unexplained bird attacks: "They said when you got here the whole thing started. . . . I think you're the cause of all this. I think you're evil. EVIL!").

As the Associated Life scene unfolds, the camera pushes in closer on the three women. That movement both invites us to scrutinize their identifications and reinforces their distance from Manny. When James finally glances toward him, the left side of the frame is blacked out in the foreground by her colleague's body, while a profile view of Manny appears in the right background, partially obscured by the bars at the counter. The camera holds for just two seconds before James yanks herself back out of Manny's sightline.

"It is the same," she whispers.

"*It* is the same." This is the most disturbing single line in the film. As author Marc Raymond Strauss has observed, the employees "have scared themselves into completely dehumanizing Manny into an 'it' in such a way that only blind, unthinking, unfeeling fear is left." The scene foreshadows Manny's impending loss of basic human rights and calls to mind the observations of philosopher David Livingstone Smith on dehumanization. Smith has explained that when people conceive of others as "subhuman," they give themselves psychological license to engage in cruelty and, ultimately, atrocity. Here the Associated Life employees relegate Manny to subhuman status, clearing the way for a rush to judgment. No thought is given to the possibility that Manny could be innocent, or to the cataclysmic effect of their accusations if wrong.

Hitchcock portrays a "chain reaction" of fear and accusation that instills a collective certainty in witnesses. By filling the frame with obstructions, though, he shows their self-assuredness is misplaced. Ironically, in each case the source of the obstruction is the body of the first employee who misidentified Manny. This visual strategy symbolizes how one eyewitness's mistake may induce another's. With James, it also highlights that her coworkers are coercing her into endorsing their accusations even as they deprive her of a clear view of Manny.

The employees' behavior recalls the portrayal of eyewitnesses in Hitchcock's *Young and Innocent* (1937), the story of a young man named Robert Tisdall (Derrick de Marney) wrongfully accused of murder. In an early scene, two women observe Tisdall running away from the victim's body, which has washed up on a beach. While Tisdall is running for help, the women conclude that he is fleeing the crime scene. Moments later, the women, the police, Tisdall, and several other locals gather near the body. The two women are shaken and on the verge of tears. When Tisdall recounts his discovery of the body and his effort to get help, the women indignantly insist that he's lying ("You were running away, you know you were!"). Hitchcock then uses three quick images to show how self-righteous indignation has produced an instant false judgment: a shot of two locals staring at Tisdall with condemning eyes, followed by a cut to Tisdall and then a cut back to the two eyewitnesses alongside the police officer, all of whom share the same wide-eyed glare. The cuts create a sense that the accusers are feeding off one another. It's a chilling moment in a film that otherwise is closer in spirit to *The 39 Steps* and other lighter Hitchcock mistaken identity thrillers.

Hitchcock and Fonda shared a preoccupation with the dangers of mob mentality. As a fourteen-year-old in Omaha in 1919, Fonda had witnessed the horrific mob lynching of Will Brown, a forty-five-year-old Black man who had been accused of the rape of a white woman. Fonda's father owned a printing shop that overlooked the courthouse square. On the night of September 28, at least four thousand people surrounded the courthouse in which Brown was being held, overcame the police, set fire to the building, and seized and murdered Brown. "They took him, strung him up to the end of a lamppost, hung him, and while his feet were still dancing in the air, they riddled his body with bullets. It was the most horrendous sight I'd ever seen," Fonda later recalled. The mob also nearly lynched the mayor, who had urged the crowds to disperse.

As Fonda biographer Devin McKinney has suggested, the actor's exposure to this horrifying mass crime informed his performance in John Ford's *Young Mr. Lincoln* (1939). In that film, Fonda plays the future president when he was a young lawyer defending two brothers accused of murder. Before trial, an angry mob storms the jail that houses the defendants, intent on a lynching. Lincoln stops them, first by using his body as a human shield and then by disarming the crowd with a speech that blends humor and an eloquent plea for the necessity of law: "Trouble is when men start taking the law into their own hands, they're just as apt in all the confusion and fun to start hanging somebody who's not a murderer as somebody who is." Lincoln adds that "we do things together that we'd be mighty ashamed to do by ourselves."

While depicting mob mentality in a more mundane context, *The Wrong Man* shows how easily a misidentification by one witness may contaminate others' memories and create a false group consensus. In Manny's case, three witnesses testified that they were positive in their identification. Some of the cases discussed in Part One were even more extreme. Five bank employees swore that Bertram Campbell was a front man for a forgery racket. At least eight people misidentified New Jersey residents Clifford Shephard and Elizabeth Lester as the couple who passed bad checks. Seven witnesses confused Indiana resident Nancy Botts with the woman who defrauded them.

In 1914, a Boston man named Herbert Andrews was convicted of forgery after *seventeen* people swore in court that he had passed them bad checks. Andrews was exonerated less than four months later based on the confession of a criminal who bore no resemblance to him.

Authorities in these cases saw multiple identifications as incontrovertible evidence of guilt. Instead, they were a form of mob justice.

The Associated Life scene also bears out an observation made by Professor Edwin Borchard in his landmark 1932 study of wrongful convictions: the experience of falling victim to a crime (or even merely witnessing one) may distort one's powers of perception. "Into the identification enter other motives, not necessarily stimulated originally by the accused personally—the desire to requite a crime, to exact vengeance upon the person believed guilty, to find a scapegoat, to support, consciously or unconsciously, an identification already made by another." These motives are on display in the Associated Life office. The women show an intense desire to make someone pay for the prior armed robberies. As described by scholar David Humbert, the women share not only a fear arising from the previous trauma, but also "a contagious desire, with the encouragement of others, to take action and to find a culprit."

Their chain of suspect conclusions continues once Manny leaves. Duffield reports the employees' collective suspicions to the office manager. Manny's actions were "so very strange" because "he put his hand in his pocket," but "all he took out was this folded paper" and "he said he just wanted a loan on his wife's policy." The description of Manny's behavior is accurate. But the conclusion drawn by his accusers—that it was "so very strange"—reflects confirmation bias. Although Manny has done nothing to warrant suspicion, the anxiety unleashed by his appearance causes the employees to adopt irrational theories that fit their assumption about him. No one wonders why Manny would return for a loan and identify himself if he were guilty. Instead, one employee theorizes that Manny "didn't do anything" because there was a man present toward the back of the office. Even if one accepts that the holdup man's plan assumed that only women would be present, that hardly explains why Manny would present the policy and ask about a loan.

The Associated Life scene marks the first of several rushes to judgment in the film. Ann James does not "dare look" at Manny, but she is quick to identify him as the holdup man. We will see a similar lack of care in the behavior of law enforcement agents (who treat Manny as guilty without a careful investigation) and jurors (who seem uninterested in his defense). And the spread of false conclusions from one employee to another foreshadows the instant judgment that the detectives will make and share inside their precinct. There is a recurring failure to appreciate the gravity of an accusation and a corresponding refusal to reckon with its calamitous effect on the innocent.

It was not until decades after *The Wrong Man*'s release that the unreliability of eyewitness identification became more widely recognized. That growing consensus emerged at first from social science research and analysis of perception and memory. One compelling study came from research at Florida State University in 1990. Using a scenario that neatly evokes Manny's experience, the study tested the ability of bank tellers to identify a suspect after a stressful encounter.

The researchers sent a "target" suspect into various banks with an obviously fraudulent money order. The target attempted to persuade a bank teller to cash the money order. When the teller refused, the target "became irate" and stormed out of the bank. The encounter lasted about a minute and a half. Later that day, a person posing as a police officer interviewed the teller on the pretense that the officer was investigating the incident. The officer showed the teller a photographic lineup—in some cases one that included the target seen by the teller and in other cases one that did not.

The results supplied compelling proof of the unreliability of eyewitness identifications. Of the tellers who viewed a lineup that included the target, only 47 percent chose the correct suspect. Of those who viewed a lineup without the suspect, 37 percent chose the wrong man.

Of course, the most potent evidence of eyewitness fallibility lies in the hundreds of convictions overturned by DNA evidence since 1989. Arriving more than thirty years before the first of these exonerations, *The Wrong Man* stands as a prescient cultural marker of the destructiveness of eyewitness errors. But the film is ultimately less an indictment of the mistaken witnesses than it is a commentary on the way the justice system uses this faulty evidence. The protection of the innocent requires searching scrutiny of accusations. Yet time and again in false conviction cases, the police either accepted eyewitness identifications unquestioningly or secured them through suggestive procedures.

Hitchcock first illustrates this point through omission. At no point do we see the detectives question the Associated Life employees about their observations. Instead, the film dissolves from an image of Manny waving goodbye to his father (itself an ironic foreshadowing) to a shot of two detectives (Bowers and Matthews) walking out of the insurance company's office. After telling the employees to expect a call within several hours, Bowers says: "All right, let's pick him up." The transition suggests that the detectives have given only cursory scrutiny to the accusations—a point confirmed by the interrogation that follows.

—THIRTEEN—
"JUST A ROUTINE MATTER"

From left: Detective Matthews (Charles Cooper), Manny, and Detective Lieutenant Bowers (Harold J. Stone) at the 110th Precinct (*Collection Christophel/Alamy Stock Photo*)

The detectives in *The Wrong Man* are neither corrupt nor motivated by any obvious bias. Under a common reading of the film, they are not to blame for Manny's predicament. Commentators have instead ascribed his suffering to bad luck and coincidence.

Director Jean-Luc Godard wrote that "chance" plays "the primordial role" in the film, "leaving its unmistakable mark on every foot of it." According to scholar Robert Ray, "Manny's troubles depended solely on absurd coincidences that piled up one after another." And in noting its absence of heroes or villains, criminologist Nicole Rafter grouped the film with *The Postman Always Rings Twice* (1946) and *A Place in the Sun* (1951) as sharing "bleak views of the world as a place where people

149

either create their own tragedies or are struck down randomly by fate."

On a closer look, though, *The Wrong Man* depicts a police investigation that is as much the cause of Manny's suffering as the hand of fate. It's just that the evil identified in the film is not a knowing attempt to frame an innocent man. It is, instead, a rush to judgment by detectives that has become part of their mode of doing business.

From the outset of the interrogation sequence, Hitchcock signals that precinct headquarters will not be a house of justice. The first exterior shot shows the building at a canted angle, suggesting that something off-kilter is going on inside. As Manny is brought in, Detective Bowers stains the doorsteps with his discarded cigar. This gesture hints at the neglect that will mark the investigation. Inside, the interrogation room has a gaping hole on the wall behind Manny's chair. As observed by Professor Nicholas Haeffner, the hole suggests that "the police station (and, by implication, the justice system) is in an advanced state of disrepair."

At the station, Bowers puts the burden on Manny to prove his innocence. "Certain people" have reported that Manny resembles a man who has committed neighborhood robberies. "We have to clear you before we can send you home," the detective says. He assures Manny that "clearing" him is a "purely a routine matter" and that "it's nothing for an innocent man to worry about." Instead, "it's the fella that has done something wrong that has to worry."

In this dialogue, *The Wrong Man* anticipates a premise of the crime control model of police work. As explained by Herbert Packer in 1964, the model assumes that "the repression of criminal conduct is by far the most important function to be performed by the criminal process." To execute on this premise, the crime control model emphasizes the need for an efficient procedure to "screen suspects" and make an early determination of a suspect's probable guilt or innocence. It applies "a presumption of guilt" to suspects who are not screened out as "probably innocent":

> *The presumption of guilt allows the Crime Control Model to deal efficiently with large numbers. The supposition is that the screening processes operated by police and prosecutors are reliable indicators of probable guilt. Once a man has been investigated without being found to be probably innocent, or, to put it differently, once a determination has been made that there is enough evidence of guilt so that he should be held for further action rather than released from the process, then all subsequent activity directed toward him is based on the view that he is probably guilty.*

One of the model's underpinnings eerily echoes the detective's assurance to Manny: since the police have no incentive to wrongfully detain and arrest people, "the innocent have nothing to fear."

The question whether innocents have cause to fear the police has surfaced in various legal and cultural contexts. A century ago, Judge Learned Hand implicitly dismissed that fear in describing wrongful convictions as "an unreal dream." The question has also shaped the legal doctrines governing when the state can infer guilt from a suspect's flight or from their silence in the face of accusatory questions.

In Arthur Miller's *The Crucible*, authorities investigating claims of witchcraft insist that no righteous person should fear the court. Judge Danforth uses the justification when ordering the "arrest for examination" of ninety-one locals who have signed a statement in support of the accused. When Francis Nurse (whose wife is in jail) tells the court that the people who signed are "all covenanted Christians," Danforth replies: "Then I am sure they may have nothing to fear." Danforth also insists that "the pure in heart need no lawyers."

More recently, in the opening episode of the HBO crime drama *The Night Of* (2016), Detective Dennis Box (Bill Camp) uses the same tactic in his interrogation of murder suspect Nasir Khan (Riz Ahmed). Box asks Nasir for permission to take DNA swabs. In response, Nasir (who seems as ignorant of police practices as Manny was) expresses uncertainty and a lack of understanding, and can only insist that "I didn't do it." Detective Box replies, "Well, there you have it. You got nothing to fear."

The durability of "nothing to fear" as a mantra is a tribute to its force as a psychological pressure tactic. It conveys to a suspect that a failure to cooperate with police will be taken as an admission of guilt. In fact, studies suggest that a substantial minority of guilty suspects waive their Miranda rights—the right to remain silent and the right to an attorney—and agree to speak with the police, "for strategic reasons, so that the detective would not infer guilt from a lack of compliance."

At the same time, innocent people often waive their Miranda rights because they believe they have "nothing to fear." That faith in the system is built into Packer's crime control model, which assumes that informal fact-finding by the authorities can "elicit and reconstruct a tolerably accurate account of what actually took place in an alleged criminal event."

The detectives intercept Manny outside his home. (*cineclassico/Alamy Stock Photo*)

The "presumption of guilt" underlying the model is not itself a legal doctrine. It is, instead, "a complex of attitudes, a mood" that expresses "confidence" in the state's ability to make early and reliable determinations of probable guilt.

That mood informs the behavior of the detectives in *The Wrong Man*. Based on the initial identifications, the detectives determine that Manny is probably guilty. Their seizure of Manny outside his home reflects this belief. At first Bowers tells Manny that "we'd like you to come down to the precinct and help us out a little." His tone is deceptively casual, and he smiles as he brushes off Manny's request to alert Rose ("You can tell her later"). But almost immediately Bowers and his partner, Detective Matthews, each grab Manny by the arm. A close-up shows their grips tightening to direct Manny to their car. While the detectives continue to insist Manny is needed only for "a routine matter," their handling has the indicia of an arrest. And once in the car, Bowers lights up a cigar, as if the case has been solved.

As this scene reflects, the physical manifestation of accusation and guilt is a motif that pervades *The Wrong Man*. The motif first appears in the Associated Life scene when the two employees who claim to recognize Manny place their hands on Ann James's shoulders as they pressure her to join in their identification. It continues in the squad car, where Manny is sandwiched between the two detectives, their shoulders operating as restraints. After that, Hitchcock gives us many shots of the detectives touching Manny's arm, shoulder, or back while directing him with varying degrees of force. The prearrest sequence alone features at least nine such images. This motif not only conveys the presumption of guilt used by the detectives, but also signals a permanent marking of Manny as a victim of false accusation.

In a potent depiction of tunnel vision, the detectives filter each new piece of information through their prejudgment of guilt. When Manny admits he has a few bills outstanding, the detectives treat this ordinary working-class predicament as incriminating—even though the same answer bears out Manny's explanation for why he went to the insurance office (to seek a loan). Likewise, when Manny says he plays the bass in a nightclub band, Detective Matthews adds that fact to the criminal profile he is constructing ("I suppose you have some pretty high old times there . . . women, drinks, dancing, that sort of thing"). The detective also takes in Manny's admission that he occasionally "played the horses" with a smirking satisfaction, as if it adds to the profile.

While preoccupied with Manny's alleged gambling, the detectives are themselves playing the odds. In their eyes, the eyewitness identifications make it probable that Manny is guilty. So the interrogation becomes a perfunctory exercise in confirmation bias rather than a search for truth. "Confirmation bias is the tendency to look for information that supports our beliefs and ignore information that doesn't," criminal justice scholar Richard Leo has explained. "It's why police develop tunnel vision, lock in on one explanation, and discount other possibilities." While arising from natural human tendencies, tunnel vision and confirmation bias are even more likely to affect police investigations, because of institutional pressures to close cases quickly.

The detectives' bet on Manny's guilt disables them from asking the right questions or fairly assessing his answers. In fact, they never even ask Manny if he has alibis for the dates of the robberies.

This phenomenon is especially disturbing because Hitchcock has shown us the hysteria and rashness of the eyewitnesses at the insurance office. Their identifications cry out for scrutiny. Instead, the detectives treat them as conclusive.

The detectives' confidence in their assessment of guilt is matched by Manny's faith that he will be cleared. Since Manny has nothing to hide, he accepts their assurances. As several scholars have noted, the depiction of Manny's obliviousness to his imperilment anticipates the Warren Court's strengthening of protections for suspects in cases like Miranda v. Arizona, which was decided in 1966 (about a decade after the film's release). The interrogation scenes also anticipate post-Miranda social science research showing that the innocent are more likely to waive their right to remain silent than the guilty. In one study, experts Saul Kassin and Rebecca Norwick found that "72% of the innocents who waived their rights said they did so, quite simply, because they were innocent and had nothing to hide or fear." And 67 percent of the innocent suspects signed the waiver even though the interrogator in the experiment "was hostile and close-minded" and had "made it clear to participants that they had nothing to gain from denial." These findings illustrate that "people have a naive faith in the power of their own innocence to set them free."

Believing that he will be proven innocent, Manny never wavers in his cooperation with the detectives. He readily complies with their request that he appear before the proprietors of local stores that have been robbed. The detectives arrange these identification parades because they believe the man who held up Associated Life also committed the other robberies.

"If you'll just walk into this liquor store, walk to the back of the store, turn around, and come back here," Bowers instructs him. Cooperative but nervous, Manny stiffly walks past the counter where the proprietor is standing and toward the

Manny is forced to parade before a liquor store proprietor (John C. Becher). In the film's final cut, the two other men pictured do not appear. (*cineclassico/Alamy Stock Photo*)

back of the store. He then looks back abruptly toward the camera, at the proprietor. His face betrays escalating anxiety. As film critic Josh Larsen has observed, Fonda transforms himself here and becomes "shifty" and "nervous."

With his tentative gait and darting eyes, Fonda conveys a mix of confusion, paranoia, and shame. You can see the emotions in his face and coursing through his body. The performance captures the inherently incriminating position in which Manny finds himself. More than that, it reveals the dehumanizing nature of the showup, with the proprietor staring as if he were looking at an animal pacing in its cage.

The liquor store scene also marks the recurrence of a gesture that Fonda ingeniously deploys throughout the film. When the detectives first call out to him outside his house, Manny looks back over his shoulder at them. At this point his face registers mere curiosity. Then, as the detectives escort him to their car and rebuff his request to alert Rose, Manny looks back toward the house—again, over his shoulder—with growing concern. By the time he repeats the gesture (twice) in the liquor store, the quick turn of the head and the widening of his eyes project fear and panic. In each case, the police have induced the gesture—once by calling out his name, once by forcibly separating him from Rose, and then by requiring him to parade before a proprietor under suspicious circumstances. The progression of the gesture becomes a metaphor for how the police have made Manny appear guilty.

The film's depiction of Manny's behavior evokes the debate over whether police can rely on furtive or nervous gestures to justify investigative stops. The Supreme Court has ruled that such stops are permitted when a police officer has a "reasonable, articulable suspicion that criminal activity is afoot." Under the court's precedents, police may consider a suspect's "nervous, evasive behavior" as a factor supporting reasonable suspicion. But nervousness alone is not a reliable basis for suspicion. Most of us get nervous when stopped by police. As one court observed, "nervousness is a natural reaction to police presence"—a point that Hitchcock himself would have endorsed. The director once said that he invariably had a "potent urge to flee" upon seeing a policeman.

The legal significance of nervous gestures came into play in the constitutional challenge to the New York City Police Department's controversial stop and frisk policy, which led to some 4.4 million stops between 2004 and 2012. Civil rights groups challenged the police practice as unsupported by reasonable suspicion and tainted by racial bias. In the ensuing litigation, a police officer relied on young Black males "looking over their shoulder" as an example of suspicious behavior. US District Court Judge Shira A. Scheindlin rejected this justification. In declaring stop and frisk unconstitutional, Scheindlin observed that "even if credited, [defendant's] alleged furtive movements—looking over his shoulder and jaywalking—in combination with the generic description of young Black male does not establish the requisite individualized suspicion that [defendant] was engaged in criminal activity."

By showing that an innocent person's nervous behavior may arise from anxiety induced by the police, The Wrong Man points at the circularity and overbreadth of the justification.

The showup scenes yield piercing insights about false arrest cases. As Manny heads out of the liquor store, a cut to the proprietor sets up a shot from his perspective. We then see Manny from behind, wearing his overcoat and hat. Beyond Manny, Detective Matthews looms outside the store's glass door, clad in a similar hat and overcoat. The image emphasizes the vulnerability of eyewitnesses to suggestiveness and the risk that a suspect might be misidentified based on his clothing. At the same time, Manny's position in the frame, with his back to us and facing the glass door, suggests that for a moment he is seeing his own reflection. But it's the detective looking back at him. The shot not only highlights Manny's loss of identity, it also invites us to consider how guilty the detective himself might appear if forced to undergo the same showup. And by trapping Manny between the proprietor and the detective, the framing calls attention to the blurred line between his private and state accusers.

Manny walks toward the liquor store door.
(*Alfred Hitchcock, director. The Wrong Man. Warner Bros., 1956*)

That theme becomes even more pronounced when the detectives require Manny to parade through a delicatessen as the owner and an employee look on. After realizing that his employee was not paying attention, the owner directs Manny to repeat the ritual: "Would you do that again, walk back with your hat off?" Manny obliges as if he received a request from an authority figure. The owner then releases Manny with the words "Okay, you can go." With the detectives waiting outside the store, the owner has assumed the role of investigator.

At this point, the detectives have not even questioned Manny about the Associated Life holdups. They have prejudged him as guilty. Manny, though, seems oblivious to that determination. As a result, he readily agrees to the detectives' request that he write out the holdup note. This leads to what may be the sole moment of humor in the film. Before reading the holdup note, Bowers says, "An innocent man has nothing to fear—remember that." Manny is about to write those words down when Bowers clarifies that "that's not the note."

Since Manny has everything to fear, the moment stings.

Upon reviewing the note, Bowers says there is "a rough similarity between your printing and the note." He asks Manny to write the note again—an indication that the interrogation will continue until something incriminating emerges. In the second version, Manny misspells "drawer" as "draw," as the holdup man did.

The requirement that Manny write the note, like the showups, forces Manny to reenact the crimes under investigation. And just as the parades induced Manny's incriminatingly nervous behavior, the detective arguably induces his mistake: when Bowers dictates the part of the note about the cash "drawer," his New York accent drops the "er" from his pronunciation.

The detectives then arrange a lineup to secure a formal identification by two Associated Life employees. The lineup includes five other men. Like Manny, each man is wearing a hat, overcoat, and tie. But otherwise none of them looks like Manny. The man to Manny's immediate left is much older, while the man on his right is much younger.

As Manny takes his place in the lineup, Detective Matthews escorts the employees, Constance Willis and Ann James, into a dark room across the hall. Each woman can hear the other's identification—an arrangement that evokes the tainted procedures used in Bertram Campbell's case. But the detective's questioning is even more prejudicial:

Matthews:	*Now look carefully at the men in the other room. I want you to count. Please look at the men from right to left. Count them off, and when you come to the one you can identify, stop.*
Willis:	*One . . . two . . . three . . . four.*
Matthews:	*You're sure?*
Willis:	*Absolutely.*

The detective then turns to Ann James, who has just witnessed Willis's identification:

Matthews:	*Look carefully at the men you see in the other room. Count them off from the right. Observe them carefully. When you come to the one you know, stop.*
James:	*One . . . two . . . three . . . four.*
Matthews:	*You're positive?*
James:	*Yes.*

The detective tells the women to identify the person they "can identify" or "know," without any reference to the robberies. Each of the women knows Manny because each saw him at Associated Life earlier that day. As observed by author Donald Laming, since "the women were simply identifying Manny Balestrero as the man they had seen in the [insurance] office the previous day . . . their identifications did not tell the police anything they did not already know."

Matthews doesn't pose the right questions at any point. During the showups, he does not linger to ask either proprietor if he recognizes Manny ("I'll give you a ring,"

Manny stands in a lineup at the 110th Precinct.
(*Collection Christophel/Alamy Stock Photo*)

he tells one as he's leaving). At the lineup he reduces Manny to a number, but never asks either witness if the suspect they identify as number four is the same man who robbed the office. And to secure the identifications he uses the impersonal convention of counting off, which seems intended to make the exercise as comfortable for the eyewitnesses as possible—especially for the trembling Ann James, who could barely bring herself to look at Manny at the office and who implores the detective not to refer to her by name.

The lineup scene points to the thin line between confirmation bias and conscious efforts at false incrimination. The identification procedure is tainted by artifice, and its outcome is preordained. As we learn later, one of the lineup fillers is Miss James's husband. As a result, the detective's direction that the witnesses should observe the lineup "carefully" plays as theatrical embellishment. This preoccupation with appearances marks the character throughout the film, as Matthews repeatedly straightens the brim of his hat.

Hitchcock does not vilify the detectives in this sequence. Their identification procedures are part of ordinary police business. They seem motivated by the day-to-day imperative of closing cases. Yet their reasonable tone never obscures the danger posed by their routines. If anything, it makes the result of those routines more frightening because, as film historian Imogen Sara Smith has noted, "it's really believable that this could happen to anyone."

With a quiet but uncompromising realism, the lineup scene captures an essential truth about what happened to Manny. If staged fairly, a lineup can be an effective investigative tool. It may support a case against the target or help clear that target. But when staged suggestively, as in Manny's case, lineups become a form of theater, with no probative value.

The editing of the scene reinforces that the police are choreographing a procedure that merely appears to generate evidence. We see the full lineup only once, from the perspective of the eyewitnesses. In that shot, Manny stands near the center of the group, behind a doorway. The shot draws on the convention of enclosing characters in "frames within the frame" used in films noir—a term coined by French critics to describe a cycle of dark American crime films released between the early 1940s and the late 1950s. Such films, which often feature falsely accused (if flawed) protagonists, use various visual techniques to create a sense that their characters are doomed or imprisoned. One of those techniques, as scholar Foster Hirsch has observed, is to frame a character behind a door or a window to evoke entrapment. Here, Manny appears at the rear of the frame, behind two doorways and most of the other men in the lineup. The perspective deepens the sense that the world is closing in on Manny. The police have arranged Manny's position in the frame, as part of a procedure that will inevitably incriminate him.

There are many noir touches in *The Wrong Man*. Other recurring noir motifs, as cataloged by Hirsch, include close-ups in a "fixed, tight space" to create a sense of claustrophobia, and "the high angle overhead shot . . . a visual signal of impending doom." Hitchcock and cinematographer Robert Burks deploy such techniques throughout the interrogation sequence. For example, when Manny protests his innocence, an abrupt cut to a high-angle overhead shot underscores his vulnerability and the futility of his denials. And as the intensity of the questioning escalates, Hitchcock transitions to tighter shots of Manny and the detectives, sometimes all in the same frame. The visual strategy heightens the sequence's unnerving intimacy.

In fact, Turner Classic Movies host Eddie Muller, whose expertise has earned him the nickname the Czar of Noir, has said of *The Wrong Man*: "The direction and cinematography are calculated noir, nothing like the flat, documentary images Hitchcock claimed he was after."

The camerawork shrewdly serves the film's thematic concerns. After showing the full lineup, Hitchcock alternates between medium close-ups of Manny and shots of the eyewitnesses with Detective Matthews across the hall. The alternating shots of Manny eliminate the other men in the lineup: each time the camera returns to the apparent perspective of the witnesses, Manny is centered in the frame, and only his face is visible. The effect signals that Manny's identification is preordained, with the camera transforming the procedure from a lineup to a showup.

In the end, the lineup scene implies the completion of a frame-up, though not one conceived in corruption. The detectives sincerely believe in Manny's guilt. But their methods are reckless and unfair. And so Matthews's comment as the lineup disbands is both devastating and farcical: "Positive identification."

—FOURTEEN—
PROSECUTORIAL OVERSIGHT

The assistant district attorney (Maurice Manson) confronts Manny as Detective Bowers looks on. (*Album/Alamy*)

As the eyewitnesses identify Manny, a prosecutor is hiding in plain sight.

When the detectives assemble the lineup, an unidentified man in a suit appears. The man is neither introduced nor ever identified by other characters. But he watches over the lineup and ultimately orders Manny's arrest.

One could easily conclude, as some authors have, that the man is another detective. Even Godard, in his acclaimed review of the film, misidentified the man as "the police chief."

The script for *The Wrong Man* reveals the character's actual identity: Assistant District Attorney John Hall.

The failure to identify Hall fits a larger narrative pattern. The detectives aren't named, either. Before the interrogation, one telephones Manny's house and speaks to his son Robert. When Rose asks who called, Robert says, "It was some man. He didn't say." Then, when first approaching Manny, Bowers announces "we're police officers" and flashes his badge. The detectives withhold not only their names, but also their reasons for seizing Manny—a concealment that deepens the terror of his predicament.

More broadly, the authorities' failure to identify themselves symbolizes how unknowable the justice system is to the Balestreros. The meaning of legal concepts repeatedly eludes Manny. At his arraignment, he registers bewilderment as his first lawyer (before O'Connor is retained) and a prosecutor parry over bail; phrases like "notice of appearance" and "waive reading of the complaint" escape his understanding. On top of that, Manny isn't even introduced to his attorney, who enters a plea without consultation.

"I guess I didn't know what happened," Manny says after leaving the courtroom.

Likewise, when pressed by Manny's mother to call Frank O'Connor, Rose replies, "I wouldn't know what to say to him." Rose's comment implies that communicating with an attorney requires a special vocabulary. Upon reaching O'Connor's wife, Rose is relieved to have the chance to tell her, rather than the attorney, of Manny's plight. "No, no I'd like to tell you," she says to Mrs. O'Connor.

Manny and Rose know little about the legal process. At their first meeting with O'Connor, the attorney warns them that "I have little experience in criminal cases" and "I shall be at a disadvantage with a skillful prosecutor." As filmmaker François Truffaut observed, this "disturbing note" creates "a feeling of apprehension and anxiety" for the viewer. But not for the Balestreros, who shrug off the comment. They are just grateful that O'Connor will take the case. "We trust you, Mr. O'Connor, and you trust us," Manny says. "We can't ask for more than that."

With their lack of experience and limited resources, the Balestreros are not well positioned to navigate the dangers of the criminal justice system. Their plight contrasts with that of wrongfully accused protagonist Guy Haines (Farley Granger) in Hitchcock's *Strangers on a Train* (1951).

In that film, when Guy learns of the murder of his estranged wife, he understands immediately that police will see him as a suspect. But Guy is a professional tennis player in a relationship with Anne Morton (Ruth Roman), the daughter of a senator. These social trappings produce a much different experience for Guy with the police than the one Manny endures. His support system includes Senator Morton, who assures Guy to "never lose any sleep over accusations—unless they can be proved, of course." Unlike Manny, Guy is not immediately picked up for interrogation. Instead, after providing his alibi to police on the phone, Guy is given the privilege of reporting to the station the next morning, where he is greeted by the avuncular Captain Turley. What follows can hardly be called an interrogation. Turley assures Guy that "I know you're a busy man, so we won't detain you any longer than necessary." The police test Guy's alibi by bringing in a man whom Guy claims to have seen on a train on the night of his wife's murder. Even though the alibi cannot be confirmed, Guy is released, apparently without much questioning.

The police then initiate surveillance of Guy, with a friendly detective named

Leslie Hennessey taking the lead. Senator Morton at first says of the detective that "I'll have him called off immediately"—another marker of the circle of privilege that protects Guy. Still, perhaps because Guy sees the detective "as a very nice fellow," the senator does not interfere. Soon after that, the likable Hennessey breezily chats with Guy as they stroll near the Jefferson Memorial. Later, despite orders to bring Guy in for more questioning, the detective allows Guy to finish his match—prompting a fellow detective to observe that "this is the first time I've waited for a murder suspect to play tennis before I pulled him in."

Manny does not move in such circles. While he performs for the rich and famous at the Stork Club, he is otherwise removed from them. So Manny is treated like any other accused criminal in the authorities' assembly line. He cannot cogently defend himself against their accusations. He does not appreciate that their endgame is to close the file as quickly as possible. And in the case of Assistant District Attorney Hall, Manny literally does not know whom he is dealing with.

By not identifying Hall, *The Wrong Man* highlights a lack of prosecutorial accountability. The state attributed false convictions to the honest mistakes of eyewitnesses. Accepting that narrative, courts seldom identified the prosecutors or detectives who engaged in misconduct. The same mindset informed the 1948 judicial council report, which emphasized the fallibility of eyewitnesses while treating law enforcement agents as anonymous, peripheral players.

The revelation of Hall's identity, in turn, allows the lineup scene to be recontextualized as an examination of the role of prosecutors in a criminal investigation.

Hitchcock tracks Hall's reactions at the lineup. As each witness counts off the men by number, Hall follows along with his eyes, moving from one member of the lineup to another. This syncing of their words with his eyes implies that the witnesses are controlling Hall; their accusations against Manny will now be adopted by the state, without further investigation.

Hall's position in the frame suggests a failure of prosecutorial oversight. We see him from Manny's perspective. Hall is in the right foreground, looking at the lineup. With his back to the witnesses, Hall has ceded control to the detective. He has deprived himself of the ability to observe the witnesses' demeanor or their interaction with Matthews. At the same time, his presence gives the detective incentive to amplify the lineup's theatrical elements.

The witnesses are enshrouded in shadows toward the rear of the frame. The lighting adds an element of menace to the accusations against Manny, who cannot see his accusers. They are voices coming out of the dark.

In the real case, Manny implored Assistant District Attorney Thomas Cullen to allow him to speak with the Prudential employees to try to convince them of their mistake. Cullen refused. From Manny's perspective, the witnesses remained nameless, faceless figures, just as they appear in this scene.

After the lineup disbands, Detective Matthews gives Hall the holdup notes. Hall looks at them for less than ten seconds. He then confronts Manny with his summary of the evidence: (1) "you made this copy of the holdup note . . . with the mistake in it" and (2) "the girls identified you—they saw you in the office and

The assistant district attorney observes the lineup.
(*Alfred Hitchcock, director. The Wrong Man. Warner Bros., 1956*)

they saw you here." Based on these points, Hall tells Manny that "there's no sense beating around the bush. You held up the office, and you might as well say so." When Manny protests his innocence, Hall reiterates that "you were in that office this afternoon." When Manny explains his purpose was to get a loan on his wife's policy, Hall responds: "You'd better think of another story, Manny. Something more plausible."

During this confrontation, Hitchcock's compositions are as oppressive as the interrogation. Manny stands against a wall, hemmed in by the detective on his right and framed by the vertical bars on a fire escape window behind him. The window, in turn, is framed by bricks, with no view of the outside world. Since the shots of Manny are from Hall's perspective, the evocation of a jail cell conveys the prosecutor's single-minded focus on an inexorable outcome: the imprisonment and ultimate conviction of the suspect.

Yet even the eyewitnesses can corroborate that Manny asked for the loan. And if questioned, they would admit that Manny did nothing else at the office that day. But, like the detectives, Hall doesn't ask basic questions. Instead, he delivers his verdict: "Okay, Manny. With the evidence before us, there's nothing to do but lock him up."

The scene tracks Manny's actual experience with Cullen at the precinct. After the lineup, Cullen twice tried to get Manny to confess. He even declared the handwriting on the two notes "identical"—a position that a police handwriting expert disavowed at trial.

In capturing these events, *The Wrong Man* reminds us that prosecutors have a duty to protect the innocent. In fact, in a report issued before Manny's arrest, the New York County district attorney assured the public that before any indictment, prosecutors "examine all the facts and question the witnesses" and "run down any lead suggesting the defendant's innocence." Such assurances sought to give meaning to the Supreme Court's statement that a prosecutor is "a servant of the law, the twofold aim of which is that guilt shall not escape or innocence suffer."

Wielding his power with a disturbing casualness, Hall plays a fateful role in Manny's suffering. But he is on screen for under three minutes. After directing that Manny be locked up, Hall does not reappear. The same is true of the eyewitness who first identifies Manny, Alice Dennerly. Neither character ever returns to defend their accusations or account for their mistakes. There will be no reckoning for Manny's accusers.

With Hall's work done, Manny is fingerprinted, booked, and searched. He takes Rose's insurance policy out of his coat pocket. As he hands the policy to Detective Matthews, the interrogation sequence comes to a crushing conclusion. We realize that Manny was so shell-shocked that it never occurred to him to offer the policy as proof of his explanation. We observe the detectives' indifference to the revelation of the document. And we grasp the recklessness of the prosecutor's dismissal of Manny's story—a story borne out by evidence in Manny's pocket.

—FIFTEEN—
A SPIRALING TRAUMA

Manny, Rose, and their children, Greg (Robert Essen), left, and Robert (Kippy Campbell)
(*Album/Alamy Stock Photo*)

Recent studies confirm that the families of the wrongfully accused may experience trauma and depression. But in the 1950s, little was known about the spiraling impact of false arrest. Films of that era, in turn, rarely explored the fallout from wrongful incarceration.

The Wrong Man stands apart in its depiction of how false arrest can devastate a family.

Hitchcock telegraphs this theme early on, when Manny gets into the squad car. Pinned between the detectives in the backseat, Manny looks toward his house. Bowers fills the left foreground. At first we can see Rose through a window in the rear right of the frame. But as the car slowly pulls away, the detective's stern profile moves

164

in front of Rose and removes her from view. When the film cuts back to Manny, a shadow descends over him, blotting out his face. With these elegant images, *The Wrong Man* signals that the accusations against Manny will remove Rose from his life and thereby imperil his own identity.

The ripple effects of the arrest come to the fore after he returns home on bail. Approaching the front door, he again looks back over his shoulder and recalls "the police car sitting over there about a million years ago." After Manny goes to lie down, his older son, Robert, walks slowly past his father's bedroom with his head down. Then, in a haunting visual echo of Manny's gesture, Robert looks back over his shoulder toward the camera—a cinematic transference of anguish from father to son.

Robert's expression betrays his heartbreak at seeing Manny diminished. It also hints at feelings of guilt: earlier, we saw Robert answer the phone and unwittingly reveal to police what time his father would be home. Now, as Robert seeks to give comfort to Manny lying in bed ("You're the best dad in the world"), Hitchcock's composition inverts the normal parent-child dynamic. It also upends the conventions of the "wrong man" plots that Hitchcock used so often. The director's other films saw the falsely accused hero as a man of action on the run from police or hunting for the real culprit. But *The Wrong Man* is truer to the experience of people like Manny Balestrero. In real life, Manny emerged from his brief stint in jail almost as a ghost of himself. Activities that once had been routine, like taking the subway to work, proved impossible. As Manny, Henry Fonda is unsteady on his feet, emotionally drained, and can only retreat to his bed. The image of a movie star like Fonda looking up at a child for support captures the reality of false arrest.

In a rare display of emotion, Manny tries to assure Robert: "I hope you won't ever have to go through anything like I did, but if you ever do, I hope you've got a son like mine to come back to." The sentiment is touching, but tragically qualified. While the circumstances call for the comforting of a frightened child, Manny is in a real nightmare and can only "hope" that his son will not see similar suffering. Robert, crying, collapses into Manny's arms. The scene ends with another inversion of their relationship, as Robert tells Manny, "You oughta get some sleep now."

If that bedroom scene implies a transference from father to son, the next movement of *The Wrong Man* depicts a deeper transference of undeserved guilt from husband to wife. As Godard observed, through Rose's unraveling, "the wrong man becomes the wrong woman." This development fits within Hitchcock's recurring motif of the "transference of guilt," which springs from the premise, as described by Professor Allen Rostron, that "all characters in the films, like all people in the world, are part of one community of sin and interchangeable guilt."

While shifting the film's focus away from Manny's impending trial, the portrayal of Rose's suffering deepens Hitchcock's injustice theme by showing how false arrest upends the lives of all it touches.

Rose Balestrero had, in the words of her son Greg, a "fragile foundation in life." She lost her mother at a young age and suffered other trauma. The film points at her anxiety in an early scene when Manny returns from work. "Oh, Manny, sometimes I'm so frightened waiting for you to come home at night," Rose says. She adds that

Manny and Rose embrace after his release on bail, as his sister Olga (Lola D'Annunzio) and brother-in-law Gene (Nehemiah Persoff) look on. (*cineclassico/Alamy Stock Photo*)

"every time we get up, something comes along and knocks us right back down again." While its immediate reference is to Rose's dental problems, the statement also hints at a fraught personal history.

The first sign of Rose's descent comes after police put Manny in a holding cell. We have just seen Manny endure a literal and symbolic manhandling during the interrogation, arrest, and booking process. In shot after shot, Detective Matthews grabs Manny's arm, back, or hand as he directs him from one location to the next. These images of subjugation continue in an extended fingerprinting procedure that marks Manny's hands with ink. Hitchcock then cuts to a scene of Manny's brother-in-law relaying details of the arrest. We see an anxious Rose cross her arms—a defensive gesture that continues the framing of false accusation's effects in physical terms. After Manny arrives home on bail, Rose clutches her biceps as she considers phoning a lawyer. The film presents the recurring gesture as a manifestation of the transfer of trauma to Rose. In fact, when Manny is reunited with Rose outside the Long Island City jail, the camera lingers on Manny's hands gripping Rose's back and shoulder, as if to suggest a physical transmission.

The strain on Rose becomes more evident after she learns that the two alibi witnesses have died. At a follow-up meeting in O'Connor's office, she sits quietly with an eerie stillness and holds her left arm, signaling an escalation of her anxiety.

Later, when Manny arrives home after work in the middle of the night, Rose is seated in the dark, despondent. The ensuing bedroom confrontation brings home the turmoil threatening to poison the Balestreros' marriage. At first, Rose proposes a full internal retreat: "We're going to lock the doors and stay in the house; we'll lock them out and keep them out." Rose's plan is a tragic reflection of her growing paranoia. But in the context of mistaken identity cases, the sentiment is not as senseless as it might first seem. Innocent people who were confused for serial offenders faced danger simply from going outside, because any chance encounter might lead to another misidentification. That's what happened to Clifford Shephard, the New Jersey man

Rose and Manny in a meeting with Frank O'Connor (Anthony Quayle)
(*cineclassico/Alamy Stock Photo*)

whose case is discussed in Chapter Two. After serving two prison terms for crimes he did not commit, Shephard was arrested a third time because he happened to walk by a store proprietor who had been bilked by the real forger. Such experiences led the woman falsely accused of being Shephard's accomplice, Elizabeth Lester, to avoid public places.

For the Balestreros, though, it's too late to try to "keep them out." The destabilizing force of false accusation has already corrupted the foundation of their lives. Indeed, as her agitation in the scene intensifies, Rose expresses doubts about Manny's innocence: "You don't tell me everything, do you? How do I know you're not guilty? You could be. You could be!" This expression of doubt, while sheathed in anxiety, speaks to the insidious power of the state's indictment, as it compels even Rose to reconsider Manny's identity. The false allegations have so unmoored Rose that she can no longer trust anything or anyone in her life.

Hitchcock's staging of the scene melds psychological horror with thematic irony. When Rose rises above the seated Manny in apparent anger, the low-angle image characterizes her as threatening and unhinged. But as Stanford Law School Professor Norman Spaulding has observed, the system's treatment of Manny makes some of Rose's hysterical statements seem "lucid" and "eerily true."

Rose is the only character who articulates the idea that the case against Manny is a form of frame-up. By rushing to judgment, the state has borne out her conclusion that "no matter how innocent you are, or how hard you try, they'll find you guilty." And when Rose exclaims that "they reached in from the outside, and they put this last thing on us," she gives expression to the film's visual motif of the system's physical branding. That motif is reinforced when Manny reaches out to touch Rose's shoulders to try to calm her. Rose steps back in horror, as if Manny was about to strike an open wound. Manny is left with his hands grasping at air in front of him, a poignant symbol of severed connections. Since the camera has moved away from him, we see only Manny's outstretched hands, on the left edge of the frame. The image calls back to the shots of Manny looking at his ink-stained fingers during the fingerprinting scene and then later staring at his hands in despair while leaning against the wall of his jail cell. The system's marking of Manny as a criminal has, in turn, caused Rose to recoil.

Rose's rant against the system reaches a crescendo with her insistence that "they'll smash us down." She then strikes Manny with a hairbrush, bloodying his forehead and cracking a mirror on the follow-through. We see Manny's face in the mirror, cracked in half, in what Donald Spoto describes as "the refraction of his shattered image in her own broken mind—and henceforth the imperfect legal situation is tragically balanced by a more agonizing personal nightmare."

The bedroom scene features the dazzling work of film editor George Tomasini. As Rose's hysteria intensifies, so does the visual pace. Her striking of Manny is shown in a series of frenetic cuts—ten shots in under ten seconds of screen time. In Hitchcock's words, "the camera becomes violent as well, with the quick flashing closeups of everything." The editing conveys the surreal and seemingly instantaneous collapse of Manny's world. It also packs an emotional wallop, leaving us as stunned as Manny. As Professor Philip J. Skerry has written, the frequency of the cuts and the "sudden, lightning-like explosion of violence" anticipate the shower scene in *Psycho* (1960), which Tomasini also edited for Hitchcock.

Miles delivers a wrenching performance. In this scene alone, she conjures a stunning range of emotions, from defensive rage to poignant resignation. Her concluding moment of insight— when Rose tells Manny she needs institutional care—is heartbreaking.

The decision to embed a critique of the system in Rose's outburst fits narratively, since the system's failure has caused her breakdown. It also permitted an artful circumvention of the Hays Production Code, which preceded Hollywood's modern ratings system. Through edicts such as "the courts of the land should not be presented as unjust," the code mandated "the positive portrayal of law enforcement and the justice system as a whole." To enforce the code, the Production Code Administration (PCA) reviewed scripts and prohibited theaters from screening films without its approval. This review process started in 1934 and remained in effect until 1968.

As shown in a comprehensive study by author John Billheimer, Hitchcock navigated around the PCA's objections throughout his career; in some cases, he had to make major adjustments to satisfy the notion that justice must triumph. For example, in an early draft of the screenplay for Hitchcock's *The Paradine Case* (1947), a woman is acquitted of murder charges based on false testimony and then later (after her guilt is revealed) commits suicide to avoid punishment. But the PCA objected to the implication that the character would "escape justice" by killing herself.

Despite the code's imperatives, Billheimer found that the PCA had only minor suggestions on *The Wrong Man*—including that no toilet should appear in Manny's cell and that the word "geez" should not be used.

The PCA's muted reaction reflects the film's understated aesthetic. Rose's tirade marks the only moment where a character attacks the justice system. By enshrouding the criticism in her apparent hysteria, Hitchcock made any potential affront to the code's principles more oblique. The scene evokes the creative strategies employed by

Rose and Manny after arriving at the sanitarium (*Photo 12/Alamy Stock Photo*).

other, lesser-known directors of the era whom Martin Scorsese has called "smugglers" because of the subtle ways they subverted the code limitations. Scorsese uses a quote from director Jacques Tourneur to articulate "the smuggler's strategy" in a way that applies to *The Wrong Man*'s subtle encoding of social commentary: "You must never try to impose your views on the viewer, but rather you must try to let it seep in, little by little."

In an ensuing scene at a psychiatrist's office, the film reinforces that Rose is as much a victim of false arrest as Manny. A shot of Manny staring out a window reveals daylight. But behind closed doors, the psychiatrist questions Rose in a dark adjacent room. Rose is sitting under a lamp, like a suspect at an interrogation. The psychiatrist lurks behind her in the darkness, asking leading questions and judging her. The scene ends with Rose's confession: "It's no good. They know I'm guilty."

The psychiatrist tells Manny that Rose "doesn't see anything as it is." This same observation applies to the Associated Life employees who identified Manny and the authorities who arrested him. It's as if the inability to see has become infectious. Even Manny shows a form of blindness: it's not until after O'Connor alerts him to Rose's obvious depression that Manny urges her to see a doctor.

Rose's suffering culminates in confinement in a sanitarium, a symbolic imprisonment. A doctor and nurse greet her, each forcing a smile that is as fake as the one worn by Detective Bowers when he first seizes Manny. In another visual echo, they grab Rose by the arms and escort her toward the stairs. The image mirrors the shot of the detectives escorting Manny to their car. But while in the earlier scene Manny looks back at the house in a gesture reflecting his fear of separation from Rose, the horror now is that Rose is oblivious to the separation. Even as Manny calls out to her, she doesn't look back. Instead, Rose ascends the stairs, up and out of the frame, and out of Manny's life.

—SIXTEEN—
WHO WILL LISTEN?

Manny and O'Connor during the trial sequence
(*Moviestore Collection Ltd./Alamy Stock Photo*)

After Manny leaves Rose, an exterior shot outside the sanitarium gives way to an interior shot of the courtroom. The transition reflects a cynicism about the law that informs *The Wrong Man*'s trial sequence. It also marks one of the film's several departures from the conventions of courtroom dramas.

As Boston University law professor Jessica Silbey has observed, many trial films use establishing shots of the courthouse exterior to announce the grandeur of the legal system. Silbey points out that these shots often glorify the "house of law" and prime the viewer to see courts as permanent and dependable dispensers of justice.

Hitchcock never shows us the outside of the Queens courthouse where Manny goes on trial. Instead, he first drops us in the benches toward the back, looking over the shoulders of spectators. As the clerk reads the charges against Manny, we can barely see the figures in the front of the courtroom. The judge's head is a speck in the rear of the frame—an image that undermines his prestige and signals that justice will be elusive.

During the reading of the indictment, Hitchcock does not cut to the participants for reaction shots, which other trial films use to build anticipation. He instead holds the distant, static view of the proceeding. The shot instills in us the same sense of disorientation that Manny will feel throughout the trial. It leaves us uncertain where to look in the frame. If we strain, though, we can see the lead prosecutor toward the rear. He slinks back into his chair and leans his face against his palm, a gesture of boredom and indifference that foreshadows the events to follow.

Hitchcock's defiance of convention continues with the opening statements. A defense lawyer's opening often provides a dramatic and engaging preview of the case. By this point, though, *The Wrong Man* has planted warning signs about O'Connor's effectiveness. He has little experience in criminal cases. His role in the pretrial investigation has been limited. In fact, after the Balestreros learn that the two alibi witnesses have died, he puts the onus on them to overcome this obstacle: "You'll have to go back . . . and dig up some more facts on your side." The resulting impression of O'Connor is inaccurate and, given his role as a technical adviser, surprising. In truth, his investigation was exhaustive and yielded multiple alibi witnesses and other exculpatory evidence.

In the film, though, O'Connor's performance bears out his earlier admission that "I shall be at a disadvantage with a skillful prosecutor." His opening statement is halting and tentative. Since "an indictment is only an accusation," O'Connor

Manny sitting in the courtroom, with the jury behind him. Fourth from left in the front row of the jury box is Barney Martin, who played Jerry's father on *Seinfeld*. (*Album/Alamy Stock Photo*)

tells the jury that he would "much prefer" that the witnesses provide the "proof" at trial. This entreating tone betrays a lack of confidence, as if O'Connor himself may not believe Manny will be acquitted. O'Connor's ultimate message to the jury is similarly qualified and nearly garbled:

> *I'm going to ask you to consider the probabilities of this case. And I'm going to ask you that when the proof is all in to see if you don't say to yourself that this is a tragic case of a mistaken identity.*

O'Connor adds that "what I say to you now or hereafter or what Mr. Tomasini has said or may say to you later on is of little or no significance in the case." An attempt to explain the familiar point that lawyers' arguments are not evidence, the statement instead comes across as a clumsy and self-diminishing admission. For these reasons, O'Connor's opening statement stymies our expectation of the drama that normally escalates during trial sequences while also dampening any hope that Manny will be acquitted.

The trial's moment of highest drama comes during the testimony of Ann James, one of the two witnesses who identified Manny at the lineup. The prosecutor asks James to point out the man who held her up. "Will you step down and put your hand on his shoulder?" he requests. Hesitating at first, James steps off the witness stand and behind the jury box. Approaching Manny from his right, she walks directly toward the camera. James then extends her shaking right hand to make the identification while grasping her pocketbook in her left hand—an unnerving image that blends the passing of judgment with the mundane.

As her outstretched hand lands on Manny's shoulder in close-up, Hitchcock holds the shot just long enough for us to feel it.

James's confrontation with Manny seizes our attention. Part of its power lies in its use of a horror trope—the image of an arm grasping at a potential victim. The moment jolts us to a state of high alert, removing the distance created by the uninspired opening statements. And when the witness's hand reaches the edge of the frame, the gesture implicates us in the stain of false accusation.

This strangely intimate ritual is no Hitchcockian embellishment. Prosecutors often directed their witnesses to make courtroom identifications in this manner. As described in Chapter Eight, assistant district attorney Frank Crisona had the first eyewitness at the real trial, Constance Ello, put her hand on Manny's shoulder.

The witness's touching of the defendant is intended to convey to the jury the certainty of the identification. But here that certainty is undermined by Hitchcock's tight close-up. During this ultimate act of identification, both the witness's eyes and Manny's face are outside the frame. It's easy to imagine that James—who didn't "dare look" at the Associated Life office—is not looking at Manny at this moment either.

The ritual reinforces how prosecutors invested dubious eyewitness assertions with the state's imprimatur. James may be a private accuser, but she is wielding the power to condemn. As her hand comes to rest on Manny's shoulder, we feel the ruinous weight of false accusation.

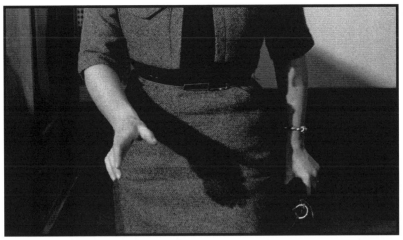

Ann James (Doreen Lang) identifies Manny in the courtroom.
(Alfred Hitchcock, director. The Wrong Man. Warner Bros., 1956)

Hitchcock then cuts to a shot of Manny tilting his head to look at his shoulder. The shot reinforces the all-enveloping nature of the prosecution from his perspective. "They come at me from all sides," Rose had said before her confinement. The same is true of Manny during the trial sequence. The prosecutor delivers part of his opening statement from behind Manny, a positioning that adds to the surrealness of the experience. Then comes the witness's symbolic assault from Manny's right. It's little wonder that Manny spends much of the trial looking behind him in the courtroom. Where will the next blow come from?

Just moments later, Hitchcock reminds us that while prosecutors have the power to employ the machinery of the state against an individual, some exercised that power with casual indifference. The point comes when O'Connor's cross-examination reveals that Ann James' husband was in Manny's lineup. Just as the witness admits this seemingly damning fact, Hitchcock cuts to a close-up of the prosecutor laughing at a remark whispered by his assistant. The image reframes the state's inattention to the recklessness of its procedures as a cruel joke.

It's not just the prosecutor who is blind to the stakes for Manny. During the same cross-examination, Hitchcock cuts to images of the banal in the courtroom as seen from Manny's perspective. The judge looks down, jabs a pencil into his binder, and frowns, as if he is being put upon. The jurors are visibly bored: Two men appear to be barely awake, while a woman impatiently cleans her glasses. Even Manny's allies are not paying attention. O'Connor's assistant doodles absentmindedly on a pad. Manny's sister puts on lipstick as her husband speaks to her. With such images, the scene realizes Hitchcock's stated goal of showing Manny's feeling "that he has no friends in the world." It is a visual expression of the awful realization that the rest of the world is going about its mundane business. As Hitchcock told Truffaut: "I've always felt a complete identification with the feelings of a person who's arrested, taken to the police station in a van, and who, through the bars of the moving vehicle, can see people going to the theater, coming out of a bar, and enjoying the comforts of everyday living."

As the trial continues, even the judge's impatience grows. He interjects repeatedly during O'Connor's ineffective cross-examination about the number system used at the precinct lineup. He obstructs the examination by implying to the jury that the questions do not warrant considered answers:

O'Connor:	*What number did Mr. Balestrero have?*
Judge:	*Do you remember? If you don't, just say so.*
Witness:	*No, I'm afraid I don't recall.*
O'Connor:	*Do you recall what number Mr. James had?*
Witness:	*No. He moved around too much.*
O'Connor:	*Did the number-one man have an overcoat on?*
Witness:	*As far as I can remember they were all dressed the same.*
O'Connor:	*Did he have an overcoat or not, the number-one man?*
Judge:	*She said as far as she knows they were all dressed alike.*
O'Connor:	*Miss, uh, can you remember how tall he was, approximately, the number-one man?*
Judge:	*If you know. If you do not know, say so.*
Witness:	*No, I don't know.*
O'Connor:	*Approximately how much did he weigh?*
Judge:	*If you know, say so. If you do not, say so.*
Witness:	*No, I do not know.*

Upon the witness's last answer, a juror stands up and asks: "Your Honor, do we have to sit here and listen to this?"

In Hitchcock's words, the outburst amounts to a "violation of the ritual" and leads to the mistrial. The moment captures the impatience and insolence of Lloyd Espenschied, who erupted with the complaint after a similar remark by a fellow juror. But it also operates as a larger and more symbolic confession of prejudgment. In that moment, the juror seems to speak for the entire criminal justice system. No one in the film—not the police, not the prosecutors, and not even the presiding judge—wants to listen to Manny's declarations of innocence or hear evidence casting doubt on his guilt. The timing of the outburst links the juror to the prosecutor who ordered Manny's arrest. Just as Assistant District Attorney Hall hastily directed the detectives to lock up Manny without listening to his explanation, the juror wants to convict Manny without scrutiny of the lineup at which Hall presided. The eruption is a systemic Freudian slip—a confirmation of institutional rashness.

By this point, the judge has exhibited the same restiveness that underlies the juror's statement. He has ceded the moral authority to condemn the outburst. The film hints at this interpretation with its camerawork and sound design. As the juror vents his frustration, the camera elevates him with a low-angle shot; with his elegant suit and ramrod straight posture, he towers over the judge in the frame. As the judge tries to assert himself in response ("The court will rule on what is proper evidence,

Mr. Juror"), the camera is suddenly in the back of the courtroom again. We can hear the judge, but barely see him.

The depiction of the judge continued a trend in the Hitchcock canon: the courts do not fare well. In *The Paradine Case,* a judge (played by Charles Laughton) coldly rebukes his wife's pleas for mercy for a murderer he has sentenced to death and then nefariously picks his teeth. In *I Confess,* the judge gratuitously criticizes a jury's verdict for an innocent man. And in *Strangers on a Train,* a judge encountered by the psychotic Bruno Antony (Robert Walker) comes across as an automaton as he explains capital punishment: "When a murderer is caught, he must be tried. When he's convicted he must be sentenced. When he is sentenced to death, he must be executed."

In *The Wrong Man,* the judge is not so heartless. But his pronouncements about justice, delivered after the mistrial, are given little weight by Hitchcock. The comments are barely audible and play like background noise while we see and hear O'Connor explain the effect of the mistrial to Manny. As the judge declares that "most importantly for all of us is that every American be guaranteed his day in court," his voice trails off and the scene fades to black—an ironic comment on the gap between what the system promises and what it has delivered for Manny.

—SEVENTEEN—
"OK, MANNY?"

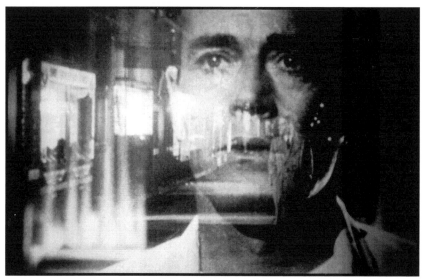

A shot of Manny dissolves as he is replaced by the actual holdup man, played by
Richard Robbins. (*Collection Christophel/Alamy Stock Photo*)

In depicting Manny's exoneration, Hitchcock bends the facts for dramatic
purposes. But even as its strays from the literal truth, *The Wrong Man* illuminates
why the calamity it depicts has been repeated many times.

At his mother's urging, Manny prays for the strength to withstand a second trial.
In one of the film's most famous flourishes, Hitchcock dissolves from Manny's face
to the real criminal, Charles Daniell. We then witness Daniell's capture in the failed
robbery of a local deli.

The prayer scene isn't as much of a dramatic liberty as it first seems. Based on the
research, Hitchcock assured coscreenwriter Maxwell Anderson that it was "factual"
to show Mrs. Balestrero beseeching Manny to pray. And Manny himself referred to

Daniell's capture as an answer to a prayer, made that very day, during his visit with Rose at the sanitarium.

The film's bigger invention gives one of the detectives who arrested Manny a role in clearing him. In real life, Daniell volunteered to police from another precinct that he had committed the Prudential holdups; the detectives from the 110th Precinct were not involved.

In the film, Detective Matthews passes by Daniell at the precinct before walking out the door and continuing down the street. Then Matthews stops and looks back at the building. Apparently grasping the man's resemblance to Manny, Matthews heads back inside. Hitchcock then cuts to the Stork Club, where Manny learns from his boss that he is wanted at the precinct because "they got the right man." The sequence implies that Matthews connected Daniell to the Associated Life robberies.

On one level, this twist softens the depiction of the police. Matthews could have continued on his way home; it would have been in his personal interest to do so. His decision to turn back reminds us that the police did not set out to imprison an innocent man. It hints at the promise of a system that is willing to correct an error rather than suppress it.

But in the ensuing scenes, Hitchcock uses this fiction to highlight the failure of state officials to learn from miscarriages of justices. As Manny meets up with O'Connor at the precinct, the police are (off-screen) showing Daniell to the same Associated Life employees who identified Manny. The rituals of Manny's lineup are repeated. Matthews can be heard instructing one of the employees, Constance Willis, to "start counting from the right" and "when you come to the man you know, stop on the number." Willis obliges, stopping on the fourth man (Daniell, having been placed in the same lineup spot as Manny earlier). When asked "Are you sure that's one?" Wills gives an unqualified, confident "yes." She and Ann James then emerge into the hallway.

The scene encapsulates the history of the mistaken identity cases discussed in Part One. Even with Manny's innocence established, there is no change in the procedures that led to his arrest. The detective stages the lineup the same way and asks the same questions. The accusing witnesses will again be credited even though they were so tragically wrong the first time.

The detective's final encounter with Manny confirms the continuation of the status quo. Matthews asks, matter-of-factly, "Okay, Manny?" It's the same phrase that the prosecutor uttered right before ordering Manny's arrest, but now punctuated by the false sense that "all's well that ends well." The detective then puts his hand on Manny's upper arm—a gesture that symbolically reverses the condemning touch of the shoulder at trial.

Matthews isn't suffering pangs of conscience. Like the eyewitnesses who hurry past Manny at the precinct, he doesn't apologize. His demeanor suggests a belief that, in the end, the system worked.

By taking license with the detective's role, then, *The Wrong Man* underlines a root cause of the Balestreros' suffering. In the decades before Manny's arrest, state officials failed to account for their role in false convictions. They neither increased their scrutiny of eyewitness identifications nor improved the procedures used to

Manny confronts the real culprit at the police station. (*cineclassico/Alamy Stock Photo*)

secure them. The same cycle of indifference to error would continue for decades after Manny's exoneration, until DNA evidence forced a reckoning with the reality of wrongful conviction.

Despite Hitchcock's view of the police, his approach is never polemical. He opts for a naturalism that makes what happened to Manny seem even more immediate and frightening. And, as in real life, Manny himself shows no resentment toward the detectives. Instead, he directs his anger at Daniell ("You realize what you've done to my wife?").

The Wrong Man's quiet rebuke of the system finds a more outspoken counterpart in another film starring Henry Fonda: *12 Angry Men*, directed by Sydney Lumet. The Lumet film was based on a 1954 installment of the television show *Westinghouse Studio One* that was written by Reginald Rose, a giant of early television who also created the acclaimed CBS-TV courtroom drama *The Defenders* (1961-1965) and wrote the 1957 *Studio One* program "The Defender" (costarring a young Steve McQueen), upon which the CBS series was loosely based.

Released only three and a half months after *The Wrong Man*, *12 Angry Men* feels at times like its spiritual sequel. The connections transcend the casting of Fonda, who in the later film stars as a juror who challenges the proof used to prosecute a criminal defendant.

From the outset, *12 Angry Men* presents apathy and snap judgments as forces that must be countered. The film opens with a judge perfunctorily charging a jury in a murder case. He rubs his forehead, then jabs the table with a pencil (much like the judge in *The Wrong Man*) while blandly noting that "one man is dead" and "another man's life is at stake." By the end of the instructions, the judge is resting his face in his palm, mirroring the bored gesture of the prosecutor at Manny's trial.

The jury is filled with men who, as law professor Norman Rosenberg has observed, show the same impatience as the juror who disrupted Manny's trial. Juror 3 (Lee J. Cobb) admits that "I almost fell asleep" and complains that "the lawyers talk and talk and talk even when it's an open-and-shut case." Other jurors show their boredom by doodling and playing games during the deliberations. The two films seem to fully converge when Juror 10 (Ed Begley) rebuffs another juror's attempt to explain his not-guilty vote with a line seemingly right out of *The Wrong Man*'s jury box: "Do we have to listen to this?" Of course, Rose wrote his *12 Angry Men* teleplay after serving jury duty in Manhattan in early 1954, more than two years before *The Wrong Man*'s release. So he did not borrow the line from Hitchcock's film. But he may have found some inspiration for the theme of jury impatience in Lloyd Espenschied's outburst at Manny's trial in April 1953, which was reported both locally and in *Life* magazine.

Unlike *The Wrong Man*, *12 Angry Men* gives voice to its concerns through Fonda's righteous indignation as Juror 8. "This isn't a game," he roars at jurors who are playing tic-tac-toe, before ripping up their paper. Throughout the film, Fonda speaks eloquently about the issues that are on display, but not expressly discussed,

Henry Fonda as Juror 8 in *12 Angry Men* (*Moviestore Collection Ltd./Alamy Stock Photo*)

in *The Wrong Man*. At one point, he notes the prosecution's entire case rests on two witnesses: "They're only people. People make mistakes. Could they be wrong?"

By contrast, while *The Wrong Man* shows us how systemic flaws enabled Manny's prosecution, the characters don't speak about those flaws. The film subverts the expectations created by its casting of Fonda, whose soulful dignity yielded moments of surpassing eloquence in earlier social justice films like *The Grapes of Wrath*. We anticipate a stirring speech from him that challenges the system, but one never arrives. Instead, consistent with the film's naturalism, Manny is left struggling to say anything at all ("How can I tell you? What can I do?" he says, after a futile effort to convince the prosecutor of his innocence). The silencing of his persona is best captured in the arraignment scene, when Manny can only silently mouth "Rose" and shake his head to indicate his innocence.

In portraying Manny, Fonda suppressed part of his emotional range as an actor: a capacity for rage. John Steinbeck once wrote that Fonda left the impression of a man "gentle but capable of sudden wild and dangerous violence." Fonda showed this dangerous side as wrongfully convicted ex-con Eddie Taylor in *You Only Live Once*

(1937). After he is sentenced to death, Eddie erupts at an angry mob outside the courthouse: "Go ahead! Take a good look! You monkeys! Have a good time! Get a big kick out of it! It's fun to see an innocent man die, isn't it?" Eddie then acts on his rage by breaking out of prison. The performance displays a fury absent from *The Wrong Man*.

Manny's quiet acceptance of his suffering is part of what scholar Murray Pomerance has described as a restrained "sonic tone" that extends even to the law enforcement agents. Even as the detectives process Manny through the system, they project an air of quiet assurance and betray no sign of malicious intent. As a result, their failures become harder to see. It's as if the film's message about the criminal justice system is cloaked by its understated realism—a veiling that may explain why some critics did not regard it as critical of the police.

The Wrong Man challenges us to look behind a facade of bureaucratic routine and tonal reasonableness to see the recklessness in the state's handling of Manny's case. Its final scene answers the detective's question of whether everything is now "okay." Manny expects the news of exoneration to restore his wife to him. But the first sight of Rose confirms her continuing psychological imprisonment. Standing in front of the window of her room, and wearing a striped outfit that evokes prison garb, Rose slowly looks back toward the camera—an echo of Manny's recurring over-the-shoulder gesture. While Manny assures her that their nightmare is over, Rose remains disconsolate. She registers no reaction even when Manny appeals to the needs of their children, who pray every night she'll come home. And in another visual echo, Rose obsessively clutches her upper arm throughout the scene. Detective Matthews's symbolic exoneration—his touch of Manny's shoulder—is thus revealed to be ineffective. The Balestreros will continue to suffer despite the withdrawal of the criminal charges.

By highlighting Rose's continuing confinement, the final scene defies the prevailing cultural narrative of exoneration. As described by law professor Lara Bazelon, this narrative fits within the structure of a fairy tale: the wrongfully accused person endures suffering and overcomes "seemingly impossible odds" before hope and happiness are restored. The media promotes this ideal with images that form "a snapshot in time: the bang of the gavel, the embrace between client and attorney, the press conference at which the exoneree gives thanks . . . ."

Not *The Wrong Man*. As a nurse escorts him out of the sanitarium, Manny faces the prospect of telling his sons that their prayers have gone unanswered. Their mother won't be coming home.

After Manny leaves Rose, the following postscript appears superimposed over him:

Two years later, Rose Balestrero walked out of the sanitarium—completely cured. Today she lives happily in Florida with Manny and the two boys . . . and what happened seems like a nightmare to them— but it did happen . . .

These words give way to a long shot of a family of four, seen in the distance, walking under palm trees.

The ending has divided commentators. Some have described the postscript as an attempt at false uplift. Film historian David Bordwell argues that "in its final seconds, *The Wrong Man* pays outrageously perfunctory obeisance to our craving for the triumph of the just and the good." Critic David Sterritt counters that "it is more likely . . . that Hitchcock is engaging in a profoundly ironic maneuver by sardonically mirroring a shallow variety of mid century optimism." And Professor Paula Marantz Cohen observes that the long shot serves the film's mistaken identity theme by reducing the characters to "pinpoints on the screen" and thereby depriving us of visual evidence that the figures are in fact the Balestreros. This observation assumes an even greater irony considering how the final image was filmed: the actors are not Fonda and Miles, but "doubles" hired by a production company in Florida to shoot the scene.

Despite these provocative readings, the immediate reason for the postscript was the need to avoid a false impression. Rose returned home more than a year before the film's release. Hitchcock could not have ended the film with the implication that she remained in the sanitarium, especially given the Balestreros' cooperation with the production.

Accused in one interview of presenting "a grafted-on upbeat ending," the director replied: "We were just doing the true story." In a March 1956 letter to Anderson, Hitchcock said of the postscript: "Not only does this give us a note of relief, but more than that they [the audience] have been seeing a factual case, and I think this is very important." In fact, on the same day that Hitchcock wrote the letter, Manny and Rose met with Fonda and Miles in Miami.

In any case, the postscript does not blunt the film's power. There is little buoyancy in the news that Rose spent another two years in an institution as her family prayed for her return. The Balestreros, as we've come to know them, are never reunited on screen. And there is no law-affirming moment of the sort that marks other films of the same era. Those films portray the justice system as central to the concept of "American exceptionalism" and present law as capable of achieving closure.

By denying both narrative and emotional closure, *The Wrong Man* leaves a disturbing aftertaste. The film's ending, and several of its themes, call to mind David Fincher's *Zodiac* (2007), which recounts a decades-long investigation into a serial killer who terrorized Northern California beginning in the late 1960s. Fincher nods to Hitchcock early on by showing a poster of *The Wrong Man* hanging behind the television of Robert Graysmith (Jake Gyllenhaal), a cartoonist who becomes obsessed with the case. The poster declares: "Somewhere . . . somewhere . . . there must be the right man!" The tagline serves as both a taunt and a warning for Graysmith and *Zodiac*'s detectives as they try to solve the maddening puzzle of the murderer's identity amid many contradictory pieces of evidence. But unlike the police in *The Wrong Man*, the lead detective in *Zodiac*, Dave Toschi (Mark Ruffalo), worries about rapid conclusions that rest on intuition rather than proof. As Professor Martin Kevorkian points out, Toschi "underlines the dangers of the will to closure" by admitting to his police captain that "I can't tell if I wanted it to be [suspect Arthur Leigh Allen] so bad because I actually thought it was him, or I just want all this to be over." In an insightful essay, Kevorkian observes that both films also explore "the intoxicating spirit of accusation," with *Zodiac* mining that theme in a scene in which Graysmith pressures a witness to recall the name of a suspect he believes to be the killer.

Fincher may have also found inspiration in Hitchcock's effort to re-create Manny's case in exacting detail. Just as the writers and producers of *The Wrong Man* conducted extensive research, Fincher and screenwriter James Vanderbilt interviewed every living detective who had worked on the case, the surviving victims, and even relatives of the suspects. "Fincher seems possessed by the need to recreate reality—to revisit the scene of the crime—piece by piece," wrote *New York Times* film critic Manohla Dargis in her review of the film. Fincher's on-screen investigation shows the police repeatedly using a handwriting expert whose inability to match a letter to a suspect derails the detectives' momentum toward an arrest. By contrast, in *The Wrong Man*, the police condemn Manny even though they have found only a "rough similarity" between his writing and the holdup note.

Zodiac's final scene shows a detective presenting a photo array of suspects to Mike Mageau, who survived an attack by the Zodiac killer. Even though the crime occurred twenty-two years earlier, Mageau points to a suspect. "It's this man," Mageau says confidently. But when asked how sure he is on a scale of one to ten, Mageau replies, "At least an eight." His identification is, in the words of critic Adam Nayman, "a claim shadowed by doubt, a fraction with a nagging reminder." The doubt about the identification is amplified by our memory of the film's depiction of the crime, which shows that Mageau saw the killer (who was holding a blinding flashlight) for no more than several seconds before the shooting.

With its meticulous attention to the evidentiary and institutional challenges faced by law enforcement, *Zodiac* warns that closing cases is arduous, and that certain premises of our justice system will lead some criminals to go unpunished. *The Wrong Man*, meanwhile, shows the cost of elevating the desire for swift retribution and resolution above the need to protect the innocent. It warns that cataclysmic harm may follow when detectives and eyewitnesses have a misplaced certainty about their ability to assign guilt.

Even though he made a false arrest, Detective Matthews does not treat the case as revelatory. Like his real-life counterpart, he sees no reason to feel remorse. The arrest was based on an error, but one made by eyewitnesses. It was just an honest mistake.

The poster for *The Wrong Man* that appears in *Zodiac* (*Album/Alamy Stock Photo*)

—EIGHTEEN—
"THE DNA OF ITS TIME"

A publicity photo featuring Fonda and Miles
(*Allstar Picture Company Ltd./Alamy Stock Photo*)

In a 2013 lecture, director Martin Scorsese cast light on the relationship between films and time. Quoting critic Manny Farber, Scorsese observed that "every movie transmits the DNA of its time." A film like 1951's sci-fi invasion classic *The Day the Earth Stood Still*, for example, was encoded with the DNA of Cold War America— "the tension, the paranoia, the fear of nuclear disaster, and the fear of the end of life on planet Earth." In both theme and mood, the film tapped into the anxieties that audiences of that era brought with them into the theaters.

A modern audience will see the same film with its own perspective and values, "uninhibited by the biases of the time when the picture was made." In Scorsese's words:

You can only see the world through your own time—which means that some values disappear, and some values come into closer focus. Same film, same images, but in the case of a great film the power—a timeless power that really can't be articulated—that power is there even when the context has completely changed.

Scorsese's insight helps explain the way *The Wrong Man* was received in 1956, and the reasons it resonates so powerfully more than sixty-five years after its release.

On one level, a viewer can locate in the film the same Cold War DNA that Scorsese linked to *The Day the Earth Stood Still*. In fact, Scorsese himself has found "paranoia" in the mood and camera movements of *The Wrong Man*. That vibe, coupled with the theme of false accusation, may well have evoked feelings of dread stirred by the hunt for communists spearheaded by Senator Joseph McCarthy. In 1954, only two years before the film's release, McCarthy had escalated his congressional inquisition with the televised Army-McCarthy hearings. These hearings followed an extensive investigation by the House Un-American Activities Committee (HUAC) into communism's alleged foothold in Hollywood, which dated back to 1947.

Perhaps because of the film's proximity to these events, some commentators see *The Wrong Man* as Hitchcock's statement about the evils of McCarthyism. Film scholar Robert Kolker, for example, calls the film "an allegory of the blacklist" and likens Manny to HUAC's victims. The critique of McCarthyism implied by this reading aligns with Hitchcock's hiring of at least two actors who had been blacklisted—Norman Lloyd (one of the stars of *Saboteur*) and Paul Henreid (Victor Laszlo in *Casablanca*)—to produce and direct for *Alfred Hitchcock Presents* on television. On the other hand, Hitchcock made no public statements linking the film to McCarthyism. The record shows that he was drawn to Manny's case as part of his lifelong preoccupation with the shadowy boundary between guilt and innocence, the inability of authorities to distinguish truth from accusation, and the convergence of his two abiding fears: police and the law.

The Wrong Man's sobering perspective on these themes limited its popular appeal. Its $1.2 million domestic box office total paled in comparison with *Rear Window* (1954, $5.3 million), *To Catch a Thief* (1955, $4.5 million), and Hitchcock's other 1956 release, *The Man Who Knew Too Much* ($4.4 million). The director's hits typically fused action, suspense, romance, and humor—elements absent from *The Wrong Man*.

Late 1956 was an especially challenging time to release a stark picture about a miscarriage of justice. Reports of spiking crime rates fueled public safety concerns. In December, when *The Wrong Man* premiered, the FBI reported that a record 2,534,000 major crimes had been committed over the previous twelve months—a 12 percent increase over 1955. In New York City, which saw a 41 percent increase in juvenile crime in the first half of 1956, Police Commissioner Stephen P. Kennedy urged the hiring of five thousand more officers to arrest "the march toward criminal chaos."

New York's rising crime rate may have dampened enthusiasm for the story of a rush to judgment that nearly destroyed an innocent family. Then, as the film was making its debut at the Paramount Theatre in Times Square, one specific threat put filmgoers' lives in jeopardy.

For more than fifteen years, police had been searching for the person responsible for planting a series of pipe bombs across the city. After two of these bombs were found, undetonated, in 1940 and 1941, the culprit resumed his crimes in 1951. Between March 1951 and April 1956, twenty-one of his bombs exploded, resulting in nine injuries but no deaths.

On December 2, the bomber struck again, at a Brooklyn movie theater showing *War and Peace*, another 1956 film starring Henry Fonda. Three people suffered cuts, and three others were treated for shock.

By the end of December, bomb threats in the city had reached what the *New York Times* called "epidemic proportions." Most were hoaxes. But then, on December 28, came a real threat, made against the Paramount during a screening of *The Wrong Man*.

At 7:25 that night, a man called the theater and warned that a bomb would explode at 7:55. Police rushed to the scene but did not evacuate the theater—either because they wanted to avoid a panic or because so many false alarms had come in. So they searched the theater in the dark, using flashlights, as some 2,500 people watched Hitchcock's film.

No explosive device went off at 7:55. But many hours after the film ended, police found a bomb buried in a seat in the theater.

The next day, during an interview promoting the film, Hitchcock credited the still-at-large and unidentified "Mad Bomber" with "a diabolical sense of humor." On a more serious note, he called the culprit "an enemy of society" and acknowledged the pressure facing the detectives on the case given that "all of us are schooled by TV to expect police miracles." Several weeks later, the police finally cracked the case and arrested a mentally disturbed former Con Edison employee named George Metesky.

According to Hitchcock biographer Donald Spoto, the bomb threat was "the most excitement the film generated." This acerbic remark captured not only the picture's subpar box office performance, but also a common thread in the critical response: *The Wrong Man* did not deliver the entertainment that audiences had come to expect from the director.

In the *New York Times*, A. H. Weiler called the film "frighteningly authentic" but complained about its lack of drama and suspense. The *Chicago Tribune* similarly commented that the "somber" story was not "as entertaining as the average Hitchcock offering."

New Yorker critic John McCarten referred to the film as "coldly factual" and saw it as proof that "simple realism is not enough." McCarten even condemned Manny as "entirely too simple-minded even to play an instrument in a Stork Club band" while mocking Rose's breakdown as raising "a tossup whether it's because of his predicament or because of a plausible hope that she can somehow get away from Daddy and the children."

Despite the director's refusal to bend the story to suit his popular brand of escapism, several critics concluded that Hitchcock had failed in his bid for authenticity. In the *Washington Post*, critic Richard Coe complained that the director had labored unsuccessfully "to make everything seem 'real.'" Coe concluded that "Hitchcock's basic fault has been in his use of the realistic technique which, perhaps out of habit, he dramatizes so that it becomes a phony realism." *Time* similarly warned that Hitchcock's "completely literal rendering" had drained Manny's story of drama and emotion.

In the *Boston Globe*, critic Marjory Adams went a step further: *The Wrong Man* was not convincing because "you can't believe that an innocent man and devoted father and husband, could get into so much trouble." She added that "there should be more reason for having him arrested and very nearly sent to prison." Adams also claimed that the film's "chief interest is what might occur in our own lives, provided we have a 'double' engaged in crime."

Still, the film had its admirers. *Variety* called it a "gripping piece of realism" that builds to "a powerful climax." *Newsweek* raved that Hitchcock had succeeded "in filling the familiar with terror." And in the New York *Daily News*, Wanda Hale described the film as "thought-provoking" and a "very fine drama"—although she cautioned readers not to "expect excitement, humor and suspense."

Hale's warning reflected audiences' expectations for a Hitchcock film. As Martin Scorsese has pointed out, the director was then "so popular it was like a franchise —every year there was a Hitchcock film." On top of that, when *The Wrong Man* was released, *Alfred Hitchcock Presents* was America's fourth-highest-rated television show. On December 31, 1956, 37.5 percent of all homes with televisions tuned in to the show, which blended mystery, humor, and plot twists.

Despite his massive popularity, Hitchcock resisted the temptation to embellish Manny's story with these elements. He instead delivered a film that French critics (and directors) Éric Rohmer and Claude Chabrol described as "stripped of romantic adventure but also of all 'suspense.'" In their words, *The Wrong Man* was "a film of winter." Rohmer and Chabrol saw it as one of Hitchcock's most artistic and uncompromising works: "Convinced that he was now strong enough to face a possible commercial failure, he decided to make the sort of film his heart was set on."

The Wrong Man is remarkable for what it withholds. It is a Hitchcock picture without the director's famous set pieces or narrative twists. A Fonda picture without the actor's eloquent defiance in the face of injustice. A legal docudrama without courtroom fireworks. An exoneration story without a catharsis.

While Hitchcock's skepticism about legal institutions infuses the film, his restraint apparently made its cautionary message elusive. Few critics saw in the story a critique of the criminal justice system. In the *Times*, Weiler characterized the arresting detectives as "dispassionate but understanding." To *The Hollywood Reporter*, the detectives were "hard and yet fair." The *Miami Daily News* noted that Manny is "questioned firmly, but given every break by the officers." The Memphis *Commercial Appeal* felt that the police "gave the suspect every opportunity to prove his story" and "could do nothing else" based on the facts before them. Rochester's *Democrat and Chronicle* described the film's perspective as showing that "the law is just but cold; the courts are fair but terrifying; the police are decent men but facts are facts."

These critical responses aligned with the state's portrayal of wrongful conviction cases as unavoidable tragedies. Authorities had a self-interest in promoting the narrative of the "double"—innocents beset by the misfortune of looking identical to a criminal. That angle may have also comforted newspaper readers and filmgoers. If Manny's ordeal stemmed from an incredible coincidence, the chances of a similar fate befalling us seem remote. The assignment of blame to police and prosecutors would have been more unsettling.

A tendency to exonerate the state showed in the reactions to Manny's case. It can be seen in the pages of the *Long Island Star-Journal*, which concluded that "there was a strong case against him . . . a case too strong for the prosecution to disregard." It informed the comments of Frank O'Connor, who declared that "the police and the district attorney's office only did their duty once the complaint was made." Given that Manny's own lawyer expressed this view, it is no surprise that the case did not register with the public as a harrowing cautionary tale. False arrests continued to be seen as isolated aberrations rather than the result of recurring systemic failures.

And so many saw in Manny a victim not of a police mistake, but of extraordinary bad luck. They saw in Manny's tale not a miscarriage of justice, but a fantastic tale of a criminal doppelgänger. Like the authorities whose tunnel vision led to Manny's prosecution, they saw what they wanted to see.

***

This conception of Manny's story—and the desire to extract from it entertainment rather than social commentary—paved the way for his appearance in January 1957 on *To Tell the Truth*. Airing shortly after the premiere of *The Wrong Man*, this installment of the popular CBS game show marks one of the most ironic moments in television history.

Manny's decision to appear on the show is itself noteworthy. While he wanted to put the false arrest behind him, a competing impulse was at work. Public appearances of this kind drew attention to his exoneration. "He wanted to make sure that everybody knew that he was innocent," said his son Greg. While Manny had generally received strong support during his ordeal, there were some "naysayers" among his friends and relatives. "Everybody's got a ballot and they are all voting, so he wanted to make sure publicly that there was no question that he was innocent. He did that until he died," Greg said.

The show featured three contestants who sought to convince a celebrity panel that they were a particular person. Two of the three were "impostors." To try to identify the impostors, the celebrities asked a series of questions. Only the "real" person was "sworn" to give truthful answers. On the episode in which Manny appears, host Bud Collyer describes it as "a game of deliberate misrepresentation in which four presumably smart people try to find out which of three challengers has sworn to tell the truth." He refers to the celebrities—actress Polly Bergen, actor Dick Van Dyke, actress Hildy Parks, and commentator John Cameron Swayze —as "our cross-examiners."

When viewed with knowledge of his suffering, Manny's appearance invests the show's conceit with an unintended moral gravity. At the start of the segment, the three contestants walk toward the front of the stage, cast at first in silhouette. When the announcer asks "What is your name, please?" each of the two impostors states confidently: "My name is Manny Balestrero." But Manny's declaration of his identity is less assertive. He blinks repeatedly and his voice trails off with "Balestrero."

To Tell the Truth's exercise in irony continues as Collyer explains to the panel that only one of the three men standing before them is "the real Manny Balestrero" while the other two "have assumed his identity in an attempt to fool our panel, our cross-examiners."

Collyer reads an "affidavit" describing pertinent details of Manny's case. The celebrities then pose a series of questions to test the contestants, such as (1) Where were you living in January 1953? and (2) How many members were in your orchestra?

In a surreal callback to the eyewitness lineup at the 110th Precinct, the celebrities refer to each of the three men by his number. Manny is Number Three. During the lineup, he was Number Four.

The panelists probe the men's knowledge of the details of Manny's experience. Van Dyke jokes that "this is worse than a police grilling."

Perhaps Manny had flashbacks to the stress of the real interrogation. When asked where people first confused him with the armed robber, he makes a mistake and doesn't mention the insurance office. "I was visiting my mother," he tells Bergen instead.

After the questioning ends, two of the four celebrities—Van Dyke and Bergen—correctly identify Manny. Parks and Swayze choose Number One, a square dance caller.

The reveal of the real Manny sets off a jubilant reaction. A giddy Van Dyke triumphantly clasps his hands. But then Bergen notes her confusion over Manny's answer about where he was first misidentified. As she points out the discrepancy, Manny nods nervously.

Collyer wraps up the segment with a serious question to Manny: "Have you learned anything specifically out of this experience?"

Manny pauses. Then, in a show of grace, he alludes not to those who made his life a nightmare, but to those who stood by him.

"People have been so wonderful to us," Manny says.

Collyer congratulates him for the "wonderful future ahead of you now." The implicit message to the audience is that Manny and Rose have put their trauma behind them. They will live happily after.

***

While television promised a blissful future for Hitchcock's real-life protagonist, the director was not ready to move on from some of the darker elements of *The Wrong Man*. He continued to explore themes of guilt and innocence, mistaken identity, and the law's inability to see truth. In fact, in his next film, his protagonist becomes the ultimate unreliable eyewitness.

In *Vertigo* (1958), Scottie Ferguson (James Stewart), a retired detective, is hired by an old college friend, Gavin Elster (Tom Helmore), to follow his possibly suicidal wife, Madeleine (Kim Novak). After falling in love with Madeleine, Scottie witnesses her appear to leap to her death from a church tower. We later learn that Scottie has been set up: the woman he was shadowing was not Elster's wife, and the apparent suicide was in fact a murder.

Vertigo riffs on the Hitchcock scenario in which police falsely accuse the protagonist. Here the lead character is an ex-cop who cannot distinguish fact from fiction, criminal from victim. At a coroner's inquest, his eyewitness account leads to the false verdict sought by the murderer: death by suicide.

In an interview, Hitchcock endorsed Peter Bogdanovich's observation that *Vertigo* is the director's "ultimate statement on illusion versus reality." This theme applies to the representation of law in the film. As embodied by the coroner, the law is duped by the same illusion that ensnared Scottie. This makes it all the more ironic when the coroner smugly condemns Scottie for failing to act to prevent the woman's death.

Two years later, Hitchcock revisited the devastating effect of false accusations in an installment of the *Startime* television series titled "Incident at a Corner," adapted by Charlotte Armstrong from her own novel. The program reteamed Hitchcock with Vera Miles, who stars as Jean, a woman whose grandfather, James Medwick, comes under false suspicion of pedophilia.

An anonymous note addressed to the PTA president accuses Medwick, a school crossing guard, of being a "vicious old man." The note warns that "you'd better get him away from the kids, especially the little girls."

In a disturbing rush to judgment, the local police chief, Taylor, discharges the "unpleasant duty" of firing Medwick. "I've had a complaint that you're a little—a little too fond of the kids, of the little girls," Taylor says. When Medwick protests his innocence, the chief tells him that "whether I believe it has nothing to do with it." Without investigation or evidence, the police treat the complaint as presumptively valid.

Jean and her fiancée, Pat (George Peppard), take up the cause of Medwick's innocence. The school principal tells them that two mothers "more or less" corroborated the accusation. Jean and Pat soon learn, though, that one girl merely said that Medwick once touched her hair (which the crossing guard may have done in helping her avoid an oncoming car). The other girl told her mother only that she "disliked" Medwick.

As Jean and Pat conduct their investigation, "Incident at a Corner" is weighted down by some clunky dialogue (when the principal warns that "any breath of this sort of thing is intolerable," Pat responds, "So is injustice") and heavy-handed symbolism (a portrait of George Washington stares knowingly at the principal). But it still packs a punch. Just as unsettling as the town's rush to judgment is the way Medwick's son urges him to accept the dismissal as a form of retirement.

In a surprising turn, Jean and Pat too succumb to the hysteria incited by the allegations. Based on circumstantial evidence, they twice rush to the wrong conclusion about who wrote the accusatory note. In the closing moments, as the characters storm from one house to another in search of the wrongdoer, they appear to be in the grip of mob mentality.

"Incident at a Corner" now plays as a prescient warning against allowing the law to be the instrument of false accusation. Its premise anticipates the notorious McMartin case of the early 1980s, when the operators of a Los Angeles day care center were arrested and accused of child molestation. The case sprung from a Manhattan Beach woman's allegation that an employee at the center had molested her son. Police subsequently sent a letter to two hundred families seeking help with the investigation and arranged for therapists to interview the children. As a result of the interviews—which were later condemned for their use of "leading and suggestive" questions—seven employees of the day care center were arrested. But the district attorney ultimately dropped the charges against five of them because the evidence was "incredibly weak." Authorities later conceded that they had made virtually no independent investigation before the arrests and instead relied almost exclusively on the therapists' "findings." The remaining two defendants were eventually tried twice but never convicted (the first trial ended in a partial acquittal and hung jury, and the second one ended in a mistrial).

***

When "Incident at a Corner" aired, Hitchcock was only five months away from the release of *Psycho*, which would become the director's biggest commercial hit. The movie that held that distinction in April 1960 was *North by Northwest*, a mistaken identity adventure starring Cary Grant. The film was still playing in theaters some thirty-nine weeks after its release in July 1959.

North by Northwest marked the apex of the cinematic escapism associated with Hitchcock. As screenwriter Ernest Lehman described the film at its inception, it was to be "a Hitchcock picture to end all Hitchcock pictures . . . a movie-movie - with glamour, wit, excitement, movement, big scenes, a larger canvas, innocent bystander caught up in great derring-do, in the *Hitchcock* manner."

Like Manny Balestrero, Roger Thornhill (Grant) is falsely suspected of a crime— the murder of a man at the United Nations. Thornhill is framed for the murder after foreign agents mistakenly conclude he is an American spy. The tone is light, and the wrong man plot operates in service of humor and thrills. As Thornhill crosses the country while evading both spies and the police, Hitchcock delivers several exciting set pieces, including a climax that takes place atop Mount Rushmore. The director likened the film to *The 39 Steps* and described it as "a fantasy."

North by Northwest raked in some $6 million at the box office, more than four times the take of *The Wrong Man*.

Hitchcock returned to the issue of eyewitness testimony in 1962 when he directed "I Saw the Whole Thing" for *The Alfred Hitchcock Hour*. As professor Nicholas Haeffner has suggested, the program is an intriguing reference point for *The Wrong Man*.

At the outset, Hitchcock shows us five people near the scene of a collision between a motorcycle and a sports car. Although most of them are not looking in the direction of the accident, all will later claim to have seen "the whole thing" and offer a definitive account of what happened.

After the accident, the sports car speeds away from the scene. The next morning, a crime writer named Michael Barnes (John Forsythe) turns himself in. He is charged with hit-and-run and passing a stop sign.

Barnes tells a lawyer friend that his wife is in labor and that he surrendered to police after driving her to the hospital. Acknowledging that he "lost his head" by leaving the scene, Barnes insists he stopped at the stop sign and expresses dismay that five eyewitnesses will swear to the contrary. His friend replies: "I'm not a criminal lawyer, but I've been around enough courtrooms to know that an eyewitness can be the weirdest animal in the zoo."

At trial, Barnes shows that the eyewitnesses were either preoccupied with other things at the time of the accident or had prejudices influencing their account. He is acquitted when a new witness surfaces and supports his story.

In a last-act twist, Barnes confides to his friend that he was not even in the sports car that collided with the motorcycle. The person driving was his wife, whose involvement Barnes concealed. The eyewitnesses had not only inaccurately described the accident, but also misidentified the driver.

"I Saw the Whole Thing" resonates as a statement about the false confidence that people have in their ability to perceive and recall events and their readiness to swear under oath to details that, in reality, eluded their observation.

In summing up the program, Hitchcock expressed a view that neither the police nor the courts were ready to accept.

"It's about the complete fallibility of witnesses," Hitchcock said.

—CONCLUSION—

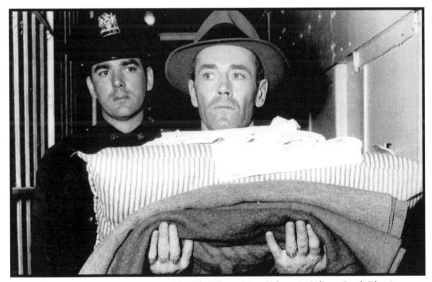

An innocent man imprisoned in *The Wrong Man* (*Photo 12/Alamy Stock Photo*)

In 2016, the podcast *Filmspotting* devoted its sixth hundredth episode to a discussion of the "Top 5 Movies Future Historians Will Remember." On that show, culture critic Chuck Klosterman predicted that one type of film that will endure is the adaptation of a significant historical event, where "anybody wanting to understand it or get a sense of it will actually go to the film interpretation of it as the main text for its memory." Klosterman cited *Titanic* as an example and speculated that in the future schools may show children the film to explain the 1912 maritime disaster.

Unlike *Titanic*, *The Wrong Man* is relatively obscure; even many Hitchcock fans have never seen it. Still, the film fits Klosterman's criteria, since it has become the main text for the memory of the Balestrero case. In fact, since its release in 1956, it has defined Manny and Rose in the public's consciousness.

But *The Wrong Man* has broader claims to make for the attention of current and future audiences. It roots the universal theme of false accusation in the details of one family's experience. It exposes the disturbing mob mentality that has doomed many suspects. It shows how authorities can be too credulous about eyewitness identifications and too quick to presume guilt. And it reveals that law enforcement routines can be just as destructive of innocent lives as corruption.

In telling Manny's story, *The Wrong Man* testifies to the experience of multiple generations of criminal defendants who became victims of a flawed justice system—a story that New York's legal institutions effectively suppressed. We can get a much better sense of what led to wrongful convictions from Hitchcock than from the New York State Judicial Council's 1948 study on erroneous identification.

At the same time, *The Wrong Man* was groundbreaking in its depiction of the spiral of devastation that comes with false arrest. Its haunting depiction of Rose's ordeal shows that the prospect of wrongful incarceration imperils not just the defendant, but their loved ones. Hitchcock paid serious attention to the family trauma even as the court system resisted recognizing it.

The issues depicted in *The Wrong Man* are just as timely today as they were sixty-five years ago. Perhaps even more so.

Since 1989, 375 people have been exonerated by DNA testing. Almost 70 percent of those cases involved at least one eyewitness misidentification. And according to the National Registry of Exonerations, which reports on both DNA and non-DNA cases, there have been more than 3,000 exonerations over the past thirty-two years. These cases have shattered the old judicial myth that wrongful convictions are an "unreal dream" and that the innocent have nothing to fear.

Even so, the criminal justice system has been slow to respond.

Hitchcock wrestled with eyewitness misidentification more than a decade before the Supreme Court. It was not until 1967 that the court first recognized that suggestiveness in police procedures was "a major factor contributing to the high incidence of miscarriage of justice in mistaken identification." In United States v. Wade, the court held that defendants have the right to counsel at postindictment lineup proceedings. In so doing, Justice William J. Brennan Jr. cited many suggestive practices, including the use of lineup fillers known to the identifying witness; the selection of fillers who were "grossly dissimilar in appearance to the suspect"; the requirement that the suspect wear "distinctive clothing"; and the showing of the witness alone to the suspect. All these elements infected Manny's case.

Less than two years later, the Supreme Court ruled that a suggestive procedure may be so prone to inducing a mistaken identification that it violates the suspect's right to due process of law. In Foster v. California (1969), the police first placed a suspect in a lineup with two men who were at least six inches shorter and made the suspect don a leather jacket similar to one worn by the culprit. Even then, the witness did not make a positive identification until after a separate, one-on-one confrontation with the suspect, followed by a second lineup with different fillers. The court recognized that these procedures fatally compromised the identification because the police effectively told the witness, "This is the man"—a point that Hitchcock had made in the showup sequences in *The Wrong Man* twelve years earlier.

In the wake of these rulings, an abundance of social science research highlighted what Hitchcock had called "the complete fallibility" of eyewitnesses. Thousands of studies have been published on eyewitness identifications since the 1970s. Supreme Court Justice Sonia Sotomayor has summarized the research this way:

> *Study after study demonstrates that eyewitness recollections are highly susceptible to distortion by postevent information or social cues; that jurors routinely overestimate the accuracy of eyewitness identifications; that jurors place the greatest weight on eyewitness confidence in assessing identifications even though confidence is a poor gauge of accuracy; and that suggestiveness can stem from sources beyond police-orchestrated procedures.*

In referencing the effect of eyewitness testimony on juries, Justice Sotomayor echoed an observation that had been endorsed by Justice Brennan about thirty years earlier: "'All the evidence points rather strikingly to the conclusion that there is almost nothing more convincing than a live human being who takes the stand, points a finger at the defendant, and says 'That's the one!'"

All the scientific research spurred cries for improved procedures. But the adoption of reforms has been, in the words of law professor Keith Findley, "spotty at best." It was not until the US Department of Justice issued eyewitness identification guidelines in 1999 that states began to follow suit. Even then, as recently as 2013 only seven states had adopted uniform eyewitness procedures to reduce erroneous identifications.

In New York, no statewide recommendations were in place until 2010, when the district attorneys association published "best practice guidelines for photo identifications and live lineups." Then, in 2017, New York passed two significant laws on eyewitness identification. The first overrode a longstanding rule prohibiting evidence of photo-based identifications at trial. The law now allows such evidence as long as a "blind or blinded procedure" was used—meaning that the person administering the procedure either did not know the identity of the suspect or did not know where the suspect's photo appears in the array viewed by the witness. This requirement ensures that the administrator cannot influence the witness (even if unintentionally) to pick the suspect's photo. The Innocence Project has described blind administration as "arguably the single most important reform."

The second law mandated the establishment of protocols for the conduct and recording of all identification procedures. In response, the Division of Criminal Justice Services issued guidelines aimed at avoiding undue suggestiveness in lineups, including the following best practices (none of which were used in Manny's case):

- lineups should include at least five fillers who are similar in appearance to the suspect with respect to "gender, clothing, facial hair, race, age, height, extraordinary physical features, or other distinctive characteristics";
- the administrator of a lineup should not use a filler who is known to the witness;

- the administrator should not know who the suspect is (although for live lineups this applies only "where practicable");
- witnesses must view the lineup separately and should not speak with each other during the identification process;
- the procedure should be documented, and "where practicable" and if the witness has consented, there should be an audio or video recording;
- photographs should be taken to preserve the lineup; and
- the witness's statement about their level of confidence or certainty of any identification made should be documented verbatim (known as a "confidence statement").

The division issued similar guidelines for photo arrays.

New York's model protocols have an inherent limitation: they are not binding on prosecutors or police as a matter of law. Instead, the minimum requirements for fairness in identification procedures are set by federal and state courts. Cases decided by the US Supreme Court continue to recognize a constitutional right, as a matter of due process, to challenge suggestive police procedures. But the test for excluding an eyewitness identification is hard to meet. The defendant must establish that police-orchestrated suggestiveness creates a "very substantial likelihood of irreparable misidentification." And even if the procedure was suggestive, the court should still permit the evidence if it finds that the identification is sufficiently reliable overall ("based on the totality of the circumstances"). In 2012, the Supreme Court summed up the law this way: "If the indicia of reliability are strong enough to outweigh the corrupting effect of the police-arranged suggestive circumstances, the identification evidence will ordinarily be admitted, and the jury will determine its worth."

In applying this rule, the Supreme Court has repeatedly rejected challenges to suggestive identification procedures. The only time the court ruled that such a procedure violated due process was in 1969, when it decided the Foster case.

While Supreme Court rulings establish baseline due process guarantees for suspects, some state courts have provided for greater protections. In New York, for example, a pretrial identification is inadmissible when it gives rise to "a substantial likelihood that the defendant would be singled out for identification"—whether or not there are other indications that the identification was reliable.

But even in New York, a suspect who has not been arrested or charged has no right to counsel at a police identification procedure. New York largely follows the federal rule that a suspect's indelible right to counsel does not apply until a formal criminal action has been initiated. While in New York the right may also be triggered by "significant judicial activity" before the commencement of a criminal action, there is no general right to have a lawyer at an investigatory lineup. This legal doctrine ignores the reality that suggestiveness in the initial display of a suspect, before an arrest, creates a great risk of misidentification—a risk underlined by research showing that once a witness makes an identification, their confidence in its accuracy grows over time.

Courts have also continued to permit showups despite the inherent suggestiveness of the procedure. In Stovall v. Denno (1967), the Supreme Court upheld a showup where police brought a murder suspect in handcuffs to the hospital room of a victim, who then made an identification. While acknowledging that showups have been "widely condemned," the court excused the procedure on the ground that it was "imperative" given the victim's medical condition.

In New York, the Court of Appeals has excluded evidence of precinct showups on the ground that they are tainted by "unreliability of the most extreme kind." Still, showups are permitted where the suspect is displayed at or near the crime scene shortly after the crime occurs or where there is an urgent need to secure the identification. In a July 2020 ruling, a New York appellate court upheld a showup identification as "reasonable and not unduly suggestive" where the suspect was illuminated by a spotlight and standing near a police car "with his hands cuffed behind his back."

Authorities across the country continue to use showups. Although police guidelines often limit showups to the immediate aftermath of the crime, a 2013 survey found that many agencies lacked clear policies on when the procedure is permitted.

***

As a result of a campaign spearheaded by the Innocence Project, police identification practices have improved in recent years. As of this writing, about half the states have adopted uniform eyewitness procedures to reduce erroneous identifications. Reforms have found support among some police groups, prosecutors, and judges.

State officials have also belatedly recognized the need to investigate claims of errors and misconduct. That more honest mindset has informed the creation of conviction integrity units across the country, including in Queens. The resulting case reexaminations confirm the persistence of the causes of wrongful conviction.

As one recent example, in 2020, the Queens DA joined in a motion to vacate the conviction of Samuel Brownridge, a man imprisoned for a deadly shooting some twenty-five years earlier. The Brownridge case has echoes of the mistaken identity cases described in Part One of this book.

In 1994, police identified Brownridge, who was then eighteen, as a suspect after an eyewitness said he saw a man nicknamed Mookie fleeing the crime scene. A detective knew Brownridge by that nickname from an unrelated matter. As a result, police put Brownridge in both a photo array and a lineup. Two eyewitnesses identified him as the shooter.

Although no forensic evidence linked Brownridge to the crime, a jury convicted him based on the eyewitness testimony. But prosecutors did not disclose that one of the witnesses had first misidentified two other men, including one who looked nothing like Brownridge. The second eyewitness suffered from schizophrenia and, according to court records, lived "in a home with other mentally challenged people."

Brownridge was sentenced to twenty-five years to life. On appeal, the Appellate Division characterized the evidence of his guilt as "overwhelming."

While Brownridge was in prison, another man confessed his involvement in the fight that led to the murder and identified someone else as the shooter. But the man refused to repeat his story in court, and Brownridge remained in prison.

Years later, with help from new lawyers, Brownridge asked the district attorney's office to reexamine the case. That reexamination was pending when Melinda Katz was elected as the new Queens County district attorney. Her newly-created Conviction Integrity Unit took up Brownridge's case and concluded he was innocent.

In June 2020, the Supreme Court for Queens County granted a joint motion to free Brownridge. The court cited the testimony of three men present at the shooting who agreed that Brownridge was innocent. But it also emphasized that the "deck had been unfairly stacked against him" because the jury never learned that the state's chief eyewitness had first misidentified as the shooter a man "who bore little resemblance to Brownridge."

"Everyone in the criminal justice system failed you in some way or another," Justice Joseph Zayas told Brownridge at the exoneration hearing.

In December 2021, the City of New York agreed to pay Brownridge thirteen million dollars to settle his claims for federal civil rights violations.

***

Another recent exoneration in Queens followed a finding that authorities wrongfully withheld exculpatory evidence about the lineup.

In February 2005, police identified Queens resident Julio Negron, then thirty-eight years old, as a suspect in a "road rage" shooting. Detectives put Negron in a lineup with fillers who were older and substantially heavier than he was and who were "clearly police officers." Of the five eyewitnesses who viewed the lineup, four failed to identify Negron. One of these witnesses told police she recognized the shooter from prior encounters and said Negron was not the man.

The only person to identify Negron was the victim of the shooting. At first he stopped short of a definitive identification and instead said, "I think it's him" and "I believe it's him." Then an assistant district attorney and two detectives met with the victim privately (and "off the record") for fifteen minutes. When the victim returned to view the lineup a second time, he declared that he was sure that Negron was the shooter. On the strength of this single identification, Negron was arrested, indicted, tried, and convicted of attempted murder and other charges.

In 2015, the Court of Appeals threw out Negron's conviction based on ineffective assistance of counsel and the prosecution's failure to disclose exculpatory evidence. Two years later, after the state moved to retry Negron, the Supreme Court for Queens County dismissed the indictment. The court found that prosecutors had wrongfully failed to advise the grand jury about the state's identification procedures: "Where the defendant was identified by only one person, and where that identification was initially equivocal and only changed after the extremely unusual circumstance of a mid-lineup, closed-door meeting, and there was such a plethora of exculpatory evidence, fundamental fairness required that the Grand Jury be given an opportunity to evaluate all of the exculpatory identification evidence."

By the time the indictment was dismissed, Negron had served ten years in prison. He subsequently sued the City of New York for federal civil rights violations. In November 2021, the city agreed to settle the suit with a payment of $6.25 million.

***

While the Negron case involved the manipulation of a lineup proceeding, the recent exoneration of Anthony Miller confirms that showups remain a threat to innocent suspects—even when used within the recognized exception for an immediate crime-scene confrontation with the victim.

At eight o'clock on the night of September 25, 2013, a man accosted a twenty-six-year-old Rochester resident outside his home. The man put a gun to the victim's head and robbed him of his iPhone, cigarettes, and ten dollars in cash. On a 911 call, the victim described the perpetrator as Black, about five feet, nine inches tall and wearing a gray hoodie and blue jeans. The victim told police that a second man, riding a bicycle, was on hand and rode off in the same direction as the gunman.

After hearing the report on a police dispatch, Rochester police came upon two men standing in a driveway about a half mile from the crime scene. One of them was Anthony Miller, a twenty-one-year-old Black man. Miller was five feet, five inches tall and wore a red hoodie and black pants.

Police brought Miller and his companion to the scene of the robbery for a showup. The victim identified Miller as the perpetrator and his companion as the man on the bicycle.

Based solely on the eyewitness identification, police arrested Miller. That night, police searched his companion's home but found no evidence linking either man to the crime. Two days after the arrest, with Miller in jail, the police used GPS tracking technology to determine that the stolen iPhone was at a location in Rochester where about thirty people were on hand. The group dispersed when police activated the phone's alarm, and the phone was not recovered.

At a pretrial suppression hearing, the trial judge upheld the showup identification and declared that he would not "dissect the miniscule, little things" that occurred during the police investigation. In November 2014, a jury convicted Miller of first-degree robbery. The court sentenced him to ten years in prison.

Six years later, after Miller had filed multiple postconviction motions, the Appellate Division exonerated him. The court relied on the suggestiveness of the showup and noted that "the reliability of an identification is affected where, as here, a gun is displayed, there is a high level of stress, the incident is brief, and the lighting is dim." More than that, there was "considerable objective evidence supporting defendant's innocence." Police had found Miller seven minutes after the crime. He was standing in a driveway half a mile from the crime scene and wearing clothes that did not match the victim's description of the culprit. He had neither a gun nor the stolen items. And the subsequent GPS search determined that someone other than Miller had the victim's iPhone.

Anthony Miller went free. But he had spent more than six years in prison.

***

Recent exonerations have also highlighted the need to ensure that police make a complete record of an eyewitness's initial identification and confidence statement. This is especially critical because research shows that an eyewitness's initial statements upon seeing a suspect are far more accurate than statements made at later viewings.

While that may sound intuitive, the judicial system continues to permit and even encourage courtroom identifications, which are invariably uttered with extreme but often misleading confidence.

In a 2021 article, a team of experts—John Wixted, Gary Wells, Elizabeth Loftus, and Brandon Garrett—show that repeating identification procedures with the same witness and suspect creates an escalating risk of error. The authors note that "by the time of trial, an eyewitness's memory has almost invariably been contaminated by a variety of factors and is therefore highly error prone." Many false convictions can be traced to an eyewitness who at the initial procedure either (1) identified the defendant with low confidence, (2) identified someone other than the defendant, or (3) made no identification at all. At trial in these cases, the same eyewitness positively identified the defendant as the culprit.

The social science research also points to a glaring limitation of judicial rules on eyewitness identification. The Supreme Court has refused to recognize a constitutional right to counsel when police subject a person to an identification procedure before an indictment. The rationale for this rule is that the right to counsel attaches only after the "initiation of adversary judicial criminal proceedings." But in the real world, the initial confrontation between the eyewitness and the suspect may determine the latter's fate. The damning phrases "that's the man" and "that's the woman" have the power to destroy even when first uttered before an arrest has been made.

***

When seen in light of all the exonerations that have occurred since 1989, *The Wrong Man*'s timeless power reasserts itself. The film insists that an innocent person's fate must not be decided by mere accusations. While the Balestreros were victims of mistaken identification, authorities bore as much responsibility for the tragedy as the complaining witnesses. Only by reckoning with its role in such cases can the state fulfill the ideal that the protection of the innocent is as sacred a duty as the prosecution of the guilty.

—EPILOGUE—

The New York State Supreme Court building, as seen in 2021 (*Photo by Rich Dubin*)

The stories of the principal players in the Balestrero case of course did not end with Manny's exoneration. Some took unexpected turns.

The Prosecutor: Frank J. Crisona

While *The Wrong Man* made Manny Balestrero into an icon of innocent suffering, the man who prosecuted him, Queens Assistant District Attorney Frank Crisona, experienced a stunning fall from grace. In a strange twist of fate, it was Crisona, not Manny, who wound up in prison.

Crisona served as an assistant district attorney in Queens until 1958. He then worked as a law secretary to his brother, James J. Crisona, who was a justice on the New York Supreme Court from 1959 to 1976.

But in 1968—some fifteen years after Manny's mistrial—Crisona was convicted of mail and wire fraud in connection with a mortgage swindling scheme. Crisona's downfall grew out of his association with John Martin Neiman, described by prosecutors as "a professional confidence man with a long criminal record." In October 1964, Crisona and Neiman made a failed attempt to save a summer camp in which Crisona had invested. In the wake of that failure, Crisona owed $15,000 to a loan shark. That debt led to a scheme engineered by Crisona, Neiman, and several other defendants to use a foreign corporation as a front for the issuance of bogus real estate financing commitments. The defendants obtained advance fees from various individuals and corporations in return for promised loans that would never materialize. As part of the scheme, Crisona represented that he would hold the advances in escrow pending the financing. In reality, the advances were doled out among the defendants. While Crisona testified at trial that he had been misled by the con man Neiman, the jury found otherwise.

It's not hard to find irony in the conviction of the man who prosecuted "the wrong man." Crisona had falsely claimed in his opening statement that Manny was "in trouble with the bookies." That made it all the more ironic that Crisona's criminal scheme grew out of *his* indebtedness to a loan shark. If that isn't enough, one of Crisona's codefendants argued unsuccessfully on appeal that there were "improper" juror discussions during the trial, including an alleged ladies' room exchange during which one juror said, "He's guilty," and another responded, "If you ask me, they're all guilty." The implication of prejudgment, while ultimately found to be unsupported by the trial judge, calls to mind the behavior of Lloyd Espenschied at Manny's trial.

Crisona was sentenced to three years in prison. As a result, the New York Appellate Division for the Second Department—the same court that ruled against Manny in his dispute with Prudential—disbarred Crisona. The court noted that Crisona's "participation in the crimes was active and knowing" and that he "knowingly gave false testimony to the Grand Jury."

Crisona was indicted again in 1977 for bribery and conspiracy to sell stolen stock certificates. The indictment accused Crisona of sending the certificates, which had been stolen from the Morgan Guaranty Trust Company, to Italy. In March 1979, Crisona pleaded guilty to the conspiracy charges and received a two-year sentence.

Crisona's crimes further upended the narrative that he was a fine officer of the law just doing his duty in prosecuting Manny.

***

The Detective: Leigh Wilson

Leigh Wilson was a living reminder of a past that Manny Balestrero wished to forget. Along with Detective Matthew Herberich, Wilson was one of the arresting officers.

In a coincidence fraught with symbolism, Wilson retired to the Miami area. By February 1957, he was living in West Hollywood, near a hotel where Balestrero was playing in a band.

After working as a private investigator, Wilson served as the police chief in Melbourne Beach for six years and then as sheriff of Brevard County, Florida, from

1963 to 1977.

In 1973, in connection with a screening of *The Wrong Man*, a newspaper in Cocoa, Florida, ran a feature on Wilson's link to the film. Wilson, whose cinematic counterpart is Detective Matthews, said he'd seen the film "a half dozen times" and concluded "it was the wrong movie." He criticized as inaccurate the scenes showing Manny parading by himself before local proprietors who had been robbed. "I always walked in with him," Wilson said, apparently blind to the point that either way the procedure was inherently suggestive.

In what now seems like a supremely candid remark, Wilson said there was nothing special about the Balestrero case.

"We treated it as an ordinary case. That's all it was," he said.

Wilson died in 1994 at the age of eighty-five; the lede of his obituary described him as a man "who tackled small-town crime with a big-city toughness."

***

The Right Man: Charles Daniell

When Charles Daniell was arrested in April 1953, newspaper coverage revealed only that he was an unemployed plastic molder whose weapon of choice was a toy pistol. The *Long Island Star-Journal* labeled him the Toy Gun Bandit.

An inmate case file obtained from the New York State Archives fills in many details about Daniell's life.

Born in 1914 in Northport, Long Island, he was orphaned by the age of eight. His father, Charles Sr., died of a "cardiac condition" at the age of thirty-three, when Daniell was only three, and his mother, Edith, died of cancer four years later, at the age of twenty-nine. Daniell lived with his grandparents on 168th Street in New York City.

Daniell left school in ninth grade and went to work as a file clerk for a cotton goods broker. In 1931, when he was seventeen, his grandfather turned him out of the house after an argument. Two years later, Daniell took a trip across the country. In 1933, he was arrested for vagrancy in Waco, Texas, and imprisoned for thirty days.

Returning to New York, he worked for several different plastic manufacturing companies before enlisting in the Army in 1941. He served for about five years, seeing action in North Africa and Italy.

In 1945, Daniell began a common law relationship with Jeanne Farra of Jackson Heights. Their home was only a mile and a half from the Balestreros'.

After the war, Daniell worked for different plastics companies and was a molder for Tech-Arts Plastics in Queens from 1950 to July 1952, when he was laid off for excessive absenteeism.

Heavily in debt, he turned to robbery apparently to support Farra and her son.

While Manny was under indictment, Daniell worked for several months at Lionel Plastic Company in Maspeth, Queens. His employment there ended on April 3, less than a month before his fateful holdup of Mank's Deli, which led to his arrest.

Having been sentenced to two concurrent prison terms, Daniell was first taken to Sing Sing on July 31, 1953. About a year later, he was transferred to Wallkill prison.

Daniell first became eligible for parole in October 1956. Before his parole hearing, Assistant District Attorney Thomas P. Cullen—the same prosecutor who had urged Manny to confess on the night of January 14, 1953—submitted a letter stating that "any action taken by the Parole Board will be satisfactory to this office." But the board considered Daniell a poor parole risk and deferred his next opportunity for another eighteen months.

Daniell was ultimately paroled in April 1958, after earlier findings that his "institutional adjustment has been most satisfactory in all respects" and that he was "highly regarded by his supervisors, as a quiet, serious-minded, ambitious worker."

After his parole, Daniell found a job as a molder in Queens. He later married and moved to Florida. Daniell died there, in Wilton Manors, on July 4, 1986.

***

The Defense Attorney: Frank O'Connor

Manny's lawyer, Frank O'Connor, had a distinguished political and jurisprudential career.

In November 1955, O'Connor was elected Queens district attorney after defeating the man whose office prosecuted Manny, T. Vincent Quinn, in the Democratic primary. O'Connor served as DA until 1966. But despite this opportunity for O'Connor to effect change from within, the DA's office continued to struggle with false arrest cases and problematic identification procedures.

During his tenure, O'Connor repeatedly requested the release of suspects who had been arrested based solely on eyewitness testimony. In November 1956, he acknowledged that mistaken identity had led to the false arrest of a Queens man for the mugging of a dancer. Several years later, O'Connor requested the release of a Queens man falsely arrested for a robbery committed by a man whom detectives called the suspect's "twin."

O'Connor left the DA's office in 1966 when he was elected president of the New York City Council. His next campaign, though, ended in defeat. In November of the same year, O'Connor lost a bid to become governor of New York to Republican Nelson Rockefeller. But that defeat paved the way for his ascendance to the bench in 1968. O'Connor served as a New York State Supreme Court justice until 1976, when Governor Hugh Carey appointed him to the Appellate Division. He remained an appellate judge until his retirement in 1986.

While on the Appellate Division, O'Connor helped free another "wrong man." In 1982, O'Connor wrote an opinion vacating the conviction of a Queens resident who had been convicted of sodomy and attempted murder. The defendant was Charles Daniels—a name with an uncanny similarity to that of Charles Daniell.

The state had prosecuted Daniels based on the testimony of a ten-year-old boy. At trial, the boy identified Daniels as the man who had dragged an infant across the roof of an adjacent three-story building and pushed the child off. A jury convicted Daniels despite the testimony of four alibi witnesses. On appeal, O'Connor found that the trial judge had issued flawed jury instructions on eyewitness identification by failing to specify the need to focus on the boy's accuracy given the varying descriptions he provided: "Bitter experience tells us . . . that the real issue is whether or not the witness is mistaken—however honest or truthful that mistake may be."

After O'Connor's ruling, the Queens district attorney dropped the charges based on new evidence that cast doubt on whether the baby had been thrown from a roof. Several years later, Daniels received $600,000 from the city in settlement of his claims for wrongful imprisonment.

The Daniels ruling reflected O'Connor's skepticism of the accuracy of eyewitness testimony; his reference to "bitter experience" with mistaken witnesses was an apparent callback to his defense of Manny.

O'Connor revisited Manny's case more explicitly in a 1974 article for the *St. John's Law Review*. O'Connor argued that defendants who face conviction based on eyewitness testimony should be able to use lie detector results if certain conditions are met. O'Connor argued that a polygraph might be the only tool that a defendant can use to counter the testimony of witnesses who swear to "positive identifications." To date, though, New York has declined to admit polygraph results in criminal cases.

O'Connor's tenure as Queen district attorney did not put an end to the identification procedures used against Manny. In fact, after O'Connor's departure, a prosecutor in that very office was subjected to similarly prejudicial procedures, with nearly calamitous results.

On the night of February 25, 1973, Queens Assistant District Attorney William G. Schrager left his home in Belle Harbor, Queens, to mail some letters. After observing his car idling near a mailbox, police pulled him over and determined that he fit the description of a man responsible for several sexual assaults. Schrager was brought to the precinct for viewing by the victims. In one lineup, the five-foot, four-inch Schrager stood among five husky police officers who were each at least four inches taller. Two of the officers wore their uniform pants. When two victims identified Schrager, the police arrested him without investigating his alibis. About a month later, Schrager was exonerated after police arrested a man they described as a "dead ringer" for the same crimes. The man, who soon confessed his guilt, was forty pounds heavier and, unlike Schrager, wore glasses. After the ordeal, Schrager said the eyewitnesses who misidentified him "were so intelligent and convincing that they almost made me believe I did it."

According to the National Registry of Exonerations, there have been forty-five exonerations in Queens since 1970. More than half of those cases involved at least one eyewitness misidentification.

The Balestreros

By early 1957, when *The Wrong Man* went into wide release, the Balestreros had been living in Miami for more than a year. Manny was playing in a band at the Lucerne Hotel. He had two main ambitions at the time: "To lead my own band and to forget."

Manny realized one of these ambitions. He successfully continued his career in Miami, playing for a popular Latin jazz band and other prominent show bands in Miami Beach. By the early 1970s, he had formed the Manny Balestrero Trio. A newspaper ad from May 1973 shows the trio performing at a Boca Raton country club.

Rose Balestrero never resolved her feelings of guilt over Manny's false arrest. "My mother felt that way because she felt if her teeth hadn't been the problem, that would have never happened," recalled Greg Balestrero.

Rose progressed with her recovery in Florida, with help from an internist. But, in Greg's words, "she was still fragile." She was also unable to discuss the arrest, or her resulting breakdown, with other family members. Even the children were instructed not to speak directly of the episode.

"There were so many guidelines about not talking about things that I was worried that if I slipped up or upset her, she would break down again and go away," Greg said. He confirmed that part of the family culture was to use euphemisms to avoid any direct reference to their ordeal, such as referring to the arrest as "the thing."

"Everything possible was done to keep us from talking about what happened, so there were code words for it, and 'the thing' was one of them," he said.

In a similar vein, Rose could never bring herself to watch *The Wrong Man*.

"She went to her grave not knowing what was in the film," Greg said.

Manny, on the other hand, saw the film in Miami after its release. Later in life, he embraced it as a form of vindication. In Manny's mind, the film helped erase any lingering stigma from his arrest. "It was proof positive that he was not guilty," Greg said.

Manny performed as a bass player into his seventies. By 1980, however, his eyesight had deteriorated severely, and he lost vision in one eye. While Manny could still play from memory, his eyesight problems prevented him from driving. He was ultimately forced to retire as a result.

Manny and Rose had their fiftieth wedding anniversary in August 1982. Four months later, Rose died in Jacksonville, Florida, at the age of seventy-two.

Manny passed away in North Carolina in 1998, at the age of eighty-eight. He was survived by his two sons, four grandchildren, and one great grandchild.

Greg Balestrero, a retired industrial engineer and project management expert now living in Florida, was only five when Manny was arrested. Greg had less of an understanding of the events that occurred in early 1953 than his older brother, Robert. But the experience disrupted both their childhoods.

"Up until they caught the guy, there was this danger that everybody would be ripped apart, that my mother would be in a mental home for the rest of her life, for that matter," Greg said.

Manny and other relatives tried to insulate Greg from any understanding of these threats.

"Because of my age, they coddled me a lot. They tried to protect me from it," he said. "But I do remember my mom getting sick, and then abruptly my mom was gone."

Robert, then twelve, was old enough to understand the threat hanging over the family.

"My brother . . . was more of a witness to what was going on," Greg said. "He took it harder . . . It was very public, and kids being kids sometimes gave him a harder time than they did me."

After the move to Miami, Greg resisted going to school because of a fear that his mother might be gone when he returned home. On the first day at his new school, Greg ran away and hid in the bushes outside the family's new home—just close enough to satisfy himself that Rose was there.

"I could hear her, and that reassured me," Greg recalled.

The emotional upheaval that Greg experienced in his early childhood stayed with him.

"What I was going through was a loss. I hated being away from my mother and my father. I mean, I really did. And that sense of loss stuck with me for a long time as an adult. The desire not to be away and be torn apart from family," he said.

In the New York area, the Balestrero name remains associated with the risk of false accusations and wrongful incarceration. In 2014, on the initiative of Queens Councilman Daniel Dromm, the intersection of Seventy-Third Street and Forty-First Avenue in Queens was renamed "Manny 'The Wrong Man' Balestrero Way." The Balestreros' former home at 41-30 Seventy-Third Street is just down the street from that intersection.

At a ceremony in September 2014, Dromm said he hoped that the sign bearing Manny's name would inspire people to investigate the history of Manny's case and "learn about their community, about cinematic history, and continue to think critically about how our justice system works."

Greg attended the ceremony with his brother. He wondered how many innocent people had suffered like his father and might deserve a sign of their own.

"My dad was only one guy, an Italian immigrant," Greg said. "He wasn't even profiled. He just had somebody pointing the finger and say, 'That was him.'"

Street sign honoring Manny Balestrero, as seen in 2021 (*Photo by Rich Dubin*)

—ACKNOWLEDGEMENTS—

In writing this book, I received invaluable assistance from many people.

Greg Balestrero was very kind and generous with his time. During two long interviews, he walked me through his family's history and reflected eloquently on his personal experience and the significance of Manny's case.

Author and editor Dawn Raffel read several early drafts and provided many excellent structural and substantive suggestions. I will be forever grateful to Dawn for both her insights and encouragement.

Liz Ohman, a senior research analyst at Hogan Lovells, was instrumental in obtaining archival prison records, old trial transcripts, and other obscure legal documents. The folks at the New York State Archives were very helpful with respect to these sources.

Melissa Flamson at With Permission did a tremendous job helping me secure the necessary licenses for the photos and find several very obscure images.

Genevieve Maxwell and Kristine Krueger of the Margaret Herrick Library, Academy of Motion Picture Arts and Sciences, provided wonderful support finding materials among the library's Alfred Hitchcock papers. So did Dr. Sandra Garcia-Myers and Billy Smith at the USC Cinematic Arts Library, who helped me access critical documents in *The Wrong Man* files there.

Thanks to Elizabeth Garver at the Harry Ransom Center at the University of Texas at Austin for providing such prompt and thorough assistance relating to materials in the Maxwell Anderson papers there.

Thanks to Christine Windheuser, a volunteer at the Smithsonian Institution's National Museum of American History Archives Center, for her excellent research assistance in reviewing the NMAH's Lloyd Espenschied papers.

For reviewing drafts along the way and sharing their insights, I thank my longtime law partner and friend Carl Chiappa, who provided many helpful and provocative comments; my brother, Stuart, with whom I've had a lifetime of engaging discussions about cinema; and my inspirational evidence and criminal procedure professor at Penn Law, the great David Rudovsky.

Thanks also to Caroline Teagle Johnson, for creating such a striking cover design; Rich Dubin, who took wonderful photos for the book in and around Jackson Heights and Manhattan; Daniel Berkowitz, for his excellent website design; and

Eric Rayman and Mona Houck for their astute and efficient advice as questions came up.

I'm grateful to David Bushman and Scott Ryan of FMP Publishing, for taking a chance on a first-time author. David's meticulous and incisive editing was indispensable, as was Scott's wonderful book design.

My daughter, Rachel, provided insightful comments on the manuscript and pitched in valuably with the notes and bibliography. Thanks also to my son, Danny, for providing much comic relief as I came down the home stretch.

Last but not least, my better half, Jen, was a constant source of inspiration and support during this project. She read many drafts, provided many excellent suggestions, and performed vital research, including on a whirlwind, last-minute trip to California. She also put aside her retired attorney status and rose to the Herculean task of reviewing the endnotes. Thank you for everything.

—NOTES—

Abbreviations (used in Notes and Bibliography)

AHPMHL = Alfred Hitchcock papers, Margaret Herrick Library, Academy of Motion Picture Arts and Sciences
GB Interview = Greg Balestrero, interviews by author, April 1, 2022, and April 8, 2022
MAPHRC = Maxwell Anderson Papers, Harry Ransom Humanities Research Center, The University of Texas at Austin
NYSA = New York State Archives
WBUSC = the Warner Bros. Archives at the USC School of Cinematic Arts

Epigraph

"behind that solid steel door": Herbert Brean, *A Case of Identity: The Balestrero Story*, Film Treatment (hereinafter "Brean Treatment"), June 29, 1955, *The Wrong Man*—Script, 1955, File 1005, AHPMHL, 19.
"my basic fears": R. Allen Leider, "Interview: Alfred Hitchcock (1978)," in *Hitchcock on Hitchcock, Volume 2: Selected Writings and Interviews*, 1st edition, ed. Sidney Gottlieb (Oakland: University of California Press, 2015), 257, 260.

Introduction

1	***Daily News* portrayed the guilty party**: Royal Riley, "Musician Learns He's Holdup Man's Double," *Daily News*, May 24, 1953, 3.
2	**"I use the 'wrong man' theme"**: Leider, "Interview: Alfred Hitchcock," 260.
2	**"everything was minutely reconstructed"**: François Truffaut, *Hitchcock* (Revised Edition) (New York: Simon & Schuster, 1985), 237.
2	**filmed many scenes on location**: Milton Esterow, "All Around the Town with 'The Wrong Man,'" *New York Times*, April 29, 1956, Section 2, 7.
3	**"the person who underwent this ordeal"**: Esterow, "All Around the Town," 7.
3	**Hitchcock cited two examples**: Truffaut, *Hitchcock*, 239.
3	**Rafter has pointed out**: Nicole Rafter, *Shots in the Mirror: Crime Films and Society*, 2d ed. (New York: Oxford University Press, 2006), 136.
3	**As Rafter observed**: Rafter, *Shots in the Mirror*, 136.
3	**only $1.2 million dollars**: John Billheimer, *Hitchcock and the Censors* (Lexington: The University Press of Kentucky, 2019), 314 (Table 1).
3	**In the headline . . . "viewer's spine tingle"**: A. H. Weiler, "A New Format for Hitchcock: Suspense Is Dropped in 'The Wrong Man,'" *New York Times*, December 24, 1956, 8.
3	***Los Angeles Times* similarly praised**: Philip K. Scheuer, "Hitchcock 'Wrong Man' Lifelike but Plodding," *Los Angeles Times*, January 24, 1957, 79.
4	***Time* magazine complained**: "Cinema: The New Pictures," *Time*, January 14, 1957.
4	**He fretted over . . . "sufficient dramatic license"**: Truffaut, *Hitchcock*, 240.
4	**Hitchcock expressed regret over:** "Interview with Alfred Hitchcock (1973)," in *Hitchcock on Hitchcock, Volume 2*, 149.
4	**"I don't feel that strongly about it"**: Truffaut, *Hitchcock*, 243.
4	***The New York Times* . . . mention the film**: Peter B. Flint, "Alfred Hitchcock Dies; A Master of Suspense," *New York Times*, April 30, 1980, A1, D32; Peter B. Flint, "Henry Fonda Dies on Coast at 77; Played 100 Stage and Screen Roles," *New York Times*, August 13, 1981, A1, A13. Each of these obituaries ran more than 2,000 words long. The *Times*'s obituary for Hitchcock mentioned "the wrong man" as a "favorite Hitchcock theme," but not the film bearing the theme's name.
4	**not among *The Essential 1,000 Films***: Manohla Dargis, A. O. Scott, and Wallace Schroeder, *The New York Times Book of Movies: The Essential 1,000 Films to See* (New York: Universal, 2019). According to the *Times* guide, the essential Hitchcock films are *The 39 Steps* (1935), *The Lady Vanishes* (1938), *Rebecca* (1940), *Suspicion* (1941), *Shadow of a Doubt* (1943), *Spellbound* (1945), *Notorious* (1946), *Strangers on a Train* (1951), *Dial M for Murder* (1954), *Rear Window* (1954), *To Catch a Thief* (1955), *The Trouble with Harry* (1955), *Vertigo* (1958), *North by Northwest* (1959), *Psycho* (1960), *The Birds* (1963), *Topaz* (1969), and *Frenzy* (1972).
4	**Thomson and Richard Schickel argued**: David Thomson, *The Big Screen: The Story of the Movies* (New York: Farrar, Straus and Giroux, 2012), 290 (describing *The Wrong Man* as a "somber, neglected warning of a film"); Richard Schickel, *Keepers: The Greatest Films—and Personal Favorites—of a Moviegoing Lifetime* (New York: Vintage Books, 2015), 200 ("*The Wrong Man* is a masterpiece that is essentially without compare in the body of his work").
4	**Kenny admires**: Glenn Kenny, "'The Wrong Man': Hitchcock's Least 'Fun' Movie Is Also One of His Greatest," *RogerEbert.com*, February 17, 2016, accessed May 7, 2022.
4	**Tobias sees it as**: Scott Tobias, "Wrong Man Movies in Honor of Hitchcock (1 of 4): *The Wrong Man*," *The A.V. Club* website, November 19, 2012, accessed May 7, 2022.

4   ***Filmspotting* podcast devoted an episode**: Adam Kempenaar and Josh Larsen, "Blindspotting: *The Wrong Man*," *Filmspotting* podcast, December 2, 2015.

4   **cited the film's camerawork and mood**: Roger Ebert, "Scorsese Learns from Those Who Went Before Him," *Chicago Sun-Times*, January 11, 1998, reprinted in Roger Ebert, *Scorsese by Ebert* (University of Chicago Press, 2008), 218-219.

4   **"over and over again"**: Scorsese made this statement in director Kent Jones's 2015 documentary, *Hitchcock/Truffaut*, which contains an excellent segment on *The Wrong Man*. *Hitchcock/Truffaut*, directed by Kent Jones, Dogwoof, 2016, DVD.

4   **"the sense of guilt and paranoia"**: Ebert, "Scorsese Learns," 219.

4   **in a short film . . . closing behind Manny**: "Martin Scorsese Reveals Lockdown 'Anxiety' and 'Relief,'" *BBC News* website, May 28, 2020, accessed May 1, 2022.

4   **It failed to make . . . *Kramer vs. Kramer*** (1979): "AFI'S 10 Top 10, The 10 Greatest Movies in 10 Categories," *American Film Institute* website, accessed May 1, 2022. As defined by AFI, "courtroom drama" refers to "a genre of film in which a system of justice plays a critical role in the film's narrative."

5   **American Bar Association's 2018 list . . . twenty-five honorable mentions**: Kevin Davis, "The 25 Greatest Legal Movies," *ABA Journal*, August 1, 2018, 38-43; Kevin Davis, "25 More Great Movies: Honorable Mentions," *ABA Journal*, August 1, 2018, 45.

5   **commentary from legal scholars**: Several professors have discussed *The Wrong Man* in writings on broader topics. Norman Rosenberg situates the film among several that use Henry Fonda's screen persona to explore the role of criminal defense attorneys. See Norman L. Rosenberg, "Constitutional History and the 'Cultural Turn': Cross-Examining the Legal-Reelist Narratives of Henry Fonda," in *Constitutionalism and American Culture: Writing the New American History*, eds. Sandra F. VanBurkleo, Kermit L. Hall, and Robert J. Kaczorowski, (Lawrence: University Press of Kansas, 2002), 381-409. More recently, Stanford University Law Professor Norman Spaulding discusses Hitchcock's depiction of juror misconduct as an example of how legal films represent "disorder." Norman W. Spaulding, "Disorder in the Court: Representations of Resistance to Law in Trial Film Dramas," in *Trial Films on Trial: Law, Justice, and Popular Culture*, eds. Austin Sarat, Jessica Silbey, and Martha Merrill Umphrey (Tuscaloosa: University of Alabama Press, 2019), 111-139. See also Allen K. Rostron, "Lawyers, Law, & the Movies: The Hitchcock Cases," 86 *California Law Review* 211 (1998) (discussing *The Wrong Man* and two other Hitchcock films in the context of a review of two books on legal themes in cinema).

5   **"the most famous penal martyr"**: Edward J. Mowery, "Dewey Orders Parole Board Inquiry into Campbell Case," *New York World-Telegram*, July 27, 1945, 1, 4.

5   **"There has been a wrong"**: Jerome Frank and Barbara Frank, *Not Guilty* (Garden City: Doubleday, 1957), 134.

5   **"tried in accordance" . . . "the result of mistaken identity"**: Campbell v. State, 62 N.Y.S.2d 638, 642 (Ct. Cl. 1946).

5   **Supreme Court justice called the case "disturbing"**: Pennekamp v. Florida, 328 U.S. 331, 357 n.6 (1946) (Frankfurter, J., concurring). Justice Felix Frankfurter cited Campbell's wrongful conviction in support of the point that the misuse of the "machinery" of justice "may deprive the individual of all that makes a free man's life dear."

6   **"It is not believed"**: *Fourteenth Annual Report of the Judicial Council of the State of New York*, 1948 ("Council Report"), 233, 234.

7   **American courts continued . . . "an unreal dream"**: U.S. v. Garsson, 291 F. 646, 649 (S.D.N.Y. 1923) ("Our procedure has been always haunted by the ghost of the innocent man convicted. It is an unreal dream"); U.S. v. Peltz, 18 F.R.D. 394, 406-407 (S.D.N.Y. 1955) (quoting Garsson).

7   **"filter all evidence in a case"**: Keith A. Findley and Michael S. Scott, "The Multiple Dimensions of Tunnel Vision in Criminal Cases," 2006 *Wisconsin Law Review* 291, 292 (2006).

7   **innocence movement that emerged**: See, e.g., Marvin Zalman, "An Integrated Justice Model of Wrongful Convictions," 74 *Albany Law Review* 1465, 1468-69 (2010) (overview of innocence movement).

7   **Innocence Project reports . . . erroneous eyewitness identification**: Innocence Project, "DNA Exonerations in the United States," Innocence Project Website, accessed May 1, 2022.

8   **"today, with the advance of forensic DNA"**: McKithen v. Brown, 481 F.3d 89, 92 (2d Cir. 2007).

8   **In 2020, the Queens district attorney . . . testimony against them**: Troy Closson, "Queens Prosecutors Long Overlooked Misconduct. Can a New D.A. Do Better?" *New York Times*, January 28, 2021, Section A, 1.

Chapter One: Prisoner 95111

10   The primary sources for this chapter are in files obtained from the New York State Archives relating to Campbell's pardon application in 1945: Bertram Campbell, Executive Clemency and Pardon Case File, NYSA, Files A0597-78-B054-F04, -F05, -F06, and -F21. Included within these files are (1) the trial transcript in People vs. Bertram M. Campbell ("Campbell Transcript"); (2) "Application for a Pardon Report: Bertram M. Campbell N-16544," State of New York Executive Department, Division of Parole, August 2, 1945 ("Campbell Parole Board Report"); and (3) the August 20, 1945, letter from Parole Board Chairman Frederick A. Moran to Governor Thomas E. Dewey, transmitting the Campbell Parole Board Report (the "Parole Board Transmittal Letter"). Another important source for this chapter is *Not Guilty*, which was written by Judge Jerome Frank of the US Court of Appeals for the Second Circuit and his daughter, Barbara. *Not Guilty* discusses the Campbell case and thirty-five other wrongful convictions, including many arising from eyewitness errors. The book was published shortly after Judge Frank's death in 1957.

10   **At 10:32 that night**: Hanson W. Baldwin, "Night Air 'Raid' Awes Long Island; Crowds Watched in 'Blacked' Area," *New York Times*, May 17, 1938, 1.

11   **Just four months earlier**: Frank and Frank, *Not Guilty*, 140-41.

11   **A native of . . . $27.50 per week**: Frank and Frank, *Not Guilty*, 140; "Bertram Campbell Victim of Mistake," *Nassau Daily Review-Star*, July 25, 1945, 1, 3; Campbell Parole Board Report, 10-11.

11   **Campbell had returned . . . firm of Kelly Brothers**: "Bertram Campbell Victim of Mistake," 3; Campbell Parole Board Report, 10-11.

11   **223 *Independence* Avenue in *Freeport***: "Bertram Campbell Victim of Mistake," 3.

11   **On January 26, 1938 . . . teller, Wesley Irvine**: Campbell Transcript, 160-162, 213-214.

11   **Campbell was mystified . . . "it absolutely is"**: Campbell Transcript, 90, 161-162.

11   **Rhinehart and Irvine identified**: Campbell Transcript, 162.

11   **A little less. . . for forgery and larceny**: Campbell Transcript, 163-64.

11   **Within a matter . . . while awaiting trial**: Edward J. Mowery, "7-Year Hell Is Ended for Forger's Double," *New York World-Telegram*, July 25, 1945, 1, 23.

11-12   **"I wish my three children"**: "Campbell Assured $40,000 From State," *New York Times*, May 8, 1946, 29.

12   **original indictment charged**: Campbell, 62 N.Y.S.2d at 640.

12   **Based on that charge . . . by many locals**: William Gilman, "The Incredible Story," *True Detective*, October 1946, 12, 76.

12	the state withdrew the November 15 forgery count: Robert Daru, *Interim and Partial Report, Bertram M. Campbell Investigation*, New York County Criminal Courts Bar Association, 1946 (hereinafter "Daru Report"), 12.
12	dates on which Campbell allegedly appeared: Campbell, 62 N.Y.S.2d at 640.
12	"I shall prove that he was in Freeport": Campbell Transcript, 3-4.
12	Conway fell ill . . . stepped in for the defense: Daru Report, 3-4.
12	Before proceeding, Wilkinson . . . "a reflection on him": Campbell Transcript, 67.
12	Joseph Brill represented . . . New York's future governor: Albin Krebs, "Joseph E. Brill, 71, Dies; Noted Criminal Lawyer," *New York Times*, May 20, 1975, 50.
12	each of the three . . . a total of $4,150: "State Parole Board Report on Campbell Case," *New York Times*, August 29, 1945, 16; Frank and Frank, *Not Guilty*, 143-44.
12	Bank president Rhinehart admitted . . . out of a lineup: Campbell Transcript, 87-89.
12	the prosecution presented . . . they had cashed: "Board Rushing Pardon Inquiry for Campbell," *New York World-Telegram*, July 30, 1945, 1, 8; Frank and Frank, *Not Guilty*, 144; "Identified 'Retouched' Campbell Photo," *Newsday*, August 24, 1945, 7.
12-13	Nott permitted the testimony: Campbell Transcript, 302-303; Daru Report, 29.
13	Wilkinson called seven witnesses: Campbell Transcript, 167-248.
13	"If ever there was an honest man . . .": Campbell Transcript, 232.
13	Campbell also took . . . the Trust Company: Campbell Transcript, 238-248; Frank and Frank, *Not Guilty*, 144-145.
13	On cross-examination . . . "That is not the fact": Campbell Transcript, 241.
13	In his closing . . . Nott overruled the objection: Campbell Transcript, 282-83; Daru Report, 30-31.
13	"I do not wonder": Campbell Transcript, 278.
13	"can consider the number that made the identification": Campbell Transcript, 297.
13-14	The jury began . . . "your verdict is correct": Campbell Transcript, 315-316.
14	In a handwritten letter . . . "of which I was convicted": Mowery, "Dewey Orders Parole Board Inquiry," 4.
14	"very rank perjury": Campbell Transcript, 322.
14	prisoner number 95111: Mowery, "7-Year Hell," 23.
14	"He was searched . . . and assigned to a cell": Campbell, 62 N.Y.S.2d at 640.
14	New prisoners like Campbell: "Sing Sing Cell Block Again Is Criticized," *New York Times*, August 15, 1937, 36.
14	This part of Sing Sing . . . six and a half feet tall: Carl Warren, "Prisons Crowded; Outbreak Feared," *Daily News*, May 16, 1938, 2, 16; John Crosson and George Dixon, "Whitney Enters a Cell Condemned as Unfit," *Daily News*, April 13, 1938, 3.
14	The old cell block . . . in the winter: Warren, "Prisons Crowded," 16.
14	"cells are unfit for human habitation": "Sing Sing Report Hits Cell Block," *New York Times*, December 16, 1934, 80.
14	A similar report issued: "Sing Sing Cell Block Again Is Criticized," 36.
14	In the spring of 1938 . . . up from 2,408 six years earlier: "Sing Sing Population at Peak," *New York Times*, April 19, 1938, 8; Warren, "Prisons Crowded," 2.
14	a "temporary dormitory": "Sing Sing Population," 8.
14	for six to nine months: "Sing Sing Cell Block Again Is Criticized." 36.
14-15	In these hellish conditions . . . Yours lovingly, 95111: "Bertram Campbell Is Dead at 60; Falsely Imprisoned for 40 Months," *New York Times*, September 7, 1946, 47 (considered suicide); Mowery, "7-Year Hell," 23 (sleepless nights, Christmas card).
15	To cope with . . . but armed guards: Mowery, "7-Year Hell," 23.
15	"What did Daddy do" . . . "could never have done that": "Campbells Face Brighter Future," *Nassau Daily Review-Star*, July 26, 1945, 2.
15	"I will never forgive": "His Double a Master Forger, He Serves Crook's Jail Term," *Newsday*, July 25, 1945, 3, 26.
15	As his sentence . . . as a bookkeeper: "His Double a Master Forger," 26.
15	more than three years: Campbell v. State, 62 N.Y.S.2d at 640.
15	After his parole . . . Floral Park, Long Island followed: "Former Haverstraw Man Was Convicted by Error," *Journal News* (Rockland County), July 25, 1945, 1, 2.
15	the Plaza Fuel Company: "Bertram Campbell Victim," 3.
15	continued to haunt: "Campbell Assured $40,000," 29.
15	visit to a probation officer: "Bertram Campbell Victim," 3.
15-16	"I knew someday": "His Double a Master Forger," 3.
16	read of the arrest: Mowery, "7-Year Hell," 23.
16	almost $500,000 from: Frederick Woltman, "Forgers, Like Artists, Are Born with Talent," *New York World-Telegram*, July 31, 1945, 4.
16	With help from a lawyer: "His Double a Master Forger," 3.
16	three of the five . . . declined to retract: Campbell Parole Board Report, 12-13. According to the Parole Board, Rhinehart did not "desire to retract his original testimony" while Morley said she was not positive that Thiel was the man she saw at the bank.
16	"I alone appeared": "Signed Confession Clears Campbell," *New York Times*, July 29, 1945, 24. In his confession, Thiel swore that Campbell did not participate in the forgeries and that "all acts . . . were acts which I myself engaged in, and from I alone profited financially, said checks being obtained, forged and deposited by me and the cash withdrawals made by me." Campbell Parole Board Report, 6. It's worth noting that Thiel specified in the confession that he appeared at the Trust Company on November 15 – the date that the district attorney removed from the indictment after Campbell and his attorney had developed an extensive alibi defense to show Campbell never left Freeport that day.
16	directed the state parole board: "Signed Confession Clears Campbell," 24.
16	granted Campbell a full pardon: "Campbell Receives a Full Pardon from Dewey as Justice, Not Mercy," *New York Times*, August 29, 1945, 1, 16.
16	to vacate Campbell's conviction: 1946 N.Y. Laws, Chapter 1.
16	Newspapers at first portrayed: John Martin, "Asks Pardon as 'Double' Clears Him," *Daily News*, July 25, 1945, 104; "Crook Admits Committing Crime for Which Broker Served Time," *New York Times*, July 25, 1945, 25 ("Mr. Campbell . . . resembles Thiel in a remarkable degree.").
16-17	*New York Times* reported: "'I'm Sorry,' Thiel Tells Campbell, Imprisoned for the Other's Crime," *New York Times*, August 11, 1945, 15.
17	"Do you think you would have mistaken": "Same Person? What Do You Think?", *New York World-Telegram*, July 30, 1945, 1.
17	two and a half inches taller and twenty five pounds heavier: Campbell Parole Board Report, 8.

17 **Photos from _World-Telegram_**: All photos from _New York World-Telegram_ are from the Library of Congress, Prints and Photographs Division, NYWT&S Collection, LCCN: sn83030206.

18 **"couldn't have looked anything alike"**: James Thrasher, "Innocent Main Imprisoned Despite Efforts of Guilty One to Warn Authorities They Had Erred," _Muncie Evening Press_, August 2, 1945, 19.

18 **brother of James Donovan**: Philip J. Bigger, _Negotiator: The Life and Career of James B. Donovan_ (Bethlehem: Lehigh University Press, 2006), 66.

18 **"Thiel does not look like me"**: "His Double a Master Forger," 3.

18 **"There are no hard feelings"**: Grace Robinson, "Innocent Term-Server Forgives Real Criminal," _Daily News_, August 11, 1945, 29.

18 **investigation initiated by**: "Lawyers Investigate Campbell Conviction," _New York. Times_, August 1, 1945, 19.

18 **Robert Daru headed**: "Bar Group Orders Campbell Probe," _New York World-Telegram_, July 31, 1945, 1.

18 **Daru traced the. . . used Mager's office often**: Daru Report, 15-16; Campbell Parole Board Report, 2.

18 **fixated on Campbell**: Daru Report, 15; Parole Board Transmittal Letter, 2.

18 **detectives apparently never considered**: Daru Report, 16. In a further twist, years after the trial, Workmaster himself was arrested for grand larceny and, as of August 1945, was awaiting sentencing. Campbell Parole Board Report, 8.

18 **The hearings . . . identified Campbell at trial**: "Pro and Con" (photo and caption), _Daily News_, August 24, 1945, 30; "Photo Faked, Campbell Trial Witness Says," _Daily News_, August 24, 1945, 119.

18-19 **Irvine and two . . . "most outstanding" feature**: Daru Report, 40; "'Retouched,' Campbell Photo," 7.

19 **investigators "pointed out" Campbell**: Daru Report, 40.

19 **"I had been practically assured"**: "State Colored His Mind, Campbell Witness Says," _New York World-Telegram_, August 28, 1945, 8.

19 **"a front man for a forgery ring"**: "State Colored His Mind," 8.

19 **"I was told that Campbell was spending"**: "Expect Dewey Pardon for Campbell Today," _Brooklyn Daily Eagle_, August 28, 1945, 1.

19 **$1,000 in large bills**: Mowery, "7-Year Hell," 23.

19 **Irvine believed that Campbell was guilty**: Daru Report, 12; "State Colored His Mind," 8.

19 **"behind the backs"**: Daru Report, 21-23.

19 **"examine all the facts . . . the defendant's innocence"**: Frank S. Hogan, _Report of the District Attorney, County of New York, 1946-48_ (1949) ("New York DA Report"), 143-144.

19 **"obligation to protect the innocent"**: New York DA Report, 143.

19 **Detective Woods and . . . be appearing there**: Campbell Transcript, 105-106.

19 **Morley similarly understood . . . "from the back and the side"**: Campbell Transcript, 57-58, 73-76.

20 **Irvine acknowledged that**: "Picture is Issue in Campbell Case," _New York Times_, August 24, 1945, 21; "'Retouched,' Campbell Photo," 7.

20 **"connected with the prosecution."**: "State Colored His Mind," 8.

20 **widely known as showups**: See, e.g, Neil v. Biggers, 409 U.S. 188, 195 (1972); Patrick M. Wall, _Eye-Witness Identification in Criminal Cases_ (Springfield, Illinois: Charles C. Thomas, 1965), 27-28. In Stovall v. Denno, 388 U.S. 293, 302 (1967), the Supreme Court noted that "the practice of showing suspects singly to persons for the purpose of identification, and not as part of a lineup, has been widely condemned." Fourteen years later, New York's highest court ruled that prosecutors are not permitted to introduce evidence of eyewitness identifications made at suggestive showup procedures. See People v. Adams, 423 N.E.2d 379, 384 (N.Y. 1981) (finding that showup procedure used at station house "could hardly have been more suggestive and there is no conceivable excuse for employing those procedures").

20 **avoid such suggestiveness**: Wall, _Eye-Witness Identification_, 40.

20 **In August 1898 . . . was inadmissible hearsay**: People v. Kennedy, 164 N.Y. 449, 455-56 (1900). Kennedy was tried twice more, with the first trial ending in a hung jury and the second trial ending in an acquittal. For a detailed account of these trials and other insights into how New York's police department evolved in the late 19th century, See John Oller, _Rogues' Gallery: The Birth of Modern Policing and Organized Crime in Gilded Age New York_ (New York: Dutton, 2021), 262-268.

20 **"lined up before them"**: People v. Cassidy, 146 N.Y.S. 15, 16 (App. Div. 1914).

20 **"placed in a line"**: People v. Jung Hing, 212 N.Y. 393, 400 (1914).

20 **issued in March 1860**: Rt. Hon. Lord Patrick Devlin, _Report to the Secretary of State for the Home Department of the Departmental Committee on Evidence of Identification in Criminal Cases_ (London: Her Majesty's Stationery Office, 1976), 112.

20 **"practice of the English police"**: John Henry Wigmore, "Identification of Accused Persons on Arrest," 25 _Illinois Law Review_ 550, 551 (1931).

20 **"it may be doubted"**: Wigmore, "Identification," 551.

20-21 **"the haste and routine of police and trial proceedings"**: John Henry Wigmore, _The Science of Judicial Proof_ (Boston: Little Brown and Company, 1937), 538.

21 **pointed to a showup**: Wigmore, _Science_, 538 and n.2.

21 **occasionally threw out criminal convictions**: See, e.g., People v. Gerace, 254 App. Div. 135 (N.Y. App. Div. 1938); People v. Davino, 284 N.Y. 486 (1940).

21 **another thirty years before**: See United States v. Wade, 388 U.S. 218 (1967) (holding that defendants have a constitutional right to have counsel at post-indictment lineup proceedings); Gilbert v. California, 388 U.S. 263 (1967) (holding that testimony on lineup identifications was inadmissible where defense counsel was not notified of or present at the lineup).

21 **assistance of counsel to an indigent farmer**: Betts v. Brady, 316 U.S. 455 (1942).

21 **To that point, the court had recognized**: See Johnson v. Zerbst, 304 U.S. 458, 463 (1938) ("The Sixth Amendment withholds from federal courts, in all criminal proceedings, the power and authority to deprive an accused of his life or liberty unless he has or waives the assistance of counsel."); Powell v. Alabama, 287 U.S. 45, 71 (1932) ("in a capital case, where the defendant is unable to employ counsel and is incapable adequately of making his own defense because of ignorance, feeble mindedness, illiteracy, or the like, it is the duty of the court, whether requested or not, to assign counsel for him as a necessary requisite of due process of law").

21 **Gideon v. Wainwright**: 372 U.S. 335 (1963).

21 **Miranda v. Arizona**: 384 U.S. 436, 479 (1966). In this pre-Miranda world, New York courts had similarly held that, prior to the commencement of actual criminal proceedings, suspects were not entitled to be informed of their rights. People v. Doran, 246 N.Y. 409, 423 (1927); People v. Leyra, 302 N.Y. 353, 363 (1951).

22 **"so inefficient, reckless and dangerous"**: Daru Report, 22.

22	**"honest mistakes" by "honest eyewitnesses"**: New York DA Report, 146.
22	**gave "considerable weight" to the eyewitnesses**: Parole Board Transmittal Letter, 13.
22	**agreed that any errant identification**: Parole Board Transmittal Letter, 13.
22	**"unimportance" of their identifications**: "Campbell Case Laid to Dewey's 100% Goal," *New York Times*, August 29, 1945, 16. Feldhusen said: "I was impressed with how unimportant our testimony would be. From indications today, our testimony seems to have become more important than anything else." "Witness Says His Testimony Called of No Importance," *Kingston Daily Freeman*, August 28, 1945, 1.
22	**original indictment accused**: Campbell, 62 N.Y.S.2d at 640.
22	**a front man**: Daru Report, 12.
22	**"Every fact which gave rise"**: Daru Report, 12.
22	**"tunnel vision"**: Findley and Scott, "Multiple Dimensions of Tunnel Vision," 293-295.
22-23	**As explained by Preet Bharara . . . "the first blunder"**: Preet Bharara, *Doing Justice: A Prosecutor's Thoughts on Crime, Punishment, and the Rule of Law* (New York: Alfred A. Knopf, 2019), 43.
23	**district attorney's office missed . . . when the crime was committed**: Parole Board Transmittal Letter, 8; Campbell Parole Board Report, 2.
23	**kept Campbell and his family . . . the prosecution overlooked**: Parole Board Transmittal Letter, 13; Campbell Parole Board Report, 5, 10. Assistant district attorney Brill told the Parole Board that he remembered that "some witnesses made some mention of" the limp, "but they apparently were not certain and were contradicted by other witnesses." Campbell Parole Board Report, 8.
23	**Detective Woods had doubts . . . "to Philadelphia was abandoned"**: Parole Board Transmittal Letter at 5; Campbell Parole Board Report at 5.
23-24	**The FBI was . . . as Campbell served his sentence**: "State Colored His Mind," 8.
24	**"it is impossible" . . . "high-pressure groups"**: State Parole Board Report on Campbell Case," *New York Times*, August 29, 1945, 16.
24	**"seems to be defending those who convicted Mr. Campbell"**: "The State's Mistake," *New York Times*, August 30, 1945, 20.
24	**"originally investigated and developed the case"**: Thomas E. Dewey, "Statement of the Governor Accompanying the Pardon of Bertram M. Campbell," August 28, 1945, in *Public Papers of Thomas E. Dewey, 1945*, 530-531 (New York: Williams Press, 1946).
24	**"Only one thing was lacking"**: "Pardon," *Time*, September 10, 1945, 22-23.
25	**headed the district attorney's office**: "Pardon," 22.
25	**the rush to judgment**: "Campbell Case Laid," 16.
25	**"Mr. Dewey's big clean-up"**: "Payment Deferred," *Time*, August 6, 1945, 23, 24.
25	**Court of Claims Act**: 1942 N.Y. Laws, Chapter 442; N.Y. Ct. of Cl. Act, section 9(3)(a); "Statutes," 21 *New York University Law Quarterly Review* 422 (1946).
25	**after April 13, 1942**: "Statutes," 422.
25	**urged the legislature**: "Gov. Dewey's Message to the Legislature Setting Forth His Program for the 1946 Session," *New York Times*, January 10, 1946, 14-15.
25	**"Only by legislative act"**: "Gov. Dewey's Message," 15.
25	**legislature acted quickly**: 1946 N.Y. Laws, Chapter 1.
25	**"compensation for the indignities"**: 1946 N.Y. Laws, Chapter 1.
25-26	**"Mr. Campbell's indictment"**: Opening Statement of Arthur W. Mattison in Bertram M. Campbell v. State, Claim No. 28125 (N.Y. Ct. of Cl. 1946), in Bertram Campbell, Executive Clemency and Pardon Case File, NYSA, A0597-78-B054-F04.
26	**"made me pretty sick" . . . experiencing continuing nightmares**: "Campbell Assured $40,000," 29.
26	**Barrett issued his ruling . . . $75,000 in additional damages"**: Campbell, 62 N.Y.S.2d at 639, 642-43.
26	**several purchases quickly**: Gordon Schendel, "The Late Bertram Campbell's Last Gesture," *Atlanta Constitution*, December 29, 1946, 70.
26	**"I want to help"**: Schendel, "Last Gesture," 70.
26	**suffered a stroke**: "Prison Term Takes Toll," *New York Times*, September 4, 1946, 22.
26	**at the age of sixty**: "Bertram Campbell Is Dead," 47.
27	**"as a result of his imprisonment"**: "Campbell Dead, His Prison Term Blamed," *Daily News*, September 8, 1946, 4.

Chapter Two: "Life Is a Dangerous Thing"

28	**thirty-three-year-old Cecelia Leib . . . for her daughter**: "Woman Jailed Five Months Cleared of Forgery," *Rochester Times-Union*, December 11, 1936, 28.
29	**Rochester police arrested . . . and awaiting trial**: "Woman Jailed Five Months," 28; "Woman Jailed 'by Error' Is Freed After Five Months," *New York Times*, December 11, 1936, 1.
29	**After the arrest . . . New York and Pennsylvania**: "Woman Jailed Five Months," 28; "Police Given Clue to Bad Check Passer," *Burlington Daily News*, July 29, 1936, 3.
29	**But while Leib . . . not in Leib's handwriting**: "Woman Jailed Five Months," 28; "Woman Jailed 'by Error,'" 1.
29	**when police finally. . . the culprit**: "Indictment in Check Case Dismissed," *Star-Gazette* (Elmira, New York), December 11, 1936, 38; "Woman Jailed Five Months," 28.
29	**declared Leib innocent**: "Rochester Woman Released from Steuben County Jail Following Exoneration on Forgery Charge," *Genesee Country Express and Advertiser*, December 17, 1936, 14.
29	***New York Times* reported**: "Woman Jailed 'by Error,'" 1.
29	**They would later . . . 1925 and 1938**: "Woman, 62, Gets Pardon in Jersey Sixteen Years After False Arrest," *New York Times*, May 17, 1951, 33. In October 1938, Theo Sullivan, then 45, was arrested in Elmira for passing bad checks. The following February, she pleaded guilty to multiple charges of forgery. "Former Elmira Woman Admits Forgery Guilt," *Star-Gazette*, February 17, 1939, 13. Edward Eugene Sullivan, 56, was also arrested in October 1938 as a "fugitive from justice" facing forgery charges in Milwaukee. "Man Arrested Here Wanted in Milwaukee," *Star-Gazette*, October 8, 1938, 2.
29	**A forty-six-year-old widow . . . the check bounced**: Roger Dove, "Clifford Shephard and the Phantom Forger," *Daily News*, July 9, 1950, 6; "Victim of Mistaken Identity Granted Full Pardon by Driscoll," *Central New Jersey Home News* (New Brunswick), May 17, 1951, 7; Edward D. Radin, *The Innocents* (New York: William Morrow and Company, 1961), 91-92.
29-30	**The baker filed . . . twenty dollars cash bail**: "Scotch Plains Woman Faced Bad Check Plaint," *Plainfield Courier-News*

(Plainfield, NJ), April 17, 1935, 1.

30   **On April 18 . . . was accompanied by**: "Couple Identified as Check Passers in Police Court," *Central New Jersey Home News*, April 19, 1935, 1, 21.

30   **former executive . . . about four months**: Clifford Shephard, "They Swore My Life Away," *Inside Detective*, October 1950, 16, 17, 60.

30   **Lester had made. . . withdrew the complaint**: "Detainer Filed Against Woman," *Plainfield Courier-News*, April 19, 1935, 15.

30   **But police saw . . . towards the back**: "Couple Identified as Check Passers," 1; "Man Imprisoned Here Is Now Held Innocent," *Central New Jersey Home News*, February 12, 1939, 1 ("Lieutenant Detective Elmer Henry invited three local businessmen, all of who had been victims of check forgers, to accompany him to the North Plainfield hearing").

30   **Liquor store proprietor . . . "That's the woman, too"**: "Couple Identified as Check Passers," 21.

30   **Joining Salva in . . . Longcoy said**: "Couple Identified," 1, 21.

30   **Lester and Shephard . . . as decisively as the other locals**: Shephard, "They Swore My Life Away," 17, 60.

30   **"merry-go-round"**: "Jailed by Mistake, Woman Asks Pardon," *Newark Star-Ledger*, June 18, 1950, 1, 10.

30   **Unable to post the $1,500**: "Pair Held for Jury on Check Charges," *Plainfield Courier-News*, April 20, 1935, 4.

30   **Their attorney implored . . . request was rejected**: Harry Brundidge and David Camelon, "Vindicated After 15 Years," *American Weekly*, October 1, 1950, 3.

30-31   **The case involving . . . $34.25 back in cash**: "Perth Amboy Couple Put on Trial Here for Passing Checks," *Central New Jersey Home News*, November 12, 1935, 7.

31   **Lester and Shephard denied . . . night of the crime**: "Two Found Guilty of Check Passing," *Central New Jersey Home News*, November 13, 1935, 15.

31   **verdict of guilty**: "Two Found Guilty of Check Passing," 15.

31   **sentenced each defendant**: Joseph O. Haff, "Jailed in Mistake, Man Wins Pardon," *New York Times*, June 15, 1950, 33.

31   **"someday I'll be free to track down that man"**: "Refuses to Plead Guilty," *Central New Jersey Home News*, November 25, 1935, 4.

31   **as soon as . . . similar forged checks**: Radin, *The Innocents*, 92-93.

31   **In June 1936 . . . women's detention home**: Haff, "Jailed in Mistake," 33.

31   **After serving her . . . time in public**: "Woman Asks Pardon," 10.

31   **Her fears were . . . when the check was passed**: "Held for Jury on Worthless Check Charge," *Plainfield Courier-News*, December 29, 1938, 8 (reporting Shephard's arrest); "Jailed Innocent Man Rejects 15G Solace," *Daily News*, March 1, 1953; New Jersey Laws of 1951, Chapter 221.

31   **In 1939, Shephard . . . Sullivan's, not Shephard's**: Haff, "Jailed in Mistake," 33, 62.

31   **the woman for whom Cecelia Leib had been mistaken**: Dove, "Clifford Shephard," 7.

31   **Shephard quickly concluded . . . a full confession**: "Man Imprisoned Here Is Now Held Innocent," *Central New Jersey Home News*, February 12, 1939, 1.

31-32   **How strong was . . . similar facial expressions**: Dove, "Clifford Shephard," 7.

32   **International Detective Agency . . . the "erroneous prosecution"**: Haff, "Jailed in Mistake," 33, 62.

32   **The Court of Pardons . . . explain its ruling**: Haff, "Jailed in Mistake," 62; Dove, "Clifford Shephard," 7.

32   **It was not until . . . outcome of Shephard's application**: "New Jersey: The Phantom Forger," *Time*, June 26, 1950; Haff, "Jailed in Mistake," 33.

32   **Finally, in June . . . signed the pardon**: Haff, "Jailed in Mistake," 62.

32   **Shephard, then sixty-four . . . "and cleaned spittoons"**: Bennett Schiff, "Cleared of Another's Forgery After 15 Years, Can't Get Job," *New York Post*, September 10, 1950, 18.

32-33   **"It's too late . . . you'd be dead"**: Jim Mulvihill and Ann Lerner, "Freed 'Forger' to Marry at 64," *Newark Star-Ledger*, June 15, 1950, 1.

33   **Shephard hoped . . . "I guess I'm still guilty"**: Schiff, "Cleared," 18.

33   **Lester, meanwhile, had . . . "a dangerous thing"**: "Former Plainfielder, Granted Full Pardon by State, Finds Years Have Lessened Much of Her Bitterness," *Plainfield Courier-News*, May 17, 1951, 1.

33   **"It's too bad the pardon"**: "Pardoned in Forgery, She's Suing for 25Gs," *Newark Star-Ledger*, May 17, 1951, 1.

33   **awarded Shephard $15,000**: New Jersey Laws of 1951, Chapter 221; "Aid for Wrongly Jailed Man," *New York Times*, January 30, 1951, 18.

33   **any legislation to compensate Wean**: Charles Walling, "Must Wait to Get Bum Rap Cash," *Daily News*, June 3, 1951, 122.

33   **On April 3, 1952 . . . her two children**: "Mrs. Harry Wean Dies, Jailed Though Innocent," *Plainfield Courier-News*, April 4, 1952, 9.

33   **New Jersey appropriated $1,000**: New Jersey Laws of 1953, Chapter 101 (approved April 17, 1952).

33   **Shephard died in . . . and a stepson**: "False Accusation Victim Dies at 71," *Plainfield Courier-News*, April 22, 1957, 10.

34   **According to the National Registry . . . after Wean's conviction**: National Registry of Exonerations website, accessed August 2022. The registry is an online resource created and maintained jointly by the University of California Irvine Newkirk Center for Science and Society, the University of Michigan Law School, and the Michigan State University College of Law.

34   **Botts's misfortune can . . . was the woman**: "Brazil Woman Suspected of Widespread Forgery," *Indianapolis Star*, October 17, 1934, 4; "Mrs. Botts Wants to See Her Double," *Indianapolis Star*, December 18, 1935, 1, 3; Martha Martin, "Her Double," *Daily News*, August 8, 1937, 62.

34   **Botts had never . . . for small purchases**: "Kokomo Police Help Solution of Check Fraud," *Kokomo Tribune*, October 17, 1934, 1; Russell E. Campbell, "Bride Serves Year in Prison-Innocent," *Indianapolis Star*, December 15, 1935, 1.

34   **other witnesses arrived**: Martha Martin, "Her Double," *Daily News*, August 8, 1937, 62.

34   **Botts was arrested . . . had a miscarriage**: 1939 Indiana Acts, Chapter 144 ("Appropriation for Nancy Louis Botts").

34   **seven witnesses identified . . . laundry in her home**: "Forgery Case Reaches Jury Before Noon," *Kokomo Tribune*, November 20, 1934, 1; Pardon Issued by Indiana Governor Paul V. McNutt ("McNutt Pardon"), December 14, 1935.

34   **Despite the alibi . . . years in prison**: "Woman Found Guilty," *Kokomo Tribune*, November 21, 1934, 1.

34   **In late 1935 . . . at the time**: Campbell, "Bride Serves Year," 13.

34-35   **Based on the . . . Botts went free**: Campbell, "Bride Serves Year," 13; McNutt Pardon, 1.

35   **"I enjoyed being"**: Campbell, "Bride Serves Year," 13.

35   **In July 1937 . . . four-year period**: "Woman Confesses Forgery Clearing Convicted 'Double,'" *Star Press*, July 20, 1937, 1.

35   In 1939, the . . . "practically an invalid": 1939 Indiana Acts, Chapter 144.
35   The use of . . . jury convicted him: State v. Hauptmann, 115 N.J.L. 41 (N.J. 1935).
35-36   increasing judicial acceptance: D. Michael Risinger, Mark P. Denbeaux and Michael J. Saks, "Exorcism of Ignorance as a Proxy for Rational Knowledge: The Lessons of Handwriting Identification 'Expertise,'" 137 *University of Pennsylvania Law Review* 731, 761 n.136, 170-71 (1989).
36   attorney Samuel Leibowitz . . . acquitted in May 1937: "Double Trouble Ends for John B. Coughlin," *Brooklyn Daily Eagle*, May 21, 1937, 8; "Handwriting Saves Man Going to Jail for Double," *Reading Times* (Reading, Pennsylvania), March 15, 1937, 7; Quentin Reynolds, *Courtroom: The Story of Samuel S. Leibowitz* (New York: Farrar, Straus and Giroux, 1950), 193-196.
36   Albert D. Osborn also performed: Haff, "Jailed in Mistake," 33, 62.
36   "our janitor could have convicted them": Brundidge and Camelon, "Vindicated," 3.

                                    Chapter Three: Phil the Ghost
37   The principal sources for this chapter are (1) People v. Caruso, 14 N.Y.S.2d 191 (Sup. Ct. 1939); (2) St. Clair McKelway, "Annals of Crime: The Innocent Man at Sing Sing," *New Yorker*, November 11, 1939 (which quotes extensively from judicial proceedings); (3) a 1939 probation officer report in Philip Caruso's Great Meadow Prison Inmate Case File, NYSA, W0024-88-14508 ("Caruso Report"); and (4) Frank and Frank, *Not Guilty*, 129-136.
37   The account of the armed robbery draws from the sources in the preceding note and "Jury Convicts 'Ghost' With A Bid For Mercy," *Daily News*, March 10, 1939, Brooklyn Section, 2, and Fred Menagh, "Innocent Men Do Go to Prison," *Akron Beacon Journal*, October 15, 1939, 57.
38   In this case . . . Street in Brooklyn: Caruso Report, 3-4; McKelway, "Annals of Crime," 28; "Jury Convicts 'Ghost,'" 2; "Court Quashes Indictment Against Youth, In Prison for Hold-Up He Did Not Commit," *New York Times*, September 7, 1939, 19.
38   In February 1930 . . . had run away: "Three Brooklyn Boys Found in Raritan Township," *Daily Home News* (New Brunswick, NJ), February 26, 1930, 1.
38   In a fateful . . . and Eighty-Sixth Street: McKelway, "Annals of Crime," 36.
38   On the night of December 8 . . . first-degree robbery: McKelway, "Annals of Crime," 27.
38   At a police lineup: Frank and Frank, *Not Guilty*, 129-30.
38   But as later reported . . . had committed the crime: McKelway, "Annals of Crime," 28-30.
38   Scaramellino's uncertainty . . . then indicted him: McKelway, "Annals of Crime," 29.
38-39   At trial in . . . "this was the man": McKelway, "Annals of Crime," 30.
39   The defense called . . . at the time of the crime: Frank and Frank, *Not Guilty*, 132; "Jailed by Error, Freedom Cost $5000," *Record-Argus* (Greenville, Pennsylvania), April 3, 1940, 2.
39   denied any involvement . . . "out of bed": Frank and Frank, *Not Guilty*, 130; McKelway, "Annals of Crime," 31.
39   During its deliberations . . . "the robbery was committed": McKelway, "Annals of Crime," 32.
39-40   "If you gentlemen can find": McKelway, "Annals of Crime," 32.
40   took Brancato's cue: McKelway, "Annals of Crime," 32.
40   On March 9 . . . the headline screamed: "Jury Convicts 'Ghost,'" 2; McKelway "Annals of Crime," 36.
40   not less than ten years: Frank and Frank, *Not Guilty*, 133.
40   After serving four: "Parallel Seen in Caruso Case and Incarceration of Campbell," *Brooklyn Daily Eagle*, August 5, 1945, 32.
40   police reopened the case: "Arrests Clear Man Wrongly Convicted," *New York Times*, July 31, 1939, 3.
40   tip led to the arrest: "Arrests Clear Man," 3; "Robbers Absolve Convict," *New York Times*, August 29, 1939, 15.
40   Complaining of news . . . "another already convicted": "Court Bids Caruso to Prove Innocence," *Brooklyn Daily Eagle*, August 7, 1939, 6.
40   "all records of police": Caruso, 14 N.Y.S.2d at 353.
40   thirty minutes after the crime: Caruso, 14 N.Y.S.2d at 353.
40   a transcript of the lineup . . . "on his upper lip": Frank and Frank, *Not Guilty*, 131, 133.
40   he now recognized Gottlieb: Caruso, 14 N.Y.S.2d at 351.
40   "Do not feel bitter . . .": Frank and Frank, *Not Guilty*, 134.
40   "neither the complaining witness": Frank and Frank, *Not Guilty*, 134.
41   "assuring and unequivocal": Caruso, 14 N.Y.S.2d at 350.
41   "any other verdict": Caruso, 14 N.Y.S.2d at 350-351.
41   "Had the Court . . . damaging errors": Caruso, 14 N.Y.S.2d at 353.
41   "At no time did he falter": Caruso, 14 N.Y.S.2d at 350.
41-42   But perhaps the . . . identification of Caruso: McKelway, "Annals of Crime," 30.
42   "there is as much difference": McKelway, "Annals of Crime," 34.
42   "there is some resemblance": Caruso, 14 N.Y.S.2d at 351.
42   he alerted firefighters: "Brooklyn Fire Injures 5," *New York Times*, November 5, 1939, 22.
42   "I originally intended": "Bill Would Make State Liable for False Conviction," *Brooklyn Daily Eagle,* January 17, 1940, 13. "Phelps Phelps" is not a typo. See Laurie Johnston, "Phelps Phelps, 84, Ambassador and Albany Legislator," *New York Times*, June 12, 1981, Section D, 15 (obituary noting that he was "christened Phelps von Rottenburg" but became "Phelps Phelps" after his parents divorced and "his mother . . . took back her family name for herself and son").
42   Two years later . . . no legal remedy: 1942 New York Laws, Chapter 442.
42   Caruso struggled . . . the business failed: "Jailed by Error," 2.
42   Caruso, who had . . . (a five-day jail term): "Court Eases Old Error," *New York Times*, July 18, 1944, 21.
42   drew comparisons to Caruso: "Parallel Seen in Caruso Case," 32.
42   passed in April 1946: 1946 N.Y. Laws, Chapter 494.
43   "To do so would be to broaden": Thomas E. Dewey, "Claim of Philip Caruso: Memorandum filed with Senate Bill, Introductory Number 2212, Printed Number 2501," 303-04, in *Public Papers of Thomas E. Dewey*, 1946 (New York: Williams Press, 1946).
43   Dewey said that: Dewey, "Claim of Philip Caruso," 303-04.
43   requested $108,750 in: "Suffolk Man's Suit Sequel to Campbell Case," *Newsday*, December 5, 1946, 64.
43   The case was not heard . . . entitled to $5,000: Decision in Caruso v. State of New York, Claim No. 28182 (N.Y. Ct. Cl. January 12, 1948), 3.

Chapter Four: The Key to Freedom

44	This chapter draws heavily on the transcript of the trial of Louis Hoffner ("Hoffner Transcript"), which was filed as part of the record in People v. Hoffner, 288 N.Y. 552 (1942), and on the Executive Clemency file for Louis Hoffner obtained from the New York State Archives, which includes the "Petition Submitted to His Excellency, Honorable Thomas E. Dewey, Governor of the State of New York Praying that a Pardon be Granted to Louis Hoffner" and the June 24, 1948 report on that petition by Parole Officers Joseph Pincus and Elias Saltman ("Hoffner Parole Report"). See Louis Hoffner, Executive Clemency and Pardon Case File, NYSA, File A0597-16-B61.
45	**donate bone marrow**: Hoffner Transcript, 94-95.
45	**At 2:35 in . . . fled into the night**: Hoffner Transcript, 26-29.
45	**An ambulance brought. . . He was thirty-eight**: "Holdup Man's Bullet Fatal to Bartender," *Long Island Daily Press*, August 9, 1940, 1.
45	**as Hoffner prepared . . . picked out Hoffner's photo**: Hoffner Parole Report, 22.
45	**Police had started maintaining**: Dan Barry, "Cheats, Swindlers and Ne'er-Do-Wells: A New York Family Album," *New York Times*, February 9, 2018.
45	**By the end of . . . the city's precincts**: Oller, *Rogues' Gallery*, 94.
45	**convicted of conspiracy**: Hoffner Transcript, 189.
45	**served more than two years**: Hoffner Parole Report, 74-76.
45	**Hoffner lived at . . . eight dollars a week**: Hoffner Transcript, 162-63.
45-46	**Hoffner had a distinctive . . . staked out Hoffner's home**: Hoffner Parole Report, 21-22; "Suspect Seized in Bar Murder," *Long Island Daily Press*, August 12, 1940, 1 (photo).
46	**Around four thirty . . . the week before**: Hoffner Transcript, 167-69.
46	**About two hours . . . of his nose**: Hoffner Parole Report, 26-27 (reporting Stotzing's comments on lineup), 30 (Halkias's comments) and 47-48 (Police Captain Fogarty's comments); Hoffner Transcript, 46-47 (Halkias testimony) and 87-88 (testimony of detective Harry Wood). See also Peter J. Donoghue and Benjamin J. Jacobsen, "Coram Nobis & the Hoffner Case," 28 *St. John's Law Review* 234, 241 (1954) ("the three detectives were all taller, heavier and older than Hoffner").
46	**With Assistant District Attorney . . . Hoffner as the gunman**: Hoffner Transcript, 46-48, 172.
46	**Two minutes later . . . identification at the lineup**: Hoffner Parole Report, 22, 27; Hoffner Transcript, 173.
46	**"That is the man"**: Hoffner Transcript, 51, 175; Donoghue and Jacobsen, "Coram Nobis," 242.
46	**Since Hoffner remained . . . died of leukemia**: Hoffner Parole Report, 81.
46	**Hoffner had no . . . fee of $1,000**: "2 North Side Lawyers to Aid Murder Defense," *Long Island Star-Journal*, October 17, 1940, 6.
46	**began on January 13**: Hoffner Transcript.
46-47	**Assistant District Attorney . . . "No doubt in my mind"**: Hoffner Transcript, 32.
47	**On cross-examination, Sheridan . . . "looked at his profile, the left side"**: Hoffner Transcript, 48-51; People v. Hoffner, 129 N.Y.S.2d 833, 836-38 (Sup. Ct. 1952).
47	**Halkias at first estimated . . . "it is exactly thirty-five seconds"**: Hoffner Transcript, 40-41.
47	**"He had [a] reddened mark"**: Hoffner Transcript, 94-95.
47	**neither Halkias nor Stotzing mentioned**: Hoffner Parole Report, 21.
47	**used his prior convictions**: Hoffner Transcript, 189-191.
47	**As for the alibi . . . Hoffner went home**: Hoffner Transcript, 164-66.
47	**Hoffner's employer, Herman . . . "about his mother"**: Hoffner Transcript, 101-102.
47	**the great Giants outfielder**: Hoffner Transcript, 103.
47	**until around 3:00 a.m.**: Hoffner Transcript, 102-103.
47-48	**The prosecution therefore. . . seemingly major details**: Hoffner Transcript, 107-110.
48	**at least one inaccuracy . . . Ott received a car**: Jack Mahon, "53,997 See Dodgers Trim Giants," *Daily News*, August 8, 1940, 46; John Drebinger, "Ott Honored as Brooklyn Beats Giants in Night Game, *New York Times*, August 8, 1940, 24.
48	**Chalowsky's lack of recall . . . not coming forward earlier**: Hoffner Transcript, 317-318.
48	**After three days . . . "a little vague on that"**: Hoffner Transcript, 364-65.
48	**"There was no reason they" . . . did not commit**: Hoffner Transcript, 371-372. "Facing Life, Asks Chair (for Appeal)," *Daily News*, January 18, 1941, 135; "Denies Guilt, Asks Chair," *New York Times*, January 19, 1941, 30.
48	**"I will not play with"**: Hoffner Transcript, 372.
48	**sentenced Hoffner to life**: Hoffner Transcript, 373-374.
48	**New York Appellate Division**: People v. Hoffner, 29 N.Y.S.2d 726 (App. Div. 1941).
48	**Court of Appeals**: People v. Hoffner, 42 N.E.2d 15 (N.Y. 1942).
48-49	**Hoffner began his . . . a "model prisoner"**: Clinton Prison Report of the Warden, April 30, 1948, in Louis Hoffner, Inmate Case File, Clinton Prison, NYSA, File W0014-77-27193.
49	**Bernard Arluck . . . the Hoffner family**: Hoffner Parole Report, 81.
49	**"do everything in my power" . . . Kings County prosecutor**: See Edward J. Mowery, "Justice . . . Went Astray," *New York World-Telegram*, May 29, 1947, reprinted in *The Hoffner Case* (New York: The Hoffner Committee, 1947), 1-4; "Retiring Cop Continues Battle," *Long Island Star-Journal*, August 11, 1960, 3.
49	**As part of their investigation . . . "could" have been mistaken**: Mowery, "Went Astray," 2; "Policeman Ends Six-Year Search for Witness in Effort to Clear Man Convicted of Murder," *New York Times*, May 30, 1947, 23; David Snell, "Life Begins All Over for Freed Convict, Thanks to Pals and Crusading Newspaper," *Knoxville New-Sentinel*, January 4, 1953, 25.
49	**Edward J. Mowery launched**: Mowery, "Went Astray," 1-4.
49	**would later win**: *1953 Pulitzer Prizes*, Pulitzer Prizes website, accessed April 30 2022; "Edward Mowery, Reporter, Dies; Won a Pulitzer Prize in 1953," *New York Times*, December 21, 1970, 38. Mowery, whose journalistic campaign to free Hoffner spanned some six years, experienced an unspeakable tragedy himself in 1958: His two teenage sons died in an accidental drowning at Lake George. "Tragic Drowning of Youths Shock to Residents of Area," *Post-Star* (Glen Falls, New York), August 29, 1958, 2.
49	**Mary Arendt . . . she said**: Edward J. Mowery, "Still Doubts," *New York World-Telegram*, May 27, 1947, reprinted in *The Hoffner Case*, 39-41.
49	**About two months . . . Arthur J. Kolb**: Edward J. Mowery, "Jurors Help," *New York World-Telegram*, July 2, 1947, reprinted in *The Hoffner Case*, 46-48.
49	**in September 1947, when Mowery reported**: Edward J. Mowery, "Perjury," *New York World-Telegram*, September 22, 1947, reprinted in *The Hoffner Case*, 57-61.
49	**Authorities had not disclosed . . . no such record**: People v. Hoffner, 129 N.Y.S.2d at 837.

49   **The minutes revealed . . . Hoffner's left profile**: Minutes of Lineup in People v. Louis Hoffner, August 11, 1940, Executive Clemency File, NYSA, A0597-16-B61.

50   **moved for a new trial**: "'I Would Never Have Voted Guilty,'" *New York Post*, November 21, 1947, 16.

50   **When the motion . . . oppose the motion**: "Would Never Have Voted," 16.

50   **motion was denied**: People v. Hoffner, 76 N.Y.S.2d 916, 921 (Sup. Ct. 1947).

50   **ruling that aged . . . adequacy of Halkias's identification**: Hoffner, 76 N.Y.S.2d at 921.

50   **Hoffner's team applied . . . in August 1948**: Charles D. Breitel, "Statement by Charles D. Breitel, Counsel to the Governor, Concerning Denial of the Application for Executive Clemency Made on Behalf of Louis Hoffner," 494-496, in *Public Papers of Thomas E. Dewey, 1948* (New York: Williams Press, 1948).

50   **"Nearly two score discrepancies"**: "1940 Murder Case Reopened by Quinn," *New York Times*, September 3, 1952, 38.

50   **"uncovering" of the lineup minutes**: "Judge Mulls Hoffner's Plea for Freedom," *Long Island Star-Journal*, October 23, 1952, 1, 15.

50   **November 1951 election**: James Desmond, "Queens, Staten Island Toss Out Their DAs," *Daily News*, November 7, 1951, 262.

50   **Quinn's office developed . . . after the meeting**: Edward J. Mowery, "DA Seeks to Give Lifer a Chance to Prove Innocence in '40 Slaying," *New York World-Telegram and The Sun*, September 3, 1952, 1, 2; Edward J. Mowery, "Lifer Risks Death to Clear Name," *New York World-Telegram and The Sun*, September 3, 1952, 1, 9.

50   **While at the prison . . . such a view**: Mowery, "DA Seeks to Give," 2.

50-51   **a lie detector test . . . about his innocence**: "Hoffner Learns Today if He's Free After 12 Years in Prison," *Long Island Star-Journal*, October 16, 1952, 4.

51   **granted his motion**: Hoffner, 129 N.Y.S.2d at 837.

51   **"the course of justice"**: Hoffner, 129 N.Y.S.2d at 837-838.

51   **"convincingly disproved by"**: Hoffner, 129 N.Y.S.2d at 837.

51   **While noting that . . . "as to require a directed verdict"**: Hoffner, 129 N.Y.S.2d at 837.

51-52   **Farrell also noted . . . "a visible blemish"**: Hoffner, 129 N.Y.S.2d at 835-36.

52   **In a 1948 interview . . . the short notice**: Hoffner Parole Report, 27, 29, 47-48.

52   **Hoffner, clad in . . . "nobody to help them"**: Edward J. Mowery, "Hoffner Life Term Set Aside," *New York World-Telegram and The Sun*, November 10, 1952, 1, 2.

53   **asked the court to dismiss**: Robert Bigelow, "Hoffner Given Freedom After 12 Years in Prison," *Long Island Star-Journal*, November 21, 1952, 1.

53   **"the dilution of an already weak case"**: Edward J. Mowery, "Presumption of Innocence - A Myth," Twenty-Fourth Address Delivered under the Don R. Mellett Memorial Fund, September 25, 1953, 14 (quoting Quinn).

53   **He spent his . . . "you hold the key"**: "Rabbi and Man He Helped Free," *Glenn Falls Times*, December 8, 1952, 2.

53   **Dewey approved legislation**: New York Laws 1955, Chapter 841

53   **awarded Hoffner $112,290**: Hoffner v. State, 142 N.Y.S.2d 630, 631 (Ct. Cl. 1955).

53   **"all the wealth of the State"**: Hoffner, 142 N.Y.S.2d at 631-632.

53   **Hoffner married . . . the earlier convictions**: "Application for Executive Clemency" dated July 1, 1961 and September 5, 1961 letter to Evelyn Hoffner from Howard A. Jones, Assistant Counsel, State of New York Executive Chamber.

53   **owned a Long Island sporting goods store**: "Where Are They Now?" *Newsweek*, July 22, 1956, 16.

53   **died in Ronkonkoma**: Ancestry.com, U.S. Social Security Death Index 1935-2014.

Chapter Five: Guilt by Association

54   My account of the case of Thomas Oliver is drawn from (1) a March 19, 1947 letter from Manhattan Assistant District Attorney Jerome Kidder to Assistant District Attorney General Marvin P. Lazarus ("Kidder letter"), which is within the case file for Eddie Lee Wilber that I obtained from the New York State Archives ("Wilber File"); (2) an undated Investigation Report by Irving W. Halpern, Chief Probation Officer, Court of General Sessions ("Halpern report"), in the Wilber file; (3) the New York DA Report, 148-49; (4) court papers filed on behalf of Thomas in the New York Court of Claims in 1947; and (5) Harold E. Danforth and James D. Horan, *The D.A.'s Man* (New York: Crown, 1957), 272-275.

54   **The widow, Sophie Wright . . . "left eye removed"**: Kidder letter, 1-2; Danforth and Horan, *D.A.'s Man*, 273.

55   **Based on a . . . and robbery charges**: Kidder letter, 1-2; New York DA Report, 148-149.

55   **The case went . . . a ten to fifteen years**: Kidder letter, 1-2; New York DA Report, 148-149.

55   **During an interview . . . that Camp patronized**: Kidder letter, 2; "Jailed by Error, Freed," *New York Times*, December 7, 1946, 23.

55   **The district attorney . . . remained in prison**: Kidder letter, 3.

55   **An investigator for . . . "they're neighborhood boys"**: Danforth and Horan, *D.A.'s Man*, 273-274.

55   **Danforth realized that . . . Danforth said**: Danforth and Horan, *D.A.'s Man*, 274.

55   **Wright had based . . . "mental association"**: New York DA Report, 148-149.

55   **retracted the identification**: Danforth and Horan, *D.A.'s Man*, 273-274; New York DA Report, 148-149.

55   **without the new suspect . . . confessed to the crime**: Kidder letter, 3. Like Wilber, Campbell retracted the confession. On the eve of trial, though, Campbell changed his plea to guilty.

56   **announced that Oliver was innocent**: Kidder letter, 3; "Jailed by Error, Freed," 23.

56   **The Oliver case . . . about eight years older**: Thomas Oliver, Inmate Record Card, NYSA, File B1222-77-50197; James W. Campbell, Elmira Reformatory In-Take Record, November 24, 1941, NYSA, File B0141-30-V137-45751.

56   **Hansley**: The facts about the Hansley case are drawn from "Dewey Frees Innocent Man in Sing Sing," *Daily News*, April 28, 1939, 31; and "Innocent Convict Freed," *New York Times*, April 28, 1939, 52.

57   *Times* **relegated the case**: "Jailed by Error, Freed," 23.

57   **devoted only five**: "Cleared Ten Months After Sentence," *New York World-Telegram*, December 6, 1946, 5.

57   **"untiring efforts"**: "Court Frees Youth Falsely Imprisoned," *Brooklyn Daily Eagle*, September 7, 1939, 1.

57   *Daily News* **described**: "Dewey Frees Innocent Man in Sing Sing," 31.

57   *New York Times* **referred**: "Innocent Convict Freed," 52.

57-58   **a three-paragraph story**: "Jailed by Error, Freed," 23.

58   **Registry of Exonerations identifies . . . approximately three hundred exonerees**: National Registry of Exonerations website, accessed August 2022.

58   **225 of the 375 defendants exonerated**: Innocence Project, "DNA Exonerations in the United States."

58   **Court of Last Resort . . . "including those involving race"**: Austin Downey, "The 'Court of Last Resort,'" *Ransom Center Magazine* website, April 25, 2019 (interview with Ian Burney), accessed September 3, 2022.

58	**In the early morning**: The facts of the Horace Wright case are based on the trial transcript in People v. Wright ("Wright Transcript"), as paginated in the Record on Appeal filed with the New York Court of Appeals, in or about 1944. The account of the crime is based on Simmons's testimony at pages 16 to 21 of the Wright Transcript.
59	**That night, Simmons . . . "lighter than the short fellow"**: Wright Transcript, 26, 36.
59	**About a month . . . "That is the man"**: Wright Transcript, 24.
59	**Wright, twenty-four . . . near his home**: Wright Transcript, 74-75.
59	**Wright denied . . . going straight home**: Wright Transcript, 76.
59-60	**Simmons, who was Black . . . "I am positive"**: Wright Transcript, 19-20.
60	**On cross-examination . . . "there were two fellows"**: Wright Transcript, 37.
60	**Simmons allowed that . . . had a mustache**: Wright Transcript, 37.
60	**wore a mustache at trial**: Wright Transcript, 75.
60	**Wright's counsel . . . made the identification**: Wright Transcript, 21, 24.
60	**Mattie Wright testified**: Wright Transcript, 53.
60	**backed Wright's claim**: Wright Transcript, 62, 71.
60	**both employees struggled**: Wright Transcript, 64-65, 72-73.
60	**near the end . . . the time of the arrest**: Wright Transcript, 87.
61	**"Now, I don't care to go"**: Wright Transcript, 102.
61	**At 4:12 p.m. . . . guilty**: Wright Transcript, 103, 109.
61	**ten to twenty years in Sing Sing**: Wright Transcript, 113.
61	**conviction was affirmed**: People v. Wright, 268 A.D. 854 (N.Y. App. Div. 1944). On further appeal, the Court of Appeals affirmed the judgment of conviction. People v. Wright, 294 N.Y. 758 (1945).
61	**"was prejudicial error"**: Wright, 268 A.D. at 854.
61	**"District Atorney Frank . . . "committed a robbery"**: Respondent's Brief, Record on Appeal in People v. Wright, 9.
61	**Untermyer . . . voted to reverse**: Wright, 268 A.D. at 854.
61-62	**In September 1947 . . . convicted of murder**: U.S. v. Williams, 323 F.2d 65, 66 (2d Cir. 1963). Relevant portions of Donald Graff's trial testimony appear at pages 103 and 132-133 in the Record on Appeal in People v. Williams, 298 N.Y. 803 (1949). During the cross-examination, the prosecution conceded that "there is no contention by the People that this witness can identify this defendant or that he ever has." Williams, 298 N.Y. at 803. The detective's testimony about the teletype alarm appears at page 206 of the Record on Appeal.
62	**conviction was affirmed**: People v. Williams, 298 N.Y. 803 (1949). Despite a jury recommendation that Williams receive a life sentence, the trial court sentenced him to death. The Court of Appeals affirmed the death sentence and so did the U.S. Supreme Court. Williams v. New York, 337 U.S. 241 (1949). But Governor Dewey commuted the sentence to life in prison. Williams, 323 F.2d at 65, 66.
62	**Second Circuit vacated**: Williams, 323 F.2d at 69.
62	**"long and exhausting interrogation"**: Williams, 323 F.2d at 69. While noting that "the record leaves the impression that Williams grossly exaggerated the story of physical abuse," the court also said that Williams's testimony about the police torture was "not without some corroboration." Williams, 323 F.2d at 67.
62	**"weakened physical condition"**: Williams, 323 F.2d at 69.
62	**"a confession obtained by these methods"**: Williams, 323 F.2d at 69.
62	**the case again . . . "the physical brutality alleged"**: Williams v. City of New York, 508 F.2d 356, 363-64 (2d Cir. 1974).
62	**no "evidence to support a reasonable belief"**: Williams, 508 F.2d at 360.
62	**campaign to highlight . . . scholars have documented**: Martha Biondi, *To Stand and Fight: The Struggle for Civil Rights in Postwar New York City* (Harvard University Press, 2003), 61-66, 70-78; Marilynn S. Johnson, *Street Justice: A History of Police Violence in New York City* (Boston: Beacon Press, 2003), 208-222.
62	**on May 30, 1949 . . . "quarrel over traffic regulations"**: "No Indictment in Death," *New York Times*, July 14, 1949, 20.
62	**Newton had been . . . killing Newton**: Richard Mason, "Group to Sift Fatal Shooting of Negro by Off Duty Cop," *Daily News*, July 27, 1949.
63	**declined to indict**: "No Indictment in Death," 20.
63	**But in a subsequent . . . the plaintiff $50,000**: Ruling on Motion for Directed Verdict, as replicated in Record on Appeal in Ferguson v. City of New York, 279 A.D. 606 (N.Y. App. Div. 1951), 150-151; "$50,000 Won by Widow," *New York Times*, January 31, 1951, 27.
63	**"a willful and intentional killing"**: Ferguson v. City of New York, 279 App. Div. 606 (N.Y. App. Div. 1951). Eight months later, the Court of Appeals affirmed the Appellate Division's ruling. See Ferguson v. City of New York, 303 N.Y. 936 (1952).
63	**John Harvey Brown . . . indications of brain damage**: My account of the John Harvey Brown case is based primarily on the trial transcript ("Harvey Brown Transcript") in the Record on Appeal in John Harvey Brown v. City of New York, 279 A.D. 741 (N.Y. App. Div. 1951). Harvey Brown's testimony describing the attack on him appears on pages 24-27 of the transcript.
63	**claimed that Brown came at them**: Harvey Brown Transcript, 164-65, 193 (Hogan testimony), 201-203 (Tyson testimony). See also "2 Deny Beating Charges," *New York Times*, January 25, 1951, 19.
63	**denied they had been out drinking**: Harvey Brown Transcript, 161-62, 193 (Hogan testimony), 199, 207 (Tyson testimony).
63	**awarded $60,000 in damages**: "$60,000 Damage Award; Jury Supports Man Who Said Policemen Beat Him," *New York Times*, January 27, 1951, 5. On appeal, the Appellate Division ordered that the amount of the judgment be reduced to $40,000. Brown v. City of New York, 109 N.Y.S.2d 101 (App. Div. 1951).
63	**Burton B. Roberts testified**: Harvey Brown Transcript, 276 (Roberts testimony).
63	**It is also now widely recognized . . . was ultimately acquitted**: People v. Boone, 30 N.Y.2d 521 (2017); Ashely Southall, "Witness IDs Led to His Conviction. Then Court Ruled on Racial Bias," *New York Times*, March 18, 2019, Section A, 15. See also National Registry of Exonerations, *Race and Wrongful Convictions in the United States 2022*, September 2022, 26 ("One of the oldest and most consistent findings of systematic studies of eyewitness identification is that white Americans are much more likely to mistake one Black person for another than to mistakenly identify members of their own race").
63	**42 percent of the 375 DNA-based exonerations**: Innocence Project, "DNA Exonerations in the United States."
64	**law permitting Oliver to recover damages**: 1947 N.Y. Laws, Chapter 785.
64	**Oliver filed . . . "the sum of $1,500"**: Proposed Findings of Fact and Conclusions of Law submitted by Hon. Nathaniel L. Goldstein, Attorney General, Court of Claims, Claim No. 28642, October 4, 1948.
64	**On December 6, 1948 . . . award him just $7,200**: Thomas Oliver v. State of New York, Claim No. 28642 (N.Y. Ct. Cl. December 6, 1948).

Chapter Six: The "Insoluble" Problem

66   **Dewey directed the Judicial Council**: Alexander Feinberg, "Dewey Seeks Way to Guard Innocent," *New York Times*, September 7, 1945, 1, 12.

66   **The council was . . . representatives of the public**: Feinberg, "Dewey Seeks Way," 12; Leonard S. Saxe, "The Judicial Council of the State of New York: Its Objectives, Methods, and Accomplishments," *American Political Science Review* 35, no. 5 (1941): 933-934.

66   **met once a month**: Harry D. Nims, "Four Judicial Councils," 27 *Canadian Bar Review*, 38, 39 (1949).

66   **regularly advised lawmakers**: Nims, "Councils," 39.

66   **saw 258 of its recommendations**: Nims, "Councils," 41.

66   **"the feasibility of erecting safeguards"**: Council Report, 233.

66   **urged a law requiring**: Feinberg, "Dewey Seeks Way," 12.

66   **Lyons brought . . . state prison system**: "John A. Lyons Dies; State Prison Head," *New York Times*, July 13, 1951, 21.

66   **"desire to break the case"**: Feinberg, "Dewey Seeks Way," 12.

66   **"I never believed"**: Feinberg, "Dewey Seeks Way," 12.

66   **"as an assistant district attorney"**: "Robert Daru Dies; Zealous Lawyer," *New York Times*, Apr. 22, 1967, 31.

66   **Daru proposed several reforms**: Daru Report, 42-43.

66   **released a report**: "Plea is Renewed to Join 2 Courts," *New York Times*, February 17, 1948, 19 (reporting on erroneous identification study, as contained in annual report submitted to state legislature).

66   **problem of erroneous identification**: Council Report, 234.

66   **not "an isolated instance"**: Council Report, 235.

66-67   **a 1932 study**: Edwin M. Borchard, *Convicting the Innocent* (London: FB &c, 2015). The council observed that "the annals of criminal law contain a number of miscarriages of justice resulting from erroneous identification." Council Report, 235.

67   **the council outlined . . . influence an identification**: Council Report at 237-241.

67   **memory is not a videotape**: Peter Hermann, "Faulty Identification Leads to Dropped Robbery Charges," *Baltimore Sun*, March 30, 2012, A1, A3 (reporting comment by James Doyle, former director of the Center for Modern Forensic Justice at John Jay College of Criminal Justice, that "memory is not like a videotape"); People v. Shirley, 723 P.2d 1354, 1377 (Cal. 1982) ("Memory does not act like a videotape recorder, but rather is subject to numerous influences that continuously alter its content."), *cert. denied*, 459 U.S. 860 (1982).

67   **"not an observation robot"**: Council Report, 239.

67   **Turning to state . . . suspect is included**: Council Report at 246.

67   **two sets of factors**: See, e.g., Deah S. Quinlivan and Gary L. Wells, "Suggestive Eyewitness Identification Procedures and the Supreme Court's Reliability Test in Light of Eyewitness Science: 30 Years Later," *Law and Human Behavior* 33, no. 1 (2009): 1, 5 (noting that "in the late 1970s, a framework emerged for distinguishing between variables that were under the control of the justice system, called system variables, and those that the justice system could not control, called estimator variables").

67   **In addressing system . . . with Daru's proposal**: Council Report, 246-47, 251-52.

67   **"those in authority"**: Council Report, 257.

67   **"an element of suggestion" . . . "the culprit is there"**: Council Report, 248.

67   **"practical reasons"**: Council Report, 249.

68   **"additional weight" . . . "as a matter of law"**: Council Report, 253.

68   **statutory requirement would**: Council Report, 253.

68   **New York Legislature ultimately passed**: N.Y. Exec. Law 837(21) (2017 law requiring Division of Criminal Justice Services to establish protocols for the conduct and recording of identification procedures).

68   **In the early evening . . . to the employees**: "Paymaster Dies From Bandits' Bullets," *New York Times*, August 16, 1925, 25. My references to the testimony at the trial of Edward Larkman are based on (1) the trial transcript ("Larkman Transcript") in the Record on Appeal in People v. Larkman, 244 N.Y. 503 (1926) (citations are to pages of the appellate record), and (2) Carlos C. Alden, "Report of Commissioner Carlos C. Alden in the Matter Pertaining to the Application for Executive Clemency in Behalf of Edward Larkman" ("Alden Report"), 418-428, in *Public Papers of Herbert H. Lehman, 1933* (Lyon, 1934) ("Lehman Papers").

68   **As the culprits fled . . . with light stripes**: Larkman Transcript, 208, 211, 214-215, 219-220.

68   **brought Littlewort to police headquarters**: Larkman Transcript, 243; Alden Report, 430.

68   **twenty-seven-year-old Edward Larkman**: Police identified Larkman as a suspect shortly after the murder. Larkman had a criminal record that included second-degree larceny and statutory rape. In February 1926, police escorted Larkman in Detroit. He was returned to Buffalo and indicted for Pierce's murder on February 5. "Girl Involved in Capture of Alleged Thugs," *Buffalo Times*, August 21, 1925, 1; "Larkman Papers Off to Detroit," *Buffalo Times*, January 30, 1926, 1; "Indicts Ed Larkman For Murder in Pierce Paymaster Robbery," *Buffalo Courier*, February 6, 1926, 3; Alden Report, 422.

69   **The procedure was . . . fled the murder scene**: Larkman Transcript, 243; Alden Report, 423.

69   **Littlewort testified**: Larkman Transcript, 242. On cross examination, Littlewort admitted that she had seen the man only briefly. "I saw a profile view of him as he walked past. It may have taken three seconds," she testified. "And I saw another full-faced view of him as he turned, and it may have taken two seconds." Littlewort also said the glasses were so large as to obscure part of the man's face. And about a month after the holdup, she failed to identify Larkman when shown a photo of him. Even so, Littlewort insisted at trial that she was sure about the identification. Larkman Transcript, 219-220, 226-227, 237-39, 242.

69   **was at a wedding**: Alden Report, 422.

69   **Seven witnesses supported**: Alden Report, 422.

69   **During forty-three hours . . . went unanswered**: Alden Report, 23. While deliberating, the jury sent the trial judge, Justice Brown, a note stating that "the possibility of an agreement seems to hinge upon an explanation as to the method employed in what is known as the 'police show-up.'" The note posed ten questions about the showup, including "how many people were at the show-up?"; "did witness know any of these people?"; and "what was the character of the people brought in at the show-up?" The judge said he could not answer these questions, because "there is no testimony whereby an answer could be made to those inquiries." He instructed the jury to resume deliberations based on the evidence. Alden Report, 422-23; Larkman Transcript, 604-605.

69   **sentenced him to death**: "Larkman to Die in April," *Buffalo Times*, March 4, 1926, 1; Alden Report, 422-23.

69   **a 5-2 ruling**: People v. Larkman, 244 N.Y. 503 (1926).

69   **Smith commuted**: "Larkman Is Saved from Execution," *New York Times*, January 14, 1927, 12.

69	**Six years later . . . was not involved**: "Lehman Frees Convict; Real Slayer Confessed," *New York Times*, December 19, 1933, 2; Alden Report, 424-26.
69	**"had this method of identification"**: Alden Report, 423.
69	**since the council cited**: Council Report, 236.
69-70	**On October 31, 1938**: "Brooklyn Fireman Killed in Hold-Up," *New York Times*, November 1, 1938, 48. My references to the eyewitness testimony in the Davino case are based on the trial transcript ("Davino Transcript") in the Record on Appeal in People v. Davino, 284 N.Y. 486 (1940) (citations are to pages of the appellate record).
70	**There were several eyewitnesses**: Davino Transcript, 192, 252, 316; People v. Davino, 284 N.Y. 486 (1940).
70	**wore a gray overcoat and a gray hat**: Davino, 284 N.Y. at 487-488.
70	**About six weeks . . . could not identify the man**: Davino, 284 N.Y. at 487-488; Davino Transcript, 217-221 (Alice Kavanaugh testimony), 294-302 (Richard Kavanaugh testimony), 320-22, 367-378 (Ryall testimony).
70	**The next day . . . his "becoming positive"**: Davino, 284 N.Y. at 487-88; Davino Transcript, 303 (Richard Kavanaugh testimony), 1253-1254 (testimony of William A. Sullivan establishing that all men in lineup were either police officers or firemen).
70	**On the strength . . . sentenced to death**: "Davino Freed in Payroll Murder After 17 Months in Death House," *New York Times*, November 10, 1942, 29.
70	**Court of Appeals reversed . . . "reasonable possibility of mistake"**: Davino, 284 N.Y. at 489 (citation omitted).
70	**only in passing**: Council Report, 250. Davino was tried and convicted again in 1941. This time, prosecutors called both the eyewitnesses from the first trial and five additional witnesses, four of whom were serving prison terms for other crimes. But again the Court of Appeals threw out the verdict, finding that the state's new evidence was unreliable and that, taken as a whole, the state's case remained "so full of doubt and uncertainty" that the guilty verdict could not stand. People v. Davino, 288 N.Y. 423 (1942). The council described the 1942 ruling as having reversed a conviction where the witnesses' observations were "obtained in haste and excitement" and their identification of the defendant was not made until after a "considerable period of time" after the crime.
70	**grew out of an armed robbery**: My account of the arrest and prosecution of Salvatore Gerace is based on the trial transcript ("Gerace Transcript") in the Record on Appeal in People v. Gerace, 254 App. Div. 135 (N.Y. App. Div. 1938) (citations are to pages of the appellate record).
70	**On September 25, 1937 . . . pockmarks on his face**: Gerace Transcript, 9-27 (Ritter testimony); Gerace, 254 App. Div. at 135-36.
70	**Bundschu went to**: Gerace Transcript, 41-43 (Bundschu testimony)
70	**prior convictions for . . . and bookmaking**: Gerace Transcript, 76-77 (Gerace testimony).
70	**Gerace did not . . . pockmarks on his face**: Gerace Transcript, 34-39; Gerace, 254 App. Div. at 136.
70	**Gerace insisted that . . . the police station**: Gerace Transcript, 42 (Bundschu testimony)
70-71	**Police then summoned . . . "the man who held you up"**: Gerace Transcript, 25, 40-41 (Ritter testimony).
71	**Ritter entered the . . . "pretty sure," but not certain**: Gerace Transcript, 47-48.
71	**"gave him time to think it over"**: Gerace Transcript, 48.
71	**"which I get paid for"**: Gerace Transcript, 47-48.
71	**Two days later . . . arrested Gerace**: Gerace Transcript, 45-46 (Bundschu testimony) and Defendant's Exhibit A (Ritter sworn statement given to police); Gerace, 254 App. Div. at 136.
71	**a verdict of guilty**: Gerace Transcript, 104.
71	**The Appellate Division . . . "this was such a case"**: Gerace, 254 App. Div. at 135-36.
71	**The state elected**: "Man Freed After Facing 15-40 Year Prison Term," *Middletown Times Herald* (Middletown, New York), June 24, 1938, 6.
71	**New York courts later cited**: People v. Williams, 3 A.D.2d 967, 968 (N.Y. App. Div. 1957) (citing Gerace for the proposition that "in the absence of a 'line-up', testimony relating to complainant's prior identification of defendants had no probative value"; court noted that complainant was "merely asked to state whether the only two men shown him were his assailants"); People v. Miller, 134 N.Y.S.3d 605 (App. Div. 2020) (citing Gerace as a case that rejected a verdict "where the only significant evidence against the defendant was an uncorroborated eyewitness identification of dubious reliability").
71	**private detectives had doctored**: Council Report, 241, 254.
71	**"before the District Attorney received"**: Council Report, 241.
71-72	**Campbell's lawyer failed to elicit**: Council Report, 254.
72	**In the end . . . "caution and prudence"**: Council Report, 268.
72	**Hogan's response . . . "in criminal cases"**: New York DA Report, 143.
72	**"one-one hundredth of one percent"**: New York DA Report, 143. Hogan also insisted that "even if there were added those defendants who continued to protest their innocence after conviction, the percentage still would be infinitesimal."
72	**"proved" to be erroneous**: In addition to the Campbell and Oliver cases, Hogan addressed the 1939 wrongful conviction of Mathew Uchansky who, along with Benny Amatsky, was charged with an armed robbery of a Brooklyn synagogue. The arrest occurred after Uchansky was seen in Amatsky's company. Uchansky was "positively identified" by "several of the victims" and had also engaged in other "similar criminal activities with Amatsky." Based on these facts, the prosecutor was "morally certain that he had the right man, and the jury accepted the positive testimony of identifying witnesses." A year after Uchansky's conviction, though, Amatksy came forward with information "that enabled this office to establish Uchansky's innocence and to secure his release." At the hearing to set aside the conviction, both the district attorney and the judge expressed the view that the three eyewitnesses against Uchansky "had made an honest mistake." The district attorney conspicuously omitted a key fact in its summary of the case: Amatsky had insisted all along that Uchansky had nothing to do with robbery. New York DA Report at 146-47; Frank and Frank, *Not Guilty*, 96-99.
72	**Hogan acknowledged that . . . "in *good faith*"**: New York DA Report, 146.
72	**"five responsible citizens"**: New York DA Report, 150.
72	**"goal of 100 per cent"**: "Campbell Case Laid to Dewey's 100% Goal," *New York Times*, August 29, 1945, 16.
72-73	**Under the heading . . . "and perhaps insoluble"**: New York DA Report, 150-151.
73	**On September 22, 1948 . . . camel hair sports coat**: The account of the Taft Cleaners armed robbery and subsequent investigation is drawn from the trial transcript in James J. Francis v. Taft Cleaners and Dyers ("Francis Transcript"), as replicated in the "Record on Appeal" filed with the New York Appellate Division, Second Department, 119 N.Y.S.2d 618 (App. Div. 1953). Citations are to the pages of the appellate record. The account of the crime is based on the deposition testimony of Florence Brennan, which was read into the record at trial. See Francis Transcript, 89-91.
73	**The next day . . . motioning urgently to her**: Francis Transcript, 63. Tafuri is identified in the trial transcript as Sue Smith. After the episode involving Francis, but before trial, Tafuri was married and changed her legal name to Smith.

73	**Brennan explained herself**: Francis Transcript, 64-65.
73	**"That's the man"**: Francis Transcript, 65.
73	**Agitated by the . . . claim the laundry**: Francis Transcript, 68.
73	**The detectives then . . . the holdup man**: Francis Transcript, 93-95.
73	**James Francis . . . for Hathaway Bakeries**: Francis Transcript, 43.
73-74	**Shortly after 9:00 . . . dark green glasses?**: Francis Transcript, 45-46.
74	**A mystified Francis . . . Hawkins said**: Francis Transcript, 46-47.
74	**Francis agreed . . . lying on a sofa**: Francis Transcript, 46-47.
74	**At the precinct . . . the tan jacket**: Francis Transcript, 49.
74	**visions of "being railroaded"**: Francis Transcript, 54.
74	**"He's not the man"**: Francis Transcript, 93.
74	**He was free to go**: Later that year, Francis sued Taft Cleaners and Dyers for false imprisonment. He alleged that Taft and its employees had given false information to police that led to his detention and imprisonment. The case went to trial in 1949. But after the plaintiff rested his case, the court dismissed the suit. The court ruled that because the Taft employees had merely given statements to the police rather than directing an arrest, there was no liability. Oral Decision of the Court, Francis Transcript, 128-134. The Appellate Division affirmed this ruling. Francis v. Taft Cleaners & Dyers, 119 N.Y.S.2d 618 (App. Div. 1953).

Chapter Seven: When the Music Stopped

76	The principal sources for the account of Manny's story in Chapters Seven, Eight, and Nine are: (1) "The Balestrero Case," which contains the trial transcript in People of the State of New York v. Christopher Balestrero ("Balestrero Transcript"), Indictment Number 271/53, Supreme Court, Queens County, April 21-23, 1953, *Wrong Man* files, WBUSC; (2) court papers filed in Manny's litigation against Prudential Insurance Company and the City of New York (which is discussed at length in Chapter Nine), including the September 15, 1954 Affidavit of Christopher Emanuel Balestrero filed in Balestrero v. Prudential Insurance Co., Index No. 6334/53 (N.Y. Sup. Ct. 1953) ("Balestrero Affidavit") (citations to the affidavit are to its original pagination); (3) reporter Herbert Brean's account of Manny's false arrest and exoneration in "A Case of Identity," *Life*, June 29, 1953, 97 (hereinafter "Brean Article"); (4) Brean's Treatment for *The Wrong Man*, which includes both Brean's reporting and extensive references to memos and correspondence from the files of Manny's attorney, Frank O'Connor; (5) dozens of newspaper articles on the case that ran between 1952 and 1956 and are cited in the notes that follow; and (6) research materials, as specified in the notes that follow, in the files for *The Wrong Man* at the Margaret Herrick Library, Academy of Motion Picture Arts and Sciences; (7) Frank O'Connor, "That's the Man: A Sobering Study of Eyewitness Identification and the Polygraph," 49 *St. John's Law Review* 1 (1974); and (8) my interviews of Greg Balestrero.
76	**An epicenter of status and glamor**: See generally Ralph Blumenthal, *Stork Club: America's Most Famous Nightspot and The Lost World of Cafe Society* (New York: Little Brown and Company, First Back Bay paperback edition, 2001). Hitchcock frequented the Club in the period after D-Day, for example. Blumenthal, *Stork Club*, 26-27.
77	**By the beginning of 1953 . . . from the club**: Blumenthal, *Stork Club*, 151-52.
77	**On Saturday night . . . million in sales**: "The Stork Club" (television review), *Variety*, January 14, 1953, 27.
77	**The lyrics**: Slim Willet (writer), *Don't Let the Stars Get in Your Eyes*.
77	**for twenty-one years**: James Louttit, "Wife of Musician Falsely Accused Lives in Constant State of Fear," *Long Island Star-Journal*, November 23, 1953, 2 (reporting Manny's statement that he and Rose have "been married for 21 years – all of them in this apartment").
77	**Before the nightmare**: Unless otherwise noted, the facts of Manny's and Rose's upbringing and life before the false arrest are based on government records available through Ancestry.com and my interviews with Greg Balestrero.
78	**"I was a puny kid"**: Brean Treatment, 1.
78	**soon taught himself**: Brean Treatment, 1.
78	**After two years . . . were twenty-two**: GB Interview; Brean Treatment, 2.
78	**joined the local musicians' union**: Brean Treatment, 2
78	**Latin music orchestras**: Brean Treatment, 2.
78	**steady employment at**: Brean Treatment, 47; Balestrero Affidavit, 18 (referring to his employment as a musician with "the Latin band" at the Stork Club).
78-79	**Manny enjoyed . . . Fifty-Third Street in Manhattan**: Brean Treatment, 3.
79	**"quiet, inoffensive, peace-loving"**: Brean Treatment, 3.
79	**"never been in a fight"**: Brean Treatment, 6.
79	**Manny was also . . . St. Malachy's Church**: Brean Treatment, 14; "Resume of Meeting with Mr. Eugene Conforti, Olga Conforti and Mr. and Mrs. Balestrero, Sr.," ("Resume of Conforti Meeting"), Unsigned memo dated February 6, 1956, *The Wrong Man* – Research, 1955-56, File 1037, AHPMHL.
79	**the Actors' Chapel**: Art Cohn, "St. Malachy's Is Haven for Actors," Troy Record (Troy, New York), October 24, 1943, 19.
79	**In early July . . . the rain resumed**: This account of the Balestreros' vacation is based on (1) "Interview with Mr. & Mrs. Ferrero on Sunday 12th Feb.," unsigned memo, *The Wrong Man* – Research, 1955-56, File 1037, AHPMHL; (2) GB Interview; and (3) Brean Treatment, 21-25, 25-26, 59-60.
79	**two blocks from his Jackson Heights home**: Brean Treatment, 3.
79	**Each day, thousands . . . Prudential Insurance Company**: Brean Treatment, 7-8.
79	**At 12:30 p.m.**: Balestrero Transcript, 23-24. My account of the first Prudential holdup is based on the testimony of Constance Ello and Yolanda Casagrande at Manny's trial as well as the front-page article headlined "Gunman Robs Busy Office in Jackson Heights," *Long Island Star-Journal*, July 9, 1952. Ello's testimony about the July 9 holdup appears at pp. 23-28 of the trial transcript and Casagrande's is at pp. 90-94.
80	**circulated the following description**: "Descriptions circulated by police of holdup man," *The Wrong Man* - Script, 1957, File 1015, AHPMHL.
80	**About five months later**: My account of the second Prudential holdup is based on (1) Ello's trial testimony, which appears at pp. 29-34 of the trial transcript; (2) the testimony of Catherine Di Clemente, which appears at pp. 69-74 of the transcript; and (3) the front-page article headlined "Insurance Firm Robbed Again," *Long Island Star-Journal*, December 18, 1952.
81	**bandit that varied**: "Descriptions circulated by police of holdup man," AHPMHL.
81	**Manny's visit to . . . pay the bills**: Balestrero Affidavit, 2; Brean Treatment, 8, 47; Brean Article, 98.
81	**Balestreros had several . . . and Rose's policies**: Brean Treatment, 47; "Stork Club Fiddler in Holdup Trial Wins Point in Clash Over Identity," *Long Island Star-Journal*, April 22, 1953, 17.

81   **For the children's policies . . . were on strike**: Brean Treatment, 47; "Agents Ordered to Quit Work," *Long Island Star-Journal*, December 1, 1951, 5 (reporting that "more than 450 insurance agents in Queens were called out on strike by the Insurance Agents International Union").

81   **on January 13 . . . for groceries nearby**: Brean Treatment, 8, 10, 48; Balestrero Affidavit, 2-3.

81-82   **the Prudential employee . . . Kopp said**: "Resume of Meeting at Prudential Office," Unsigned and undated memo, *The Wrong Man* – Research, 1955-56, File 1037, AHPMHL.

82   **Kopp and Miller . . . "I'm not getting up from this desk"**: "Resume of Meeting at Prudential Office," AHPMHL. Balestrero Transcript, 35-37 (Ello testimony).

82   **Catherine Di Clemente . . . the same conclusion**: Balestrero Transcript, 75-77, 84 (Di Clemente testimony).

82   **After Manny left . . . to Manny's arrest**: "Resume of Meeting at Prudential," AHPMHL.

82   **On January 14 . . . around 5:45 p.m**: Balestrero Affidavit, 3; Brean Treatment, 3.

82   **He then heard . . . went to the precinct**: Brean Treatment, 4-5.

82   **Herberich and Leigh Wilson**: Tom Sander, "Alfred Hitchcock Presents Leigh Wilson," *Florida Today*, July 29, 1973, 1B.

82   **They told Manny . . . "just for identification"**: Brean Treatment, 5-6, 13.

82   **situation was ridiculous**: Brean Treatment, 48 (quoting from Frank O'Connor's January 23, 1953 memo).

82   **"nothing to fear"**: Brean Article, 97.

82   **paraded him through**: Balestrero Affidavit, 3; Brean Article, 97.

82   **"under the gaze"**: Balestrero Affidavit, 3.

82   **None of the proprietors**: Balestrero Affidavit, 3.

82-83   **Back at the 110th . . . pay the policy premiums**: Brean Treatment, 6-7, 13-14.

83   **he had nothing to worry about**: Brean Treatment, 48 (citing O'Connor's January 23 memo).

83   **declined to let him call Rose**: Brean Treatment, 14.

83   **Instead, the detectives . . . and Yolanda Casagrande**: Balestrero Affidavit, 4; Balestrero Transcript, 55-56 (Ello testimony).

83   **positioned the hat**: Balestrero Affidavit, 4.

83   **After telling Manny . . . use block letters**: Brean Treatment, 11.

83   **At the detectives'. . . in his guilt**: O'Connor, "That's the Man," 6.

83   **Assistant District Attorney . . . they were mistaken**: Brean Treatment, 49.

83   **Instead, Cullen directed . . . as the bandit**: Balestrero Affidavit, 4; Balestrero Transcript, 38-39 (Ello testimony); Brean Treatment, 13.

84   **Cullen then confronted . . . actual holdup note**: Brean Treatment, 50.

84   **Over Manny's continuing . . . prayed for deliverance**: Brean Treatment, 14.

84   **When Manny did . . . had been reported**: "Resume of Conforti Meeting," AHPMHL.

84   **"There was a lot of crying"**: GB Interview.

84   **The mystery of . . . about a loan**: This account of the detective's visit is based on a February 29, 1956 letter from Alfred Hitchcock to coscreenwriter Malcolm Anderson. In that letter, Hitchcock describes a telephone discussion between Rose and associate producer Herbert Coleman, who was assisting with research for *The Wrong Man*. While Brean reported in *Life* magazine that two detectives searched the Balestrero home for the blue overcoat, Rose told Coleman that only one detective was present. See Alfred Hitchcock, Letter to Maxwell Anderson, February 29, 1956, *The Wrong Man* – Script, 1955-56, File 1012, AHPMHL. See also "Resume of Conforti Meeting," AHPMHL.

84   **Queens Felony Court**: "Resume of Conforti Meeting," AHPMHL.

84   **On the morning of . . . to signal his innocence**: "Resume of Conforti Meeting," AHPMHL.

84   **set at $7,500**: "7,500 Bail Set for Musician," *Long Island Star-Journal*, January 16, 1953, 3; Brean Treatment, 50.

84-85   **After that appearance . . . an individual cell**: Herbert Coleman, "Notes re: Int. Long Island City Jail," March 5, 1956, *The Wrong Man* – Research, 1955-56, File 1037, AHPMHL.

85   **Around 5:00 p.m. . . . being released on bail**: Brean Treatment, 17-18.

85   **Guards escorted Manny . . . fell into Gene's arms**: Brean Treatment, 18.

85   **Earlier, Gene had . . . secured Manny's release**: "Resume of Conforti Meeting," AHPMHL; "Information on Bailing from Peerless Casualty Company," *The Wrong Man* - Script, 1957, File 1015, AHPMHL.

85   **read about the arrest**: "Her Memory Pins Robbery on Man," *Daily News*, January 16, 1953, 15; "Was It Mistaken Identity? Musician Accused as Holdup Man," *Long Island Star-Journal*, January 15, 1953, 1.

85   **both papers misspelled**: "Her Memory Pins," 15; "Was It Mistaken Identity?" 1.

85   **Manny retained Frank . . . doctor recommended him**: "Resume of Conforti Meeting," AHPMHL; Brean Treatment, 20.

85   **In a disquieting . . . the two offices**: Brean Treatment, 20; Ruth Reynolds, "A Tragedy of Errors," *Daily News*, October 3, 1954, 94.

85   **On the same . . . the December 18 Prudential holdup**: Brean Treatment, 7-8, 23.

85   **met with O'Connor**: Brean Treatment, 20.

85   **"Manny would walk five blocks"**: Brean Treatment, 21.

85   **By the end of the meeting . . . "she sold me"**: Brean Treatment, 21.

86   **Rose was a child**: The background about Rose's upbringing and personal history is based on my interview with Greg Balestrero and records at Ancestry.com.

86   **Another devastating blow . . . only twenty-four**: "One Killed, Five Hurt as Autos Crash," *Standard Union* (Brooklyn), January 30, 1931, 4.

87   **Before her husband's arrest . . . "my right hand"**: Brean Treatment, 17.

87   **Rose's behavior changed . . . "a state of depression"**: Brean Treatment, 54.

87   **In the days . . . "slipping away from us"**: Louttit, "Wife of Musician," 2.

87   **On February 20 . . . "a large vanity mirror"**: Brean Treatment, 57-58.

87   **Several days later . . . "deeply despondent"**: "Resume of Meeting with Drs. Banay & Rouke," Unsigned memo, *The Wrong Man* – Research, 1955-56, File 1037, AHPMHL; "Dr. Ralph Banay, Psychiatrist, Dies," *New York Times*, May 17, 1970, 88 (referring to Banay's tenure at Sing Sing).

87   **Banay did not believe . . . charges against Manny**: Alfred Hitchcock, Letter to Maxwell Anderson, March 15, 1956, MAPHRC. In his letter, Hitchcock indicates that Dr. Banay relayed this information to Angus MacPhail.

87   **immediately to Greenmont**: "Resume of Meeting with Drs. Banay & Rouke," AHPMHL.

87   **Heeding this . . . "breakdown and collapse"**: Balestrero Affidavit, 8.

87   **Out on bail . . . to and from work**: "Resume of Conforti Meeting," AHPMHL; Brean Treatment, 19.

87-88   **Manny's mother moved**: "Resume of Conforti Meeting," AHPMHL.
88   **His extended family . . . "in a big way"**: GB Interview.
88   **Meanwhile, O'Connor tried . . . not be wrong**: Brean Treatment, 50-52.
88   **O'Connor then made . . . seven years earlier**: "Says Bandit Must Be His Double," *Long Island Daily Press*, April 22, 1953, 1.
88   **grand jury indicted**: Brean Treatment, 57.
88   **With Rose institutionalized . . . April 21, 1953**: Brean Treatment, 57-58.
88   **arranged a lie detector test**: O'Connor, "That's the Man," 2; Brean Treatment, 58.
88   **not admissible evidence**: Brean Treatment, 52 (citing February 24, 1953 memorandum from O'Connor). Polygraph evidence remains inadmissible in criminal cases in New York. See, e.g., People v. Shedrick, 66 N.Y.2d 1015, 1018 (1985) ("The reliability of the polygraph has not been demonstrated with sufficient certainty to be admissible in this State.").
88   **routinely used the tests**: Editorial, "Lie Detectors," *Long Island Star-Journal*, May 1, 1953, 8 (describing several Queens cases in which police relied on lie detector results to eliminate suspects).
88   **Quinn relied on**: Bigelow, "Hoffner Given Freedom," 1.
88   **O'Connor retained . . . West Ninety-Eighth Street in Manhattan**: Brean Treatment, 58.
88   **Yet Manny himself . . . "like a reed in the wind"**: O'Connor, "That's the Man," 2.
88   **Rouke posed questions**: "Original Copy of Questions Dr. Rouke Asked of Manny on His First Visit for Lie Detection Test on Feb. 23," *The Wrong Man* - Script, 1957, File 1015, AHPMHL.
88-89   **Manny's anxiety was eased . . . prosecution would proceed**: O'Connor, 2; Brean Treatment, 58; "Resume of Meeting with Drs. Banay & Rouke," AHPMHL.
89   **In February 1953 . . . at the farm on that date**: "Interview with Mr. & Mrs. Ferrero," AHPMHL.
89   **But then came . . . died of a heart attack**: "Interview with Mr. & Mrs. Ferrero," AHPMHL; "Resume of Conforti Meeting," AHPMHL; Brean Treatment, 25.
89   **Manny learned of the deaths**: Resume of Conforti Meeting, AHPMHL.
89   **powerful alibi defense**: The details about Manny's alibis are based on: (1) Brean Treatment, 21-28, 56, 59-62; (2) "Interview with Mr. & Mrs. Ferrero," AHPMHL; and (3) "Resume of Conforti Meeting," AHPMHL.
89   **Ferrero agreed to sign an affidavit**: Brean Treatment, 56, 60.
89-90   **O'Connor also tracked . . . "exceptionally fine witness"**: Brean Treatment, 25-29, 56-57.
90   **He lost weight . . . missed his cues**: Brean Treatment, 31-32, 36.
90   **fear that a police officer would seize him**: Brean Treatment, 36.

Chapter Eight: Trial

91   **Crisona's opening statement**: The opening appears at pages 5-17 of the Balestrero Transcript.
91   **a jury of ten men and two women**: "Stork Club Fiddler in Holdup Trial," 17.
91   **"was in trouble with the bookies"**: Balestrero Transcript, 16-17.
91-92   **Herberich claimed that**: "Additional Notes on Balestrero Case," *The Wrong Man* - Script, 1957, File 1015, AHPMHL.
92   **And Manny himself acknowledged**: Brean Treatment, 11.
92   **But he did not gamble . . . "that it wasn't"**: GB Interview.
92   **In his opening . . . "I don't want to tip my hand"**: Balestrero Transcript, 18-22.
92   **Crisona's first witness**: Ello's testimony appears at pages 22-68 of the Balestrero Transcript. Her identification of Manny by touching of the shoulder is recorded on page 28.
92   **Ello trembled with . . . table for support**: Brean Treatment, 33-35.
92   **The trauma had . . . she nearly fainted**: Brean Treatment, 14, 33-34.
92-93   **On cross-examination . . . "Yes, I do"**: Balestrero Transcript, 47-48.
93   **the jurors turned**: "Stork Club Fiddler in Holdup Trial," 17.
93   **"quite dark, almost black"**: "Says Bandit Must Be His Double," *Long Island Daily Press*, April 22, 1953, 1, 7.
93   **admitted she told police**: Balestrero Transcript, 48.
93   **O'Connor then questioned . . . "lighted doorway"**: Balestrero Transcript, 55-56.
93   **O'Connor then secured . . . "Yes, one of the men"**: Balestrero Transcript, 56-58.
93   **also included police officers**: O'Connor, "That's the Man," 6.
93-94   **Ello betrayed doubt . . . "No, sir"**: Balestrero Transcript, 38.
94   **Crisona next called . . . "Yes, sir"**: Balestrero Transcript, 73, 77.
94   **During a short . . . the payment receipt**: Balestrero Transcript, 65 (Ello cross-examination), 80-82 (Di Clemente cross-examination).
94   **Manny faced a . . . undergoing "psychiatric treatment"**: Balestrero Transcript, 106. During the lie detector exam, Dr. Rouke was sufficiently alarmed about Manny's "extreme nervousness" that he asked Dr. Banay (the same psychiatrist who would later treat Rose) to examine him. "Resume of Meeting with Drs. Banay & Rouke," AHPMHL.
94   **"I will continue the bail"**: Balestrero Transcript, 106-107.
94   **The trial resumed . . . "of questioned documents"**: Balestrero Transcript, 108.
95   **the handwriting on the two notes was "identical"**: Brean Treatment, 50.
95   **"does not show enough similarity"**: Balestrero Transcript, 112.
95   **In a short examination . . . "That is correct"**: Balestrero Transcript, 114-115.
95   **Groat was not impressed . . . "after that testimony"**: Balestrero Transcript, 115.
95   **more than 100 questions**: O'Connor's cross-examination of Sang appears at pages 115-150 of the transcript.
95   **He drew out . . . any apparent payoff**: Balestrero Transcript, 127-141.
95-96   **Near the end . . . "different people wrote them?"**: Balestrero Transcript, 143-144. The book O'Connor quoted from was Albert S. Osborn, *Questioned Documents* (Albany: Boyd Printing Company, 1946).
96   **On July 9 she had returned**: Balestrero Transcript, 90-92.
96-97   **O'Connor got Casagrande . . . "exactly thirty-five seconds"**: Balestrero Transcript, 28, 160-163.
97   **Having punctured Casagrande's. . . "No, I do not know"**: Balestrero Transcript, 171-174.
97   **Suddenly, O'Connor heard . . . "to this nonsense?"**: Balestrero Transcript, 174, 179-180.
97   **"do we have to sit here"**: Balestrero Transcript, 174-175.
97   **an engineer from Kew Gardens**: "Juror's Gripe Forces Robbery Case Mistrial," *Long Island Star-Journal*, April 23, 1953, 1, 2. The *Long Island Star-Journal* reported Espenschied's name, occupation and address. While Espenschied is not named as juror number four in the trial transcript, Brean also identified Espenschied as the juror in his *Life* article and in his treatment for the film. Brean Article, 104; Brean Treatment, 34. See also Donald Spoto, *The Dark Side of*

Genius: The Life of Alfred Hitchcock (New York: Ballantine Books, 1983), 407 (noting that during research conducted for *The Wrong Man*, Judge Groat confirmed that Espenschied's remark led to the mistrial).

97   **"The Court is the sole judge"**: Balestrero Transcript, 175.

98   **O'Connor doubted . . . a complete breakdown**: Brean Treatment, 35.

98   **heard juror number five**: Balestrero Transcript, 180, 187-88.

98   **"audible stage whisper"**: "Juror's Gripe Forces Robbery Case Mistrial," *Long Island Star-Journal*, April 23, 1953, 1, 2.

98   **"very clear indication"**: Balestrero Transcript, 180.

98   **"I do not think . . . a similar nature around here"**: Balestrero Transcript, 180-181.

98   **Back in court . . . oppose O'Connor's motion**: Balestrero Transcript, 187-189.

98   **declared a mistrial . . . "rights of a defendant"**: Balestrero Transcript, 189-190. In granting O'Connor's motion, Judge Groat directed the clerk to "withdraw a juror." Historically in New York and elsewhere, this step was taken in any circumstance where the court determined a new trial was necessary (including in cases where the reason for mistrial was unrelated to juror misconduct). So, for example, if a party moved for a mistrial on the ground that the jury had heard prejudicial testimony that should not have come into evidence, withdrawing a juror was the procedural vehicle for granting the motion. Clarence N. Callender, *American Courts: Their Organization and Procedure* (New York: McGraw Hill, 1927), 100. The removal of a juror meant that the jury was incomplete and the trial could not continue. David D. Siegel and Patrick M. Connors, *New York Practice* (Sixth Edition), Section 4.03 - "Motion for a Mistrial," (Thomson Reuters, 2022); Schultze v. Huttlinger, 150 A.D. 489 (N.Y. App. Div. 1912). In Manny's case, in response to Judge Groat's direction to "withdraw a juror," the clerk read the name of a juror ("John Newmar"), the judge responded that "he has stepped aside" and both the clerk and the judge announced that "the jury is incomplete." Balestrero Transcript, 189.

98   **Espenschied worked as . . . airplanes and other objects**: Joan Cook, "Lloyd Espenschied, One of the Inventors of the Coaxial Cable" (obituary), *New York Times*, July 4, 1986, A16.

98   **Espenschied made plans . . . the day before**: Espenschied, Lloyd, Letter to Hotel Shoreham (Washington, DC), March 30, 1953, Series Four, Box 28, Lloyd Espenschied Papers, Archives Center, National Museum of American History.

99   **In 1944, for example . . . the war effort**: Jon Gertner, *The Idea Factory: Bell Labs and the Great Age of American Innovation* (New York: Penguin Press, 2012), 63-64 and n.10 (quoting from Lloyd Espenschied, "Memo: Visit by a Young Investigator of the War Department," January 25, 1944, 4:50 p.m., AT&T archives). I obtained a copy of the memo from the Espenschied papers housed at the Smithsonian. See Lloyd Espenschied, "Visit by a Young Investigator of the War Department," January 25, 1944, Series Four, Box 25, Lloyd Espenschied Papers, Archives Center, National Museum of American History.

99   **"I spent the rest of the time"**: Lloyd Espenschied, "American Background of the Espenschieds During the War," April 9, 1951, 4, located in Lloyd Espenschied Genealogical Research Papers, NYGB Coll 157, [01-004], The Irma and Paul Milstein Division of United States History, Local History and Genealogy, The New York Public Library.

99   **a visit by Espenschied . . . "by the Jews"**: Lloyd Espenschied, *The German Background of the Espenschied-Esbenshade Families* (Reynolds Historical Genealogy Collection, 1938), 61-62, 65.

99   **made him "a marked man"**: "American Background of the Espenschieds," 3.

99   **"of having been a German agent" . . . "catering to the Jews"**: Lloyd Espenschied, Letter to Paul Hardaway, September 24, 1953, 3, located in Lloyd Espenschied Genealogical Research Papers, NYGB Coll 157, [01-031], The Irma and Paul Milstein Division of United States History, Local History and Genealogy, The New York Public Library.

99-100   **"keep an eye on my home"**: Lloyd Espenschied, Letter to Police Department, 102nd Precinct, April 24, 1953, Series Four, Box 28, Lloyd Espenschied Papers, Archives Center, National Museum of American History.

100   **accepted each of the 12 jurors**: Brean Treatment, 33.

100   **O'Connor claimed that**: Brean Treatment, 64.

100   **it would have convicted**: Riley, "Musician Learns," 3.

100   **jury would not have believed**: Robert Bigelow, "'The Wrong Man' Is a Story of Horror, Not Suspense," *Long Island Star-Journal*, December 24, 1956, 3.

100   **In preparing for . . . changed expression**: "2/7 – Meeting with Mr. Joseph Vincent Micucci," Unsigned memo, *The Wrong Man* – Research, 1955-56, File 1037, AHPMHL.

100   **another obstacle . . . the stand at all**: "Resume of Conforti Meeting," AHPMHL.

100   **traveled to a resort**: "Resume of Conforti Meeting," AHPMHL.

100   **"a *Dirty Dancing* vacation spot"**: GB Interview.

100   **Groat set the date**: Brean Treatment, 36.

100-01   **On the afternoon of . . . promised to do so**: The details concerning the Greenmont visit are based on Manny's comments to the *Long Island Star-Journal* immediately after his exoneration. See "Fiddler in Fog at News, 'Went Right on Playing,'" *Long Island Star-Journal*, April 30, 1953, 1.

101   **Shortly before eleven o'clock . . . was a toy**: Robert Bigelow, "Toy Gun Bandit Admits Robberies Laid to Jackson Heights Musician," *Long Island Star-Journal*, April 30, 1953, 1, 2; Royal Riley, "Cleared, He Hopes It Will Cure Wife," *Daily News*, May 1, 1953. The details of how Daniell was subdued varied in press accounts. According to Brean's *Life* magazine story, Joseph Mank seized Daniell from behind and threw him into a corner right before the police arrived. Brean Article, 104.

101   **Daniell quickly confessed . . . "I was going to try"**: Bigelow, "Toy Gun Bandit," 1, 2.

101   **Manny was on . . . about 1:30**: "Miscellaneous Questions & Answers – as per Danny – Feb. 7th 1956," *The Wrong Man* - Research, 1955-56, File 1037, AHPMHL.

101   **A piano player . . . "Don't you understand?'"**: "Fiddler in Fog," 1; Robert Bigelow, "Double, Caught Red-Handed, Clears Fiddler in Holdups," *Long Island Daily Press*, April 30, 1953, 1, 67; "Double's Arrest Clears Musician," 16.

102   **Shortly after 2:00 . . . did not answer**: Bigelow, "Double, Caught Red-Handed," 1.

102   **The next night . . . identification of Manny**: "Musician May Ask $150,000 False Arrest Damages," *Long Island Daily Press*, May 1, 1953, 1.

102   **"I never wanted to send"**: Brean Treatment, 68.

102   **"We are going to reexamine the case"**: Robert Bigelow, "D.A. to Reexamine Case of 'Cleared' Musician," *Long Island Star-Journal*, May 1, 1953, 1, 2. By May 10, Quinn had told the *Daily News* that he expected to join in a motion to dismiss the indictments against Manny. Frank Ross, "Musician Will Seek Clearing of Reputation," *Daily News*, May 10, 1953.

102   **"answer to those prayers"**: "Fiddler in Fog," 1.

102	**On June 15 . . . on the books**: "'Double' Pleads Guilty of 2 Insurance Holdups," *Long Island Star-Journal*, June 15, 1953, 1; "Holdup Double Indicted Too," *Long Island Star-Journal*, June 1, 1953. While the indictment was not dismissed until July, the state effectively cleared Manny of the charges when it decided, by late May, to indict Daniell for the Prudential holdups.
102	**indictment was dismissed**: Brean Treatment, 63.
102	**About two weeks later . . . "after he was caught"**: "Balestrero's 'Double' Given Maximum Term," *Long Island Star-Journal*, July 29, 1953, 7.
102	**Rose's continuing absence . . . "doesn't say much about coming home"**: Louttit, "Wife of Musician," 2 (photo of six-year-old Greg at kitchen table looking up at Manny).
102	**"looked enough like Daniell"**: "Held in $10,000 In Insurance Firm Holdups," *Daily News*, May 7, 1953.
102	**a "striking resemblance"**: "Double's Arrest Clears Musician," *New York Times*, May 1, 1953, 16. The *Times* continued this theme in subsequent coverage. See "'Double' Admits His Guilt," *New York Times*, June 16, 1953 (reporting that Daniell pleaded guilty to the insurance office robbery).
102-03	**all referred to Daniell**: See, e.g., Bigelow, "D.A. to Reexamine Case," 1 (reporting that Daniell "looks enough like Balestrero to be his 'double'"); Bigelow, "Double, Caught Red-Handed," 1.
103	**papers across the country**: "Double Saves Him from Prison," *Miami Herald*, May 3, 1953, 84; "Freed as Double Confesses," *Lancaster Eagle Gazette* (Lancaster, Ohio), May 4, 1953, 1; "'Double' Frees Man in Holdups," *Tipton Daily Tribune* (Tipton, Indiana), May 5, 1953, 1.
103	**"a fleeting resemblance"**: Brean Article, 107. See also O'Connor, "That's the Man," 2 (noting that Daniell "resembled Balestrero only remotely").
104	**"trousers clearly visible"**: O'Connor, "That's the Man," 6. According to O'Connor, the lineup included a uniformed desk lieutenant and police officer as well as Ello's husband. Herbert Brean's summary of O'Connor's case file notes that most of the men in the lineup were "evidently detectives." Brean Treatment, 49.
104	**Manny had it even worse**: Another aspect of Manny's lineup that made it even worse than Hoffner's was that the two eyewitnesses (Ello and Casagrande) viewed the lineup at the same time. See Wall, *Eye-Witness Identification*, 49 and n.100.
104	**not the first time Cullen had used . . . on their height**: Meyer Berger, "Sutton Fails to Take Stand; Jury Will Get Case Monday," *New York Times*, March 29, 1952, 1, 32; Robert Conway and James Desmond, "Sutton Avoids Stand and Both Sides Rest," *Daily News*, March 29, 1952, 3, 6. At trial, the lawyer who stood in the lineup, James A. McDonald, testified that the bank manager saw Sutton in the Queens District Attorney's office before the lineup.
104	**Sutton was convicted**: "Thomas P. Cullen, Legislator, Dies," *New York Times*, January 25, 1968, 37.
104	**Di Clemente . . . did not witness**: Balestrero Transcript, 69. Di Clemente testified that she was on vacation on July 9.
104	**Kopp . . . was not in the office**: Balestrero Transcript, 44-45. Ello testified that, before Yolanda Casagrande walked into the office, the only two women there besides Ello were a "Miss Trisano and Miss di Giovanni." Neither Trisano nor di Giovanni witnessed the robbery.
104	**towards the rear of the office**: Brean Treatment, 9.
104	**Only Ello signed**: "Her Memory Pins Robbery," 15; "Was It Mistaken Identity?", 1.
104	**But based on . . . Di Clemente and Ello**: Balestrero Transcript, 35-38, 75-78, 84-86.
104-05	**"a motion that she recognized"**: Balestrero Transcript, 74-75.
105	**"it was the same man"**: Balestrero Transcript, 85.
105	**"A few seconds"**: Balestrero Transcript, 85.
105	**As Ello recounted . . . "the previous occasions"**: Balestrero Transcript, 35-37.
105	**"I was afraid"**: Balestrero Transcript, 35.
105	**far from the public counter**: Brean Treatment, 9.
106	**in an example of "tunnel vision"**: Findley and Scott, "Multiple Dimensions of Tunnel Vision," 292.
106	**Daniell confessed to thirty-eight**: Bigelow, "Double, Caught Red-Handed," 67.
106	**Similar thinking would . . . so soon after the crime**: Patrick O'Shaughnessy, "Don't Bank on Robber's Smarts," *Daily News*, November 25, 2001, 6.
106	**Schreiner was exonerated**: Herbert Lowe, "The Right Man Gets Cleared," *Newsday*, December 19, 2001, 13; John Marzulli, "Wrong Man Is Arrested in Queens Bank Heist," *Daily News*, December 18, 2001, 30.
106	**"'knew' they had the right man"**: O'Connor, "That's the Man," 6.
106-07	**pronounce the word as "draw"**: Serena Tara, "New Study Shows Thirteen Words New Yorkers Say Differently," *thrillist* website, May 27, 2022, accessed September 9, 2022 (reporting on study finding New Yorkers tend to say "draw" rather than "drawer"); Let's Go Inc., *Roadtripping USA 2nd Edition: The Complete Coast-to-Coast Guide to America* (Let's Go Publications, 2007), 45 (in context of a "linguistic tour of the Northeast," travel guide advises that in Boston and New York, "drawer is pronounced draw").
107	**Supreme Court of South Carolina**: State v. Hughes, 493 S.E.2d 821, 822 (S.C. 1997).
107	**Images of holdup notes**: These images appeared in Ordway Hilton, "Handwriting Identification vs. Eye Witness Identification," 45 *Journal of Criminal Law, Criminology and Police Science* 207, 208-210 (1954-1955).
107	**"repeated, small differences"**: Hilton, "Handwriting Identification," 209.
108	**"sufficient to give rise to a serious doubt"**: Hilton, "Handwriting Identification," 210.
108	**no ordinary expert . . . including New York**: See Robert McG. Thomas, Jr., "Ordway Hilton, 84, Authority Who Detected Forged Papers," *New York Times*, May 10, 1998, 37 (obituary); "The 1950 Short Course for Prosecuting Attorneys at Northwestern University School of Law," 41 *Journal of Criminal Law and Criminology* 533, 538 and n. 16 (1950).
108	**been regularly consulted**: "Elbridge Stein, Signature Expert," *New York Times*, September 19, 1970, 30.
108	**police lab confirmed**: "Jackson Heights Musician Cleared of Holdups Admitted by Double," *Long Island Star-Journal*, July 14, 1953, 4.
108	**O'Connor told the . . . until after Daniell's confession**: Brean Treatment, 56; "Musician's Double in 2 Stickups for Jury Under $10,000 Bail," *Long Island Star-Journal*, May 7, 1953, 1 (reporting that in response to O'Connor's stated intention to seek dismissal of the indictment, "at present Quinn is obtaining statements from alibi witnesses who were to testify."); "Musician Fights to Clean Slate of 2 Robberies," *Long Island Star-Journal*, March 18, 1953, 26 (reporting on O'Connor's claim about the alibi witnesses).
108-09	**he had "great faith"**: "Lie Test Backs Mate's Story in Wife's Slaying," *Daily News*, August 13, 1952, 77.
109	**in the Hoffner case**: Robert Bigelow, *Hoffner Given Freedom After 12 Years in Prison*, *Long Island Star-Journal*, November 21, 1952, 1.
109	**he had "learned"**: "Jackson Heights Musician Cleared," 4.

109 **O'Connor had the results sent**: "Resume of Meeting with Drs. Banay & Rouke," AHPMHL (noting that O'Connor asked Dr. Rouke to send a copy of the results to the district attorney); "Musician Fights to Clean Slate," 26 (reporting O'Connor's statements about Manny's lie detector test).

109 **"I am not a judge or jury"**: Herb Kelly, "Detective Who Seized Musician Lives Here," *Miami News*, February 1, 1957, 25.

109 **"it wasn't necessary"**: Sander, "Leigh Wilson," 1B.

109 **"never accused us"**: Kelly, "Detective Who Seized," 25.

109 **"there wasn't a finger laid on him"**: Sander, "Leigh Wilson," 2B.

109 **Perhaps Wilson saw . . . of the charges**: "3 Policemen Indicted," *New York Times*, May 8, 1945, 21; "3 Policemen Are Cleared of Assault," *Long Island Daily Press*, June 12, 1945, 6.

109 **Herberich had served**: "2 Sleuths, with 76 Years' Service, Retire," *Long Island Star-Journal*, June 5, 1961, 8.

109 **"until they made a movie out of it"**: Sander, "Leigh Wilson," 1B.

109 **"God's will"**: James M. Doyle, "Learning from Error in American Criminal Justice," 100 *Journal of Criminal Law and Criminology* 109, 125 (2010).

109-10 **Doyle cites . . . "man who did this"**: Doyle, "Learning from Error," 125; Maria Cramer, "Police Head Defends Role After Wrongful Imprisonment," *Boston Globe*, December 25, 2008, B1, B5.

110 **"a strong case against him"**: "Lie Detectors," 8.

110 **"given every right"**: Brean Article, 99.

110 **"acting as agents"**: Brean Treatment, 68.

110 **"They couldn't help it"**: Brean Article, 107. In his groundbreaking 1965 book on eyewitness identification, criminal defense attorney Patrick Wall referred to Manny's comment that the police "couldn't help it" and asserted that "they most surely could have." Wall's book is a rare source that cited Manny's case as an example of the need for reform in identification procedures. Wall, *Eye-Witness Identification*, 216 ("And as long as those procedures and rules which foster erroneous identification are tolerated by those who have the power to eliminate them, then those persons must share the blame for the miscarriages of justice which will inevitably occur").

110 **"only did their duty"**: Bigelow, "D.A. to Reexamine Case," 2.

110 **"was behind this action"**: Bigelow, "D.A. to Reexamine Case," 2.

110 **an election he won**: Dennis Hevesi, "Frank O'Connor, 82, Is Dead; Retired New York Appellate Judge," *New York Times*, December 3, 1992, D21.

Chapter Nine: Stricken Again: The Fight for Compensation

111 **"All's Well That Ends Well"**: Bigelow, "D.A. to Reexamine Case," 1. The quoted phrase appeared as the lead-in to a caption photo of Manny and his sons in their Jackson Heights home with Manny's mother and O'Connor.

111 **"hazy world of self-incrimination"**: Louttit, "Wife of Musician," 2.

111 **"it was really not a lot of engagement"**: GB Interview.

112 **With Rose still . . . minded the boys**: Louttit, "Wife of Musician," 2.

112 **Greenmont Sanitarium charged $125 per week**: Balestrero Affidavit, 8.

112 **cumulative cost of Rose's care**: Affidavit of Frank O'Connor in Support of Motion for Preference, September 15, 1954, filed in Balestrero v. Prudential Insurance Co., Index No. 6334/53 (N.Y. Sup. Ct. 1953).

112 **added up to about $6,300**: Balestrero Affidavit, 9.

112 **lacked probable cause**: Davis v. Carroll, 159 N.Y.S. 568 (App. Div. 1916) (police officers who arrested man on train without a warrant were not liable where they had "reasonable grounds for believing that a felony had been committed and that plaintiff was one of the guilty parties"). A subsequent acquittal does not remove the "reasonable cause" that police had at the time of arrest. Schultz v. Greenwood Cemetery, 190 N.Y. 276, 278 (1907) ("innocent parties may sometimes be subjected to inconvenience and mortification; but any more lax rule would be greatly dangerous to the peace of the community and make the escape of criminals frequent and easy.").

112 **New York courts had long held**: Bass v. State, 92 N.Y.S.2d 42 (Ct. Cl. 1949) (state trooper's arrest was lawful, even without a warrant, where felony victim had made "positive identification of the person arrested"); Stearns v. N.Y. City Transit, 200 N.Y.S.2d 272 (Sup. Ct. 1960) ("The arrest by a peace officer of a person for a felony, upon the positive identification of the victim of the felony, is a lawful arrest, even when made without a warrant"), *affirmed*, 209 N.Y.S.2d 264 (App. Div. 1960).

112 **grand jury indictment created a presumption**: Levy v. Chasnoff, 283 N.Y.S. 891 (App. Div. 1935).

112 **"fraud, perjury or suppression of evidence"**: Langley v. City of New York, 337 N.Y.S.2d 460 (App. Div. 1972) (citing Morgan v. New York Cent. R. R. Co., 9 N.Y.S.2d 32 (App. Div. 1939)).

112 **within the scope of their employment**: Stearns, 200 N.Y.S.2d at 274.

112 **"does not act at his peril"**: Barnes v. Bollhorst, 225 N.Y.S 2d 286, 288 (Sup. Ct. 1962) (even though liquor store owner misidentified plaintiff as the man who assaulted him and the identification led to plaintiff's arrest, the store owner was not liable for false arrest where he "did no more than furnish information to the police for their guidance").

112 **instigated or procured the arrest without reasonable justification**: Grinnell v. Weston, 88 N.Y.S. 781 (App. Div. 1904) (where defendant procured plaintiff's arrest, jury had to decide whether defendant was justified in believing plaintiff to be guilty of the crime and was justified in bringing about the arrest); Stearns, 200 N.Y.S.2d at 276-277 (in claim for false imprisonment, it was a question of fact whether the defendant had reasonable cause to believe plaintiff was the criminal at the time defendant mistakenly identified him).

112-13 **he had to prove "malice"**: Stearns, 200 N.Y.S.2d at 276 (employee's signing of complaint and mistaken identification did not establish cause of action for malicious prosecution "since malice was absent"); Schultz, 190 N.Y. at 278 ("plaintiff must allege and prove not only the want of probable cause for the prosecution, but also that it was inspired by malice").

113 **Manny sued Prudential . . . not have indicted Manny**: Complaint, Balestrero v. Prudential Insurance Co., Index No. 6334/53 (N.Y. Sup. Ct. 1953), replicated in Record on Appeal, Balestrero v. Prudential Ins. Co., 307 N.Y. 709 (1954).

114 **On April 27, 1905**: The facts of the Hutchinson case are drawn from Hutchinson v. Stern, 115 A.D. 791, 791-792 (N.Y. App. Div. 1906).

114 **His wife . . . "the sum of One thousand Dollars"**: Hutchinson, 115 A.D. at 792.

114 **They moved to strike . . . the alleged wrong**: Hutchinson, 115 A.D. at 791-793; Hampton v. Jones, 58 Iowa 317, 320 (1882).

114 **Only a year earlier . . . "anguish in such circumstances"**: Roher v. State, 112 N.Y.S. 2d 603 (App. Div. 1952).

114-15 **In October 1953 . . . Manny's "unfortunate experience"**: "Prudential Claims Wife's Illness Not an Issue in Balestrero's Suit," *Long Island Star-Journal*, October 22, 1953, 7.

115   **"one of the worst experiences that can happen"**: "Prudential Claims," 7.

115   **Even so, on . . . from the complaint**: Balestrero v. Prudential Ins. Co., 126 N.Y.S.2d 792, 793 (Sup. Ct. 1953).

115   **Manny moved Rose . . . dollars per week**: Balestrero Affidavit, 8.

115   **Appellate Division affirmed . . . based on Rose's injury**: Balestrero v. Prudential Ins. Co., 128 N.Y.S.2d 295 (App. Div. 1954).

115   **denied the appeal**: Balestrero v. Prudential Ins. Co., 307 N.Y. 709 (1954).

115   **"causation was not established"**: Maricle v. Glazier, 307 N.Y. 738, 742 (1954) (Van Voorhis, J., dissenting).

115   **never been treated for mental disorders**: Balestrero Affidavit, 8.

115   **"She was badly frightened for me"**: Louttit, "Wife of Musician," 2.

115   **"causation" required . . . "almost unlimited"**: Maricle v. Glazier, 307 N.Y. 738, 742 (1954) (Van Voorhis, J., dissenting).

115   **close to $10,000**: Balestrero Affidavit, 9.

115-16   **filed an amended complaint . . . "any probable cause"**: Amended Verified Complaint in Balestrero v. Prudential Insurance Co., Index No. 6334/53 (N.Y. Sup. Ct. 1953).

116   **an average of forty-two months to get to trial**: Note, "Trial Calendar Advancement," 6 *Stanford Law Review* 323, Appendix One (1954).

116   **moved for a "preference"**: Balestrero v. Prudential Ins. Co., 137 N.Y.S.2d 134 (1955).

116   **where "the interests of justice will be served"**: This language appeared in Section 151(3) of the Rules of Civil Practice, which was the forerunner to Rule 3403 of the New York Civil Practice Law and Rules.

116   **Manny submitted an affidavit . . . was "completely destitute"**: Balestrero Affidavit, 10.

116   **The city and Prudential opposed . . . New York's public's institutions**: See "Brief on Behalf of the Defendants-Appellants The Prudential Insurance Company of America, and Constance Ello" and "Brief of Defendant-Appellant The City of New York" filed in Appellate Division, Second Department.

116   *Life* **magazine had published**: Brean Article.

116   **appeared in** *Reader's Digest*: Brean Treatment, 15.

116   **an installment of the television show Robert Montgomery Presents**: "Balestrero's Nightmare," *Life*, February 1, 1954, 45; Steven DeRosa, "Revisiting Hitchcock's *The Wrong Man*," *Writing with Hitchcock Blog*, November 10, 2010. To my knowledge, that installment is not available on DVD or to stream. Greg Balestrero mentioned to me that he had searched far and wide to try to get access to it, without success.

116   **Manny received about $3,000**: Reply Affidavit of Christopher Emanuel Balestrero, October 1, 1954, 1, filed in Balestrero v. Prudential Insurance Co., Index No. 6334/53 (N.Y. Sup. Ct. 1953).

116   **"As fast as these moneys were received"**: Balestrero Reply Affidavit, 1.

116   **On October 14 . . . after a car accident**: October 14, 1954 order at 2 (citing Rogers v. Derris, 117 N.Y.S.2d 594 (App. Div. 1952)).

117   **On January 31, 1955 . . . "in excess of $100 per week"**: Balestrero, 137 N.Y.S.2d at 134.

117   **"shock therapy treatments are given to her"**: Balestrero Reply Affidavit, 2.

117   **reserved for the most extreme cases**: Certain rulings directed that a plaintiff's financial condition was to be used sparingly to justify a preference and that the plaintiff had to show complete or near destitution. See, e.g., Healy v. Healy, 99 N.Y.S.2d 874 (Sup. Ct. 1950).

117   **"command a very high price"**: Brief on Behalf of Prudential, 13.

117   **"Warners would like to cast Frank Sinatra"**: Dorothy Kilgallen, "Broadway" (column), *Elmira Star-Gazette* (Elmira, New York), January 12, 1955, 18.

117   **intended to allow trial judges to exercise discretion**: Neil R. Farmelo, "Civil Practice in Docketing Denied Though Party Aged, Infirm and Destitute," 1 *Buffalo Law Review* 172, 173 (1951).

117   **moved to Kings County Hospital**: "Mrs. Balestrero's Confinement," *The Wrong Man* – Research, 1955-56, File 1037, AHPMHL.

117-18   **"I had to get away from that house"**: Brean Treatment, 45.

118   **received a $7,000 payment**: Jack Grady, "The 'Wrong Man' Happy After 3-Yr. Nightmare," *New York Post*, April 16, 1956; "Plans Florida Trip for Wife, Mind Healed," *Daily News*, September 30, 1955, B3.

118   **declared "well enough"**: "Balestreros Reunited After 2 Years," *Long Island Star-Journal*, September 29, 1955, 2.

118   **"My life did not start over"**: Grady, "Happy After 3-Yr. Nightmare."

118   **One week after . . . "nothing to fear"**: Arthur Miller, *The Crucible* (Penguin Orange Collection) (Reprint Edition) (New York: Penguin Books, 2016), 94, 98; J. P. Shanley, "New Miller Play Opening Tonight," *New York Times*, January 22, 1953, 20 (reporting on Broadway premier).

Chapter Ten: "My Basic Fears"

121   **"a pattern of the innocent man"**: Anthony Macklin and Alfred Hitchcock, "'It's the Manner of Telling': An Interview with Alfred Hitchcock (1976)," in *Hitchcock on Hitchcock, Volume 2*, 49, 52.

124   **is found guilty and executed**: Amy Lawrence, "Constructing a Priest, Silencing a Saint: The PCA and *I Confess*," *Film History* 1, no. 19 (2007): 58, 68 and n.53.

124   **tracks the 1902 French play**: Patrick McGilligan, *Alfred Hitchcock: A Life in Darkness and Light* (New York: HarperCollins paperback edition, 2004), 401.

124   **opposed the death penalty**: McGilligan, *Alfred Hitchcock*, 383-84.

124   **"an anti-capital punishment thriller"**: McGilligan, *Alfred Hitchcock*, 401.

124   **Warner Bros. insisted**: Billheimer, *Hitchcock and the Censors*, 177-78.

124   **"Policemen and the law"**: Leider, "Interview: Alfred Hitchcock," 260.

124   **"I was terrified"**: Leider, "Hitchcock," 260. Hitchcock told several versions of this story. As recounted in the Leider interview, his cell time lasted "several hours." But in the version he told to Truffaut, the police chief locked Hitchcock in a cell for a few minutes and told him "this is what we do to naughty boys." Truffaut, *Hitchcock*, 25.

124   **perspective of the accused**: Truffaut, *Hitchcock*, 239.

124   **"suddenly deprived of freedom"**: Truffaut, *Hitchcock*, 174.

125   **regretted not being a criminal lawyer**: "Surviving: An Interview with John Russell Taylor," in *Hitchcock on Hitchcock, Volume 1*: Selected Writings and Interviews, 1st edition, ed. Sidney Gottlieb (Berkeley and Los Angeles: University of California Press, 1997), 59, 62.

125   **"a seemingly happy home"**: Edward White, *The Twelve Lives of Alfred Hitchcock: An Anatomy of the Master of Suspense* (New York: W.W. Norton & Company, 2021) at 24, 163.

125   **As White observes**: White, *Twelve Lives*, 163.

125   **Warner Bros. had . . . but no salary**: DeRosa, "Revisiting Hitchcock's *The Wrong Man*."

125-26   **Anderson's inspiration was the Sacco-Vanzetti case**: McGilligan, *Alfred Hitchcock*, 533.

126   **There remains substantial debate**: William Grimes, "Prejudice and Politics: Sacco, Vanzetti and Fear," *New York Times*, August 15, 2007.

126   **"any stigma and disgrace"**: "Sacco, Vanzetti Names Cleared of 'Any Stigma,'" *Boston Globe*, July 20, 1977, 1.

126   **"moral implications of false indictment"**: Spoto, *Dark Side of Genius*, 406.

126   **future Supreme Court Justice . . . as a "farce"**: Felix Frankfurter, *The Case of Sacco and Vanzetti* (Universal Library Edition) (Little, Brown and Co., 1927), 30-32.

126   **Anderson drew on**: Maxwell Anderson and Harold Hickerson, *Gods of the Lightning* (Longmans, Green and Co., 1928).

126-27   **"When you identified Capraro . . . to incriminate the defendants"**: Anderson and Hickerson, *Gods*, 59.

127   **"They told me"**: Anderson and Hickerson, *Gods*, 44.

127   **"You don't have to say"**: Anderson and Hickerson, *Gods*, 48.

127   **Bartlet uses . . . the cross-examination**: Anderson and Hickerson, *Gods*, 58-59.

127   **a "noble outlaw"**: DVD Commentary (Joseph McBride, with Susan Shillinglaw), *The Grapes of Wrath*, directed by John Ford (1940: 20th Century Fox, 2004), DVD.

128   **"sense of moral outrage"**: Spoto, *Dark Side of Genius*, 402.

128   **As in the real case . . . the Lynn job**: "Question Two in Lynn Holdup," *Boston Daily Globe*, January 6, 1934, at 1; "Six Identify Suspects at Lynn," *Boston Evening Globe*, January 6, 1934, 1; Louis M. Lyons, "Two Men Freed with Apologies," *Boston Daily Globe*, February 28, 1934, 1.

129   **warned Columbia Pictures that they**: Carlos Clarens, *Crime Movies* (New York: Da Capo Press, 1997), 165-66.

129   **insisted that the credits not even mention**: Frank S. Nugent, "The Screen: Fact Adds Its Bit of Drama to 'Let Us Live,' at the Globe," *New York Times*, March 30, 1939, 26.

129   **Fonda's estranged wife**: "Fonda's Wife, Ill, Commits Suicide," *New York Times*, April 15, 1950, 34.

129-30   **McKinney writes . . . "haunts" the film**: Devin McKinney, *The Man Who Saw a Ghost: The Life and Work of Henry Fonda* (New York: St. Martin's Press, 2012), 189, 191-92.

130   **"Tragedy had touched my own life"**: Charlotte Chandler, *It's Only a Movie: Alfred Hitchcock: A Personal Biography* (New York: Simon & Schuster, 2005), 236-37.

130   **learned to play Manny's instrument**: "Court Is Turned into a Movie Set," *New York Times*, April 9, 1956, 21.

130   **"the same element"**: Peter Bogdanovich, *Who the Devil Made It: Conversations with Legendary Film Directors* (New York: Ballantine Books, 1997), 525.

131   **Hitchcock's relationship with Miles . . . during a break in shooting**: Spoto, *Dark Side of Genius*, 408-409. In a 2016 memoir, actress Tippi Hedren, star of *The Birds* and *Marnie*, alleged that Hitchcock assaulted her during the filming of *Marnie*. For a discussion of Hedren's experience placed in the larger context of Hitchcock's behavior towards women generally, See White, *Twelve Lives*, 99-104.

131   **Miles would work**: Hitchcock also initially cast Miles to play the role of Judy in *Vertigo*. But when Miles became pregnant before shooting started, she was replaced by Kim Novak. Dan Aulier, *Vertigo: The Making of a Hitchcock Classic* (New York: St. Martin's Press, 1998), 23.

131-32   **Frances Reid, who . . . ordered Adler shoes**: Ray Neilsen, "Harold Stone – The Wrong Man,'" *Classic Images*, October, 1993, 22. The scene with Frances Reid was not used, and a related scene in which Rose calls Mrs. O'Connor was edited so that we see only Rose's end of the conversation.

132   **"want to be *taller*"**: Advertisement, Adler Shoes for Men, *Daily News*, February 28, 1950.

132   **"almost impossible to walk"**: Neilsen, "Harold Stone," 22.

132   **Laurinda Barrett, who . . . "to the letter"**: Murray Pomerance, *Alfred Hitchcock's America* (Cambridge: Polity Press, 2013), 15.

132   **"he blueprinted every scene"**: McGilligan, *Alfred Hitchcock*, 537.

132   **loved working with Hitchcock**: McGilligan, *Alfred Hitchcock*, 537.

132   **sometimes dozed off . . . "excited about everything"**: Michael Barnum, "Just the Facts, Ma'am: Peggy Webber," *Scarlet Street*, 2004, 62.

132   **Harold Berman and Charles Gulotta both played themselves**: William A. Raidy, "The Wrong Man: This Is Where It Happened," *Long Island Sunday Press*, April 22, 1956, 21.

132   **influenced by the neorealist movement**: McGilligan, *Alfred Hitchcock*, 533.

132   **"film must breathe reality"**: Raidy, "This Is Where It Happened," 21.

132-33   **The Balestreros, who . . . "everything, to come down here"**: Jack Grady, "The 'Wrong Man' Happy After 3-Yr. Nightmare," *New York Post*, April 16, 1956.

133   **In February 1956 . . . details of the visit**: Alfred Hitchcock, Letter to Maxwell Anderson, February 29, 1956, AHPMHL.

133   **met at their home in Miami**: "Visit to the home of Manny Balestrero - Sunday, 20th March 1956," Unsigned memo, *The Wrong Man* – Research, 1955-56, File 1037, AHPMHL.; "Court Is Turned into a Movie Set," 21 (noting that Hitchcock sent Fonda and Miles to Florida to meet with the Balestreros) .

133   **"looked like a cruise liner"**: GB Interview.

133   **"Vera Miles and Henry Fonda"**: GB Interview.

133   **Over the course . . . nightmare at bay**: "Visit to the home of Manny Balestrero," AHPMHL.

133   **"we were warned not to talk to her"**: Scott Eyman, *Hank and Jim: The Fifty-Year Friendship of Henry Fonda and James Stewart* (New York: Simon & Schuster, 2017), 228 (citing Bill Kelley, "Henry Fonda: On Peter, Jane, Movies Past and Present," *The Acquarian*, December 26 1979-January 2, 1980).

133-34   **her father and her sister . . . about five blocks away**: George Schiffer, "Memo to Files," March 13, 1956, *The Wrong Man* – Legal, 1956-57, File 1031, AHPMHL.

134   **a directive came down**: Coleman, *Man Who Knew Hitchcock*, 228.

134   **"We had hoped we might be able to get"**: Alfred Hitchcock, Letter to Maxwell Anderson, February 28, 1956, *The Wrong Man* – Script, 1955-56, File 1012, AHPMHL.

134   **record number of crimes**: Charles Grutzner, "City Crime at Peak In '54, Adams Says, But He Cites Gains," *New York Times*, February 4, 1955, 1 (reporting that there were a total of 295,622 felonies and misdemeanors in 1954, compared to 261,980 a year earlier).

134   **In August of . . . seven thousand more police officers**: Paul Crowell, "City Crime-Ridden, Adams Declares in Plea for Police," *New York Times*, August 2, 1954, 1, 11.

134   **"larger and better-paid police"**: "Kennedy Renews Plea for Police; Reminds 5,500 of High Civic Role," *New York Times*, March 19, 1956, 33.

134   **a formal public relations policy . . . Manual of Procedure stated**: Cedric Larson, "New York City Police Department Launches New Public Relation Policy," 41 *Journal of Criminal Law and Criminology* 364, 369 (1950).

134   **"Our police are a law enforcement agency"**: Murray Schumach, "Kennedy Warns Aides Not to Balk His Police Policy," *New York Times*, August 9, 1955, 1.

135   **"wanted no part of the Balestrero story"**: Coleman, *Man Who Knew Hitchcock*, 228.

135   **hired a retired detective**: Coleman, *Man Who Knew Hitchcock*, 230.

135   **O'Connor had hoped to play himself**: James F. O'Donnell, *Against the Tides and The Times (on occasion): Grace-Notes in a Celtic Mist* (USA: James F. O'Donnell, 2012). O'Connor makes a cameo appearance in the Stork Club during the opening credits sequence.

135   **"are temporarily benevolent"**: Esterow, "All Around the Town," 7.

135   **developed a very bad cold . . . "everything was going wrong"**: Neilsen, "Harold Stone," 22.

136   **died in a car crash**: "2 Actresses Die in Kansas Auto Crash," *Variety*, June 6, 1956, 59. Television actress Phyllis Palumbo, 26, was also killed. Palumbo was driving the car and D'Annunzio was one of her passengers. Palumbo's four-year-old son survived the accident, suffering only minor injuries.

136   **only after Hitchcock agreed**: Robert McMillan, "Remembering Alfred Hitchcock," *Manhasset Press*, April 14, 2011, 21. McMillan recounts that Hitchcock made good on his promise and that the director "could not have been funnier and serious at the same time."

136   **In an interview . . . needs of his cameraman**: Charles Bitsch and François Truffaut, "Encounter with Alfred Hitchcock," in *Hitchcock on Hitchcock, Volume 2*, 84.

136   **"The judge is wrong"**: "John Player Lecture (1967)" in *Hitchcock on Hitchcock, Volume 2*, 236, 250.

Chapter Eleven: Nothing but the Truth

138   **scholars William Rothman and D.A. Miller**: William Rothman, *Must We Kill the Thing We Love? Emersonian Perfectionism and the Films of Alfred Hitchcock* (New York: Columbia University Press, 2014), 188 (noting that the figure "could be anyone"); D.A. Miller, *Hidden Hitchcock* (University of Chicago Press, 2016), Kindle, Chapter Three, "The Long Wrong Man" ("In a film about mistaken identity . . . it cannot be a negligible fact that, if the well-known voice did not intone 'This is Alfred Hitchcock speaking,' we would not be able to identify him any more than we could establish, say, the truth of the film's every word").

138   **"Hitchcock's physical self"**: White, *Twelve Lives*, xii.

140   **In preparing for . . . Bickford's cafeteria**: "Notes from Stork Club Visit and Musicians' Departure," Unsigned and undated memo, *The Wrong Man* – Research, 1955-56, File 1037, AHPMHL; Don Ross, "Alfred Hitchcock, a Very Crafty Fellow," *New York Herald Tribune*, March 4, 1956, Section 4, 3; Ad for Brand Names Foundation ("Can you trust your husband with your shopping money?"), *Kingston Daily Freeman* (Kingston, New York), September 1, 1955, 3.

140   **Coleman and MacPhail . . . "really happened there"**: Alfred Hitchcock, Letter to Maxwell Anderson, March 20, 1956, *The Wrong Man* – Script, 1955-56, File 1012, AHPMHL.

140   **his retention of a handwriting expert**: O'Connor tells the Balestreros that he intends to bring in a handwriting expert, but the point is not mentioned again.

140   **As Professor Marshall Deutelbaum has observed**: Marshall Deutelbaum, "Finding the Right Man in *The Wrong Man*," in *A Hitchcock Reader*, second edition, eds. Marshall Deutelbaum and Leland Poague (Blackwell Publishing, 2009), 212-214.

140   **"It would have looked phony"**: Ross, "Very Crafty Fellow," 3.

140   **when in fact O'Connor lined up three such witnesses**: Hitchcock did have MacPhail write a scene highlighting Manny's alibi defenses. In the scene, which was to take place the night before trial, O'Connor and his assistant discuss their strategy, including their intention to call a witness who was at a card game with Manny at the farm. O'Connor also reveals that he will show, through the testimony of a dentist and others, that Manny's jaw was "swollen with toothache" at the time of the second robbery. But the scene does not appear in the film. Maxwell Anderson & Angus MacPhail, *The Wrong Man* (1956) (unpublished screenplay housed at The Morgan Library, New York, NY), 134-137.

140   **"the preparation of the defense"**: Alfred Hitchcock, Letter to Maxwell Anderson, March 6, 1956, *The Wrong Man* – Script, 1955-56, File 1012, AHPMHL.

140-41   **"deliberately designed to allow"**: Hitchcock, March 20 Letter to Anderson, AHPMHL.

141   **As Professor Mark Osteen has noted**: Mark Osteen, "Introduction," in *Hitchcock and Adaptation: On the Page and Screen*, ed. Mark Osteen (Rowman & Littlefield, 2014), xxvi. Osteen provides an excellent discussion of the evolution of the screenplay, based on the correspondence between Hitchcock and Anderson.

141   **"if we allowed the juror to interrupt"**: Hitchcock, March 20 Letter to Anderson, AHPMHL.

141   **feared that "sticking to the transcript"**: Hitchcock, March 20 Letter to Anderson, AHPMHL.

141   **"the public is weary of the trial scene"**: Alfred Hitchcock, "Making *Murder!*" in *Hitchcock on Hitchcock, Volume 2*, 164, 167.

141   **almost 70 percent of the 375**: Innocence Project, "DNA Exonerations in the United States."

141   **Professor Herbert Packer . . . extensive legal scholarship**: Herbert L. Packer, "Two Models of the Criminal Process," 113 *University of Pennsylvania Law Review* 1, 9 (1964); Keith A. Findley, "Toward a New Paradigm of Criminal Justice: How the Innocence Movement Merges Crime Control and Due Process," 41 *Texas Tech Law Review* 133, 139 (2008) (observing that Packer's competing models provided the "scholarly foundation" for the paradigm that suggests that crime control and due process are conflicting goals).

141-42   **"select and filter the evidence"**: Findley and Scott, "Multiple Dimensions of Tunnel Vision," 292. See also Jon B. Gould and Richard A. Leo, "One Hundred Years Later: Wrongful Convictions after a Century of Research," 100 *Journal of Criminal Law and Criminology* 825, 838-858 (2010) (outlining sources of wrongful convictions, including "mistaken eyewitness identification" and "tunnel vision").

142   **"one of the bleakest movies ever"**: James Naremore, *An Invention Without A Future: Essays on Cinema* (University of California Press, 2014), 146.

142   **was based on the concept of a Ferris wheel**: *Guilt Trip: Hitchcock and The Wrong Man*, directed by Laurent Bouzereau (Warner Bros., 2004) (DVD).

142   **"images of order disrupted"**: Donald Spoto, *The Art of Alfred Hitchcock: Fifty Years of His Motion Pictures* (New York: Doubleday, Second Edition, 1992), 194.

142   **machines that generate empathy**: Roger Ebert, "Ebert's Walk of Fame Remarks," *RogerEbert.com*, June 24, 2005, accessed July 18, 2020.

Chapter Twelve: "I Don't Dare Look"

144   ***Is this man reaching for a gun?***: As Professor Osteen noted, Hitchcock and MacPhail reworked the scene to make Manny's act of reaching for the policy to "'look as though he is taking out a gun from its holster.'" Osteen, "Introduction," xxvi (quoting Hitchcock's February 15 letter to Anderson).

145   **"scared themselves into completely dehumanizing"**: Marc Raymond Strauss, *Hitchcock Nonetheless: The Master's Touch in His Least Celebrated Films* (North Carolina: McFarland & Co., 2007), 161.

145   **conceive of others as "subhuman"**: "'Less than Human': The Psychology of Cruelty" (interview with author David Livingstone Smith), *WBUR* website, March 29, 2011, accessed July 29, 2022. See also David Livingstone Smith, *Less Than Human: Why We Demean, Enslave, and Exterminate Others* (New York: St. Martin's Press, 2011).

145   **"chain reaction"**: See David Humbert, *Violence in the Films of Alfred Hitchcock: A Study in Mimesis* (East Lansing: Michigan State University Press, 2017), 81 (stating that Dennerly's recognition "sets off a chain reaction of desires that find the culprit in Balestrero"). In an excellent analysis supported by images from the scene, Humbert notes that "we see how an emotion like fear escalates and how it leaps contagiously from one person to the next." Humbert, *Study in Mimesis*, 81.

146   **Hitchcock and Fonda shared**: Hitchcock warned against the mob mentality in one of his earliest "wrong man" films, *The Lodger: A Story of the London Fog* (1927), in which a crowd chases down a man wrongfully suspected to be a serial murderer and nearly kills him. Humbert, *A Study in Mimesis*, 79.

146   **"the most horrendous sight"**: Henry Fonda and Howard Teichmann, *Fonda: My Life* (New York: New American Library, 1981), 24-25. For details concerning this horrific episode, see, e.g., Micah Mertes, "The Lynching of Will Brown," *Omaha World-Herald* website, August 27, 2017, accessed July 29, 2022.

146   **McKinney has suggested**: McKinney, "Man Who Saw a Ghost," 332-342. Fonda also starred in the searing western *The Ox-Bow Incident* (1943), which depicts a mob's capture of three men falsely accused of the murder of a local rancher. As cattleman Gil Carter, Fonda tries to stop the mob but fails, and the three men are hanged. For more on the connection between the murder of Will Brown and Fonda's work, see Sean Hogan, "Turning on the Light: Henry Fonda and Will Brown," *RogerEbert.com*, January 31, 2018, accessed July 29, 2022.

146   **In 1914, a Boston man . . . no resemblance to him**: Borchard, *Convicting the Innocent*, 1-6. When the prosecutor saw Andrews and the culprit in court, he "wondered how so many persons could have sworn that the innocent man was the one that had cashed the bad checks. The two men were as dissimilar in appearance as could be. There was several inches difference in height and there wasn't a similarity about them." Borchard, *Convicting the Innocent*, 5.

146-47   **Into the identification**: Borchard, *Convicting the Innocent*, 367.

147   **"a contagious desire"**: Humbert, *A Study in Mimesis*, 81.

147-48   **One compelling study . . . 37 percent chose the wrong man**: R. K. Bothwell, J. C. Brigham, and M. A. Pigott, "A Field Study on the Relationship Between Quality of Eyewitness' Descriptions and Identification Accuracy," *Journal of Police Science and Administration* 17 (1990): 84-88.

Chapter Thirteen: "Just a Routine Matter"

149   **neither corrupt nor motivated by any obvious bias**: See Spaulding, "Disorder in the Court," 112 (noting that "Hitchcock has taken care not to suggest official corruption"). For examples of how scholars specializing in law and culture have characterized the depiction of the police in the film, see Michael Asimow and Paul Bergman, *Reel Justice: The Courtroom Goes to the Movies* (Kansas City, Missouri: Andrews McMeel Publishing, LLC 2006), 59-60 (stating the police "act in complete good faith" toward Manny); Rosenberg, "Legal-Reelist Narratives of Henry Fonda," 391 (characterizing the detectives as "competent (if uncaring) professionals" who "do their job with plodding efficiency").

149   **"the primordial role"**: Jean-Luc Godard, "The Wrong Man," in *Godard on Godard*, eds. Jean Narboni and Tom Milne (De Capo Press 1972), 48

149   **"solely on absurd coincidences"**: Robert B. Ray, *A Certain Tendency of the Hollywood Cinema* (Princeton University Press, 1995), 157.

149-50   **"bleak views of the world"**: Rafter, *Shots in the Mirror*, 136.

150   **shows the building at a canted angle**: This image fits within the film's visual strategy of imbalance and subjectivity, which presents, in Donald Spoto's words, "a world increasingly off center." Spoto, *Art of Alfred Hitchcock*, 258.

150   **"an advanced state of disrepair"**: Nicholas Haeffner, *Alfred Hitchcock* (Harlow: Pearson Longman, 2005), 62.

150   **"the repression of criminal conduct"**: Packer, "Two Models," 9.

150   **"screen suspects"**: Packer, "Two Models," 10.

150   **"The presumption of guilt allows"**: Packer, "Two Models," 11.

150   **"the innocent have nothing to fear"**: Packer, "Two Models," 25.

150   **"an unreal dream"**: U.S. v. Garsson, 291 F. 646, 649 (S.D.N.Y. 1923).

150   **when the state can infer guilt from a suspect's flight**: In Illinois v. Wardlow, 528 U.S. 119 (2000), the Supreme Court upheld the legality of an investigative stop that led to the defendant's arrest. The Court ruled that the suspect's flight from police justified the officer's suspicion that the suspect "was involved in criminal activity." In a partial dissent, Justice John Paul Stevens noted that there are reasons innocent people (especially minorities) may flee at the sight of police, including a belief "that contact with the police itself can itself be dangerous." Wardlow, 528 U.S. at 132.

150   **from their silence in the face of accusatory questions**: For example, in Salinas v. Texas, 570 U.S. 178 (2013), the Supreme Court held that a prosecutor did not violate the Fifth Amendment by using, as evidence of guilt, the defendant's silence when asked during a precustodial interview whether a ballistic test of shell casings would match his shotgun. In a dissenting opinion, Justice Stephen Breyer noted that even innocent suspects may refrain from answering an accusatory question to avoid revealing "prejudicial facts, disreputable associates, or suspicious circumstances." Salinas, 570 U.S. at 195. See also Lisa Kern Griffin, "Silence, Confessions, and the New Accuracy Imperative," 65 *Duke Law Journal* 697, 730 (2016) ("the idea that innocents have nothing from fear from responding to police is flat wrong").

151   **In Arthur Miller's . . . "need no lawyers"**: Miller, *The Crucible*, 93- 94, 98.

151   **studies suggest . . . "nothing to fear"**: Saul M. Kassin and Rebecca J. Norwick, "Why People Waive Their Miranda Rights: The Power of Innocence," *Law and Human Behavior* 28, no. 2 (2004): 211, 217.

151   **"elicit and reconstruct"**: Packer, "Two Models," 14.

152   **"a complex of attitudes, a mood"**: Packer, "Two Models," 12.

152   **"police develop tunnel vision"**: Mark Leviton, "The Whole Truth," *Sun Magazine*, July 2017, 8. See also Findley and Scott, "Multiple Dimensions of Tunnel Vision," 309-17 (explaining confirmation bias and how it contributes to tunnel vision in police investigations).

152	**pressures to close cases**: Richard A. Leo, *Police Interrogation and American Justice* (Cambridge: Harvard University Press 2009), 264
153	**As several scholars have noted**: See, e.g., McGilligan, *Alfred Hitchcock*, 538 (2003) (noting that the film's concern about the rights of criminal suspects "prefigures the Miranda ruling"); Robert Genter, "Cold War Confessions and the Trauma of McCarthyism: Alfred Hitchcock's *I Confess* and *The Wrong Man*," Quarterly Review of Film and Video, 29:2 (2012): 129, 132-34 (discussing Hitchcock's critique of interrogation tactics in *I Confess* and *The Wrong Man* in relation to Supreme Court rulings on police tactics and analyzing the films as commentaries on "the causes and effects of confession" in the McCarthy era).
153	**Miranda v. Illinois**: 384 U.S. 436 (1966).
153	**"72% of the innocents . . . to set them free"**: Kassin and Norwick, "Why People Waive," 217-18 (2004).
154	**appear "shifty" and "nervous"**: Kempenaar and Larsen, "Blindspotting: *The Wrong Man*," Filmspotting.
154	**the progression of the gesture**: After the liquor store scene, Manny repeats the gesture throughout the film: three times during the next eyewitness parade in the deli, once in the precinct cell where he is held overnight after his arrest, once at his bail hearing (looking back at Rose, who is sitting on the spectator benches), and once during his brief stint in the Long Island City jail.
154	**"reasonable, articulable suspicion"**: Wardlow, 528 U.S. at 123 (2000) (citing Terry v. Ohio, 392 U.S. 1, 30 (1968)).
154	**"nervous, evasive behavior"**: Wardlow, 528 U.S. at 124. See, e.g., U.S. v. Campbell, 843 F.2d 1089, 1094-95 (8th Cir. 1988) (in upholding a narcotic agent's investigative stop, court relied on the fact that a suspect "looked at least three times over his shoulders" while at an airport, along with other evidence of "nervousness").
154	**"nervousness is a natural reaction"**: United States v. McKoy, 402 F. Supp. 2d 311, 317 (D. Mass. 2004) (while police may consider "nervousness" as a factor in considering an investigative stop, "it alone is not sufficient").
154	**"a potent urge to flee"**: Beth Twiggar, "Hitchcock, Master Maker of Mystery", in *Hitchcock on Hitchcock, Volume 2*, 31.
154	**the constitutional challenge . . . "engaged in criminal activity"**: Floyd v. City of N.Y., 959 F. Supp. 2d 540, 556, 614, 630 (S.D.N.Y. 2013).
156	**In the second version**: Here Hitchcock compresses the actual events, which saw the detectives require Manny to write the note six times.
156	**"the women were simply identifying"**: Donald Laming, *Human Judgment: The Eye of the Beholder* (University of Cambridge, 2011), 216.
157	**Manny stands in a lineup (photo)**: The photo appearing here is a zoomed-in image of the lineup. As discussed on page 158, the film shows the lineup in a wider shot from the perspective of the witnesses across the hallway.
157	**"it's really believable that this could happen to anyone"**: Imogen Sara Smith, "Audio Commentary," *Boomerang!*, directed by Elia Kazan (1947: Kino Lorber, 2016), DVD. Smith sees *The Wrong Man* as sharing this element with *Boomerang!*, a film in which the police arrest an innocent man but are not "demonized." Smith points out that the restrained approach "in a sense makes it more chilling."
158	**"frames within the frame"**: Foster Hirsch, *The Dark Side of the Screen: Film Noir*, 2nd edition (Da Capo Press, 2008), 21, 89. See also Eric Rohmer and Claude Chabrol, *Hitchcock, the First Forty-Four Films* (New York: Frederick Ungar Publishing, 1979), 150 (noting that after Manny is jailed Hitchcock uses the "frame within a frame" device "in the form of the prison-door window which the camera penetrates").
158	**as scholar Foster Hirsch has observed**: Hirsch, *Dark Side of the Screen*, 89, 134.
158	**Other recurring noir motifs**: Hirsch, *Dark Side of the Screen*, 89, 96-97.
158	**"are calculated noir"**: Eddie Muller, *Dark City: The Lost World of Film Noir, Revised and Expanded Edition* (New York: Hachette Book Group, 2021), 145. *The Wrong Man* is also classified as a film noir in, among other places, Ed Sikov, *Film Studies: An Introduction* (New York: Columbia University Press, 2010), 153, and Hirsch, *Dark Side of the Screen*, 139.

Chapter Fourteen: Prosecutorial Oversight

159	**as some authors have**: See, e.g., Michael Walker, *Hitchcock's Motifs* (Amsterdam: Amsterdam University Press, 2005) 213 (describing the man who confronts Manny in this scene as a "detective"); Jane E. Sloan, *Alfred Hitchcock: The Definitive Filmography* (Berkeley & Los Angeles: University of California Press, 1993), 286 (describing the man who tells Manny he must come up with a better story as a "third detective").
159	**"the police chief"**: Godard, "The Wrong Man," 50 (describing the man observing the lineup as "the police chief").
159	**reveals the character's actual identity**: Anderson and MacPhail, *The Wrong Man*, 69. See also *The Wrong Man* Full Cast and Crew, IMDB website, accessed April 4, 2020 (listing Maurice Manson as the actor in the "uncredited" role of "District Attorney John Hall").
159-60	**detectives aren't named**: Some of the detectives' names appear once on signs hanging behind Manny during the lineup. The detectives' withholding of their names is ironic given their misidentification of Manny, whom they repeatedly refer to as "Chris" (which they derive from Manny's given name, Christopher).
160	**enters a plea without consultation**: The scenario is repeated during the trial scene: Only after O'Connor moves for a mistrial does he explain to Manny what's happened.
160	**"a feeling of apprehension and anxiety"**: Truffaut, *Hitchcock*, 16.
161	**the likable Hennessey**: Hennessey is linked as a character type to the similarly likable but ineffective detectives in *Shadow of a Doubt*.
161	**courts seldom identified**: As discussed in Part One, the rulings in the Caruso and Hoffner cases criticized officials for withholding information, but did not name those officials. A notable exception from that era was People v. Riley, 191 Misc. 888, 891 (N.Y. Sup. Ct. 1948), which named a Brooklyn prosecutor who suppressed expert handwriting evidence that would have exonerated a falsely accused defendant.
162	**framed by the vertical bars**: As one author has noted, Manny "is constantly framed and visually incarcerated by architecture." See Steven Jacobs, *The Wrong House: The Architecture of Alfred Hitchcock* (Rotterdam: 010 Publishers, 2007), 115.
162	**"examine all the facts and question the witnesses"**: New York DA Report, 143-44.
162-63	**"guilt shall not escape or innocence suffer"**: Berger v. United States, 295 U.S. 78, 88 (1935).

Chapter Fifteen: A Spiraling Trauma

164	**Recent studies confirm**: See Samantha K. Brooks and Neil Greenberg, "Psychological Impact of Being Wrongfully Accused of Criminal Offences: A Systematic Literature Review," *Medicine, Science and the Law*, 61(I) (2020): 44, 48 (reporting on studies finding "secondary trauma" among family members of the wrongfully accused, including anxiety, depression and feelings of stigma and shame). See also Robert I. Simon, MD, "The Psychological and Legal

Aftermath of False Arrest and Imprisonment," *Journal of the American Academy of Psychiatry and the Law* 21, no. 4 (December 1993): 523, 525 ("the family itself may be so traumatized as to be emotionally unavailable to the arrest victim on his or her release.").

165   **"[t]he wrong man becomes"**: Godard, "The Wrong Man," 53.

165   **"[a]ll characters in the films"**: Rostron, "The Hitchcock Cases," 225.

165   **while shifting the film's focus**: See, e.g., Naremore, *Invention Without A Future*, 146 (arguing that in its second half, the film becomes "less about crime and punishment than about the breakdown of a fragile lower-middle-class-marriage under the pressure of debt and patriarchy, and the slow descent of one of its members into an unglamorous darkness").

165   **"fragile foundation in life"**: GB Interview.

166   **clutches her biceps**: Notes of the March 1956 meeting between Fonda, Miles and the Balestreros refer to Rose's habit of "scratching her left arm" out of anxiety. "Visit to the home of Manny Balestrero," AHPMHL.

167   **"lucid" and "eerily true"**: Spaulding, "Disorder in the Court," 112.

168   **"the refraction of his shattered image"**: Spoto, *Art of Alfred Hitchcock*, 260.

168   **ten shots in under ten seconds**: Philip J. Skerry, *Psycho in the Shower: The History of Cinema's Most Famous Scene* (New York: Continuum International Publishing, 2008), 208.

168   **"camera becomes violent"**: Hitchcock, Letter to Anderson, March 15, 1956, MAPHRC.

168   **"lightning-like explosion of violence"**: Skerry, *Psycho in the Shower*, 208. See also Strauss, *Hitchcock Nonetheless*, 166 (describing Rose's attack as a precursor to the murder scene in *Psycho*).

168   **the Hays Production Code . . . without its approval**: Naomi Mezey and Mark Niles, "Screening the Law: Ideology and Law in American Popular Culture," 28 *Columbia Journal of Law and the Arts* 91, 136-37 (2005).

168   **started in 1934 . . . system in 1968**: Billheimer, *Hitchcock and the Censors*, 20-22, 291.

168   **Hitchcock navigated around . . . by killing herself**: Billheimer, *Hitchcock and the Censors*, 131-32.

168   **Billheimer found that the PCA**: Billheimer, *Hitchcock and the Censors*, 216.

168-69 **"smugglers"**: Martin Scorsese and Michael Henry Wilson, *A Personal Journey with Martin Scorsese Through American Movies* (Miramax Books, 1997), 98.

169   **"'You must never try'"**: Scorsese and Wilson, *A Personal Journey*, 98.

Chapter Sixteen: Who Will Listen?

170   **often glorify the "house of law"**: Jessica M. Silbey, "Patterns of Courtroom Justice," 28 *Journal of Law and Society* 97, 99-100 (2001). In a fascinating article, Silbey draws examples from movies like *And Justice for All*, *The Verdict*, and *A Few Good Men* to examine how trial films use courthouse structures and spaces to comment on "the power and legitimacy of legal institutions." Silbey, "Patterns of Courtroom Justice," 98.

171   **warning signs about O'Connor's effectiveness**: As professor Norman Spaulding observes, this depiction of O'Connor is one of several elements that points to the apparent impossibility of exoneration. Spaulding, "Disorder in the Court," 112 (by the time trial arrives, "Hitchcock has already primed the viewer to accept that the system would not likely rectify the error"). See also Rosenberg, "Legal-Reelist Narratives of Henry Fonda," 392 (observing that "the film assigns the burden of gathering exculpatory evidence to a romantic couple rather than to agents of the legal system").

172   **gesture implicates us**: See also Spaulding, "Disorder in the Court," 113 (describing the witness's laying of her hand on Manny's shoulder as a "'physical mark of shame' and conditional guilt") (quoting Godard, "The Wrong Man," 50).

173-74 **"I've always felt a complete identification"**: Truffaut, *Hitchcock*, 205.

174   **ineffective cross-examination**: Critic Adam Kempenaar unsparingly describes O'Connor's performance as "the worst cross-examining you've ever seen in a film." Kempenaar and Larsen, "Blindspotting: *The Wrong Man*."

174   **"violation of the ritual"**: Truffaut, *Hitchcock*, 235.

Chapter Seventeen: "OK, Manny?"

176-77 **answer to a prayer**: "Fiddler in Fog," 1. According to Hitchcock, the fact that the mother "begs Manny to pray for strength" (as opposed to exoneration) was included "so that we do not feel the arrival of Daniell in the picture will look like an answer to Manny's prayer." Hitchcock, March 20 Letter to Anderson, AHPMHL. Reporter Robert Bigelow credited the film for capturing the "one major truth that cannot be argued with . . . the truth that Divine Providence, and that alone, intervened to save Balestrero from prison." Bigelow, "Story of Horror," 3.

177   **the detectives from the 110th precinct were not involved**: Bigelow noted this discrepancy in his review of the film for the *Long Island Star-Journal*. Bigelow, "Story of Horror," 3.

177   **willing to correct an error**: See also Rosenberg, "Legal-Reelist Narratives of Henry Fonda," 407 n. 49 (noting possible reading that film celebrates "the ability of the legal bureaucracy to dispense 'blind justice'").

177   **the detective stages the lineup the same way**: See also Spoto, *Art of Alfred Hitchcock*, 261-62 ("when the 'right man' is sent before the police lineup to be identified by the insurance office workers, their sincere, certain identification of him is repeated in exactly the same tones as when Manny is brought in").

178   **the casting of Fonda**: See Jennifer L. Mnookin and Nancy West, "Theaters of Proof: Visual Evidence and the Law in *Call Northside 777*," 13 *Yale Journal of Law and the Humanities* 329, 351 n.82 (2001) (noting that *12 Angry Men* director Sydney Lumet likely "was capitalizing" on Fonda's association with *The Wrong Man* "by casting Fonda as the juror most skeptical of [eyewitness] testimony").

178   **show the same impatience**: Rosenberg, "Legal-Reelist Narratives of Henry Fonda," 392.

179   **wrote his *12 Angry Men* teleplay**: Phil Rosenzweig, *Reginald Rose and the Journey of 12 Angry Men* (Fordham University Press, 2021), 61-62.

179   **"capable of sudden wild and dangerous"**: John Steinbeck, "Henry Fonda," *Harper's Bazaar*, November 1966, 215.

180   **a low-key "sonic" tone**: Pomerance, *Hitchcock's America*, 153-54. Pomerance points out that except for the scene in which Rose hits Manny, no one "ever raises a voice, dramatizes, exaggerates, or melodizes."

180   **some critics did not regard it as critical**: See the discussion of the film's critical reception in Chapter Eighteen.

180   **As described by . . . "the exoneree gives thanks"**: Lara Bazelon, *Rectify: The Power of Restorative Justice After Wrongful Conviction* (Boston, Beacon Press, 2018), 93. Bazelon explains that in reality exoneration is "an earthquake" that "leaves upheaval and ruin in its wake." Bazelon, *Rectify*, 93-94.

181   **"outrageously perfunctory obeisance"**: David Bordwell, "Happily Ever After, Part Two," *The Velvet Trap* no. 19 (1982): 2, 5 (available at www.davidbordwell.net).

181   **"profoundly ironic maneuver"**: David Sterritt, *The Films of Alfred Hitchcock (Cambridge Film Classics)* (Cambridge University Press, 1993), 77-78.

181   **"pinpoints on the screen"**: Paula Marantz Cohen, *Alfred Hitchcock: The Legacy of Victorianism* (Lexington: The University Press of Kentucky, 1995), 134. Cohen also presents a competing interpretation, informed by the film's "documentary" aspirations, that the small figures "are, in fact, the real Balestreros (as opposed to the actors who played them) and, as such, prefer . . . to be invisible than to be misrecognized and coerced." Cohen, *Legacy of Victorianism*, 134.

181   **the actors are not Fonda and Miles**: Bill Krohn, *Hitchcock at Work* (London, Phaidon Press, 2000), 180.

181   **"We were just doing the true story"**: Macklin, "It's the Manner of Telling," 52.

181   **"Not only does this give"**: DeRosa, "Revisiting Hitchcock's *The Wrong Man*."

181   **met with Fonda and Miles**: "Visit to the home of Manny Balestrero," AHPMHL.

181   **concept of "American exceptionalism"**: See Paul Bergman, "Guilt or Innocence: Lessons About the Legal Process in American Courtroom Films," in *Oxford Encyclopedia of Crime, Media, and Popular Culture*, eds. Nicole Rafter and Michelle Brown (Oxford University Press, 2018), 251 (discussing courtroom films that present legal processes as essential to America's democratic character).

181   **achieving narrative closure**: Norman Rosenberg, "Hollywood on Trials: Courts and Films, 1930-1960," *Law and History Review* 12, no. 2 (1994): 341, 365-66 and n. 67 (pointing to *12 Angry Men*, *The Young Philadelphians* and *On the Waterfront* as examples of this "powerful, perhaps dominant trend during the 1950s and early 1960s").

181   **"underlines the dangers of the will to closure"**: Martin Kevorkian, "The Dantesque Desires of David Fincher's *Zodiac*," in *David Fincher's Zodiac: Cinema of Investigation and (Mis)Interpretation*, eds. Matthew Sorrento and David Ryan (Fairleigh Dickinson University Press, 2022), 163-64.

181-82   **"the intoxicating spirit of accusation"**: Kevorkian, "Dantesque Desires," 163.

182   **interviewed every living detective**: Al Horner, "*Zodiac* with James Vanderbilt," *Script Apart* podcast, November 17, 2020.

182   **"Fincher seems possessed"**: Manohla Dargis, "Hunting a Killer as the Age of Aquarius Dies," *New York Times*, March 2, 2007.

182   **"a claim shadowed by doubt"**: Adam Nayman, *David Fincher: Mind Games* (New York: Abrams, 2021), 66. On top of that, while Mageau has identified the same man (Arthur Leigh Allen) that the film's protagonists believe is the killer, a subsequent title card tells us that eleven years later, a partial DNA profile developed from one of the killer's envelopes did not match Allen (who died not too long after Mageau's identification, before police could interrogate him further).

182   **Like his real-life counterpart**: Matthews is based on Detective Leigh Wilson. Sander, "Leigh Wilson," 2B.

Chapter Eighteen: "The DNA of Its Time"

184-85   **In a 2013 lecture . . . "the context has completely changed"**: Martin Scorsese, 2013 Jefferson Lecture, available at National Endowment for the Humanities website, accessed July 17, 2022.

185   **Scorsese has himself found "paranoia"**: Ebert, "Scorsese Learns," 218-219.

185   **"an allegory of the blacklist"**: Robert P. Kolker, *Triumph Over Containment: American Film in the 1950s* (Rutgers University Press, 2021), 101-102. See also Genter, "Cold War Confessions," 131.

185   **actors who had been blacklisted**: Stephen Whitty, *The Alfred Hitchcock Encyclopedia* (Lanham, Maryland: Rowman & Littlefield, 2016), 512 (noting that Hitchcock "had seen several friends and associates banned or 'gray-listed' by nervous moguls after the Washington witch trials"); Eric Nagourney, "Norman Lloyd, Associate of Welles, Hitchcock, and Others, Dies at 106," *New York Times*, May 11, 2021, B14; Glenn Collins, "Paul Henreid, Actor, Dies at 84; Resistance Hero in 'Casablanca,'" *New York Times*, April 3, 1992, 16.

185   **paled in comparison**: Billheimer, *Hitchcock and the Censors*, 314 (Table 1).

185   **a record 2,534,000 major crimes**: Luther A. Huston, "Major Crimes in '56 at 2.5 Million Peak," *New York Times*, December 30, 1956, 1, 23.

185   **"the march toward criminal chaos"**: Murray Schumach, "Kennedy Reports Juvenile Crimes Up 41.3% in Year," *New York Times*, July 30, 1956, 1.

186   **For more than fifteen years . . . treated for shock**: "6 Hurt in Bombing at Theatre Here," *New York Times*, December 3, 1956, 1, 24; "15 Were Injured by Bomb Blasts," *New York Times*, January 23, 1957, 20; Charles Delafuente, "Terror in the Age of Eisenhower," *New York Times*, September 10, 2004.

186   **reached what the *New York Times* called "epidemic proportions"**: Alexander Feinberg, "Bomb Hoax Wave Compels Police to Limit Checks," *New York Times*, December 29, 1956, 1.

186   **Most were hoaxes . . . in the theater**: Michael Cannell, *Incendiary: The Psychiatrist, the Mad Bomber, and the Invention of Criminal Profiling* (New York: St. Martin's Press, 2017), 135-137; Feinberg, "Bomb Hoax," 30 (reporting that 2,500 people were in the theater). Cannell provides the definitive account of the "Mad Bomber" case.

186   **"a diabolical sense of humor" . . . "to expect police miracles"**: Cannell, *Incendiary*, 137.

186   **"the most excitement the film generated"**: Spoto, *Dark Side of Genius*, 414.

186   **"frighteningly authentic"**: Weiler, "A New Format for Hitchcock," 8.

186   **the "somber" story**: Mae Tinee, "Somber Story Told in Movie by Hitchcock," *Chicago Tribune*, February 8, 1957, B8.

186   ***New Yorker* critic . . . "from Daddy and the children"**: John McCarten, "The Current Cinema: Hitchcock, Documentary Style," *New Yorker*, January 5, 1957, 61-62.

186-87   **In the *Washington Post* . . . "a phony realism"**: Richard L. Coe, "Story's 'True' But Not 'Real,'" *Washington Post*, January 18, 1957, A17.

187   **"completely literal rendering"**: "Cinema: The New Pictures," *Time*, January 14, 1957.

187   **In the *Boston Globe* . . . "engaged in crime"**: Marjory Adams, "'Wrong Man' Hitchcock Drama," *Boston Globe*, January 21, 1957, 28.

187   **"gripping piece of realism"**: "The Wrong Man," *Variety*, January 2, 1957, 6.

187   **"the familiar with terror"**: "Iceberg of Chills: The Wrong Man," *Newsweek*, January 7, 1957, 68.

187   **"very fine drama"**: Wanda Hale, "Fonda in 'Wrong Man' Title Role," *Daily News*, December 23, 1956.

187   **"it was like a franchise"**: "Martin Scorsese and Farran Smith Nehme" (interview), *The Criterion Collection*, 2020.

187   **America's fourth-highest-rated . . . 37.5 percent**: Robert E. Kapsis, *Hitchcock: The Making of a Reputation* (Chicago: The University of Chicago Press, 1992), 46-47, 256 and n.28.

187   **Rohmer and Claude Chabrol . . . "his heart was set on"**: Rohmer and Chabrol, *Hitchcock*, 145, 151.

187   **"dispassionate but understanding"**: Weiler, "A New Format for Hitchcock," 8.

187   **"hard and yet fair"**: "'Wrong Man' Strong Drama," *Hollywood Reporter*, December 21, 1956, 3, 30.

187   **"given every break"**: Herb Kelly, "Hitchcock Has Field Day," *Miami Daily News*, February 2, 1957, 6.

187   **"gave the suspect every opportunity"**: Ben S. Parker, "True-Life Story Portrayed in 'Wrong Man' at Warner," *Commercial Appeal* (Memphis), January 24, 1957, 32.

187   "the law is just but cold": "Paramount's 'Wrong Man' Weighted with Woes," *Democrat & Chronicle* (Rochester, NY), January 31, 1957, 12.
188   "there was a strong case against him": "Lie Detectors," 8.
188   "only did their duty": Bigelow, "D.A. to Reexamine Case," 2.
188   *To Tell the Truth*: As of September 2022, the episode was available on YouTube. *To Tell the Truth* (CBS Television Broadcast January 15, 1957).
188   "He wanted to make sure that everybody knew": GB Interview.
188   "naysayers": GB Interview.
188   "Everybody's got a ballot": GB Interview.
190   his eyewitness account leads to the false verdict: Since we share Scottie's perspective, we too are implicated in his mistaken conclusion. Like Scottie, we think we have observed Mrs. Elster's suicide. It's not until later in the film, through a flashback, that we learn of the deception.
190   "ultimate statement on illusion versus reality": "Alfred Hitchcock," *The Plot Thickens* (TCM podcast, interview by Peter Bogdanovich), June 30, 2020.
191   the McMartin case . . . ended in a mistrial: Alan Yuhas, "It's Time to Revisit the Satanic Panic," *New York Times*, March 31, 2021; Marcia Chambers, "Officials Drop Case Against 5 on Child Abuse," *New York Times*, January 18, 1986, 6.
191   some thirty-nine weeks after its release: Hy Hollinger, "Never-Retired 'Re-Issued' Pix," *Variety*, May 11, 1960, 3.
191   "a Hitchcock picture to end all Hitchcock pictures'": Spoto, *The Dark Side of Genius*, 423.
191   "fantasy": Bogdanovich, "Who the Devil Made It," 531.
191   an intriguing reference point: Nicholas Haeffner, *Alfred Hitchcock* (Harlow: Pearson Longman, 2005), 66 ("The view of the world presented in *I Saw the Whole Thing* and *The Wrong Man*, as in so many other Hitchcock dramas, is located at the crossroads between seeing, feeling, truth, and illusion.").

Conclusion

193   the podcast *Filmspotting* . . . the 1912 maritime disaster: Adam Kempenaar and Josh Larsen, "Top 5 Movies Future Historians Will Remember w/ Chuck Klosterman," *Filmspotting* podcast, August 26, 2016.
194   375 people have been exonerated by DNA testing: Rebecca Brown and Peter Neufeld, "Chimes of Freedom Flashing: For Each Unharmful Gentle Soul Misplaced Inside A Jail," 76 *New York University Annual Survey of American Law* 235, 236 (2021).
194   more than 3,000 exonerations: National Registry of Exonerations, *Race and Wrongful Convictions*, Preface (reporting that as of September 23, 2022, there have been 3,248 known exonerations in the United States since 1989).
194   It was not until 1967 . . . alone to the suspect: United States v. Wade: 388 U.S. 218, 228 (1967).
194-195 Foster v. California . . . "This is the man": 394 U.S. 440, 443 (1969).
195   Sotomayor has summarized the research this way: Perry v. New Hampshire, 565 U.S. 228, 262 (2012) (Sotomayor, J., dissenting).
195   "there is almost nothing more convincing": Watkins v. Sowders, 449 U.S. 341, 352 (1981) (Brennan, J., dissenting) (emphasis in original omitted) (quoting Elizabeth Loftus, *Eyewitness Testimony* 19 (1979)).
195   "spotty at best": Findley, "Lessons from Wrongful Convictions," 381-382. A historical survey found that no published lineup procedures were issued in the United States until 1967. C.A.E. Brimacombe et al., "Eyewitness Identification Procedures: Recommendations for Lineups and Photospreads," *Law and Human Behavior* 22, no. 6 (December 1998): 609-610. In 1967, the New York City Police Department adopted written lineup regulations in response to Supreme Court rulings on eyewitness identification. See New York City Regulations, Police Department, City of New York, July 26, 1967, reprinted in Frank T. Read, "Lawyers at Lineups: Constitutional Necessity or Avoidable Extravagance," 17 *UCLA Law Review* 339, 399-402 (1969) (noting that trio of Supreme Court rulings "indicated that certain procedural safeguards must be established before law enforcement officers submit a person in custody to a 'line-up'").
195   states began to follow suit: Neil Brewer et al., "Policy and Procedure Recommendations for the Collection and Preservation of Eyewitness Identification Evidence," *Law and Human Behavior* 44, no. 1 (2020): 3, 28.
195   as recently as 2013: Brown and Neufeld, "Chimes of Freedom Flashing," 251.
195   "best practice guidelines": New York State Lineup Procedure Guidelines (2010) (available at the website for the District Attorneys Association of the State of New York). See New York State Justice Task Force Recommendations for Improving Eyewitness Identifications, February 2011, 2 n.1 (until the district attorneys association released its recommendations, "there had been no uniform guidelines for the administration of identification procedures throughout New York State although many individual law enforcement agencies had their own internal written guidelines").
195   The first overrode . . . the array viewed by the witness: New York Criminal Procedure Law 60.25(1)
195   "arguably the single most important reform": Brown and Neufeld, "Chimes of Freedom Flashing," 251.
195   The second law mandated: N.Y. Exec. Law 837(21).
195-96 Division of Criminal Justice . . . for photo arrays: New York State Division of Criminal Justice Services, "Identification Procedures: Photo Arrays and Line-Ups, Municipal Police Training Council Model Policy and Identification Procedures and Forms" (2017); Miriam J. Hibel, *New York Identification Law: The Wade Hearing/The Trial*, Section 4.03[7] (Matthew Bender & Company, 2021) (summarizing legislation).
196   not binding on prosecutors or police: See Hibel, *New York Identification Law*, Section 4.03[7], 4-24 n.44 (noting that "the model protocols themselves do not have the force of law").
196   "likelihood of irreparable misidentification": Perry v. New Hampshire, 565 U.S. 228, 232 (2012) (citing Simmons v. United States, 390 U.S. 377, 384 (1968)).
196   "If the indicia of reliability": Perry v. New Hampshire, 565 U.S. at 232.
196   the only time the court ruled: Perry v. New Hampshire, 565 U.S. at 261 (Sotomayor, J., dissenting) ("To date, Foster is the only case in which we have found a due process violation"); Erwin Chemerinsky, *Presumed Guilty: How the Supreme Court Empowered the Police and Subverted Civil Rights* (New York: Liveright, 2021), 179-180.
196   "a substantial likelihood that the defendant": People v. Chipp, 75 N.Y.2d 327, 336, *cert. denied*, 498 U.S. 833 (1990).
196   But even in New York . . . an investigatory lineup: People v. Hawkins, 55 N.Y.2d 474, 486-87 (1982); People v. Brown, 26 A.3d 392 (N.Y. App. Div. 2006) ("generally there is no constitutional right to counsel at an investigatory lineup prior to the commencement of formal adversarial proceedings"); Hibel, *New York Identification Law*, Section 3.02[2][b]("If the right to counsel has not attached, either indelibly or otherwise, law enforcement officials generally have no duty to provide, or notify, counsel for the suspect at an identification procedure").

196-97	**Stovall v. Denno**: 388 U.S. 293, 302 (1967).
197	**"unreliability of the most extreme kind"**: People v. Riley, 70 N.Y.2d 523, 529-530 (1987) (precinct showup was unduly suggestive where stolen property and gun were set on table near suspects).
197	**at or near the crime scene shortly after the crime**: People v. Smith, 185 A.D.3d 1203, 1207 (N.Y. App. Div. 2020) (showups are permitted "in close geographic and temporal proximity" or where there is an "exigent" circumstance requiring an immediate identification).
197	**where there is an urgent need**: Riley, 70 N.Y.2d at 529.
197	**"illuminated by a spotlight"**: Smith, 185 A.D.3d at 1206-1207.
197	**Authorities across the country . . . procedure is permitted**: Police Executive Research Forum, "A National Survey of Eyewitness Identification in Law Enforcement Agencies," March 8, 2013, 58; Emily Bazelon, "I Write About the Law. But Could I Really Help Free a Prisoner?" *New York Times Magazine*, June 30, 2021. Bazelon provides a striking account of the 2021 exoneration of twenty-seven-year-old Yutico Briley, a Louisiana man who had served almost eight years of a sixty-year prison term for armed robbery. In 2012, Briley was misidentified at a showup that police conducted about twenty hours after the crime. Police told the victim they had a suspect in custody and brought Briley to the station. They secured the identification by displaying a handcuffed Briley alone, his face illuminated by the headlights from a nearby squad car as he stood about fifteen feet from the victim. Bazelon notes that the showup violated the police's own guidelines on the timing of the procedure.
197	**police identification procedures have improved**: Brown and Neufeld, "Chimes of Freedom Flashing," 251; Michael Ollove, "Police Are Changing Lineups to Avoid False IDs," *Pew Charitable Trusts*, July 13, 2018.
197	**about half the states have now adopted**: Brown and Neufeld, "Chimes of Freedom Flashing," 251.
197	**the conviction of Samuel Brownridge**: The facts of the Brownridge case are based on People v. Brownridge, 126 N.Y.S.3d 894, 895-896 (Sup. Ct. 2020), and Jan Ransom, "He Spent 25 Years in Prison for Murder, But Was Innocent All Along," *New York Times*, June 23, 2020.
197	**characterized the evidence of his guilt as "overwhelming"**: People v. Brownridge, 267 A.D.2d 318, 319 (N.Y. App. Div. 1999).
198	**In June 2020 . . . "little resemblance to Brownridge"**: Brownridge, 126 N.Y.S.3d at 899-900.
198	**"Everyone in the criminal justice system failed you"**: Ransom, "He Spent 25 Years in Prison."
198	**thirteen million dollars**: Stipulation of Settlement, Brownridge v. City of New York, 21 Civ. 4603 (PKC), U.S. District Court for the Eastern District of New York.
198	**Queens resident Julio Negron . . . and other charges**: Dismissal Order, People v. Negron, Index No. 398/05 (Supreme Court, Queens County, September 6, 2017), 2-5, 10-11; Brief for Respondent, 2013 Westlaw 12200523, August 5, 2013, at 48.
198	**the Court of Appeals threw out**: People v. Negron, 26 N.Y. 262 (2015).
198	**dismissed the indictment . . . "exculpatory identification evidence"**: 2017 Dismissal Order, People v. Negron, 14.
198	**agreed to settle the suit**: Graham Rayman, "10 Years for Crime He Didn't Commit Leaves Mental, Physical Scars," *Daily News*, December 12, 2021, 3.
199	**exoneration of Anthony Miller**: People v. Miller, 134 N.Y.S.3d 605 (N.Y. App. Div. 2020) (vacating Miller's conviction).
199	**At eight o'clock . . . as the gunman**: Miller, 134 N.Y.S.3d at 607-608; Robert Bell, "After Six Years in Prison, An Exonerated Rochester Man Searches for Meaning," *Rochester Democrat & Chronicle*, December 19, 2021, A14-15.
199	**After hearing the report . . . and black pants**: Miller, 134 N.Y.S.3d at 607-608.
199	**Police brought Miller . . . was not recovered**: Miller, 134 N.Y.S.3d at 608.
199	**At a pretrial suppression . . . ten years in prison**: Miller, 134 N.Y.S.3d at 610; Bell, "After Six Years in Prison," A14-15.
199	**Six years later . . . the victim's iPhone**: Miller, 134 N.Y.S.3d at 609. The court added that the arresting officer "seized the first young black man in a hooded sweatshirt who he found. It must be plainly stated—the law does not allow the police to stop and frisk any young black man within a half-mile radius of an armed robbery based solely upon a general description." Miller, 134 N.Y.S.3d at 609.
200	**permit and even encourage courtroom identifications**: Brandon L. Garrett, "Eyewitnesses and Exclusion," 65 *Vanderbilt Law Review* 451, 452 (2019).
200	**In a 2021 article . . . as the culprit**: John T. Wixted et al. "Test a Witness's Memory of a Suspect Only Once," *Psychological Science in the Public Interest* 22, no. 1 (2021): 1S-18S. One of the article's co-authors, Duke Law Professor Brandon Garrett, conducted an earlier study of wrongful convictions involving eyewitness errors. He found that "in 57% of the trial transcripts . . . the witness who misidentified an innocent suspect with high confidence at trial recalled having initially done so with low confidence (34 cases); they recalled having identified a filler, another suspect, or no one at all (64 cases); or they reported not having seen the culprit's face (15 cases)." See Wixted, "Test a Witness's Memory," 12S-13S (citing Brandon L. Garrett, *Convicting the Innocent: Where Criminal Prosecutions Go Wrong* (Harvard University Press, 2011)).
200	**"adversary judicial criminal proceedings"**: Kirby v. Illinois, 406 U.S. 682, 689 (1972). See Chemerinsky, *Presumed Guilty*, 291 ("Counsel is required for such identifications after an indictment, but as a result of *Kirby*, police can easily circumvent that requirement simply by conducting the identification before it occurs").

Epilogue

201	**assistant district attorney in Queens until 1958**: Joseph Giardini, "Political Roundup," *Long Island Star-Journal*, April 15, 1969, 18.
201	**law secretary to his brother**: Giardini, "Political Roundup," 18.
201	**justice on the New York Supreme Court**: "James J. Crisona, 96, Lawyer, Legislator and New York Judge," *New York Times*, Sep. 10, 2003, C15.
202	**convicted of mail and wire fraud**: U.S. v. Crisona, 416 F.2d 107 (2d Cir. 1969); "Crisona Is Given A 3-Year Sentence for Loan Swindle," *New York Times*, December 12, 1968, 48.
202	**Crisona's downfall . . . "they're all guilty"'**: Crisona, 416 F.2d at 110, 119.
202	**three years in prison**: Crisona, 416 F.2d at 109.
202	**the New York Appellate Division . . . "testimony to the Grand Jury"**: Matter of Frank Crisona, 43 A.D.2d 299 (N.Y. App. Div. 1974).
202	**indicted again in 1977**: "Ex-Official Pleads Not Guilty in Bribe," *New York Times*, June 17, 1977, B3
202	**The indictment accused . . . a two-year sentence**: "Former Prosecutor Sentenced," *Newsday*, March 10, 1979, 5.
202	**was living in West Hollywood**: Kelly, "Detective Who Seized," 25.

202-03   **After working as . . . "I always walked in with him"**: Sander, "Leigh Wilson," 2B.
203   **"an ordinary case"**: Sander, "Leigh Wilson," 1B.
203   **"tackled small-town crime"**: "Former Brevard Sheriff, Leigh Wilson, Dies at 85," *Orlando Sentinel*, July 13, 1994, 43.
203   **"Toy Gun Bandit"**: Robert Bigelow, "Toy Gun Bandit Admits Robberies Laid to Jackson Heights Musician," *Long Island Star-Journal*, April 30, 1953, 1, 2.
203-04   **An inmate case file . . . in October 1956**: Charles Daniell Wallkill Prison Inmate Case File, NYSA, W0054-87-05753. Daniell's file contains several parole reports that detail his personal and employment history before his imprisonment.
204   **"any action taken by the Parole Board"**: "Pre-Parole Summary," Daniell Case File.
204   **But the board . . . "serious-minded, ambitious worker"**: "Pre-Parole Summary," Daniell Case File.
204   **After his parole . . . later married**: Parole Officer Reports, Daniell Case File.
204   **died there, in Wilton Manors**: "Charles J. Daniell," (obituary), *South Florida Sun Sentinel*, July 7, 1986, 13.
204   **was elected Queens District Attorney**: Leo Egan, "Democrats in City Sweep," *New York Times*, November 9, 1955, 1; Leo Egan, "O'Connor Defeats Quinn; Loser May Ask Recount," *New York Times*, Sep. 14, 1955, 1.
204   **DA until 1966**: Dennis Hevesi, "Frank O'Connor, 82, Is Dead; Retired New York Appellate Judge," *New York Times*, December 3, 1992, D21.
204   **requested the release**: Hevesi, "Frank O'Connor," D21 ("Four times, he recommended that grand juries throw out robbery cases where the only evidence was the victim's testimony").
204   **acknowledged that mistaken identity**: "Plans to Sue Over Arrest for Mugging," *Daily News*, November 1, 1956, B3.
204   **release of a Queens man**: "Convicted Suspected Paroled in Queens; 'Double' Confesses," *New York Times*, May 9, 1959, 23.
204   **O'Connor left . . . retirement in 1986**: Hevesi, "Frank O'Connor," D21.
204   **While on the Appellate Division . . . and attempted murder**: People v. Daniels, 88 A.D.2d 392 (N.Y. App. Div. 1982).
204-05   **The state had . . . "that mistake may be"**: Daniels, 88 A.D.2d at 400. The eyewitness in the case was "a student assigned to a class for emotionally handicapped children." He identified the defendant after a detective asked a "suggestive question" ("was it Charles?"). In highlighting that the state's case rested entirely on the boy's testimony, O'Connor noted that "because of its persuasive power and inherent unreliability, eyewitness identification is always fraught with peril but when, as here, it is suspect, it is frightening indeed." Daniels, 88 A.D.2d. at 393, 399-400.
205   **After O'Connor's ruling . . . for wrongful imprisonment**: Selwyn Raab, "Man Wrongfully Imprisoned Is to Get $600,000 From City," *New York Times*, January 18, 1985, A1, B5.
205   **O'Connor revisited . . . to "positive identifications"**: O'Connor, "That's the Man," 26-28.
205   **New York has declined to admit polygraph results**: People v. Shedrick, 66 N.Y.2d 1015 (1985). See also People v. Brewer, 151 N.Y.S.3d 784, 797 (App. Div. 2021) (citing Shedrick in holding that court did not err in denying defendant's "request to admit in evidence the results of his polygraph examination").
205   **On the night of February 25 . . . by the victims**: Robert Hanley, "Reforms Advised in Police Line-Ups," *New York Times*, September 16, 1973, 21; Manny Topol, "A Quiet Man's Ordeal by Law," *Newsday*, March 25, 1973, at 4, 17.
205   **among five husky police officers**: Topol, "Quiet Man's Ordeal," 4.
205   **wore their uniform pants**: Hanley, "Reforms Advised," 21.
205   **without investigating his alibis**: Topol, "Quiet Man's Ordeal," 17.
205   **Schrager was exonerated . . . wore glasses**: Topol, "Quiet Man's Ordeal," 17; Irving Spiegel, "Assistant District Attorney Cleared of Sex Crimes Will Get His Job Back," *New York Times*, March 18, 1973, 61.
205   **"they almost made me believe I did it"**: "Oh Say Can You See," *Time*, April 2, 1973, 59.
205   **forty-five exonerations in Queens . . . at least one eyewitness misidentification**: National Registry of Exonerations website, accessed August 2022.
205   **the Lucerne Hotel**: Kelly, "Detective Who Seized," 25.
205   **"To lead my own band"**: "Life's a Song Now for Musician Once Falsely Accused as Robber," *Miami Herald*, January 27, 1957, 35.
205-06   **newspaper ad from May 1973**: Ad for Boca Teeca Country Club and the Manny Balestrero Trio, *Fort Lauderdale News*, May 5, 1973, 24.
206   **"My mother felt"**: GB Interview.
206   **Rose progressed . . . of the episode**: GB Interview.
206   **"There were so many guidelines" . . . forced to retire as a result**: GB Interview.
206   **Rose died in Jacksonville**: Obituary for Rose Giolito Balestrero, *Miami News*, December 22, 1982, 6.
206   **Manny passed away**: Obituary for Christopher Emanuel Balestrero, *Charlotte Observer*, March 3, 1998, 57.
206-07   **Greg Balestrero . . . "apart from family"**: GB Interview.
207   **In the New York area . . . "how our justice system works"**: Jason D. Antos, "Jackson Heights Co-Naming Immortalizes 'Wrong Man,'" *Queens Gazette*, October 1, 2014.
207   **"My dad was only one guy"**: GB Interview.

—SELECTED BIBLIOGRAPHY—

Adams, Marjory. "'Wrong Man' Hitchcock Drama." *Boston Globe*, January 21, 1957.

Albright, Thomas D. and Brandon L. Garrett. "The Law and Science of Eyewitness Evidence." 102 *Boston University Law Review 511* (2022).

Anderson, Maxwell, and Angus MacPhail. *The Wrong Man*. Unpublished Screenplay. New York: The Morgan Library & Museum, 1956.

Anderson, Maxwell and Harold Hickerson. *Gods of the Lightning*. Longmans, Green and Co., 1928.

Antos, Jason D. "Jackson Heights Co-Naming Immortalizes 'Wrong Man.'" *Queens Gazette*, October 1, 2014.

Asimow, Michael and Paul Bergman. *Reel Justice: The Courtroom Goes to the Movies*. Kansas City, Missouri: Andrews McMeel Publishing, 2006.

Aulier, Dan. *Vertigo: The Making of a Hitchcock Classic*. New York: St. Martin's Press, 1998.

"The Balestrero Case." Trial Transcript in *People of the State of New York v. Christopher Balestrero*, Indictment Number 271/53, Supreme Court, Queens County, April 21-23, 1953, *Wrong Man* files, WBUSC.

Barnum, Michael. "Just the Facts, Ma'am: Peggy Webber." *Scarlet Street*, no. 52, 2004.

Barry, Dan. "Cheats, Swindlers and Ne'er-Do-Wells: A New York Family Album." *New York Times*, February 9, 2018.

Bazelon, Emily. "I Write About the Law. But Could I Really Help Free a Prisoner?" *New York Times Magazine*, June 30, 2021.

Bazelon, Lara. *Rectify: The Power of Restorative Justice After Wrongful Conviction*. Boston: Beacon Press, 2018.

Bell, Robert. "After Six Years in Prison, an Exonerated Rochester Man Searches for Meaning." *Rochester Democrat & Chronicle*, December 19, 2021.

Bharara, Preet. *Doing Justice: A Prosecutor's Thoughts on Crime, Punishment, and the Rule of Law*. New York: Alfred A. Knopf, 2019.

Bigelow, Robert. "D.A. to Reexamine Case of 'Cleared' Musician." *Long Island Star-Journal*, May 1, 1953.

———. "Double, Caught Red-Handed, Clears Fiddler in Holdups." *Long Island Daily Press*, April 30, 1953.

———. "'The Wrong Man' Is a Story of Horror, Not Suspense." *Long Island Star-*

Journal, December 24, 1956.

———. "Toy Gun Bandit Admits Robberies Laid to Jackson Heights Musician." *Long Island Star-Journal*, April 30, 1953.

Billheimer, John. *Hitchcock and the Censors*. Lexington: The University Press of Kentucky, 2019.

Biondi, Martha. *To Stand and Fight: The Struggle for Civil Rights in Postwar New York City*. Harvard University Press, 2003.

Blumenthal, Ralph. *Stork Club: America's Most Famous Nightspot and the Lost World of Cafe Society*. New York: Little Brown and Company, First Back Bay paperback edition, 2001.

Bogdanovich, Peter. *Who the Devil Made It: Conversations with Legendary Film Directors*. New York: Ballantine Books, 1997.

Bothwell, R. K., J.C. Brigham, and M.A. Pigott. "A Field Study on the Relationship Between Quality of Eyewitnesses' Descriptions and Identification Accuracy." *Journal of Police Science and Administration* 17 (1990): 84-88.

Bouzereau, Laurent, director. *Guilt Trip: Hitchcock and The Wrong Man*. Warner Bros., 2004, DVD.

Borchard, Edwin M. *Convicting the Innocent*. London: FB &c, 2015.

Brean, Herbert. "A Case of Identity." *Life*, June 29, 1953.

———. *A Case of Identity: The Balestrero Story*, Film Treatment. June 29, 1955, *The Wrong Man*—Script, File 1005, AHPMHL.

Brewer, Neil, Amy Bradfield Douglass, Margaret Bull Kovera, Christian A. Meissner, Gary L. Wells, and John T. Wixted. "Policy and Procedure Recommendations for the Collection and Preservation of Eyewitness Identification Evidence." *Law and Human Behavior* 44, no. 1 (2020): 3-36.

Brimacombe, C. A. E., S. M. Fulero, R. S. Malpass, S. Penrod, M. Small, and G. L. Wells. "Eyewitness Identification Procedures: Recommendations for Lineups and Photospreads." *Law and Human Behavior* 22, no. 6 (December 1998): 603-647.

Brooks, Samantha K. and Neil Greenberg. "Psychological Impact of Being Wrongfully Accused of Criminal Offences: A Systematic Literature Review." *Medicine, Science and the Law* 61, No. 1 (2020): 44-54.

Brown, Rebecca and Peter Neufeld. "Chimes of Freedom Flashing: For Each Unharmful Gentle Soul Misplaced Inside a Jail." 76 *New York University Annual Survey of American Law* 235 (2021).

Brundidge, Harry and David Camelon. "Vindicated After 15 Years." *American Weekly*, October 1, 1950.

Campbell, Bertram. Executive Clemency and Pardon Case File, NYSA, Files A0597-78-B054-F04, -F05, -F06, and -F21.

Cannell, Michael. *Incendiary: The Psychiatrist, the Mad Bomber, and the Invention of Criminal Profiling*. New York: St. Martin's Press, 2017.

Caruso, Philip. Great Meadow Prison Inmate Case File, NYSA, W0024-88-14508.

Chandler, Charlotte. *It's Only a Movie: Alfred Hitchcock: A Personal Biography*. New York: Simon & Schuster, 2005.

Chemerinsky, Erwin. *Presumed Guilty: How the Supreme Court Empowered the Police and Subverted Civil Rights*. New York: Liveright, 2021.

Clarens, Carlos. *Crime Movies.* New York: Da Capo Press, 1997.

Closson, Troy. "Queens Prosecutors Long Overlooked Misconduct. Can a New D.A. Do Better?" *New York Times,* January 28, 2021.

Coe, Richard L. "Story's 'True' But Not 'Real.'" *Washington Post,* January 18, 1957.

Cohen, Paula Marantz. *Alfred Hitchcock: The Legacy of Victorianism.* Lexington: The University Press of Kentucky, 2006.

Coleman, Herbert. *The Man Who Knew Hitchcock: A Hollywood Memoir.* Lanham, Maryland: Scarecrow Press, 2007.

Cook, Joan. "Lloyd Espenschied, One of the Inventors of the Coaxial Cable" (obituary). *New York Times,* July 4, 1986.

Daily News (New York). "Held in $10,000 in Insurance Firm Holdups." May 7, 1953.

———. "Her Memory Pins Robbery on Man." January 16, 1953.

———. "Plans Florida Trip for Wife, Mind Healed." September 30, 1955.

Danforth, Harold E. and James D. Horan. *The D.A.'s Man.* New York: Crown, 1957.

Daniell, Charles. Wallkill Prison Inmate Case File. NYSA, W0054-87-05753.

Dargis, Manohla. "Hunting a Killer as the Age of Aquarius Dies." *New York Times,* March 2, 2007.

Dargis, Manohla, A.O. Scott, and Wallace Schroeder. *The New York Times Book of Movies: The Essential 1,000 Films to See.* New York: Universal, 2019.

Daru, Robert. *Interim and Partial Report, Bertram M. Campbell Investigation.*

New York County Criminal Courts Bar Association, 1946.

Davis, Kevin. "The 25 Greatest Legal Movies." *ABA Journal,* August 1, 2018.

Democrat & Chronicle (Rochester, NY). "Paramount's 'Wrong Man' Weighted with Woes." January 31, 1957.

Deutelbaum, Marshall. "Finding the Right Man in The Wrong Man," in *A Hitchcock Reader,* second edition, edited by Marshall Deutelbaum and Leland Poague. Blackwell Publishing, 2009.

Dewey, Thomas E. "Statement of the Governor Accompanying the Pardon of Bertram M. Campbell." *Public Papers of Thomas E. Dewey,* 1945. New York: Williams Press, 1946.

Donoghue, Peter J. and Benjamin J. Jacobsen. "Coram Nobis & the Hoffner Case." 28 *St. John's Law Review* 234 (1954).

Doyle, James M. "Learning from Error in American Criminal Justice." 100 *Journal of Criminal Law and Criminology* 109 (2010).

Ebert, Roger. *Scorsese by Ebert.* University of Chicago Press, 2008.

Espenschied, Lloyd. "American Background of the Espenschieds During the War," April 9, 1951. Lloyd Espenschied Genealogical Research Papers, NYGB Coll 157, [01-004], The Irma and Paul Milstein Division of United States History, Local History and Genealogy, The New York Public Library.

———. Letter to Hotel Shoreham (Washington, DC), March 30, 1953. Series Four, Box 28, Lloyd Espenschied Papers, Archives Center, National Museum of American History.

———. Letter to Paul Hardaway, September 24, 1953. Lloyd Espenschied

Genealogical Research Papers, NYGB Coll 157, [01-031], The Irma and Paul Milstein Division of United States History, Local History and Genealogy, The New York Public Library.

———. Letter to Police Department, 102nd Precinct, April 24, 1953. Series Four, Box 28, Lloyd Espenschied Papers, Archives Center, National Museum of American History.

———. *The German Background of the Espenschied-Esbenshade Families.* Reynolds Historical Genealogy Collection, 1938.

———. "Visit by a Young Investigator of the War Department," January 25, 1944. Series Four, Box 25, Lloyd Espenschied Papers, Archives Center, National Museum of American History.

Esterow, Milton. "All Around the Town with 'The Wrong Man.'" *New York Times,* April 29, 1956.

Eyman, Scott. *Hank and Jim: The Fifty-Year Friendship of Henry Fonda and James Stewart.* New York: Simon & Schuster, 2017.

Feinberg, Alexander. "Bomb Hoax Wave Compels Police to Limit Checks." *New York Times,* December 29, 1956.

———. "Dewey Seeks Way to Guard Innocent." *New York Times,* September 7, 1945.

Findley, Keith A. "Toward a New Paradigm of Criminal Justice: How the Innocence Movement Merges Crime Control and Due Process." 41 *Texas Tech Law Review* 133 (2008).

Findley, Keith A. and Michael S. Scott. "The Multiple Dimensions of Tunnel Vision in Criminal Cases." 2006 *Wisconsin Law Review* 291 (2006).

Flint, Peter B. "Alfred Hitchcock Dies; a Master of Suspense." *New York Times,* April 30, 1980.

———. "Henry Fonda Dies on Coast at 77; Played 100 Stage and Screen Roles." *New York Times,* August 13, 1981.

Fonda, Henry and Howard Teichmann. *Fonda: My Life.* New York: New American Library, 1981.

Frank, Jerome and Barbara Frank. *Not Guilty.* Garden City: Doubleday, 1957.

Frankfurter, Felix. *The Case of Sacco and Vanzetti* (Universal Library Edition). Little, Brown and Co., 1962.

Garrett, Brandon L. "Eyewitnesses and Exclusion." 65 *Vanderbilt Law Review* 451 (2019).

Garrett, Brandon L., Elizabeth F. Loftus, Gary L. Wells, and John T. Wixted. "Test a Witness's Memory of a Suspect Only Once." *Psychological Science in the Public Interest* 22, no. 1S (2021): 1S-18S.

Gertner, Jon. *The Idea Factory: Bell Labs and the Great Age of American Innovation.* New York: Penguin Press, 2012.

Gilman, William. "The Incredible Story." *True Detective,* October 1946.

Godard, Jean-Luc. "The Wrong Man," in *Godard on Godard,* edited by Jean Narboni and Tom Milne, 48-55. De Capo Press, 1972.

Gottlieb, Sidney, ed. *Hitchcock on Hitchcock, Volume 1: Selected Writings and Interviews.* Berkeley and Los Angeles: University of California Press, 1997.

———. *Hitchcock on Hitchcock, Volume 2: Selected Writings and Interviews.* Oakland: University of California Press, 2015.

Grady, Jack. "The 'Wrong Man' Happy After 3-Yr. Nightmare." *New York Post*, April 16, 1956.

Haeffner, Nicholas. *Alfred Hitchcock*. Harlow: Pearson Longman, 2005.

Haff, Joseph O. "Jailed in Mistake, Man Wins Pardon." *New York Times*, June 15, 1950.

Hale, Wanda. "Fonda in 'Wrong Man' Title Role." *Daily News*, Dec. 23, 1956.

Hevesi, Dennis. "Frank O'Connor, 82, Is Dead; Retired New York Appellate Judge." *New York Times*, December 3, 1992.

Hibel, Miriam J. *New York Identification Law: The Wade Hearing/The Trial*. Matthew Bender & Company, 2021.

Hilton, Ordway. "Handwriting Identification vs. Eye Witness Identification," 45 *Journal of Criminal Law, Criminology and Police Science* 207 (1954-1955).

Hirsch, Foster. *The Dark Side of the Screen: Film Noir*, second edition. Da Capo Press, 2008.

Hitchcock, Alfred. Letter to Maxwell Anderson, February 28, 1956. *The Wrong Man*—Script, 1955-56, File 1012, AHPMHL.

———. Letter to Maxwell Anderson, February 29, 1956. *The Wrong Man*—Script, 1955-56, File 1012, AHPMHL.

———. Letter to Maxwell Anderson, March 6, 1956. *The Wrong Man*—Script, 1955-56, File 1012, AHPMHL.

———. Letter to Maxwell Anderson, March 15, 1956. MAPHRC.

———. Letter to Maxwell Anderson, March 20, 1956. *The Wrong Man*—Script, 1955-56, File 1012, AHPMHL.

Hoffner, Louis, Executive Clemency and Pardon Case File, Series, NYSA, A0597-16-B61.

Hogan, Frank S. *Report of the District Attorney, County of New York, 1946-48* (1949).

Hogan, Sean. "Turning on the Light: Henry Fonda and Will Brown." *RogerEbert.com*, January 31, 2018.

The Hollywood Reporter. "'Wrong Man' Strong Drama." December 21, 1956.

Humbert, David. *Violence in the Films of Alfred Hitchcock: A Study in Mimesis*. East Lansing: Michigan State University Press, 2017.

Innocence Project. "DNA Exonerations in the United States." Innocence Project website, accessed August 17, 2022.

"Interview with Mr. & Mrs. Ferrero on Sunday 12th Feb." Unsigned memo, *The Wrong Man*—Research, 1955-56, File 1037, AHPMHL.

Johnson, Marilynn S. *Street Justice: A History of Police Violence in New York City*. Boston: Beacon Press, 2003.

Jones, Kent, director. *Hitchcock/Truffaut*. Dogwoof, 2016, DVD.

Judicial Council of the State of New York. *Fourteenth Annual Report of the Judicial Council of the State of New York*, 1948.

Kapsis, Robert E. *Hitchcock: The Making of a Reputation*. Chicago: The University of Chicago Press, 1992.

Kassin, Saul M. and Rebecca J. Norwick. "Why People Waive Their Miranda Rights:

The Power of Innocence." *Law and Human Behavior* 28, no. 2 (2004): 211-221.

Kelly, Herb. "Detective Who Seized Musician Lives Here." *Miami News*, February 1, 1957.

———. "Hitchcock Has Field Day." *Miami Daily News*, February 2, 1957.

Kempenaar, Adam and Josh Larsen. "Blindspotting: *The Wrong Man*." *Filmspotting* podcast, December 2, 2015.

Kenny, Glenn. "'The Wrong Man': Hitchcock's Least 'Fun' Movie Is Also One of His Greatest." *RogerEbert.com*, February 17, 2016.

Kevorkian, Martin. "The Dantesque Desires of David Fincher's *Zodiac*," in *David Fincher's Zodiac: Cinema of Investigation and (Mis)Interpretation*, edited by Matthew Sorrento and David Ryan. Fairleigh Dickinson University Press, 2022.

Kolker, Robert P. *Triumph Over Containment*. Rutgers University Press, 2021.

Krohn, Bill. *Hitchcock at Work*. London: Phaidon Press, 2000.

Laming, Donald. *Human Judgment: The Eye of the Beholder*. University of Cambridge, 2011.

Lawrence, Amy. "Constructing a Priest, Silencing a Saint: The PCA and *I Confess* (1953)." *Film History* 1, no. 19 (2007): 58-72.

Leo, Richard A. *Police Interrogation and American Justice*. Cambridge: Harvard University Press 2009.

Long Island Daily Press. "Musician May Ask $150,000 False Arrest Damages." May 1, 1953.

———. "Says Bandit Must Be His Double." April 22, 1953.

Long Island Star-Journal. "Agents Ordered to Quit Work." December 1, 1951.
———. "Balestrero's 'Double' Given Maximum Term." July 29, 1953.

———. "Balestreros Reunited After 2 Years." September 29, 1955.

———. "'Double' Pleads Guilty of 2 Insurance Holdups." June 15, 1953.

———. "Fiddler in Fog at News, 'Went Right on Playing.'" April 30, 1953.

———. "Gunman Robs Busy Office in Jackson Heights." July 9, 1952.

———. "Holdup Double Indicted Too." June 1, 1953.

———. "Insurance Firm Robbed Again." December 18, 1952.

———. "Jackson Heights Musician Cleared of Holdups Admitted by Double." July 14, 1953.

———. "Juror's Gripe Forces Robbery Case Mistrial." April 23, 1953.

———. "Lie Detectors." May 1, 1953.

———. "Musician Fights to Clean Slate of 2 Robberies." March 18, 1953.

———. "Musician's Double in 2 Stickups for Jury Under $10,000 Bail." May 7, 1953.

———. "Prudential Claims Wife's Illness Not an Issue in Balestrero's Suit." October 22, 1953.

———. "7,500 Bail Set for Musician." January 16, 1953.

———. "Stork Club Fiddler in Holdup

Trial Wins Point in Clash Over Identity." April 22, 1953.

———. "Toy Gun Bandit Admits Robberies Laid to Jackson Heights Musician." April 30, 1953.

———. "Was It Mistaken Identity? Musician Accused as Holdup Man." January 15, 1953.

Louttit, James. "Wife of Musician Lives in Constant State of Fear." *Long Island Star-Journal*, November 23, 1953.

McCarten, John. "The Current Cinema: Hitchcock, Documentary Style," *New Yorker*, January 5, 1957.

McGilligan, Patrick. *Alfred Hitchcock: A Life in Darkness and Light*. New York: HarperCollins paperback edition, 2004.

McKelway, St. Clair. "Annals of Crime: The Innocent Man at Sing Sing." *New Yorker*, November 11, 1939.

McKinney, Devin. *The Man Who Saw a Ghost: The Life and Work of Henry Fonda*. New York: St. Martin's Press, 2012.

McMillan, Robert. "Remembering Alfred Hitchcock." *Manhasset Press*, April 14, 2011.

Miami Herald. "Life's a Song Now for Musician Once Falsely Accused as Robber." January 27, 1957.

Miller, Arthur. *The Crucible* (Penguin Orange Collection) (Reprint Edition). New York: Penguin Books, 2016.

Miller, D. A. *Hidden Hitchcock*. University of Chicago Press, 2016.

Mowery, Edward J. "DA Seeks to Give Lifer a Chance to Prove Innocence in '40 Slaying." *New York World-Telegram and The Sun*, September 3, 1952.

———. "Dewey Orders Parole Board Inquiry into Campbell Case." *New York World-Telegram*, July 27, 1945.

———. *The Hoffner Case*. New York: The Hoffner Committee, 1947.

———. "Hoffner Life Term Set Aside." *New York World-Telegram and The Sun*, November 10, 1952.

———. "7-Year Hell Is Ended for Forger's Double." *New York World-Telegram*, July 25, 1945.

"Mrs. Balestrero's Confinement," *The Wrong Man*—Research, 1955-56, File 1037, AHPMHL.

Muller, Eddie. *Dark City: The Lost World of Film Noir, Revised and Expanded Edition*. New York: Hachette Book Group, 2021.

Naremore, James. *An Invention Without a Future: Essays on Cinema*. University of California Press, 2014.

Nayman, Adam. *David Fincher: Mind Games*. New York: Abrams, 2021.

Newsday. "Former Prosecutor Sentenced." March 10, 1979.

Newsweek. "Iceberg of Chills: The Wrong Man." January 7, 1957.

New York Times. "Bertram Campbell Is Dead at 60; Falsely Imprisoned for 40 Months." September 7, 1946.

———. "Campbell Case Laid to Dewey's 100% Goal." August 29, 1945.

———. "Campbell Receives a Full Pardon from Dewey as Justice, Not Mercy." August 29, 1945.

———. "Court Is Turned into A Movie Set." April 9, 1956.

———. "Crisona Is Given a 3-Year Sentence for Loan Swindle." December 12, 1968.

———. "'Double' Admits His Guilt." June 16, 1953.

———. "Double's Arrest Clears Musician." May 1, 1953.

———. "Fonda's Wife, Ill, Commits Suicide." April 15, 1950.

———. "Innocent Convict Freed." April 28, 1939.

———. "Woman, 62, Gets Pardon in Jersey Sixteen Years After False Arrest." May 17, 1951.

Neilsen, Ray. "Harold Stone—'The Wrong Man.'" *Classic Images*, October, 1993.

Niles, Mark and Naomi Mezey, "Screening the Law: Ideology and Law in American Popular Culture." 28 *Columbia Journal of Law and the Arts* 91 (2005).

"Notes from Stork Club Visit and Musicians' Departure," Unsigned and undated memo, *The Wrong Man—Research*, 1955-56, File 1037, AHPMHL.

O'Connor, Frank. "That's the Man: A Sobering Study of Eyewitness Identification and the Polygraph." 49 *St. John's Law Review* 1 (1974).

Oller, John. *Rogues' Gallery: The Birth of Modern Policing and Organized Crime in Gilded Age New York*. New York: Dutton, 2021.

Orlando Sentinel. "Former Brevard Sheriff, Leigh Wilson, Dies at 85." July 13, 1994.

Osteen, Mark. "Introduction," in *Hitchcock and Adaptation: On the Page and Screen*, edited by Mark Osteen. Rowman & Littlefield, 2014.

Packer, Herbert L. "Two Models of the Criminal Process." 113 *University of Pennsylvania Law Review* 1 (1964).

Parker, Ben S. "True-Life Story Portrayed in 'Wrong Man' at Warner." *Commercial Appeal* (Memphis), January 24, 1957.

Pomerance, Murray. *Alfred Hitchcock's America*. Cambridge: Polity Press, 2013.

Quentin Reynolds. *Courtroom: The Story of Samuel S. Leibowitz*. New York: Farrar, Straus and Giroux, 1950.

Radin, Edward D. *The Innocents*. New York: William Morrow and Company, 1961.

Rafter, Nicole. *Shots in the Mirror: Crime Films and Society*, second edition. New York: Oxford University Press, 2006.

Raidy, William A. "The Wrong Man: This Is Where It Happened." *Long Island Sunday Press*, April 22, 1956.

Ransom, Jan. "He Spent 25 Years in Prison for Murder, But Was Innocent All Along." *New York Times*, June 23, 2020.

Ray, Robert B. *A Certain Tendency of the Hollywood Cinema*. Princeton University Press, 1995.

"Resume of Meeting with Drs. Banay & Rouke." Unsigned memo, *The Wrong Man* –Research, 1955-56, File 1037, AHPMHL.

"Resume of Meeting at Prudential Office." Unsigned and undated memo, *The Wrong Man*–Research, 1955-56, File 1037, AHPMHL.

"Resume of Meeting with Mr. Eugene Conforti, Olga Conforti and Mr. and Mrs. Balestrero, Sr." Unsigned memo dated February 6, 1956, *The Wrong Man—Research, 1955-56*, File 1037, AHPMHL.

Reynolds, Ruth. "A Tragedy of Errors." *Daily News*, October 3, 1954.

Riley, Royal. "Cleared, He Hopes It Will Cure Wife." *Daily News*, May 1, 1953

———. "Musician Learns He's Holdup Man's Double." *Daily News*, May 24, 1953.

Rohmer, Eric and Claude Chabrol. *Hitchcock, the First Forty-Four Films*. New York: Frederick Ungar Publishing, 1979.

Rosenberg, Norman L. "Constitutional History and the 'Cultural Turn': Cross-Examining the Legal-Reelist Narratives of Henry Fonda," in *Constitutionalism and American Culture: Writing the New American History*, edited by Sandra F. VanBurkleo, Kermit L. Hall, and Robert J. Kaczorowski, 381-409. Lawrence: University Press of Kansas, 2002.

Rosenzweig, Phil. *Reginald Rose and the Journey of 12 Angry Men*. Fordham University Press, 2021.

Ross, Don. "Alfred Hitchcock, a Very Crafty Fellow." *New York Herald Tribune*, March 4, 1956.

Rostron, Allen. K. "Lawyers, Law, & the Movies: The Hitchcock Cases." 86 *California Law Review* 211 (1998).

Rothman, William. *Must We Kill the Thing We Love? Emersonian Perfectionism and the Films of Alfred Hitchcock*. New York: Columbia University Press, 2014.

Sander, Tom. "Alfred Hitchcock Presents Leigh Wilson." *Florida Today*, July 29, 1973.

Scheuer, Philip K. "Hitchcock 'Wrong Man' Lifelike but Plodding." *Los Angeles Times*, January 24, 1957.

Schickel, Richard. *Keepers: The Greatest Films—and Personal Favorites—of a Moviegoing Lifetime*. New York: Vintage Books, 2015.

Schiffer, George. "Memo to Files," March 13, 1956, *The Wrong Man—Legal, 1956-57*, File 1031, AHPMHL.

Scorsese, Martin and Michael Henry Wilson. *A Personal Journey with Martin Scorsese Through American Movies*. Miramax Books, 1997.

Shephard, Clifford. "They Swore My Life Away." *Inside Detective*, October 1950.

Silbey, Jessica M. "Patterns of Courtroom Justice." 28 *Journal of Law and Society* 97 (2001).

Simon, Robert I. "The Psychological and Legal Aftermath of False Arrest and Imprisonment." *Journal of the American Academy of Psychiatry and the Law* 24, No. 4 (1993): 523-528.

Skerry, Philip J. *Psycho in the Shower: The History of Cinema's Most Famous Scene*. New York: Continuum International Publishing, 2008.

Sloan, Jane E. *Alfred Hitchcock: The Definitive Filmography*. Berkeley & Los Angeles: University of California Press, 1993.

Southall, Ashely. "Witness IDs Led to His Conviction. Then Court Ruled on Racial Bias." *New York Times*, March 18, 2019.

Spaulding, Norman W. "Disorder in Court: Representations of Resistance to Law in Trial Film Dramas," in *Trial Films on Trial: Law, Justice, and Popular Culture*, edited by

Austin Sarat, Jessica Silbey, and Martha Merrill Umphrey, 111-139. Tuscaloosa: The University of Alabama Press, 2019.

Spoto, Donald. *The Art of Alfred Hitchcock: Fifty Years of His Motion Pictures.* New York: Doubleday, Second Edition, 1992.

———. *The Dark Side of Genius: The Life of Alfred Hitchcock.* New York: Ballantine Books, 1983.

Standard Union (Brooklyn). "One Killed, Five Hurt as Autos Crash." January 30, 1931.

Steinbeck, John. "Henry Fonda." *Harper's Bazaar*, November 1966.

Sterritt, David. *The Films of Alfred Hitchcock* (Cambridge Film Classics). Cambridge University Press, 1993.

Strauss, Marc Raymond. *Hitchcock Nonetheless: The Master's Touch in His Least Celebrated Films.* North Carolina: McFarland & Co., 2007.

Thomson, David. *The Big Screen: The Story of the Movies.* New York: Farrar, Straus and Giroux, 2012.

Tinee, Mae. "Somber Story Told in Movie by Hitchcock." *Chicago Tribune*, February 8, 1957.

Time. "Cinema: The New Pictures" (review of *The Wrong Man*). January 14, 1957.

Tobias, Scott. "Wrong Man Movies in Honor of Hitchcock (1 of 4): *The Wrong Man.*" *The A.V. Club* website, November 19, 2012.

Truffaut, François. *Hitchcock* (Revised Edition). New York: Simon & Schuster, 1985.

Variety. "The Stork Club" (television review). January 14, 1953.

———. "The Wrong Man." January 2, 1957.

———. "2 Actresses Die in Kansas Auto Crash." June 6, 1956.

"Visit to the home of Manny Balestrero—Sunday, 20th March 1956." Unsigned memo, *The Wrong Man*—Research, 1955-56, File 1037, AHPMHL.

Walker, Michael. *Hitchcock's Motifs.* Amsterdam: Amsterdam University Press, 2005.

Wall, Patrick M. *Eye-Witness Identification in Criminal Cases.* Springfield, Illinois: Charles C. Thomas, 1965.

Weiler, A. H. "A New Format for Hitchcock: Suspense Is Dropped in 'The Wrong Man.'" *New York Times*, December 24, 1956.

White, Edward. *The Twelve Lives of Alfred Hitchcock: An Anatomy of the Master of Suspense.* New York: W. W. Norton & Company, 2021.

Whitty, Stephen. *The Alfred Hitchcock Encyclopedia.* Lanham, Maryland: Rowman & Littlefield, 2016.

Wigmore, John Henry. "Identification of Accused Persons on Arrest." 25 *Illinois Law Review* 550 (1931).

———. *The Science of Judicial Proof.* Boston: Little Brown and Company, 1937.

—INDEX—

12 Angry Men (1957), 4–5, 125, 178–179
The 39 Steps (1935), 2, 121, 146, 191, 210
Adams, Francis W. H., 134
Adams, Marjory, 187
Affel, Herman, 98, 99
Alden, Carlos C., 69, 220
The Alfred Hitchcock Hour, 191-192
Alfred Hitchcock Presents, 130, 138, 185, 187
American Bar Association, 5, 211
American Film Institute, 4, 211
Anderson, Alfred, 98
Anderson, Harry, 49, 52
Anderson, Maxwell, 125–127
  correspondence with Hitchcock, 133-134, 140-41,
    176, 181
  Gods of the Lightning, 126–127
  Winterset, 125-26
Andrews, Dana, 3
Andrews, Herbert, 146, 231
Arluck, Bernard, 49, 52
Armstrong, Charlotte, 190

Bacall, Lauren, 76, 77
Balestrero, Greg
  appearance in press photos, 1–2, 102, 111
  early childhood, 76, 78
  father's arrest, effect on, 206-207
  on Manny's appearance on *To Tell the Truth*, 188
  mother, memories of, 86–88, 111–112, 165, 206
  recollections relating to father's case, 84, 88, 92, 100,
    206–207
  reflections on father's case, 207
  on visit by Henry Fonda and Vera Miles, 133
Balestrero, Manny
  alibis, 79, 89–90, 92, 100, 108, 226
  attorney, retention of, 85. *See also O'Connor, Frank*
  bail, out on, 84-85, 87–88
  booking, 84
  civil lawsuit for damages, 111–118
  confrontation with Charles Daniell, 102
  continuation of music career in Florida, 205-206
  courtroom identifications of, 92–94, 96
  decision to move Rose to sanitarium, 87
  exoneration of, 1–2, 101–102, 109, 226
  family background, 77–78
  financial stresses on, 81, 112–113, 116–117
  handwriting samples, 83–84, 95–96, 106–108
  indictment against, 88, 102, 225-226
  lie detector test, 88–89, 108–109
  life before arrest, 76–79
  lineup at precinct, 83–84, 93, 97, 104, 226
  meeting with Henry Fonda and Vera Miles, 133, 181
  misidentification, initial, 81–82
  mistrial, 6, 97–98, 107, 108, 225

  music and, 77–78
  police, lack of criticism for, 110
  Prudential, visits to, 81–82, 94
  request for trial preference for false arrest claims, 116–117
  resemblance to holdup man, 102–103
  showups, 82–83, 93, 103, 105–106
  street sign honoring, 207
  Stork Club, employment at, 76, 78–79, 87
  To Tell the Truth, appearance on, 188–189
  trial of, 91–100
  visits with Rose at sanitarium, 90, 100–101, 102,
    111–112, 225
Balestrero, Peter, 77–78, 116
Balestrero, Robert
  appearance in press photos, 1–2, 102, 111
  early childhood, 76, 78
  father's arrest, effect on, 206–207
  as potential alibi witness, 90
  in *The Wrong Man*, 160, 165
Balestrero, Rose
  compensation for suffering, 113–116
  detective, encounter with, 84, 223
  Kings County Hospital, transfer to, 117–118
  life before Manny's arrest, 78, 86–87, 165
  meeting with Henry Fonda and Vera Miles, 133, 181
  meeting with Frank O'Connor, 85
  nervous breakdown after Manny's arrest, 1–2, 86–87
  recovery from breakdown, 118, 206
  time in sanitariums, 1–2, 87, 90, 102, 111–112, 117, 225
Banay, Ralph, 87, 116, 134
Barrett, James J., 25–26
Barrett, Laurinda, 132
Bastien, August J., 89–90
Bazelon, Emily, 236
Bazelon, Lara, 180, 233
Bergen, Polly, 188–189
Berrett, Louis, 128
Bharara, Preet, 22–23
Bigelow, Robert, 100, 233
Billheimer, John, 168
Billingsley, Sherman, 77, 87
The Birds (1963), 145, 210
Bogart, Humphrey, 76, 77
Bogdanovich, Peter, 130, 190
Bohan, Owen W., 55
Boomerang! (1947), 3, 232
Boone, Otis, 63, 219
Boone, People v. (N.Y. 2017), 63, 219
Borchard, Edwin M., 66–67, 146
Bordwell, David, 181
Boston Globe, 109, 187
Botts, Nancy Louise, 34–35, 146
Brancato, Peter J., 39–42, 127
Brean, Herbert, 79, 85, 103, 110, 116, 125

Brennan, William J., Jr., 194, 195
Bridge of Spies (2015), 18
Briley, Yutico, 236
Brill, Joseph, 12–13, 25
Brown, Charles H., 69
Brown, Edwin S., 29
Brown, John Harvey, 63
Brown, Will, 146, 231
Brownridge, Samuel, 8, 197–198
Browser, Harry, 59–60
Burks, Robert, 158
Burney, Ian, 58
Burns International Detective Agency, 31–32

Callahan, Joseph M., 61
Call Northside 777 (1948), 3
Campbell, Bertram, 10–27
  arrest, 11
  Court of Claims case, 25–26
  death, 26–27
  exoneration of, 5, 15–20, 57
  handwriting evidence, 22–23
  imprisonment, 14–15
  pardon of, 5, 16, 24-25
  parole, 15
  resemblance to actual forger, 16–18
  showups used against, 11, 19-20
  trial of, 10, 12–14
Campbell, James (J. Camp), 55
Campbell, Kippy, 164
Caruso, Philip, 37–43
  damages for wrongful conviction, 42–43
  exoneration of, 40–42, 57
  misidentification of, 38-39, 64
  imprisonment, 40
  trial of, 38–40
Casagrande, Yolanda, 80, 83, 93, 96–99, 104
Chabrol, Claude, 187
Clift, Montgomery, 123
Coe, Richard, 186–187
Cohen, Paula Marantz, 181
Coleman, Herbert, 133–135, 140
Collins, Charles, 36
Collyer, Bud, 188–189
Como, Perry, 77
Confirmation bias, 22, 147, 152, 157
Conforti, Gene, 84–85, 134
Conviction integrity units, 8, 197-198
Conway, Charles, 12-13
Cooper, Charles, 149
Corey, Wendell, 122
Cotten, Joseph, 121
Coughlin, John B., 36
Court of Claims Act (New York), 25, 42, 214
The Court of Last Resort, 58
Crime control model of police work, 141, 150–151
Crisona, Frank, 91–92, 94–95, 98, 100, 172, 201–202
Crisona, James J., 201
Crosby, Harley, 71
Cross-racial identifications, 63, 219

Cullen, Thomas P., 83–84, 95, 104, 161-162, 204, 226
Cummings, Robert, 120–121

Danforth, Harold, 55
Daily News (New York), 1-2, 27, 32, 40, 57, 85, 100, 102-103, 113, 187
Daniell, Charles, 101–103, 106, 107–109, 111, 144, 176–78, 203–204, 225
Daniels, Charles, 204–205
D'Annunzio, Lola, 136, 166, 230
Dargis, Manohla, 182
Daru, Robert, 18–23, 25, 66, 67, 72
Davino, Frank, 69–70, 221
Davino, People v. (N.Y. 1940), 69-70, 221
The Day the Earth Stood Still (1951), 184–185
Deutelbaum, Marshall, 140
Dewey, Thomas E., 6, 12, 16, 24–25, 42–43, 50, 53, 57, 66, 72
Di Clemente, Catherine, 80, 94, 104-105
DNA evidence, exonerations based on, 7–8, 36, 58, 63, 141, 148, 178, 194
Donnellan, George L., 57
Donoghue, Peter J., 50
Donovan, James, 18
Donovan, John, 17–18, 23–24
"Don't Let the Stars Get in Your Eyes," 77
Doubleday, Wallace, 80, 82, 88, 96
Downs, Thomas, 50
Doyle, James, 109–110
Driscoll, Alfred E., 32, 33
Dromm, Daniel, 207
Dukakis, Michael, 126

Ebert, Roger, 142
Ello, Constance, 79–81, 82, 83, 92–94, 96, 97, 102, 104, 105, 110, 113, 144–145, 172
Espenschied, Lloyd, 97–100, 174, 179, 202, 224–225
Essen, Robert, 164
Eyewitness identification
  escalating risk of error, 200, 236
  handwriting evidence and, 36.
  in Hitchcock films before *The Wrong Man*, 121-125
  jury instructions on, 204–205
  reforms to reduce risk of errors, 5–7, 65–68, 195–197
  right to counsel at identification procedures 194, 196, 200, 235

Farber, Manny, 184
Farrell, Peter T., 51–53
FBI, 16–17, 23–24, 185
Ferrero, Enrique and Mariannina, 89, 134
Filmspotting podcast, 4, 193
Fincher, David, 181–182
Findley, Keith A., 141, 195
Fogarty, James, 49, 52
Fonda, Frances, 129–130
Fonda, Henry, 2, 127–130, 132. *See also The Wrong Man*
  in *12 Angry Men*, 178–179
  Balestreros, meeting with, 133, 181
  in *The Grapes of Wrath*, 127–128, 179

in *Let Us Live*, 128-129
in *The Ox-Bow Incident*, 231
in *Young Mr. Lincoln*, 146
in *You Only Live Once*, 128, 179-180
mob mentality, preoccupation with, 146, 231
New York Times obituary, 4, 210
performance as Manny, 127-130, 139, 153–154, 165, 178–180, 232
preparation for *The Wrong Man*, 130, 133
Ford, John, 127, 146
Foster v. California (1969), 194–195
Francis, James, 73–74, 222
Frankfurter, Felix, 126, 211
Frenzy (1972), 2, 210

Gardner, Erle Stanley, 58
Garrett, Brandon, 200
Garsson, United States v. (S.D.N.Y.1923), 211, 231
Gerace, Salvatore, 70–71
Gertner, Jon, 99, 225
Gideon v. Wainwright (1963), 21
Gilbert v. California (1967), 213
Giolito, Bartholomew, 78, 86-87, 116, 133–134
Glaser, Vaughan, 120–121
Godard, Jean-Luc, 149, 159, 165, 232
Graff, Selma and Donald, 61–62
Granger, Farley, 160
Grant, Cary, 191
The Grapes of Wrath (1940), 127–128, 179
Groat, William B., 88, 93–95, 97–98, 100, 102, 105, 135-136, 225
Groves, George, 135

Haeffner, Nicholas, 150, 191, 235
Haff, Joseph O., 32
Hale, Wanda, 187
Halkias, James, 45–47, 49–52
Hallinan, James T., 116–117
Hand, Learned, 7-8, 150, 211
Handwriting evidence
in Balestrero case, 94–96, 106-108, 162
in Campbell case, 22–23
in Hauptmann case, 35–36
in Leib case, 29
in Lester/Shephard case, 30-32, 35, 64
Hansley, William, 56–57
Hauptmann, Bruno Richard, 35–36
Hays Production Code, 168
Hedren, Tippi, 145, 229
Henreid, Paul, 185
Herberich, Matthew, 82–83, 92, 105–106, 109, 202
Hickerson, Harold, 126
Hill, L. Barron, 114–115
Hilton, Ordway, 107-108
Hirsch, Foster, 158
Hitchcock, Alfred, 2–7, 120–194. *See also The Wrong Man; specific movies & television episodes*
appearance in *The Wrong Man*, 137-138
childhood encounter with police, 124, 228
correspondence with Maxwell Anderson, 133, 134,

140–41, 176, 181
death penalty, opposition to, 124
eyewitness testimony, views on 192, 194, 195
father, death of, 125
image of Hitchcock as promotional tool, 138
Miles, Vera, relationship with, 130–131, 229
mob mentality, depiction of, 124, 146, 190–191, 194, 231
New York Times obituary, 4, 210
police, depiction of in films before *The Wrong Man*, 120–124
police, views on, 121, 134, 135, 154
Stork Club, visits to, 76, 222
"wrong man" theme, use of, 2, 120–124
Hitchcock/Truffaut (2015), 211
Hitter, Thomas, 69–70
Hoffner, Louis, 44–53
after exoneration, 53
compensation for wrongful conviction, 53
conviction of, 48
exoneration, 49–53, 103
identification of, 46-47, 52, 64
lie detector test, 50–51
mother's leukemia, 45–46
trial of, 46–48
Hogan, Frank S., 61, 72, 221
House Un-American Activities Committee (HUAC), 185
Hubbell, Carl, 48
Humbert, David, 147, 231
Hutchinson, Herbert, 114

I Confess (1953), 2, 123–124, 175
Innocence Project, 7, 58, 63, 141, 195, 197
"I Saw the Whole Thing" (*The Alfred Hitchcock Hour*), 191–192

Jacobson, Jack, 40
Johnson v. Zerbst (1938), 213
Jones, Kent, 211
Judicial Council of the State of New York, 6, 65–73, 103, 161, 194
Juries
in *12 Angry Men*, 178–179
in Balestrero case, 97-100
in Campbell case, 12–13
in *Murder!*, 125
in *The Wrong Man*, 7, 100, 173, 174–175

Kassin, Saul and Rebecca Norwick, 153
Kelly, Grace, 122
Kempenaar, Adam, 4, 233
Kendrick, Jaython, 8
Kennedy, Samuel, 20, 213
Kennedy, Stephen P., 134–135
Kenny, Glenn, 4
Kevorkian, Martin, 181–182
Kilgallen, Dorothy, 117
Klosterman, Chuck, 193
Kolker, Robert, 185
Kopp, Joan, 81–82, 104–105, 144

Kramer vs. Kramer (1979), 4
Krogman, John, 46
Kubis, Joseph F., 50–51

Laming, Donald, 156
Lang, Doreen, 145, 173
Larkman, Edward, 68–69, 220
Larsen, Josh, 4, 154
Laughton, Charles, 175
Lehman, Ernest, 191
Leib, Cecelia, 28–29, 31, 36
Leibowitz, Samuel, 36
Leo, Richard, 152
Lester, Elizabeth, 28–36
  exoneration, 33–34
  false convictions, effect of, 33, 167
  misidentification of, 30, 64, 146
  wrongful conviction of, 29-31, 35
Let Us Live (1939), 128–129
Lie detector tests, 50–51, 53, 88, 108–110, 112, 134,
  140, 205, 224
Life magazine, 79, 102, 103, 110, 116. 125, 179
Lineups
  best practices for (NY), 195–196
  in Balestrero case, 83–84, 93, 97, 104, 226
  in Caruso case, 38, 40
  fillers in, 21, 93, 195-196
  Foster v. California, 194–195
  in Hoffner case, 46, 49–50, 52
  in Negron case, 198
  origins of, 20
  in *The Wrong Man*, 156–159, 161-162
Littlewort, Dorothy, 68, 69, 220
The Lodger: A Story of the London Fog (1927), 231
Lloyd, Norman, 185
Lockdown Culture with Mary Beard, 4
Loftus, Elizabeth, 200
Lonergan, Joseph, 46
Long Island Daily Press, 102-103
Long Island Star-Journal, 81, 85, 87, 100, 102-103, 110-
  111, 188, 203
Lumet, Sydney, 178
Lummis, Dayton, 136
Lyons, John A., 66

MacPhail, Angus, 126, 127, 140, 223, 230
Malicious prosecution, 62, 112-114, 116
Malden, Karl, 123
Mank, Frieda, 101
Mankiewicz, Ben, 4
Manson, Maurice, 159, 232
The Man Who Knew Too Much (1956), 3, 125–126,185, 210
Mattison, Arthur, 25–26
McBride, Joseph, 127
McCarten, John, 186
McCarthy, Joseph, 185
McGilligan, Patrick, 124
McKelway, St. Clair, 38, 41–42
McKinney, Devin, 129–130, 146
McMartin case, 191

McNutt, Paul V., 34–35
Metesky, George, 186
Miles, Vera
  Balestreros, meeting with, 133, 181
  in "Incident at a Corner" (*Startime*), 190
  performance as Rose, 130–131, 166-168, 181
  in "Revenge" (*Alfred Hitchcock Presents*), 130
  working relationship with Hitchcock, 131, 229
Miller, Anthony, 199
Miller, Arthur: *The Crucible*, 118, 151
Miller, D.A., 138, 230
Miranda v. Arizona (1966), 21, 109, 151, 153, 213
Mistrials
  Balestrero case, 6, 97–98, 100, 107–108, 139, 225
  in *The Wrong Man*, 174–175
Molway, Clement, 128
Mowery, Edward J., 49–50, 52, 217
Muller, Eddie, 158
Murder! (1930), 125, 141

Naremore, James, 142, 233
National Association of Colored People (NAACP), 62
National Registry of Exonerations, 34, 58, 194, 205, 215
Nayman, Adam, 182
Negron, Julio, 198
Neiman, John Martin, 202
Neufeld, Peter, 7
Newsweek, 53, 187
Newton, Herman, 62–63
Newton, Lottie, 62-63
New York Post, 50, 133
New York Times, 3-4, 16–17, 24, 29, 32, 57, 102, 182,
  186–187, 210
The Night Of (2016), 151
North by Northwest (1961), 2, 191–192, 210
Nott, Charles C., 12–14, 22

O'Connor, Frank. *See also The Wrong Man* (1956)
  belief in Manny's innocence, 85
  career after Manny's case, 204–205
  efforts to obtain compensation for Manny's false arrest,
    112–113, 115–116
  jury selection, 100
  Manny's hiring of, 85
  on Manny's prosecution, 110, 142, 188
  mistrial motion decision, 97–98
  opening statement at Manny's trial, 92
  preparation for Manny's trial, 88–90, 171
  on Rose's breakdown, 87
  witness examinations at Manny's trial, 92–97
Oliver, Thomas, 54–64
  damages for wrongful conviction, 63–64
  exoneration, 55–56
  press coverage of exoneration, 57–58
  trial of, 55
Oller, John, 213
Osborn, Albert S. and Albert D., 36, 95
Osteen, Mark, 141, 230, 231
Ott, Mel, 47–48
The Ox-Bow Incident (1943), 231

Packer, Herbert, 141, 150–151, 230
The Paradine Case (1947), 125, 168, 175
Parks, Hildy, 188–189
Pennekamp v. Florida (1946), 211
Perry v. New Hampshire (2012), 195–196, 235
Phelps, Phelps, 42, 216
Pierce, Ward J., 68–69
A Place in the Sun (1951), 149–150
Pomerance, Murray, 132, 180, 233
The Postman Always Rings Twice (1946), 149–150
Powell v. Alabama (1932), 213
Production Code Administration (PCA), 168
Proestos, Trifon, 45, 53
Psycho (1960), 131,168, 191, 210, 233

Quayle, Anthony, 135, 167
Quinn, T. Vincent, 50, 53, 88, 102–103, 108–109, 204, 225

Rafter, Nicole, 3, 149–150
Ray, Robert, 149
Rear Window (1954), 122-123, 185, 210
Reese, Pee Wee, 48
Reid, Frances, 131, 229
"Revenge" (*Alfred Hitchcock Presents*), 130
Robert Montgomery Presents, 116, 228
Roberts, Burton B., 63
Rohmer, Éric, 187
Roman, Ruth, 160
Rose, Reginald, 178–179
Rosenberg, Norman, 178, 211, 234
Rostron, Allen, 165
Rothman, William, 138, 230
Rouke, Fabian, 50–51, 88, 134

Saboteur (1942), 2, 120-121, 185
Sacco-Vanzetti case, 125–126
Salinas v. Texas (2013), 231
Sang, Hugh L., 94–96, 107–108
Scaramellino, Eugene, 37–41
Scheck, Barry, 7
Scheindlin, Shira A., 154
Schickel, Richard, 4, 210
Schoenfeld, Jack, 59
Schrager, William G., 205
Schreiner, Jack, 106
Scorsese, Martin, 4–5, 169, 184–185, 187, 211
Scott, Gordon, 131
Scott, Michael S., 141
Shadow of a Doubt (1943), 121–123, 210
The Shawshank Redemption (1994), 15
Shedrick, People v. (N.Y. 1985), 224, 237
Shephard, Clifford, 28-36, 58, 64, 166-167
    exoneration attempts, 32–33
    misidentification of, 30-32, 146
    pardon of, 32–33
    third arrest, 31
    wrongful convictions, 30-31
Short, Albert E., 46–48, 51

Showups
    definition of, 20
    in Balestrero case, 82–83, 93, 105–106
    in Campbell case, 11, 19-20
    in *Gods of the Lightning*, 127
    in *Stovall v. Denno*, 196–197
    New York rulings on use of, 197
    in *The Wrong Man*, 153–155
    Supreme Court rulings on, 196-197, 213
Silbey, Jessica, 170, 233
Skerry, Phillip J., 168
Smith, Alfred E., 69
Smith, David Livingstone, 145
Smith, Imogen Sara, 157, 232
Sotomayor, Sonia, 195
Spaulding, Norman, 167, 211, 231, 233
Spellbound (1945), 2, 126, 210
Spielberg, Steven, 18
Spoto, Donald, 126, 131, 142, 168, 186
Startime: "Incident at a Corner," 190–191
Stein, Elbridge W., 108
Steinbeck, John, 179
Sterritt, David, 181
Stewart, James, 3, 122, 189
Stone, Harold J., 131–132, 136, 149
Stop and frisk policy (NYPD), 154
Stork Club
    in 1953, 76–77
    Hitchcock's visits to, 76, 222
    Manny's work at, 78–79, 87, 90, 101–102, 112
    in *The Wrong Man*, 133, 136, 138–140, 143, 161,177, 186
Stotzing, William, 45–46, 47, 48, 52
Stovall v. Denno (1967), 196–197, 213
Strangers on a Train (1951), 2, 142, 160–161, 175, 210
Strauss, Marc Raymond, 145, 233
Sullivan, Charles, 50
Sullivan, Theo and Edward Eugene, 29, 31–32, 214
Sutton, Willie, 104, 226
Swayze, John Cameron, 188–189
Sylbert, Paul, 142

Taxi Driver (1976), 4
Thiel, Alexander D. L., 16-19, 22, 24, 212
Thomson, David, 4, 210
Titanic (1997), 193
Time magazine, 4, 24, 187
Tobias, Scott, 4
To Catch a Thief (1955), 185, 210
To Kill a Mockingbird (1962), 4–5
Tomasini, George, 168
To Tell the Truth, 188–189
Tourneur, Jacques, 169
Transit Authority (New York City), 135, 140
Truffaut, François, 2, 4, 160, 173, 228
Tunnel vision
    in Balestrero case, 106-108, 188
    in Campbell case, 22-23
    defined, 7, 22, 141
    in *The Wrong Man*, 7, 141-142, 152-153

Uchansky, Matthew, 221
Underwood, Kennard, 46
Untermyer, Irwin, 61
Vanderbilt, James, 182
Van Dyke, Dick, 188–189
Van Voorhis, John, 115
Variety, 187
Vertigo (1958), 189–190, 210, 229, 235
Victor Moore Arcade complex, 79–81, 83, 85, 90, 133

Wade, United States v. (1967), 194, 213
Walker, Dixie, 48
Wall, Patrick, 227
War and Peace (1956), 186
Wardlow, Illinois v. (2000), 231

Wean, Elizabeth (nee Lester), 28–36. *See also Lester, Elizabeth*
Webber, Peggy, 132, 143
Weiler, A. H., 3, 186–187
Wells, Gary, 200
White, Edward, 125, 138
Wigmore, John Henry, 20–21
Wilber, Eddie Lee, 55–56
Wilkinson, James, 12–13
Williams, Samuel Tito, 61–62, 219
Willis, Constance, 133
Wilson, Leigh, 82–83, 105–106, 202–203
Winterset (1935), 125–126
Wixted, John, 200
Woods, Archibald, 11, 19, 23
Woods, Harry, 46
Wright, Horace, 59–61
Wright, Sophie, 54–55
Wright, Teresa, 121
The Wrong Man (1956)
  alibi defenses, cut scene, 230
  authorities' failure to identify themselves in, 159–161, 232
  bomb threat at Manhattan screening of, 186
  box office performance, 3, 185
  camerawork, 4, 143–145, 155, 158, 168, 170–171, 174–175
  chance, role of, 149–150
  confirmation bias, 147, 152–153, 157
  criminal justice issues explored in, 7, 141–142, 153, 168–169, 193–194
  detectives' interrogation of Manny in, 150–153
  deviations from record, 139–141, 171, 176-77, 233
  ending, 180–181
  eyewitnesses, portrayal of, 144–148, 172–173
  factual detail, Hitchcock's attention to, 2–3, 139–142
  family trauma from false arrest, 165–169, 194
  film noir, classification as, 158
  Fonda, casting of, 127–130
  Hitchcock's ambivalence toward, 4
  Hitchcock's appearance in, 137–138
  holdup note in, 155–156
  judge, depiction of, 173–175
  lineups in, 156–159, 161–162
  McCarthyism, interpretations relating to, 185, 234
  Manny's perspective used in, 3, 7, 124, 161,173
  Miles, casting in, 130–131

Miranda, anticipation of, 151, 232
  opening credits sequence, 143–144
  plot synopsis, 138–139
  police, depiction in, 147, 149–160, 161–163, 177–178, 180–182
  police, lack of cooperation with production, 134
  prayer scene in, 176–177, 233
  production history of, 124-136
  prosecutors, depiction of, 159–163, 171, 173, 174
  reviews of, 3–4, 186–188
  Robert Balestrero in, 160, 165
  Rose Balestrero's story in, 125, 130–131, 139–141, 160, 164–169, 180–181
  showups in, 153–155
  subway scene, filming of, 2, 135, 140
  timeliness of, 7–8, 141–142, 193–195, 200
  trial sequence, 136, 141, 170–175
  visual motifs, 7, 152, 154, 165-169, 176–177, 180
Wuechner, Karl, 79, 89–90

Young and Innocent (1937), 145
Young Mr. Lincoln (1939), 146
You Only Live Once (1937), 128, 179–180

Zayas, Joseph, 198
Zodiac (2007), 181–183, 234

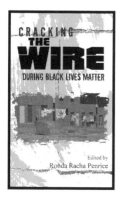
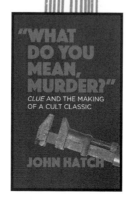
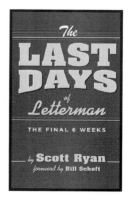